THE THOUGHTFUL READER

Second Edition

THE THOUGHTFUL READER

Second Edition

MARY C. FJELDSTAD
LAGUARDIA COMMUNITY COLLEGE
CITY UNIVERSITY OF NEW YORK

Harcourt Brace College Publishers

Fort Worth Philadelphia San Diego New York Orlando Austin San Antonio
Toronto Montreal London Sydney Tokyo

Publisher	Christopher P. Klein
Acquisitions Editor	Carol Wada
Product Manager	Ilse Wolf-West
Production Manager	Diane Gray
Art Director	Vicki Whistler
Production Services	The Page Group, Inc.

ISBN: 0-15-503946-6

Library of Congress Catalog Card Number: 97-073500

Address for Editorial Correspondence: Harcourt Brace College Publishers, 301 Commerce Street, Suite 3700, Fort Worth, TX 76102.

Address for Orders: Harcourt Brace & Company, 6277 Sea Harbor Drive, Orlando, Florida 32887. 1-800-782-4479 or 1-800-433-0001 (in Florida).

Website address: http://www.hbcollege.com

Harcourt Brace College Publishers may provide complimentary instructional aids and supplements or supplement packages to those adopters qualified under our adoption policy. Please contact your sales representative for more information. If, as an adopter or potential user, you receive supplements you do not need, please return them to your sales representative or send them to: Attn: Returns Department, Troy Warehouse, 465 South Lincoln Drive, Troy, MO 63379.

To Sam

ANNOTATED TABLE OF CONTENTS

UNIT ONE
READING AND THINKING ABOUT EDUCATION

Think about the kind of world you want to live and work in. What do you need to know to build that world? Demand your teachers teach you that.
—Prince Kropotkin

UNIT TWO
READING AND THINKING ABOUT CULTURE

Culture is that which binds men together.
—Ruth Benedict

UNIT THREE
READING AND THINKING ABOUT LANGUAGE

All words are pegs to hang ideas on.
—Henry Ward Beecher

UNIT FOUR
READING AND THINKING ABOUT WORK
AND THE WORLD OF BUSINESS

Who built the seven towers of Thebes?
The books are filled with the names of kings.
Was it kings who hauled the craggy blocks of stone?
—Bertolt Brecht

UNIT FIVE
CRITICAL READING AND THINKING
ABOUT CONTROVERSIAL ISSUES

It is better to debate a question without settling it, than to settle it without debate.
—Joseph Joubert

UNIT SIX
READING AND THINKING ABOUT TEXTBOOKS

Knowledge itself is power.
—Francis Bacon

ALTERNATE TABLE OF CONTENTS

TO THE INSTRUCTOR

The second edition of this textbook remains committed to the fundamental conviction of the first: reading is a joy. It is not hard work. It is not something to suffer through. It is not an activity relegated to school. No doubt, any instructor using this book is what *Atlantic* magazine used to call an "Avid Reader." No one has to force us to read. We read because we love it; it gives us pleasure, as well as information, solace, and escape. Unfortunately, the situation is quite different for many of our students. They regard most reading, and certainly most "school" reading, as, at best, a chore. I hope that, with the help of this book, you can change your students' minds and help them become "Avid Readers."

Many of our students have difficulty reading not because they can't understand the words and sentences on the printed page, but rather because they cannot tie those words and sentences to a fund of information. In other words, they lack the background knowledge that makes new text meaningful. Recall the old story of John Dewey's visit to a class that had studied how the earth probably was formed. Dewey asked the students whether they would find the center of the earth hot or cold. No one answered. The teacher then told Dewey that he had asked the wrong question. She turned to the class and asked, "What is the condition at the center of the earth?" All responded in unison: "In a state of igneous fusion." Just as these students read and understood at a rote level, so do many entering college students read and understand at a superficial level.

Many of our students have not read widely or deeply. They are not independent learners because of gaps in their background knowledge and because they have not learned the strategies they need to succeed in college courses. How can we help students to function as fluent readers, rather than as constantly struggling beginning readers? The answer must focus on *content* rather than on *skill* and *process*. Reading fluently is not the laborious assembling of a set of discrete skills (for example, finding the main idea, drawing an inference, etc.) independent of content. It is like any skill: it must be "practiced as it is played" in order to learn to do it right. If you want to learn to run fast, you practice by running fast. If you want to learn to run with stamina, as for a marathon, you practice by running long distances. If you had to learn to play tennis by analyzing each stroke in detail, never putting the sections together and taking a satisfying whack at the ball, you'd lose interest in tennis pretty quickly. This is the frustrating experience many of our students have with reading. Reading for them has always been a chore, a school exercise, another assignment—not something that is an exhilarating part of their everyday lives.

This book is thematically organized. Because students often do not have a broad base of information, they rarely experience the joy of reading fluently.

Because most of what they read is unfamiliar, they constantly struggle as novice, rather than sophisticated, readers. By reading extensively on one theme, students build a fund of knowledge, which then allows them to read at a higher level. They are not searching to comprehend at the base level; rather they are able to connect ideas to previous knowledge—to analyze, synthesize, and evaluate what they read. The topics represented are of particular interest to students and lend themselves to application to students' real-life experiences.

CHANGES IN THE SECOND EDITION

Many new reading selections appear in this edition. For instance, there are intriguing new articles about the difference in the way boys and girls are treated in schools, a touching story of the effect one wonderful teacher had on an immigrant child, and a story of two people who chose unusual careers—for their gender. There are recent stories about cultural differences, for example, in the expectations about love and marriage in the United States and Japan, or about the problems African immigrants in France have because they practice polygamy. There are several articles that discuss whether English should be made the official language of the United States. A series of articles describes the agonizing choices made available by advances in genetic testing. And more.

At the end of each unit there are now two, rather than one, reading selections that call for collaborative work. Students work in groups to read and understand the selection and then create their *own* exercises to accompany the text.

Finally, there is a new Unit Six. This unit contains textbook chapters that focus on each of the themes of the book—thus, there are chapters on education, culture, language, work, and critical thinking. Students will have the valuable experience of working with actual college-level materials.

WRITING AND READING

A major underlying assumption of this book is that reading and writing are inextricably linked. Writing helps students become co-creators of the texts they read. In creating their own written versions and interpretations of, and reactions to, the content, they become masters of what they read. Writing about what they read allows them to monitor their own progress, to check whether they really understand what they read. It forces them to infer structure and make connections between the varying levels of information in the selection itself and their own background knowledge. In simple terms, writing can help readers make sense of what they read.

The book is also meant to be a "course model." Much as in a textbook for history, literature, sociology, or business, the reading selections contain information that students are expected to master. They read and study the reading selections with several goals similar to those of a college-content course: learning vocabulary and information specific to a field, producing reaction and argumentation papers, and finally, passing exams. The major difference is that, in the reading course, students are given more support from the textbook and from the teacher. The strategies and knowledge students gain can transfer immediately to their primary concern—the concepts and processes of their content courses.

ORGANIZATION AND CONTENT OF THE BOOK

The book begins with an introduction to its own philosophy and structure. Here, the student is introduced to the features of the book and works through the first chapter. The first unit contains essays that consider the question "What is education?" It begins with a thought-provoking essay on the nature of education in which students are compared to "sausages" teachers are supposed to "stuff" with education, rather than "oysters" to be opened to reveal the riches within. Unit One, *Education,* includes some melancholy musings on learning by such well-known thinkers as Russell Baker and Barbara Jordan. Each unit contains at least one narrative selection; in Unit One the selection is a delightful essay—almost more poetry than prose—on the joys of summer school by Gary Soto. It functions nicely as an icebreaker and gives students a chance to think about why they are in college and what they expect from school. The next four units are organized around the following themes: culture, language, work and the world of business, and controversial issues. These themes were selected for five reasons: first, they are topics with which students already have some familiarity; second, they are of great interest to students; third, connections can easily be drawn between the information in one section and that in another, as well as to what students will be reading in newspapers and magazines; fourth, each theme lends itself to exposition in a variety of sources and styles—readings are drawn from newspapers, magazines, essays, narratives, and textbooks; fifth, the content is presented in a way similar to that of college-content courses—for example, a history, psychology, or business course. Thus the skills students learn here may be easily transferred to their other courses.

Many of the reading selections in this book are challenging. Students are insulted and demeaned when given materials they see as childish. They are challenged and interested when presented with work they see as college level.

STRUCTURE OF THE BOOK

The reading selections are not arranged in an artificial sequence of increasing complexity but rather in a logical order one might expect in a college textbook. The ideas in each selection build upon those that came before. To provide the greatest support to students in their acquisition of ideas and skills, each unit contains the following features:

Thinking about the Theme. Each of the units begins with a section that invites students to think about the subject they are about to read. It consists of a quotation and a brief introduction to the theme of the unit, then uses questions to actively engage students by stimulating them to remember what they already know about the topic, to imagine some new aspect or application of the topic, and to think about how the topic affects them personally. In short, to "turn on" the engines of their minds and get them ready to read.

Introduction to the Reading Selection. Once the theme of the unit has been introduced, each reading selection in the unit is briefly introduced—first, to encourage students to activate the knowledge they already have about the specific topic at hand; second, in some cases, to provide them with crucial background knowledge they may lack; and, finally, to stimulate their interest in new information to come. The reading selection itself follows.

Vocabulary. Because they are drawn from "real" sources, many of the reading selections contain fairly complex language. Students will find many of the new words are comprehensible because of the context. In some cases, students will need to look words up in order to understand the author's point. In this case, and where the word is one that students will find valuable to have in their own vocabulary, the word is "attacked": students read it in context, try to determine its meaning, evaluate their guess, and, if necessary, confirm their guess. This technique most closely resembles the way fluent readers naturally learn new words. Students are encouraged to investigate other words they find hard to understand in the reading.

Guide Questions. After the vocabulary has been considered, guide questions are presented. These questions have several goals. First, they guide students to a basic understanding of the major ideas presented in the reading selection; thus, some questions are geared to the lowest levels of cognitive activity—that is, knowledge and comprehension. Second, students are asked to apply the new ideas presented in the selection to their own experiences or to other situations they may read or hear about. Students then may be asked to synthesize the new information with ideas they previously possessed, or, where appropriate, to evaluate the new content. The main ideas generally are attacked in the same sequence in which they appear, thus students discern text organization in a natural way.

Application. The themes addressed in this book are of interest to most college students and lend themselves to application to students' own lives and experiences. Transferring information to novel situations is an excellent way to promote and demonstrate mastery of the content. Application questions are personal, interesting, and even enjoyable ways of stretching the mind.

Writing. Students are encouraged to see the connections among all communication skills. There is a special emphasis here on writing. The guide questions are meant to be answered in writing and discussed and argued about in class. Some reading selections lend themselves naturally to creative-writing assignments, others to underlining and summary writing, extremely valuable skills our students need to master. Research has shown that underlining, annotating, and summarizing improve both comprehension and recall of information. Thus, underlining, annotating, and summarizing assignments appear progressively through a unit. Each skill is introduced the first time it is presented in a unit and the student is directed to turn to the Appendix, where these skills are taught. In succeeding reading selections students are reminded that information on underlining, annotating, and summarizing is available in the Appendix for review. Of course the instructor is free to introduce and reinforce these skills whenever it is appropriate.

Special Projects At the end of Units Two through Five is a project designed to allow students to use the knowledge gained through reading the unit and to spur them to investigate topics independently.

Short Takes Set off from other reading selections in the unit, "Short Takes" are brief stories, examples, or explanations of ideas contained in the text. They are included for their high interest, for elaboration, or for humor.

Special Features of Units Five and Six Units One through Four of the text are organized identically, in the manner described above. Unit Five of the text, *Critical Reading and Thinking about Controversial Issues,* contains the added feature of collaborative work on an argumentation paper. Several topics of controversy are presented in this section. After each topic (which consists of several reading selections), students are asked to work in groups to research and write an essay arguing for or against a position on one of the controversial ideas. This kind of concluding exercise fosters synthesis of all that students have learned about one topic from a variety of sources and encourages them to operate as fluent readers and thinkers.

Unit Six of the text, *Reading and Thinking about Textbooks,* is different from the first five parts. Here, students tackle real, college-level textbook material. Instructions guide them through previewing, comprehension of new terminology, underlining, and annotating. Finally, actual review, discussion, and exam questions are presented. Students can see what they will face in an actual course.

Please note that answers to the exam questions in Unit Six can be found in the instructor's manual that accompanies this textbook.

FLEXIBILITY

An important feature of this book's organization is its flexibility. Instructors may choose any theme they wish. It is not necessary to complete the first unit in order to understand the following units. If a particular reading selection does not appeal to the instructor, it may be skipped without any significant problem. (Note, however, that after the first reading in each unit, instructions for vocabulary and guide questions are abbreviated.) The skills addressed (such as underlining, annotating, and summarizing) are taught in an appendix and may be presented at any point the teacher considers appropriate. Too often, textbooks are set up so rigidly that instructors have very little say in their own curricula and are forced to teach topics that bore them or that they don't feel confident teaching. This book offers a wide range of subjects that can be organized to suit the individual instructor and class. In addition, it offers both collaborative and independent activities that can be assigned to accommodate the learning styles of individual students.

ACKNOWLEDGMENTS

I very much appreciate the comments and insights of colleagues who reviewed for this new edition: Marcia Oppenheim, Pima Community College; Monica Wyatt, Northern Illinois University; Donna Wood, State Technical Institute at Memphis; Claire Hite, University of Southern Florida; Janice McIntyre, Kansas City Kansas Community College; and Patricia Daughrity, Gordon College.

I send special thanks to Stacy Moser-Simpson for her expertise, professionalism, and good humor throughout the production of this second edition, and whose help went far beyond that of copyediting.

I am very grateful to the staff at Harcourt Brace: Diane Gray, Vicki Whistler, Charlie Dierker, Aimé Merizon, and Beverly Wyatt.

To my editor, Carol Wada, I owe special thanks for her indispensable advice, patience, and guidance throughout this project.

Finally, I'd like to thank my friends and colleagues at LaGuardia Community College, who have never failed to encourage and support me on good days and bad. To my students, who never cease to surprise, hearten, and teach me, thanks.

TO THE STUDENT

Reading makes me happy. Reading is entertainment. Reading helps me forget my troubles. Reading is a pathway to knowledge. Reading is the essential tool for education. Reading is an escape from the cares and difficulties of my life. Reading is fun. Reading is relaxing. Reading is a part of my daily life, just like eating and sleeping.

All of the statements above are answers people have given to the question "What does reading mean to you?" Every person has his or her own answer. Maybe yours is "Reading is hard!" or "Reading is work!" If so, the goal of this book is to change your mind.

Reading is not a problem or a task or a school assignment. Reading is part of everyday life. It is essential for college, of course. It is also necessary for almost any career you want to pursue. It can help us in every part of our lives: reading about health and nutrition will help us to be healthier and happier; reading about current events in newspapers and magazines exercises our minds and makes us better citizens; reading for pleasure can take us out of our sometimes troubled lives to a happier or more exciting place in our imaginations. The virtues and delights of reading are endless.

Learning to read better is a natural process. To become a better reader, you must READ!

If you like to play tennis or soccer or if you like to skate or dance, you know that, to get better, you must practice. But the practice is fun in itself. And the better you get, the more fun it is. It's exactly the same thing with reading. The practice can be pleasure; and the better you get, the more pleasure it is.

If you get into the habit of reading, if you expand your vocabulary so that you are not running to the dictionary constantly, if you build enough background knowledge so that reading is not work, but pleasure, you, too, will say that reading is a joy.

In this textbook, you can read about many subjects that you are already familiar with—education, people and their customs, language, work and careers, and some of the controversial issues of our time. You will find these topics interesting and entertaining to read about. You will also learn things that will be useful in your daily life and things that will help you in the other courses you take in college.

HOW TO USE THIS BOOK

THEMES

This book is organized around five themes: 1) education, 2) culture, 3) language, 4) work and the world of business, and 5) controversial issues.

THINKING ABOUT

Each of the five thematic units of this book begins with a section called *Thinking About*. In this introductory section, ideas are presented to get you thinking about what you will be reading and studying. Often, you will find questions intended to stimulate you to remember what you already know about the subject the unit will cover. These questions will help you "turn on the engine" of your mind and get ready to learn.

INTRODUCTION

A short introduction precedes each reading selection. You should read it and answer any questions it contains. This will help you get ready to read.

THE READING

The reading selection itself then follows. You should read it straight through one time without stopping. Then go back and read it a second time, making notes and marking any words you don't know and ideas you think are important.

VOCABULARY

Each reading selection is followed by a list of important words selected from the text and instructions to help you figure out their meanings. These words were chosen because they are crucial to your understanding of the selection.

GUIDE QUESTIONS

Each reading selection is also followed by guide questions. Their purpose is to "guide" your understanding of the text. Some of the questions are simple fact questions, meant to ensure that you understand the basic information the author is trying to get across. Other questions are more sophisticated and ask you to *analyze* information, to *synthesize* information, to *evaluate* information.

APPLICATION

Following the guide questions in each chapter are one or more questions that ask you to take some of the things you have learned and apply them to some different situation or to your own life. The ability to apply information to new situations is a high-level thinking skill. It proves that you truly comprehend what you have read.

WRITING

Because reading and writing are closely linked, each chapter includes one or more writing assignments. Writing is the skill most college students need to develop.

Writing about what you have read is an interesting and valuable way to make the new information truly yours. As with all the features above, your instructor will select which exercises you are to do and will give you all the support you need to complete them successfully.

PREPARATION

Now, to become familiar with the structure of the book, let's read through the first unit and do the following exercises.

The first unit of the text focuses on the theme of *education.* This seems an appropriate topic to begin with—you may be in college for the first time or returning to school after some time away. Thinking about goals and how education can help achieve them is something all students ought to do. Read the selection called "Thinking about Education." It poses a number of questions. Think about them and try to answer them. Write your answers in a notebook. It is useful to discuss your answers with friends and classmates—this kind of give-and-take will help to clarify your reasons for being in school.

Now go to the first selection in Unit One, "What True Education Should Do" by Sydney Harris. Note the introduction before the reading selection. Always read these introductions and, if there are questions, answer them. This will help you prepare to read with understanding. In this case, we learn that the author compares students to both *sausages* and *oysters.* Does this seem strange to you? How can a student, a person, be like a sausage? What do you already know about sausages? Well, they are often tasty—no, that's probably not what the author is getting at. Just what is a sausage anyway? It is a casing stuffed with chopped meat and other filler. How could this be like a student? What could "stuff" a student? With this question in mind, read the selection.

Remember: Read the selection through quickly one time without worrying about unfamiliar words or whether you understand everything. This "once-over" will give you a good picture of what the selection is saying. Then return and read it carefully, noting any unfamiliar words you need to guess about or look up. Mark any ideas that you think are important or that you want to ask your teacher about. Jot them down in the margin of the text. When you get to class, your notes will remind you to ask your teacher to explain.

When you finish reading the selection, go to the vocabulary section. Read the directions carefully:

VOCABULARY

Directions: Find each of the key words in the reading selection. Study each word in its context and try to determine its meaning. Write what you think it means in the margin of the text, near the word. Then read over the sentence, mentally substituting your guess for the key word. Does the sentence still make sense? Does it retain its original meaning? If it does, you've probably figured out the key word correctly. In any case, confirm your guess by checking a dictionary or thesaurus.

If you take your meaning from a dictionary or thesaurus, be sure the definition includes words you already know and feel comfortable using. If it doesn't, you will be worse off than when you started—you will have begun with one word you didn't know and ended with *two* words you don't know!

Record the new words you've learned below. (Note: After the first reading in each unit, instructions for the vocabulary section appear in abbreviated form.)

The key words that follow in the chart were chosen because they are necessary to fully understand the chapter and also because they are words you will find valuable to have in your working vocabulary. Be sure to mark the words in the margin of the text. This marking of text is one of many ways you interact with the words on the page and thus become an active reader.

Let's do the first vocabulary word as an example. The word *animate* can be found in paragraph 1. Return to the paragraph and reread it:

> When most people think of the word *education,* they think of a pupil as a sort of animate sausage casing. Into this empty casing, the teachers are supposed to stuff "education."

The author is comparing a pupil to a "sort of animate sausage casing" into which teachers stuff education. What kind of sausage casing could "animate" be? Empty? A good guess—the sentence would then read ". . . they think of a pupil as a sort of [empty] sausage casing." Could be right. But then note the following sentence: "Into this empty casing, the teachers are supposed to stuff 'education.'" Why would the author repeat this notion of "empty"? No, *animate* probably means something else. If you are stuck, your next move should be to the dictionary, where you will find something like "alive" or "living" as meanings of *animate.* Does this make sense? Read the sentence again: ". . . they think of a pupil as a sort of [living] sausage casing." Sounds good, makes sense—it's probably right. Remember, if you're not sure, confirm your meaning by looking up the word in the dictionary. Then write it in the margin of the text. When you get to class, check your meanings with your instructor. Then enter your correct words in the chart in the book.

If you find other words you don't know, follow the same procedure with them. A box at the end of the vocabulary chart says "Others?" Enter the unfamiliar words you've found here and check their meanings in the same way you would the key words. For example, you may want to check the meaning of the word *cultivate* in paragraph 10.

Remember to write the meanings of all the new words in the margin of the text. When you finish the vocabulary section, your text should look something like this:

In the following reading selection, the author says students are usually treated as if they were sausages to be "stuffed" with information. He urges, instead, that students be treated as oysters—that is, something that education should "open" to reveal the riches within.

WHAT TRUE EDUCATION SHOULD DO

Sydney J. Harris

1   When most people think of the word *education*, they think of a pupil as a sort of animate sausage casing. Into this empty casing, the teachers are supposed to stuff "education." *empty? living*

2   But genuine education, as Socrates knew more than two thousand years ago, is not inserting the stuffings of information into a person, but rather eliciting knowledge from him; it is the drawing out of what is in the mind. *drawing out   I think elicit is explained here*

3   "The most important part of education," once wrote William Ernest Hocking, the distinguished Harvard philosopher, "is this instruction of a man in what he has inside of him."

4   And as Edith Hamilton has reminded us, Socrates never said, "I know, learn from me." He said, rather, "Look into your own selves and find the spark of truth that God has put into every heart, and that only you can kindle to a flame."

5   In the dialogue called the "Meno," Socrates takes an ignorant slave boy, without a day of schooling, and proves to the amazed observers that the boy really "knows" geometry—because the principles and axioms of geometry are already in his mind, waiting to be called out.

6   So many of the discussions and controversies about the content of education are futile and inconclusive because they are concerned with what should "go into" the student rather than with what should be taken out, and how this can best be done. *useless*

7   The college student who once said to me, after a lecture, "I spend so much time studying that I don't have a chance to learn anything" was succinctly expressing his dissatisfaction with the sausage-casing view of education. *briefly + clearly*

8   He was being so stuffed with miscellaneous facts, with such an indigestible mass of material, that he had no time (and was given no encouragement) to draw on his own resources, to use his own mind for analyzing and synthesizing and evaluating this material.

9   Education, to have any meaning beyond the purpose of creating well-informed dunces, must elicit from the pupil what is latent in every human being—the rules of reason, the inner knowledge of what is proper for men to be and do, the ability to sift evidence and come to conclusions that can generally be agreed to by all open minds and warm hearts. *not yet developed*

10   Pupils are more like oysters than sausages. The job of teaching is not to stuff them and then seal them up, but to help them open and reveal the riches within. There are pearls in each of us, if only we knew how to cultivate them with ardor and persistence. *make them grow*

VOCABULARY

Directions: Find each of the key words in the reading selection. Study each word in its context and try to determine its meaning. Write what you think it means in the margin of the text, near the word. Then read over the sentence, mentally substituting your guess for the key word. Does the sentence still make sense? Does it retain its original meaning? If it does, you've probably figured out the key word correctly. In any case confirm your guess by checking a dictionary or thesaurus.

If you take your meaning from a dictionary or thesaurus, be sure the definition includes words you already know and feel comfortable using. If it doesn't, you will be worse off than when you started—you will have begun with one word you didn't know and ended with *two* words you don't know!

Record the new words you've learned below.

Key Word	Paragraph	Meaning
1. animate	1	*living/alive*
2. eliciting	2	*drawing out/bringing out*
3. futile	6	*useless*
4. succinctly	7	*briefly and clearly*
5. latent	9	*not yet developed/potential*
Others?		
cultivate	*10*	*make something grow*

When you have completed the vocabulary section go on to the next section, *Guide Questions.* Again, read the directions carefully:

GUIDE QUESTIONS

Directions: The purpose of guide questions is to "guide" your analysis of the text. Your thoughtful answers will ensure that you understood the main ideas the author wanted to convey. Some questions require that you simply find the stated facts in the reading selection; others ask you to do more difficult tasks, such as paraphrasing information (putting the author's ideas into your own words), synthesizing several ideas into one complex thought, evaluating (making judgments about) an idea, or taking information from the reading and applying it to a new situation or to your own life.

Write answers to the questions in your notebook or on a separate sheet of paper if your instructor wishes to collect it. Your answers will form the basis of class discussion. (Note: After the first reading in each unit, directions for guide questions appear in abbreviated form.)

Notice that some of the questions are quite simple and straightforward, while others are much more demanding. Some may ask you to consider your own experience or knowledge of the world in answering, not just to consider ideas from the text.

Read the first guide question:

1. Write what you think is Harris's definition of a "true education."

No one sentence in the selection directly states Harris's definition of a true education, but it is certainly clear that he expects true learning to come from within the student rather than to be imposed by the teacher. The comments he makes in paragraph 9 begin to answer the question:

> Education, to have any meaning beyond the purpose of creating well-informed dunces, must elicit from the pupil what is latent in every human being—the rules of reason, the inner knowledge of what is proper for men to be and do, the ability to sift evidence and come to conclusions that can generally be agreed to by all open minds and warm hearts.

But to properly answer, you should create your own conclusion of *what you think Harris would say if he were asked this question.* In other words, draw an inference based on all the information in the selection.

Complete the guide questions. Note that the third question asks you to take the ideas from the chapter and apply them to your own life.

Go on to the next section, called "Application." This section will vary with each selection. Here, you will be asked to think about the education you have received so far and discuss with your classmates what you would still like to learn.

Last is a section called "Writing." Here, you have two questions to consider. Your instructor will tell you whether to do one or both. In one, you are asked to write a short essay based on the ideas you generated in the Application section. In the second, you are asked to *react* to Harris's view of education. To *react* means to respond with your point of view and the reasons you feel the way you do.

Many of the questions in this book begin with special *direction words.* These are words you see frequently on college assignments and exams. Some examples are *cite, define, paraphrase, summarize,* and so on. It is important to respond accurately to these words. Turn to Appendix C to study and practice using direction words.

SPECIAL PROJECTS

At the end of Units Two through Five in the text you will find a special project. The goal of the project is to allow you to use the knowledge and skills you have gained from reading extensively about one particular topic.

SPECIAL FEATURES OF UNITS FIVE AND SIX

Unit Five of the text, *Critical Reading and Thinking about Controversial Issues,* contains the added feature of collaborative work on an argumentation paper. Several topics of controversy are presented in this section. After each topic, you will be asked to work with some of your classmates in groups to research and write an essay arguing for or against one of the controversial ideas. This kind of concluding exercise will allow you to synthesize all you have learned, to operate as a fluent reader and thinker.

Unit Six of the text, *Reading and Thinking about Textbooks,* is different from the first five parts. Here, you will work with actual excerpts from college textbooks. With these chapters, you can practice your reading and studying skills with "the real thing." An important feature of this section is the inclusion of the actual test questions given to students who use these texts.

Now, before you begin this book, read the hints for productive study of textbooks in Appendix A, "Previewing."

UNIT ONE

READING AND THINKING ABOUT EDUCATION

Think about the kind of world you want to live and work in. What do you need to know to build that world? Demand your teachers teach you that.

—Prince Kropotkin

In oneself lies the whole world, and if you know how to look and learn, then the door is there and the key is in your hand. Nobody on earth can give you either that key or the door to open, except yourself.

—J. Krishnamurti

THINKING ABOUT EDUCATION

As you begin this new chapter in your college career, take a moment to think about what you are doing. Why are you in college? You may respond that you are "getting an education." But what does the word *education* really mean? Do you envision learning lots of new facts, memorizing them, and repeating them back to the instructor on exams? Is the possession of a piece of paper (a degree or certificate) your only goal? Is education simply a stepping-stone to a well-paying job? Or is it the key to becoming a happier, more fulfilled person? Perhaps education means something different to you. Take a few moments to think about your definition of education before you read this section of the book.

In the following reading selection, the author says students are usually treated as if they were sausages to be "stuffed" with information. He urges, instead, that students be treated as oysters—that is, something that education should "open" to reveal the riches within.

WHAT TRUE EDUCATION SHOULD DO

Sydney J. Harris

1 When most people think of the word *education,* they think of a pupil as a sort of animate sausage casing. Into this empty casing, the teachers are supposed to stuff "education."

2 But genuine education, as Socrates knew more than two thousand years ago, is not inserting the stuffings of information into a person, but rather eliciting knowledge from him; it is the drawing out of what is in the mind.

3 "The most important part of education," once wrote William Ernest Hocking, the distinguished Harvard philosopher, "is this instruction of a man in what he has inside of him."

4 And as Edith Hamilton has reminded us, Socrates never said, "I know, learn from me." He said, rather, "Look into your own selves and find the spark of truth that God has put into every heart, and that only you can kindle to a flame."

5 In the dialogue called the "Meno," Socrates takes an ignorant slave boy, without a day of schooling, and proves to the amazed observers that the boy really "knows" geometry—because the principles and axioms of geometry are already in his mind, waiting to be called out.

6 So many of the discussions and controversies about the content of education are futile and inconclusive because they are concerned with what should "go into" the student rather than with what should be taken out, and how this can best be done.

7 The college student who once said to me, after a lecture, "I spend so much time studying that I don't have a chance to learn anything" was succinctly expressing his dissatisfaction with the sausage-casing view of education.

8 He was being so stuffed with miscellaneous facts, with such an indigestible mass of material, that he had no time (and was given no encouragement) to draw on his own resources, to use his own mind for analyzing and synthesizing and evaluating this material.

9 Education, to have any meaning beyond the purpose of creating well-informed dunces, must elicit from the pupil what is latent in every human being—the rules of reason, the inner knowledge of what is proper for men to be and do, the ability to sift evidence and come to conclusions that can generally be agreed to by all open minds and warm hearts.

10 Pupils are more like oysters than sausages. The job of teaching is not to stuff them and then seal them up, but to help them open and reveal the riches within. There are pearls in each of us, if only we knew how to cultivate them with ardor and persistence.

VOCABULARY

Directions: Find each of the key words in the reading selection. Study each word in its context and try to determine its meaning. Write what you think it means in the margin of the text, near the word. Then read over the sentence, mentally substituting your guess for the key word. Does the sentence still make sense? Does it retain its original meaning? If it does, you've probably figured out the meaning of the key word correctly. In any case, confirm your guess by checking a dictionary or thesaurus.

If you take your meaning from a dictionary or thesaurus, be sure the definition includes words you already know and feel comfortable using. If it doesn't, you will be worse off than when you started—you will have begun with one word you didn't know and ended with *two* words you don't know!

Record the new words you've learned below.

Key Word	Paragraph	Meaning
1. animate	1	
2. eliciting	2	
3. futile	6	
4. succinctly	7	
5. latent	9	
Others?		

GUIDE QUESTIONS

Directions: The purpose of guide questions is to "guide" your analysis of the text. Your thoughtful answers will ensure that you understood the main ideas the author wanted to convey. Some questions require that you simply find the stated facts in the reading selection; others ask you to do more difficult tasks, such as paraphrasing information (putting the author's ideas into your own words), synthesizing several ideas into one complex thought, evaluating (making judgments about) an idea, or taking information from the reading and applying it to a new situation or to your own life.

Write answers to the questions in your notebook or on a separate sheet of paper if your instructor wishes to collect it. Your answers will form the basis of class discussion.

1. Write what you think is Harris's definition of a "true education."
2. Explain what Harris means by his comparison of students to sausages and oysters.

3. Have teachers treated you like a sausage or like an oyster? Would a different comparison better describe your personal experience? Explain.

APPLICATION

Directions: Read the following observations by Alan Watts on what he feels would have been an ideal education for him; then answer the questions that follow.

It is perhaps idle to wonder what, from my present point of view, would have been an ideal education. If I could provide such a curriculum for my own children they, in their turn, might find it all a bore. But the fantasy of what I would have liked to learn as a child may be revealing, since I feel unequipped by education for problems that lie outside the cloistered, literary domain in which I am competent and at home. Looking back then, I would have arranged for myself to be taught survival techniques for both natural and urban wildernesses. I would want to have been instructed in self-hypnosis, in *aikido* (the esoteric and purely self-defensive style of judo); in elementary medicine; in sexual hygiene; in vegetable gardening; in astronomy, navigation, and sailing; in cookery and clothesmaking; in metalwork and carpentry; in drawing and painting; in printing and typography; in botany and biology; in optics and acoustics; in semantics and psychology; in mysticism and yoga; in electronics and mathematical fantasy; in drama and dancing; in singing and in playing an instrument by ear; in wandering; in advanced daydreaming; in prestidigitation; in techniques of escape from bondage; in disguise; in conversation with birds and beasts; in ventriloquism; in French and German conversation; in planetary history; in morphology; and in classical Chinese. Actually, the main thing left out of my education was a proper love for my own body, because one feared to cherish anything so obviously mortal and prone to sickness.

1. What do you think Watts does for a living? What evidence in the paragraph supports your guess?
2. When Watts says there is one area in which he feels competent and at home, what does he mean by "at home"?
3. In a small group, discuss the ideas addressed in this essay. Choose a director for your group whose job is to ask group members to discuss their own personal lists of: 1) the areas where they feel "competent and at home"; and 2) things they wish they had been taught. At the end of the discussion, each person should have two lists that can be developed into the essay described in assignment 1 below.

WRITING

Directions: Choose one of the following assignments.

1. Write a short essay similar to the one by Alan Watts. In the first paragraph, describe, as Watts does, the areas in which you feel "competent." In the second paragraph, name and describe the things you wish you had been taught.
2. React to the argument presented in Sydney J. Harris's "What True Education Should Do." Do you agree or disagree with the author? Write one paragraph stating your reaction, giving reasons to support your opinion.

In 1957, Sputnik, the first satellite to fly into space, was launched by the Russians. It created a panic in Russia's Cold War enemy, the United States. Speeches were given and essays written bemoaning America's fall to second place in technological development, and many became convinced it reflected a failure of the United States educational system. President Kennedy promised that the United States would be the first to put a man on the moon and made good on his promise in 1969. But the crisis in self-confidence in American education remains. The questions "What is education?" and "Is America educating its youth?" are as current today as they were forty years ago.

ANGELS ON A PIN

Alexander Calandra

Some time ago, I received a call from a colleague who asked if I would be the referee on the grading of an examination question. He was about to give a student a zero for his answer to a physics question, while the student claimed he should receive a perfect score and would if the system were not set up against the student. The instructor and the student agreed to submit this to an impartial arbiter, and I was selected. 1

I went to my colleague's office and read the examination question: "Show how it is possible to determine the height of a tall building with the aid of a barometer." 2

The student had answered: "Take the barometer to the top of the building, attach a long rope to it, lower the barometer to the street, and then bring it up, measuring the length of the rope. The length of the rope is the height of the building." 3

I pointed out that the student really had a strong case for full credit, since he had answered the question completely and correctly. On the other hand, if full credit were given, it could well contribute to a high grade for the student in his physics course. A high grade is supposed to certify competence in physics, but the answer did not confirm this. I suggested that the student have another try at answering the question. I was not surprised that my colleague agreed, but I was surprised that the student did. 4

I gave the student six minutes to answer the question, with the warning that his answer should show some knowledge of physics. At the end of five minutes, he had not written anything. I asked if he wished to give up, but he said no. He had many answers to this problem; he was just thinking of the best one. I excused myself for interrupting him, and asked him to please go on. In the next minute, he dashed off his answer which read: 5

"Take the barometer to the top of the building and lean over the edge of the roof. Drop the barometer, timing its fall with a stopwatch. Then, using the formula $S = \frac{1}{2}at^2$, calculate the height of the building." 6

At this point, I asked my colleague if he would give up. He conceded, and I gave the student almost full credit. 7

In leaving my colleague's office, I recalled that the student had said he had other answers to the problem, so I asked him what they were. "Oh, yes," said the student. "There are many ways of getting the height of a tall building with the aid of a barometer. For example, you could take the barometer out on a sunny day and measure 8 the height of the barometer, the length of its shadow, and the length of the shadow of the building, and by the use of a simple proportion, determine the height of the building."

9   "Fine," I said. "And the others?"

10   "Yes," said the student. "There is a very basic measurement method that you will like. In this method, you take the barometer and begin to walk up the stairs. As you climb the stairs, you mark off the length of the barometer along the wall. You then count the number of marks, and this will give you the height of the building in barometer units. A very direct method.

11   "Of course, if you want a more sophisticated method, you can tie the barometer to the end of a string, swing it as a pendulum, and determine the value of g at the street level and at the top of the building. From the difference between the two values of g, the height of the building can, in principle, be calculated."

12   Finally, he concluded, there are many other ways of solving the problem. "Probably the best," he said, "is to take the barometer to the basement and knock on the superintendent's door. When the superintendent answers, you speak to him as follows: 'Mr. Superintendent, here I have a fine barometer. If you will tell me the height of this building, I will give you this barometer.'"

13   At this point, I asked the student if he really did not know the conventional answer to this question. He admitted that he did, but said that he was fed up with high school and college instructors trying to teach him how to think, to use the "scientific method," and to explore the deep inner logic of the subject in a pedantic way, as is often done in the new mathematics, rather than teaching him the structure of the subject. With this in mind, he decided to revive scholasticism as an academic lark to challenge the *Sputnik*-panicked classrooms of America.

VOCABULARY

Directions: Locate each of the key words in the reading selection. Then read and study each word in its context and try to determine its meaning. Use a dictionary or thesaurus to check your guess. Write the meanings of the words in the margin of the text.

Record the new words you've learned below.

Key Word	Paragraph	Meaning
1. arbiter	1	
2. pedantic	13	
3. lark	13	
Others?		

GUIDE QUESTIONS

Directions: The purpose of these guide questions is to ensure your understanding of what you have read. They will also help you to analyze and evaluate the author's ideas and apply them to the real world and your own life.

Write answers to the questions in your notebook or on a separate sheet of paper if your instructor wishes to collect them. Your answers will form the basis of class discussion.

1. The topic of this story is education. What point is the author making about education today?
2. Why do you think the student in the story refused to give the answer he knew the instructor wanted?
3. Evaluate the different answers the student gave to the test question. Which answer do you think is the best one?
4. Why do you think the narrator gave the student almost full credit (paragraph 7)? Why didn't he give him 100 percent credit? What score would you have given him?
5. a. In your opinion, what are the purposes of exams and tests?
   b. In your experience, have school exams achieved their purpose? If not, how could they be improved?
6. In the Middle Ages, theologians and philosophers engaged in debates that seem like a waste of time to us today. The most famous was a long-running argument about how many angels could dance on the head of a pin. What is the relation of the title of this selection to the point the author wants to make?

APPLICATION

Directions: Read this paragraph by Paul Goodman and answer the questions that follow:

In my opinion, the only justification for high schools is as therapeutic halfway houses for the deranged. Normal adolescents can find themselves and grow further only by coping with the jobs, sex, and chances of the real world—it is useless to feed them curricular imitations. I would simply abolish the high schools, substituting apprenticeships and other alternatives and protecting the young from gross exploitation by putting the school money directly in their pockets. The very few who have authentic scholarly interests will gravitate to their own libraries, teachers, and academies, as they always did in the past, when they could afford it. In organic communities, adolescents cluster together in their own youth houses, for their fun and games and loud music, without bothering sober folk. I see no reason whatsoever for adults to set up or direct such nests or to be there at all unless invited.

1. What argument is Goodman making in this paragraph? Restate his thesis in your own words.
2. Agree or disagree with Goodman. Discuss your opinion with your classmates. Write a paragraph stating your opinion and reasons to support it.

WRITING

Directions: Now that you have read and thought about the topic of education, take a moment to consider the quality of the education you have received so far. Has it been good, fair, or poor? Explain why you feel the way you do. Give specific examples of how your education has helped you to solve problems or to achieve a goal. Or give examples that describe how your education failed you. Write at least one page.

Most people would say that education *is something that occurs in school. Here, noted New York Times* columnist Russell Baker uses his characteristic dry humor to interpret the word *education as having two very different meanings. As you read, try to imagine what Baker's definition of* education *is.*

Before you read, write your own definition of education.

SCHOOL VS. EDUCATION
Russell Baker

By the age of six the average child will have completed the basic American educa- 1
tion and be ready to enter school. If the child has been attentive in these preschool
years, he or she will already have mastered many skills.

From television, the child will have learned how to pick a lock, commit a fairly 2
elaborate bank holdup, prevent wetness all day long, get the laundry twice as white,
and kill people with a variety of sophisticated armaments.

From watching his parents, the child, in many cases, will already know how to 3
smoke, how much soda to mix with whiskey, what kind of language to use when angry, and how to violate the speed laws without being caught.

At this point, the child is ready for the second stage of education, which occurs 4
in school. There, a variety of lessons may be learned in the very first days.

The teacher may illustrate the economic importance of belonging to a strong 5
union by closing down the school before the child arrives. Fathers and mothers may
demonstrate to the child the social cohesion that can be built on shared hatred by
demonstrating their dislike for children whose pigmentation displeases them. In the
latter event, the child may receive visual instruction in techniques of stoning buses,
cracking skulls with a nightstick, and subduing mobs with tear gas. Formal education
has begun.

During formal education, the child learns that life is for testing. This stage lasts 6
twelve years, a period during which the child learns that success comes from telling
testers what they want to hear.

Early in this stage, the child learns that he is either dumb or smart. If the teacher 7
puts intelligent demands upon the child, the child learns he is smart. If the teacher expects little of the child, the child learns he is dumb and soon quits bothering to tell
the testers what they want to hear.

At this point, education becomes more subtle. The child taught by school that he 8
is dumb observes that neither he, she, nor any of the many children who are even
dumber ever fails to be promoted to the next grade. From this, the child learns that,
while everybody talks a lot about the virtue of being smart, there is very little incentive to stop being dumb.

What is the point of school, besides attendance? the child wonders. As the end 9
of the first formal stage of education approaches, school answers this question. The
point is to equip the child to enter college.

Children who have been taught they are smart have no difficulty. They have been 10
happily telling testers what they want to hear for twelve years. Being artists at telling

testers what they want to hear, they are admitted to college joyously, where they promptly learn that they are the hope of America.

11   Children whose education has been limited to adjusting themselves to their schools' low estimates of them are admitted to less joyous colleges which, in some cases, may teach them to read.

12   At this stage of education, a fresh question arises for everyone. If the point of lower education was to get into college, what is the point of college? The answer is soon learned. The point of college is to prepare the student—no longer a child now—to get into graduate school. In college, the student learns that it is no longer enough simply to tell the testers what they want to hear. Many are tested for graduate school; few are admitted.

13   Those excluded may be denied valuable certificates to prosper in medicine, at the bar, in the corporate boardroom. The student learns that the race is to the cunning and often, alas, to the unprincipled.

14   Thus, the student learns the importance of destroying competitors and emerges richly prepared to play his role in the great simmering melodrama of American life.

15   Afterward, the former student's destiny fulfilled, his life rich with Oriental carpets, rare porcelain, and full bank accounts, he may one day find himself with the leisure and the inclination to open a book with a curious mind, and start to become educated.

VOCABULARY

Directions: Locate each of the key words in the reading selection. Then read and study each word in its context and try to determine its meaning. Use a dictionary or thesaurus to check your guess. Write the meanings of the words in the margin of the text.

Record the new words you've learned below.

Key Word	Paragraph	Meaning
1. armaments	2	
2. cohesion	5	
3. pigmentation	5	
4. cunning	13	
5. melodrama	14	
Others?		

GUIDE QUESTIONS

Directions: The purpose of these guide questions is to ensure your understanding of what you have read. They will also help you to analyze and evaluate the author's ideas and apply them to the real world and your own life.

Write answers to the questions in your notebook or on a separate sheet of paper if your instructor wishes to collect them. Your answers will form the basis of class discussion.

1. a. In this essay, Baker implicitly criticizes the American education system. Explain the meaning of the word *implicit.*
   b. At what point in the essay did you first realize Baker was criticizing the education system?
2. Why do you think Baker titled this essay "School vs. Education"?
3. List the skills Baker says children learn before they start school.
4. Describe some of the lessons children learn in the "second stage" of education.
5. According to Baker, how do children find out if they are "smart" or "dumb"? Does this ring true to you? Or is Baker exaggerating?
6. a. According to Baker, at what point may a person actually find himself with the "leisure and inclination" to become educated?
   b. How does this support his criticism of education?
7. Discuss Baker's tone in this essay. Is it humorous? Angry? Choose an adjective you think best describes his attitude here. Compare your description to those of your classmates.

APPLICATION

Directions: Choose one of the questions below. Discuss the question in a small group. When you have finished, compose a paragraph in response to the question.

1. If you read "What True Education Should Do," consider the following question: Would Harris and Baker agree or disagree on the requirements of a good education? State your opinion and support it with facts from the two essays.
2. React to Baker's description of school. Does he describe your experience in school or not? Explain.

WRITING

Directions: Write two paragraphs. In the first, list the things Baker says children learn in school. In the second, list the things *you* feel children *should* be learning in school.

Barbara Jordan was born in Texas in 1936 and died there in 1996. She began her life in the largest black ghetto in the biggest state of the union. She graduated magna cum laude from Texas Southern University and went on to Boston Law School. She was the first woman and the only black in the Texas State Senate; she was the first woman and the only black member of the U.S. Congress from Texas: she was the first woman and the only black member of Congress from the entire South. To quote Molly Ivins's essay on Jordan, which appeared in the New York Times, *"The degree of prejudice she had to overcome by intelligence and sheer force of personality is impossible to overestimate. She wasn't just black and female: she was homely, she was heavy, and she was dark black. When she first came to the Texas Senate, it was considered a great joke to bring racist friends to the gallery when B. J. was due to speak. They would no sooner gasp, 'Who is that nigger?' than she would open her mouth and out would roll language Lincoln would have appreciated. Her personal dignity was so substantial even admirers hesitated to approach her. No one will ever know how lonely she was at the beginning." Jordan won national acclaim for her intelligence and oratory during the House Judiciary Committee's proceedings to impeach President Richard Nixon in 1974 and later for her keynote speech to the Democratic National Convention in 1976. She retired from Congress after three terms and became an immensely popular and respected teacher at the University of Texas. In 1992, Jordan returned to the podium of the Democratic National Convention and electrified the nation with her speech. She spoke of her fierce passion for her country and for its ideals. She proclaimed, "My faith in the Constitution is whole, it is complete, it is total." To quote Ivins again, "She sounded like God." Suffering from multiple sclerosis and other ailments, Barbara Jordan died on January 17, 1996. President Clinton called her death the "loss of a national treasure." Today, she is the first and only black woman buried in the Texas State Cemetery.*

In this excerpt from her autobiography, Jordan describes learning to "think and read and understand and reason."

BECOMING EDUCATED

Barbara Jordan

1   So I was at Boston University in this new and strange and different world, and it occurred to me that if I was going to succeed at this strange new adventure, I would have to read longer and more thoroughly than my colleagues at law school had to read. I felt that, in order to compensate for what I had missed in earlier years, I would have to work harder, and study longer, than anybody else. I still had this feeling that I did not want my colleagues to know what a tough time I was having understanding the concepts, the words, the ideas, the process. I didn't want them to know that. So I did my reading not in the law library, but in a library at the graduate dorm, upstairs where it was very quiet, because apparently nobody else there studied. So I would go there at night after dinner. I would load my books under my arm and go to the library, and I would read until the wee hours of the morning and then go to bed. I didn't get much sleep during those years. I was lucky if I got three or four hours a night, because I had to stay up. I had to. The professors would assign cases for the next day, and these cases had to be read and understood or I would be behind, further behind than I was.

I was always delighted when I would get called upon to recite in class. But the   2
professors did not call on the "ladies" very much. There were certain favored people
who always got called on, and then on some rare occasions a professor would come
in and would announce: "We're going to have Ladies Day today." And he would call
on the ladies. We were just tolerated. We weren't considered really top drawer
when it came to the study of the law.

At some time in the spring, Bill Gibson, who was dating my new roommate,   3
Norma Walker, organized a black study group, as we blacks had to form our own.
This was because we were not invited into any of the other study groups. There
were six or seven in our group—Bill, and Issie, and I think Maynard Jackson—and
we would just gather and talk it out and hear ourselves do that. One thing I learned
was that you had to talk out the issues, the facts, the cases, the decisions, the process.
You couldn't just read the cases and study alone in your library as I had been doing;
and you couldn't get it all in the classroom. But once you had talked it out in the
study group, it flowed more easily and made a lot more sense.

And from time to time I would go up to the fourth floor at 2 Rawley Street to   4
check on how Louise was doing. She was always reading *Redbook*. Every time I was
in there and wanted to discuss one of the cases with her, she was reading a short
story in *Redbook*. I don't know how she could do that. She was not prepared in class
when the professors would call on her to discuss cases, but that did not bother her.
Whereas it was a matter of life and death with me. I had to make law school. I just
didn't have any alternatives. I could not afford to flunk out. That would have been
an unmitigated disaster. So I read all the time I was not in class.

Finally I felt I was really learning things, really going to school. I felt that I was get-   5
ting educated, whatever that was. I became familiar with the process of thinking. I
learned to think things out and reach conclusions and defend what I had said.

In the past I had got along by spouting off. Whether you talked about debates   6
or oratory, you dealt with speechifying. Even in debate it was pretty much canned
because you had, in your little three-by-five box, a response for whatever issue
might be raised by the opposition. The format was structured so that there was no
opportunity for independent thinking. (I really had not had my ideas challenged
ever.) But I could no longer orate and let that pass for reasoning. Because there was
not any demand for an orator in Boston University Law School. You had to think and
read and understand and reason. I had learned at twenty-one that you couldn't just
say a thing is so because it might not be so, and somebody brighter, smarter, and
more thoughtful would come out and tell you it wasn't so. Then, if you still thought
it was, you had to prove it. Well, that was a new thing for me. I cannot, I really cannot describe what that did to my insides and to my head. I thought: I'm being educated finally.

VOCABULARY

Directions: Locate each of the key words in the reading selection. Then read and
study each word in its context and try to determine its meaning. Use a dictionary
or thesaurus to check your guess. Write the meanings of the words in the margin
of the text.

Record the new words you've learned on the next page.

Key Word	Paragraph	Meaning
1. compensate	1	
2. top drawer	2	
3. spouting off	6	
4. oratory	6	
Others?		

GUIDE QUESTIONS

Directions: The purpose of these guide questions is to ensure your understanding of what you have read. They also will help you to analyze and evaluate the author's ideas and apply them to the real world and your own life.

Write answers to the questions in your notebook or on a separate sheet of paper if your instructor wishes to collect them. Your answers will form the basis of class discussion.

1. What can you infer from this story about the status of women and minorities in law schools at the time Barbara Jordan attended Boston University?
2. What did Jordan learn about the value of studying with a group of fellow students while she was at Boston University?
3. At the end of the piece, Jordan says, "I'm being educated finally." What had happened to make her feel this way?

APPLICATION

Directions: Learn a little more about this interesting American, Barbara Jordan. Visit the library to find out more about her extraordinary life. Share what you discover with your classmates.

WRITING

Directions: Complete at least two of the assignments below.

1. Do you ever feel discouraged about school? Many students juggle work and family responsibilities as well as college. Many students find their course work just plain hard! Try this mental exercise: Write a letter to Barbara Jordan. Describe the problems you are having. Try to be specific: Is scheduling a problem? Do you have difficulty finding enough time to study? Are your classes extremely difficult? Is the material too advanced?

Is there a problem with an instructor? Or with other students? Are your grades lower than you would like? Try to define and describe any trouble you are having. Write at least a page—you may need to write more.

2. Put the letter you wrote in assignment 1 above in a drawer for a few days. Then take it out and read it carefully. Imagine you are Barbara Jordan and write an answer to your letter. What do you think she might say in response to you?

3. Read the selection "Darkness at Noon" by Harold Krents on page 223. Write an imaginary letter from Mr. Krents that responds to your letter written in assignment 1.

During the 1980s and 1990s, the number of older people returning to school grew enormously. Many return to improve their employment potential. Others return simply for the pleasure of learning. In the essay below, we learn of a thirty-year-old woman who feels handicapped by her lack of education—and of her determination to help herself overcome it.

OVERCOMING AN INVISIBLE HANDICAP
Thomas J. Cottle

1   On her thirtieth birthday, Lucille Elmore informed her husband that she was going through a crisis. "I was thirty years old, active, in good health—and I was illiterate," she recalls. "I didn't know books, I didn't know history, I didn't know science. I had the barest understanding of the arts. Like a physical condition, my knowledge limped, my intelligence limped."

2   She was not only the mother of two young children but also was working full time as an administrative assistant in a business-consulting firm. Nevertheless, at age thirty, with her husband's agreement, Lucille Elmore enrolled in college. "I thought getting in would be difficult," she says. "It was easy. I thought I couldn't discipline myself, but that came. Half the people in the library the first day thought I was the librarian, but that didn't deter me."

3   For Lucille, the awareness of her invisible limp came only gradually. As a young woman, she had finished high school, but she had chosen not to go on with her education. Her parents, who had never completed high school themselves, urged her to go to college but she refused. At the time, she was perhaps a bit timid and lacked a certain confidence in her own intellectual or academic abilities. Besides, a steady job was far more important at that point to Lucille than schooling; she felt she could read on her own to make up for any lack of education.

4   At twenty, working full time, she married Ted Elmore, a salesman for a food-store chain, a man on his way to becoming more than modestly successful. There was no need for her to work, but she did so until her first child was born; she was then twenty-two. A second child was born two years later, and three years after that, she went back to work. With her youngest in a day-care program, she felt no reservations about working, but her lack of education began to nag at her as she approached the age of thirty. She thus gave up her job, entered a continuing-education program at a nearby university, and began what she likens to a love affair.

5   "I'm carrying on an open affair with books, but like a genuinely good lover, I'm being guided. Reading lists, suggested reading, recommended readings—I want them all. I must know what happened in the twelfth, thirteenth, and eighteenth centuries. I want to know how the world's major religions evolved. Papal history, I know nothing of papal history and succession, or the politics involved. I read the Bible, but I never studied it. It's like music: I listened, but it wasn't an informed listening. Now all of this is changing.

6   "I must tell you, I despise students when they talk about 'the real world,' as if college were a dream world. They simply don't understand what the accumulation of knowledge and information means. Maybe you have to be thirty at least, and going through a personal crisis, to fully appreciate what historical connections are.

"A line of Shakespeare challenges me more than half the jobs I'll be equipped   7
for when I'm finished. I'm having an affair with him, too, only it's called Elizabethan
Literature 606. I think many people prefer the real world of everyday work because
it's less frightening than the larger-than-life world of college.

"There's a much more important difference between the rest of the students   8
and me. We don't agree at all on what it means to be a success. They think in terms
of money, material things. I suppose that's normal. They don't understand that, with
a nice home, and decent job prospects, and two beautiful children, I know I am a
failure. I'm a failure because I am ignorant. I'm a failure until I have knowledge, until
I can work with it, be excited by and play with ideas.

"I don't go to school for the rewards down the line. I want to reach the point   9
at which I don't measure knowledge by anything but itself. An idea has value or it
doesn't. This is how I now determine success and failure.

"'How can I use it?' That's what students ask. 'What good will this do me?' They   10
don't think about what the question says about them, even without an answer attached to it. Questions like that only build up competition. But competition is the
bottom line for so many students, I guess, getting ahead, getting a bit of a step up on
the other guy. I know, it's my husband's life.

"I'll tell what I think I like most about my work: the library. I can think of no   11
place so exclusive and still so open and public. Millions of books there for the taking.
A chair to sit in, a row of books, and you don't need a penny. For me, the library is
a religious center, a shrine.

"Students talk about the real world out there. What about the free world in   12
here? Here, no one arrests you for what you're thinking. In the library, you can't
talk, so you have to think. I never knew what it meant to think about something, to
really think it through. I certainly never understood what you had to know to even
begin to think. I always thought it was normal to limp."

VOCABULARY

Directions: Locate each of the key words in the reading selection. Then read and
study each word in its context and try to determine its meaning. Use a dictionary
or thesaurus to check your guess. Write the meanings of the words in the margin
of the text.

Record the new words you've learned below.

Key Word	Paragraph	Meaning
1. deter	2	
2. shrine	11	
Others?		

GUIDE QUESTIONS

Directions: The purpose of these guide questions is to ensure your understanding of what you have read. They will also help you to analyze and evaluate the author's ideas and apply them to the real world and your own life.

Write answers to the questions in your notebook or on a separate sheet of paper if your instructor wishes to collect them. Your answers will form the basis of class discussion.

1. Define the word *illiterate* as it is generally used; then define *illiterate* as it is used by Elmore in this essay.
2. Why did half of the people in the library on the first day think Elmore was the librarian?
3. In this essay, Elmore uses two powerful comparisons in describing her return to school: a "handicap," or "limp," and a "love affair." Explain each of these comparisons.
4. In paragraph 8, Elmore describes herself as a failure. Why does she say this? Do you agree that she was a failure?
5. Contrast Elmore's view of what it means to be a success with the view of her fellow students.
6. a. Why does Elmore say she despises students when they talk about "the real world"?
   b. List some of the other differences of opinion between Elmore and her younger classmates.
7. a. Why does Elmore describe the library as "a religious center"?
   b. Compare and contrast your opinion of the library with Elmore's.

APPLICATION

Directions: Compare Lucille Elmore's view of education with that of Sydney Harris ("What True Education Should Do") or Alexander Calandra ("Angels on a Pin"). Would they agree on the purpose of education? Give evidence to support your answer. Write at least one paragraph.

WRITING

Directions: If you are a "returning student" (say, returning to school after an absence of five or more years), discuss your view of education with a younger student (someone who came to college directly from high school). If you are a young student, discuss education with an older classmate. Then write one or two paragraphs comparing and contrasting your views.

Studies show a clear relationship between teachers' expectations of students and the students' academic performance. For example, if a child sees that a teacher expects him or her to do well in math, chances are that the child will do well. The opposite is also true: if teachers show that they expect a child to do poorly, the child probably will do poorly. In this article from Newsweek *magazine, the author reports on a study that shows teachers pay more attention to boys than to girls and the effect of this bias on the children.*

SEXISM IN THE SCHOOLHOUSE
A Report Charges That Schools Favor Boys over Girls

Barbara Kantrowitz

The girls in Jill Gugisberg Wall's science class at Farnsworth Elementary School in   1
St. Paul, Minnesota, get angry when they think about the bad old days. At the
schools they attended before coming to Farnsworth, "the boys got all the attention,"
says Carrie Paladie, twelve. "Every time *we* asked a question, the teacher would just
ignore us." Her classmate, eleven-year-old Jennie Montour, agrees: "The boys got
to participate in everything." Jennie says the teachers made her feel "that I was stupid." Their new science teacher's mission is to change all that. "In my classroom,"
she says, "I encourage everyone to be involved."

Unfortunately, there are too few teachers like Wall. Sexism may be the most   2
widespread and damaging form of bias in the classroom, according to a report released last week by the American Association of University Women. The report,
which summarized 1,331 studies of girls in school, describes a pattern of downward
intellectual mobility for girls. The AAUW found that girls enter first grade with the
same or better skills and ambitions as boys. But, all too often, by the time they
finish high school, "their doubts have crowded out their dreams."

In elementary school, the researchers say, teachers call on boys much more of-   3
ten and give them more encouragement. Boys frequently need help with reading, so
remedial reading classes are an integral part of many schools. But girls, who just as
often need help with math, rarely get a similar chance to sharpen their skills. Boys
get praised for the intellectual content of their work while girls are more likely to
be praised for neatness. Boys tend not to be penalized for calling out answers and
taking risks; girls who do the same are reprimanded for being rude. Research indicates that girls learn better in cooperative settings, where students work together,
while boys learn better in competitive settings. Yet most schools are based on a
competitive model. The report also indicates that schools are becoming more tol-
erant of male students sexually harassing female students.

Despite these problems, girls get better grades and are more likely to go on to   4
college, according to the report. But even these successful girls have less confidence
in their abilities than boys, have higher expectations of failure and more modest
aspirations. The result, the report concludes, is that girls are less likely to reach their
potential than boys.

5   The differences between the sexes are greatest in science. Between 1978 and 1986, the gap between the national science achievement test scores of nine- and thirteen-year-old boys and girls widened—because girls did worse and boys did better. Girls and boys take about the same number of science courses, but girls are more likely to take advanced biology and boys are more likely to take physics and advanced chemistry. Even girls who take the same courses as boys and perform equally well on tests are less likely than boys to choose technical careers. A Rhode Island study found that 64 percent of the boys who had taken physics and calculus in high school were planning to major in science or engineering, compared with only 18.6 percent of the girls who had taken those courses.

6   More than two-thirds of the nation's teachers are women. Presumably, their gender bias is unintentional but no less apparent. American University researchers Myra and David Sadker have taped hundreds of hours of class sessions in schools around the country and have studied how teachers react to boys and girls. "When researchers have asked teachers to remember their favorite students, it always ends up being kids who conformed to gender stereotypes," says David Sadker. "The ones they like best are assertive males and the ones they like least are assertive females."

"Wrong Target"

7   Critics of the report's conclusions point out that girls have come a long way in the last twenty years. "If you're talking equity," says Diane Ravitch, assistant secretary of education, "you have to acknowledge that there are more women enrolled in college today than men. Women have the edge." Rather than sexism in education, she says, the problem is sexist attitudes encouraged by TV, advertising, and the movies: the researchers "picked the wrong target." Ravitch thinks much of the educational gap could be closed by simply telling girls to take more science and advanced math.

8   Other education experts say the remedy is much more complicated. Keith Geiger, president of the National Education Association, the largest teachers union, advocates incorporating gender awareness into teacher training and classroom reviews. Also, he says, as schools upgrade their math and science standards, they should encourage more participation by girls. A more controversial solution might be single-sex schools or sex segregation at crucial points in a girl's development. "For most girls, it's a very affirming experience," says Agnes Underwood, headmistress of the all-girls National Cathedral School in Washington, D.C. "You get a level of support you absolutely do not get in a coed classroom."

9   In Jill Wall's class, girls get a lot of support from their teacher. Wall learned more about teaching girls after receiving an AAUW fellowship in 1990 during which she studied elementary science education. Last year she ran a science program for inner-city girls. At Farnsworth, her students give her straight As. "She treats us all the same," says Tamika Aubert, eleven. Equity in the classroom won't turn all girls—or boys—into physicists. But maybe we'll get a generation of teachers who can delight in assertive girls and shy boys with a talent for the arts.

VOCABULARY

Directions: Locate each of the key words in the reading selection. Try to figure out each word's meaning by using the context. Confirm your guess by checking the dictionary or thesaurus. Write the meanings of the words in the margin of the text. Then record the meanings in the chart below.

Key Word	Paragraph	Meaning
1. integral	3	
2. reprimanded	3	
3. bias	6	
4. assertive	6	
Others?		

GUIDE QUESTIONS

Directions: These questions will guide your understanding of what you have read. Write your answers in your notebook or on a separate sheet of paper if your instructor wishes to collect it. Your answers to these questions will be the basis of class discussion.

1. a. Describe the study that is cited in the reading selection: Who conducted it? What method was used?
   b. Summarize the results of the study.
2. React to the opinion of Diane Ravitch, a critic of the study.
3. One suggested solution to the problem of sexism in schools is the creation of single-sex or sex-segregated schools. What would be the benefits of such schools? What would be the drawbacks?
4. Have you observed or experienced incidents of gender bias in any of your classrooms? If you have, describe what happened.
5. Many people would say that gender bias begins at home, long before children go to school. Consider this: In a different study, preschool youngsters were shown a drawing of a house and asked, "How far can you go from your own house?" Most girls pointed to an area quite near the house and said that was how far their parents permitted them to go and how far they actually went. Most boys pointed to a much wider perimeter of permission and generally said they exceeded it.

   Can you supply other examples from your own experience that illustrate differences in the way parents treat little boys and little girls?

APPLICATION

Directions: In a small group, discuss the information in the article. Do the results of the AAUW study ring true? What have your personal experiences been? Suggest some solutions to the problem of gender bias in school.

If you found this article interesting, you may also enjoy reading "Women in Science" on page 178.

WRITING

1. *Directions:* If you have experienced gender bias in your schooling, write a brief account describing what happened.
2. *Directions:* Write a summary of "Sexism in the Schoolhouse." To review summary writing, turn to Appendix B.

Most people associate "summer school" with failure and frustration—held prisoner in steamy classrooms, bored by repetition, barred from the delights of summer. Here, however, the author of the book Living up the Street *recalls summer school as pure pleasure.*

SUMMER SCHOOL
Gary Soto

The summer before I entered sixth grade I decided to go to summer school. I had never gone, and it was either school or mope around the house with a tumbler of Kool-Aid and watch TV, flipping the channels from exercise programs to soap operas to game shows until something looked right. 1

My sister decided to go to summer school too, so the two of us hopped onto our bikes and rode off to Heaton Elementary, which was three miles away, and asked around until we were pointed to the right rooms. I ran off without saying good-bye to Debra. 2

These were the home rooms where the teachers would check roll, announce bulletins, and read us a story before we dashed off to other classes. That morning I came in breathing hard, smiling a set of teeth that were fit for an adult, and took a seat behind a fat kid named Yodelman so I couldn't be seen. 3

The teacher, whose name is forgotten, told us that summer school classes were all electives—that we could choose anything we wanted. She had written them on the blackboard, and from her list I chose science, history, German, and square dancing. 4

Little John, a friend from our street, sat across the room. I had not seen him at first, which miffed him because he thought I was playing stuck-up for some reason, and so he threw an acorn at me that bounced harmlessly off Yodelman's shoulder. Yodelman turned his head slowly, turtle-like, blinked his small dull eyes, and then turned his head back to the teacher who was telling us that we had to fill out cards. She had two monitors pass out pencils, and we hovered and strained over the card: Date of birth, address, grade, career goals. At the last one I thought for the longest time, pencil poised and somewhat worried, before I raised my hand to ask the teacher how to spell paleontology. Surprised, as if someone had presented her flowers, she opened her mouth, searched the ceiling with her eyes, and gave it a stab: p-a-y-e-n-t-o-l-o-g-y. I wrote it in uneven capitals and then wrote "bone collector" in the margin. 5

Little John glared at me, made a fist, and wet his lips. When class was dismissed he punched me softly in the arm and together the two of us walked out of class talking loudly, happy that we were together. 6

While Little John went to typing I went to science class. The teacher stood before us in a white shirt, yardstick in hand, surrounded by jars of animal parts floating in clear liquids. Those scared me, as did a replica of a skeleton hanging like a frayed coat in the corner. On the first day we looked carefully at leaves in groups of threes, after which the teacher asked us to describe the differences. 7

"This one is dried up and this one is not so dried up," one kid offered, a leaf in each hand. 8

9 The teacher, who was kind, said that that was a start. He raised his yardstick and pointed to someone else.

10 From there I went to history, a class I enjoyed immensely because it was the first one ever in which I would earn an A. This resulted from reading thirty books—pamphlets to be more exact. I was a page-turner, and my index finger touched each paragraph before the thumb peeled a new page, as I became familiar with Edison, Carnegie, MacArthur, Eli Whitney. . . . At the end of the five-week summer school, the teacher would call me to the front of the class to tell about the books I had read. He stood behind the lectern, looking down at his watch now and then, and beamed at me like a flashlight.

11 "Who was Pike?"

12 "Oh, he was the guy that liked to go around in the mountains."

13 "Who was Genghis Khan?"

14 "He was a real good fighter. In China."

15 With each answer the teacher smiled and nodded his head at me. He smiled at the class and some of the students turned their heads away, mad that I knew so much. Little John made a fist and wet his lips.

16 From history we were released to the playground, where we played softball, sucked on popsicles, and fooled around on the monkey bars. We returned to our classes, sweating like the popsicles we had sucked to a rugged stick. I went to German, where, for five weeks, we sang songs we didn't understand, though we loved them and loved our teacher who paraded around the room and closed his eyes on the high notes. On the best days he rolled up his sleeves, undid his tie, and sweated profusely as he belted out songs so loudly that we heard people pounding on the wall for quiet from the adjoining classroom. Still, he went on with great vigor:

> Mein Hut der hat drei Ecken
> Drei Ecken hat mein Hut
> Und wenn er das nicht haste
> Dan war's auch nicht mein Hut

17 And we joined in every time, faces pink from a wonderful beauty that rose effortlessly from the heart.

18 I left, humming, for square dancing, Debra was in that class with me, fresh from science class, where, she told me, she and a girlfriend had rolled balls of mercury in their palms to shine nickels, rings, and earrings, before they got bored and hurled them at the boys. The mercury flashed on their shoulders, and they pretended to be shot and they staggered and went down to their knees.

19 Even though Debra didn't want to do it, we paired off the first day. We made ugly faces at each other as we clicked our heels, swished for a few steps, and clicked again.

20 It was in that class that I fell in love with my corner gal who looked like Hayley Mills, except she was not as boyish. I was primed to fall in love because of the afternoon movies I watched on television, most of which were stories about women and men coming together, parting with harsh feelings, and embracing in the end to marry and drive big cars.

21 Day after day we'd pass through do-si-does, form Texas stars, spin, click heels, and bounce about the room, released from our rigid, school-children lives to let our

bodies find their rhythm. As we danced I longed openly for her, smiling like a lantern and wanting very badly for her eyes to lock onto mine and think deep feelings. She swung around my arm, happy as the music, and hooked onto the next kid, oblivious to my yearning.

When I became sick and missed school for three days, my desire for her didn't   22
sputter out. In bed with a comic book, I became dreamy as a cat and closed my eyes to the image of her allemanding left to "The Red River Valley," a favorite of the class's, her long hair flipping about on her precious shoulders. By Friday I was well, but instead of going to school I stayed home to play "jump and die" with the neighbor kids—a game in which we'd repeatedly climb a tree and jump until someone went home crying from a hurt leg or arm. We played way into the dark.

On Monday I was back, stiff as new rope, but once again excited by science, his-   23
tory, the guttural sounds of German, and square dancing! By Sunday I had almost forgotten my gal, so when I walked into class my heart was sputtering its usual tiny, blue flame. It picked up, however, when I saw the girls come in, pink from the afternoon heat, and line up against the wall. When the teacher clapped her hands, announced something or another, and asked us to pair off, my heart was roaring like a well-stoked fire as I approached a girl that looked like my girlfriend. I searched her face, but it wasn't her. I looked around as we galloped about the room but I couldn't spot her. Where is she? Is that her? I asked myself. No, no, my girlfriend has a cute nose. Well, then, is that her? I wondered girl after girl and, for a moment in the dizziness of spinning, I even thought my sister was my girlfriend. So it was. All afternoon I searched for her by staring openly into the faces of girls with long hair, and when class was dismissed I walked away bewildered that I had forgotten what the love of my life looked like. The next day I was desperate and stared even more boldly, until the teacher pulled me aside to shake a finger and told me to knock it off.

But I recovered from lost love as quickly as I recovered from jumping from trees,   24
especially when it was announced, in the fourth week of classes, that there would be a talent show—that everyone was welcome to join in. I approached Little John to ask if he'd be willing to sing with me—"Michael Row the Boat Ashore," "If I Had a Hammer," or "Sugar Shack"—anything that would bring applause and momentary fame.

"C'mon, I know they'll like it," I whined at him as he stood in center field. He told   25
me to leave him alone, and when a fly ball sailed in his direction he raced for it but missed by several feet. Two runs scored, and he turned angrily at me: "See what you did!"

I thought of square dancing with Debra, but I had the feeling that she would   26
screw up her face into an ugly knot if I should ask. She would tell her friends and they would ride their bikes talking about me. So I decided that I'd just watch the show with my arms crossed.

The talent show was held on the lawn, and we were herded, grade by grade, into   27
an outline of a horseshoe. The first and second grades sat Indian-style, the third and fourth graders squatted on their haunches, and the fifth and sixth graders stood with their arms across their chest. The first act was two girls—sisters I guessed—singing a song about weather. Their fingers made the shape of falling rain, their arching arms made rainbows, and finally their hands cupped around smiling faces made sunshine.

We applauded like rain while some of the kids whistled like wind from a mountain pass.

28   This was followed with a skit about personal hygiene—bathing and brushing one's teeth. Then there was a juggling act, another singing duo, and then a jazz tap dancer, who, because he was performing on the grass, appeared to be stamping mud off his shoes. After each act my eyes drifted to a long table of typewriters. What could they possibly be for? I asked myself. They were such commanding machines, big as boulders lugged from rivers. Finally, just as the tap routine was coming to an end, kids began to show up behind them to fit clean sheets of paper into the rollers. They adjusted their chairs as they looked at one another, whispering. A teacher called our attention to the typewriters and we whistled like mountain wind again.

29   "All summer we have practiced learning how to type," the teacher said in a clear, deliberate speech. "Not only have we learned to type letters, but also to sing with the typewriters. If you listen carefully I am sure that you will hear songs that you are familiar with." She turned to the kids, whose hands rested like crabs on the keys, raised a pencil, and then began waving it around. Click-clickclick-click-click-click, and I recognized "The Star Spangled Banner"—and recognized Little John straining over his keyboard. Damn him, I thought, jealous that everyone was looking at him. They then played "Waltzing Matilda," and this made me even angrier because it sounded beautiful and because Little John was enjoying himself. Click-click-click, and they were playing "Michael Row the Boat Ashore," and this made me even more mad. I edged my way in front of Little John and, when he looked up, I made a fist and wet my lips. Smiling, he wet his own lips and shaped a cuss word, which meant we would have a fight afterward, when the music was gone and there were no typewriters to hide behind.

VOCABULARY

Directions: Locate each of the key words in the reading selection. Then read and study each word in its context and try to determine its meaning. Use a dictionary or thesaurus to check your guess. Write the meanings of the words in the margin of the text.

Record the new words you've learned below and on the next page.

Key Word	Paragraph	Meaning
1. mope	1	
2. miffed	5	
3. paleontology	5	
4. replica	7	
5. primed	20	
6. oblivious	21	

Key Word	Paragraph	Meaning
7. skit	28	
Others?		

GUIDE QUESTIONS

Directions: These questions will guide your understanding of what you have read. Write your answers in your notebook or on a separate sheet of paper if your instructor wishes to collect it. Your answers to these questions will be the basis of class discussion.

1. Explain Soto's reasons for attending summer school.
2. Explain "elective courses" and why this type of course was probably crucial to Soto's enjoyment of summer school.
3. In paragraph 5, why do you think the teacher was "surprised, as if someone had presented her flowers" when Soto asked how to spell paleontology?
4. Describe some of the other pleasurable experiences Soto had in his classes.
5. Describe Soto's brief experience with summer school romance.
6. Briefly describe the talent show. Why didn't Soto participate? Why did he make a fist and wet his lips at Little John?

APPLICATION

Directions: Discuss the following questions with your classmates.

1. Based on Soto's description of the school and the teachers, do you think they were of good quality?
2. Was Soto a good student? Support your opinion with evidence from the story.
3. Note the author's frequent use of comparisons in the story. Here are a few examples:

   (paragraph 16) "We returned to our classes, sweating like the popsicles we had sucked to a rugged stick."
   (paragraph 23) "On Monday I was back, stiff as new rope . . ."
   (paragraph 29) "She turned to the kids, whose hands rested like crabs on the keys, . . ."

   Comparisons like these are examples of figurative language. To learn more about figurative language, turn to Appendix D.

   Go through the story and find as many uses of figurative language as you can. What effect do they have on the reader?

WRITING

Directions: Write at least two paragraphs on one of the following topics.

1. If you have ever attended summer school, compare and contrast your experiences with Soto's.
2. If you have never attended summer school, write a description of an experience in school that you enjoyed.

COLLABORATIVE LEARNING

WORKING IN GROUPS TO GUIDE YOUR OWN READING

Along with each of the reading selections in this unit, you were provided with questions and exercises to guide your understanding of the text. However, in most of your college reading you will not be given exercises to help you understand vocabulary or given questions that guide your understanding of a textbook chapter. You will be expected to master the material on your own.

Research has shown that one of the most effective ways to study is in groups—working with classmates to master the material of a college course. The give-and-take that comes naturally when working with other people helps us to avoid falling into bad habits like *passive reading.* (We have all had this experience: reading a whole chapter, then realizing that we don't remember one single thing we read.) Working with other students will help you avoid such problems. For this assignment, form groups of four to six students. In your group you will consider the two reading selections that follow, "The Teacher Who Changed My Life," by Nicholas Gage, and "How to Mark a Book," by Mortimer Adler. You will create your own vocabulary chart, guide questions, an application exercise, and a writing assignment for the reading selections.

Follow these steps to complete this assignment.

1. Preview the selection before you read—look at and think about the title, the headings, the first paragraph, the last paragraph, and the first sentence of each paragraph.
2. Read through the selection one time quickly.
3. Read the selection carefully a second time; this time mark the pages. Underline words you want to look up and ideas that you think are important. Put a question mark next to things you don't understand and want to discuss with your group members or your instructor. Ask yourself questions as you read along and try to find the answers to your questions.
4. Brainstorm with your group. Ask yourselves: What important issues is the author discussing? What new information did you learn? Can the issues discussed in the selection be connected to those you have studied in earlier lessons? Can any of the information here be applied to situations in your own life?
5. Now, *create* a set of exercises similar to those you have completed in previous chapters:
   a. *Vocabulary.* Make a list of key vocabulary words from the text. Set them up in chart format, as on page 3.
   b. *Guide questions.* Write questions that will guide understanding of the major ideas in the reading.
   c. *Application.* Prepare an application exercise that takes one or more of the important ideas in the reading and relates them to real life.
   d. *Writing.* Prepare a writing assignment to conclude the chapter.

Before you begin, it would be a good idea to review the questions and exercises included in the previous reading selections of this unit for reference.

When you are finished, submit your work to your instructor for review. Your instructor may then review and combine the work of all the groups and return the exercises to the class. You will have the opportunity to *answer* the questions you and your classmates have developed.

Now, use your skills as an active, independent reader to tackle the following reading selections. Good luck!

"If it weren't for her . . ." begins Nicholas Gage as he speaks of Miss Hurd, the English teacher and school newspaper-club advisor who changed the whole course of his life. She was "the catalyst that sent me into journalism and indirectly caused all the good things that came after." This powerful and emotional story comes from Gage's book, A Place for Us. *In it, he describes his life after coming to the United States at the age of nine. Earlier, during the Greek civil war, Gage's mother had been captured and killed for sending her children to safety and freedom in America. It was Miss Hurd who "directed [his] grief and pain into writing," inspired him to become an investigative reporter, foreign correspondent, and writer of the much-acclaimed book about his mother's life,* Eleni. *Can you recall a teacher who had a special effect on your life?*

THE TEACHER WHO CHANGED MY LIFE
Nicholas Gage

1   The person who set the course of my life in the new land I entered as a young war refugee—who, in fact, nearly dragged me onto the path that would bring all the blessings I've received in America—was a salty-tongued, no-nonsense schoolteacher named Marjorie Hurd. When I entered her classroom in 1953, I had been to six schools in five years, starting in the Greek village where I was born in 1939.

2   When I stepped off a ship in New York Harbor on a gray March day in 1949, I was an undersized nine-year-old in short pants who had lost his mother and was coming to live with the father he didn't know. My mother, Eleni Gatzoyiannis, had been imprisoned, tortured, and shot by Communist guerrillas for sending me and three of my four sisters to freedom. She died so that her children could go to their father in the United States.

3   The portly, bald, well-dressed man who met me and my sisters seemed a foreign, authoritarian figure. I secretly resented him for not getting the whole family out of Greece early enough to save my mother. Ultimately, I would grow to love him and appreciate how he dealt with becoming a single parent at the age of fifty-six, but at first our relationship was prickly, full of hostility.

4   As Father drove us to our new home—a tenement in Worcester, Massachusetts—and pointed out the huge brick building that would be our first school in America, I clutched my Greek notebooks from the refugee camp, hoping that my few years of schooling would impress my teachers in this cold, crowded country. They didn't. When my father led me and my eleven-year-old sister to Greendale Elementary School, the grim-faced Yankee principal put the two of us in a class for the mentally retarded. There was no facility in those days for non-English-speaking children.

5   By the time I met Marjorie Hurd four years later, I had learned English, been placed in a normal, graded class and had even been chosen for the college preparatory track in the Worcester public school system. I was thirteen years old when our father moved us yet again, and I entered Chandler Junior High shortly after the beginning of seventh grade. I found myself surrounded by richer, smarter, and better-dressed classmates who looked askance at my strange clothes and heavy accent. Shortly after I arrived, we were told to select a hobby to pursue during "club hour"

on Fridays. The idea of hobbies and clubs made no sense to my immigrant ears, but I decided to follow the prettiest girl in my class—the blue-eyed daughter of the local Lutheran minister. She led me through the door marked "Newspaper Club" and into the presence of Miss Hurd, the newspaper advisor and English teacher who would become my mentor and my muse.

6   A formidable, solidly built woman with salt-and-pepper hair, a steely eye, and a flat Boston accent, Miss Hurd had no patience with layabouts. "What are all you goof-offs doing here?" she bellowed at the would-be journalists. "This is the Newspaper Club! We're going to put out a *newspaper*. So if there's anybody in this room who doesn't like work, I suggest you go across to the Glee Club now, because you're going to work your tails off here!"

7   I was soon under Miss Hurd's spell. She did indeed teach us to put out a newspaper, skills I honed during my next twenty-five years as a journalist. Soon I asked the principal to transfer me to her English class as well. There, she drilled us on grammar until I finally began to understand the logic and structure of the English language. She assigned stories for us to read and discuss; not tales of heroes, like the Greek myths I knew, but stories of underdogs—poor people, even immigrants, who seemed ordinary until a crisis drove them to do something extraordinary. She also introduced us to the literary wealth of Greece—giving me a new perspective on my war-ravaged, impoverished homeland. I began to be proud of my origins.

8   One day, after discussing how writers should write about what they know, she assigned us to compose an essay from our own experience. Fixing me with a stern look, she added, "Nick, I want you to write about what happened to your family in Greece." I had been trying to put those painful memories behind me and left the assignment until the last moment. Then, on a warm spring afternoon, I sat in my room with a yellow pad and pencil and stared out the window at the buds on the trees. I wrote that the coming of spring always reminded me of the last time I said good-bye to my mother on a green and gold day in 1948.

9   I kept writing, one line after another, telling how the Communist guerrillas occupied our village, took our home and food, how my mother started planning our escape when she learned that the children were to be sent to re-education camps behind the Iron Curtain and how, at the last moment, she couldn't escape with us because the guerrillas sent her with a group of women to thresh wheat in a distant village. She promised she would try to get away on her own, she told me to be brave, and hung a silver cross around my neck, and then she kissed me. I watched the line of women being led down into the ravine and up the other side, until they disappeared around the bend—my mother a tiny brown figure at the end who stopped for an instant to raise her hand in one last farewell.

10   I wrote about our nighttime escape down the mountain, across the minefields, and into the lines of the Nationalist soldiers, who sent us to a refugee camp. It was there that we learned of our mother's execution. I felt very lucky to have come to America, I concluded, but every year, the coming of spring made me feel sad because it reminded me of the last time I saw my mother.

11   I handed in the essay, hoping never to see it again, but Miss Hurd had it published in the school paper. This mortified me at first, until I saw that my classmates reacted with sympathy and tact to my family's story. Without telling me, Miss Hurd

also submitted the essay to a contest sponsored by the Freedoms Foundation at Valley Forge, Pennsylvania, and it won a medal. The Worcester paper wrote about the award and quoted my essay at length. My father, by then a "five-and-dime-store chef," as the paper described him, was ecstatic with pride, and the Worcester Greek community celebrated the honor to one of its own.

For the first time I began to understand the power of the written word. A secret ambition took root in me. One day, I vowed, I would go back to Greece, find out the details of my mother's death and write about her life, so her grandchildren would know of her courage. Perhaps I would even track down the men who killed her and write of their crimes. Fulfilling that ambition would take me thirty years.   12

Meanwhile, I followed the literary path that Miss Hurd had so forcefully set me on. After junior high, I became the editor of my school paper at Classical High School and got a part-time job at the Worcester *Telegram and Gazette*. Although my father could only give me $50 and encouragement toward a college education, I managed to finance four years at Boston University with scholarships and part-time jobs in journalism. During my last year of college, an article I wrote about a friend who had died in the Philippines—the first person to lose his life working for the Peace Corps—led to my winning the Hearst Award for College Journalism. And the plaque was given to me in the White House by President John F. Kennedy.   13

For a refugee who had never seen a motorized vehicle or indoor plumbing until he was nine, this was an unimaginable honor. When the Worcester paper ran a picture of me standing next to President Kennedy, my father rushed out to buy a new suit in order to be properly dressed to receive the congratulations of the Worcester Greeks. He clipped out the photograph, had it laminated in plastic and carried it in his breast pocket for the rest of his life to show everyone he met. I found the much-worn photo in his pocket on the day he died twenty years later.   14

In our isolated Greek village, my mother had bribed a cousin to teach her to read, for girls were not supposed to attend school beyond a certain age. She had always dreamed of her children receiving an education. She couldn't be there when I graduated from Boston University, but the person who came with my father and shared our joy was my former teacher, Marjorie Hurd. We celebrated not only my bachelor's degree but also the scholarships that paid my way to Columbia's Graduate School of Journalism. There, I met the woman who would eventually become my wife. At our wedding and at the baptisms of our three children, Marjorie Hurd was always there, dancing alongside the Greeks.   15

By then, she was Mrs. Rabidou, for she had married a widower when she was in her early forties. That didn't distract her from her vocation of introducing young minds to English literature, however. She taught for a total of forty-one years and continually would make a "project" of some balky student in whom she spied a spark of potential. Often these were students from the most troubled homes, yet she would alternately bully and charm each one with her own special brand of tough love until the spark caught fire. She retired in 1981 at the age of sixty-two but still avidly follows the lives and careers of former students while overseeing her adult stepchildren and driving her husband on camping trips to New Hampshire.   16

Miss Hurd was one of the first to call me on December 10, 1987, when President Reagan, in his television address after the summit meeting with Gorbachev, told the   17 nation that Eleni Gatzoyiannis's dying cry, "My children!" had helped inspire him to seek an arms agreement "for all the children of the world."

18   "I can't imagine a better monument for your mother," Miss Hurd said with an uncharacteristic catch in her voice.

19   Although a bad hip makes it impossible for her to join in the Greek dancing, Marjorie Hurd Rabidou is still an honored and enthusiastic guest at all family celebrations, including my fiftieth birthday picnic last summer, where the shish kebab was cooked on spits, clarinets and *bouzoukis* wailed, and costumed dancers led the guests in a serpentine line around our Colonial farmhouse, only twenty minutes from my first home in Worcester.

20   My sisters and I felt an aching void because my father was not there to lead the line, balancing a glass of wine on his head while he danced, the way he did at every celebration during his ninety-two years. But Miss Hurd was there, surveying the scene with quiet satisfaction. Although my parents are gone, her presence was a consolation, because I owe her so much.

21   This is truly the land of opportunity, and I would have enjoyed its bounty even if I hadn't walked into Miss Hurd's classroom in 1953. But she was the one who directed my grief and pain into writing, and if it weren't for her I wouldn't have become an investigative reporter and foreign correspondent, recorded the story of my mother's life and death in *Eleni*, and now my father's story in *A Place for Us*, which is also a testament to the country that took us in. She was the catalyst that sent me into journalism and indirectly caused all the good things that came after. But Miss Hurd would probably deny this emphatically.

22   A few years ago, I answered the telephone and heard my former teacher's voice telling me, in that won't-take-no-for-an-answer tone of hers, that she had decided I was to write and deliver the eulogy at her funeral. I agreed (she didn't leave me any choice), but that's one assignment I never want to do. I hope, Miss Hurd, that you'll accept this remembrance instead.

VOCABULARY

Directions: Mark any important words in the reading selection that you don't know. Then list them in the chart below along with their paragraph numbers. Try to figure out each word's meaning by reading over the context carefully for clues to help you guess the meaning of the unfamiliar word. Check your dictionary or thesaurus to confirm your guess. After you discuss the words with your group members, write the meanings in the margin of the text, near the word. Then enter them in the chart below and on the next page.

Key Word   **Paragraph**   **Meaning**

Key Word   Paragraph   Meaning

_____

_____

_____

_____

GUIDE QUESTIONS

Directions: Develop a list of questions that elicit the important ideas in the reading selection. Start at the beginning and work your way sequentially through the text until you have addressed all of the author's major ideas.

APPLICATION

Directions: When you have a list of guide questions, read through the selection again. This time, write one or more questions that require application of the information in the text to a situation in the real world.

WRITING

Directions: Your last task is to prepare a writing assignment. For example, you might ask for a paragraph in which the writer comments on the ideas in the reading selection. You might also ask for a summary of the selection.

Mortimer Adler is well-known as the chairman of the Board of Editors of Encyclopaedia Britannica, *as a prolific writer, and as the originator of the "Great Books" program in which people from all backgrounds meet to read and discuss the classics. Dr. Adler is a philosopher who believes that "philosophy is everybody's business" and that a better understanding of the great ideas is essential if we are to cope with the political, moral, and social issues that we all confront.*

Dr. Adler has written extensively about the joys of reading and the "how-to"s of reading. In this essay, which appeared in the Saturday Review of Literature *in 1940, he explains how to "own" a book.*

HOW TO MARK A BOOK

Mortimer Adler

1   You know you have to read "between the lines" to get the most out of anything. I want to persuade you to do something equally important in the course of your reading. I want to persuade you to "write between the lines." Unless you do, you are not likely to do the most efficient kind of reading.

2   I contend, quite bluntly, that marking up a book is not an act of mutilation but of love.

3   You shouldn't mark up a book which isn't yours. Librarians (or your friends) who lend you books expect you to keep them clean, and you should. If you decide that I am right about the usefulness of marking books, you will have to buy them. Most of the world's great books are available today, in reprint editions.

4   There are two ways in which one can own a book. The first is the property right you establish by paying for it, just as you pay for clothes and furniture. But this act of purchase is only the prelude to possession. Full ownership comes only when you have made it a part of yourself, and the best way to make yourself a part of it is by writing in it. An illustration may make the point clear. You buy a beefsteak and transfer it from the butcher's icebox to your own. But you do not own the beefsteak in the most important sense until you consume it and get it into your bloodstream. I am arguing that books, too, must be absorbed in your bloodstream to do you any good.

5   Confusion about what it means to *own* a book leads people to a false reverence for paper, binding, and type—a respect for the physical thing—the craft of the printer rather than the genius of the author. They forget that it is possible for a man to acquire the idea, to possess the beauty, which a great book contains, without staking his claim by pasting his bookplate inside the cover. Having a fine library doesn't prove that its owner has a mind enriched by books; it proves nothing more than that he, his father, or his wife, was rich enough to buy them.

6   There are three kinds of book owners. The first has all the standard sets and best-sellers—unread, untouched. (This deluded individual owns woodpulp and ink, not books.) The second has a great many books—a few of them read through, most of them dipped into, but all of them as clean and shiny as the day they were bought. (This person would probably like to make books his own, but is restrained by a false respect for their physical appearance.) The third has a few books or many—every

one of them dog-eared and dilapidated, shaken and loosened by continual use, marked and scribbled in from front to back. (This man owns books.)

Is it false respect, you may ask, to preserve intact and unblemished a beautifully printed book, an elegantly bound edition? Of course not. I'd no more scribble all over a first edition of *Paradise Lost* than I'd give my baby a set of crayons and an original Rembrandt! I wouldn't mark up a painting or a statue. Its soul, so to speak, is inseparable from its body. And the beauty of a rare edition or of a richly manufactured volume is like that of a painting or a statue.

But the soul of a book *can* be separated from its body. A book is more like the score of a piece of music than it is like a painting. No great musician confuses a symphony with the printed sheets of music. Arturo Toscanini reveres Brahms, but Toscanini's score of the C-minor Symphony is so thoroughly marked up that no one but the maestro himself can read it. The reason why a great conductor makes notations on his musical scores—marks them up again and again each time he returns to study them—is the reason why you should mark your books. If your respect for magnificent binding or typography gets in the way, buy yourself a cheap edition and pay your respects to the author.

Why is marking up a book indispensable to reading? First, it keeps you awake. (And I don't mean merely conscious; I mean wide awake.) In the second place, reading, if it is active, is thinking, and thinking tends to express itself in words, spoken or written. The marked book is usually the thought-through book. Finally, writing helps you remember the thoughts you had, or the thoughts the author expressed. Let me develop these three points.

If reading is to accomplish anything more than passing time, it must be active. You can't let your eyes glide across the lines of a book and come up with an understanding of what you have read. Now an ordinary piece of light fiction, like say, *Gone with the Wind,* doesn't require the most active kind of reading. The books you read for pleasure can be read in a state of relaxation, and nothing is lost. But a great book, rich in ideas and beauty, a book that raises and tries to answer great fundamental questions, demands the most active reading of which you are capable. You don't absorb the ideas of John Dewey the way you absorb the crooning of Mr. Vallee. You have to reach for them. That you cannot do while you're asleep.

If, when you've finished reading a book, the pages are filled with your notes, you know that you read actively. The most famous active reader of great books I know is President Hutchins, of the University of Chicago. He also has the hardest schedule of business activities of any man I know. He invariably reads with a pencil, and sometimes, when he picks up a book and pencil in the evening, he finds himself, instead of making intelligent notes, drawing what he calls "caviar factories" on the margins. When that happens, he puts the book down. He knows he's too tired to read, and he's just wasting time.

But, you may ask, why is writing necessary? Well, the physical act of writing, with your own hand, brings words and sentences more sharply before your mind and preserves them better in your memory. To set down your reaction to important words and sentences you have read, and the questions they have raised in your mind, is to preserve those reactions and sharpen those questions.

13   Even if you wrote on a scratch pad, and threw the paper away when you had finished writing, your grasp of the book would be surer. But you don't have to throw the paper away. The margins (top and bottom, as well as side), the end-papers, the very space between the lines, are all available. They aren't sacred. And, best of all, your marks and notes become an integral part of the book and stay there forever. You can pick up the book the following week or year, and there are all your points of agreement, disagreement, doubt, and inquiry. It's like resuming an interrupted conversation with the advantage of being able to pick up where you left off.

14   And that is exactly what reading a book should be: a conversation between you and the author. Presumably, he knows more about the subject than you do; naturally, you'll have the proper humility as you approach him. But don't let anybody tell you that a reader is supposed to be solely on the receiving end. Understanding is a two-way operation; learning doesn't consist in being an empty receptacle. The learner has to question himself and question the teacher. He even has to argue with the teacher, once he understands what the teacher is saying. And marking a book is literally an expression of your differences, or agreements of opinion, with the author.

15   There are all kinds of devices for marking a book intelligently and fruitfully. Here's the way I do it:

1. *Underlining:* of major points, of important or forceful statements.
2. *Vertical lines at the margin:* to emphasize a statement already underlined.
3. *Star, asterisk, or other doo-dad at the margin:* to be used sparingly, to emphasize the ten or twenty most important statements in the book. (You may want to fold the bottom corner of each page on which you use such marks. It won't hurt the sturdy paper on which most modern books are printed, and you will be able to take the book off the shelf at any time and, by opening it at the folded-corner page, refresh your recollection of the book.)
4. *Numbers in the margin:* to indicate the sequence of points the author makes in developing a single argument.
5. *Numbers of other pages in the margin:* to indicate where else in the book the author made points relevant to the point marked; to tie up the ideas in a book, which, though they may be separated by many pages, belong together.
6. *Circling of key words or phrases.*
7. *Writing in the margin, or at the top or bottom of the page, for the sake of:* recording questions (and perhaps answers) that a passage raised in your mind; reducing a complicated discussion to a simple statement; recording the sequence of major points right through the books. I use the end-papers at the back of the book to make a personal index of the author's points in the order of their appearance.

16   The front end-papers are, to me, the most important. Some people reserve them for a fancy bookplate. I reserve them for fancy thinking. After I have finished reading the book and making my personal index on the back end-papers, I turn to the front and try to outline the book, not page by page, or point by point (I've already done that at the back), but as an integrated structure, with a basic unity and an order of parts. This outline is, to me, the measure of my understanding of the work.

If you're a die-hard anti-book-marker, you may object that the margins, the space between the lines, and the end-papers don't give you room enough. All right. How about using a scratch pad slightly smaller than the page-size of the book—so that the edges of the sheets won't protrude? Make your index, outlines, and even your notes on the pad, and then insert these sheets permanently inside the front and back covers of the book.   17

Or, you may say that this business of marking books is going to slow up your reading. It probably will. That's one of the reasons for doing it. Most of us have been taken in by the notion that speed of reading is a measure of our intelligence. There is no such thing as the right speed for intelligent reading. Some things should be read quickly and effortlessly, and some should be read slowly and even laboriously. The sign of intelligence in reading is the ability to read different things according to their worth. In the case of good books, the point is not to see how many of them you can get through, but rather how many can get through you—how many you can make your own. A few friends are better than a thousand acquaintances. If this be your aim, as it should be, you will not be impatient if it takes more time and effort to read a great book than it does a newspaper.   18

You may have one final objection to marking books. You can't lend them to your friends because nobody else can read them without being distracted by your notes. Furthermore, you won't want to lend them because a marked copy is a kind of intellectual diary, and lending it is almost like giving your mind away.   19

If your friend wishes to read your *Plutarch's Lives, Shakespeare,* or *The Federalist Papers,* tell him gently but firmly to buy a copy. You will lend him your car or your coat—but your books are as much a part of you as your head or your heart.   20

VOCABULARY

Directions: Mark any important words in the reading selection that you don't know. Then list them in the chart below along with their paragraph numbers. Try to figure out each word's meaning by reading over the context carefully for clues to help you guess the meaning of the unfamiliar word. Check your dictionary or thesaurus to confirm your guess. After you discuss the words with your group members, write the meanings in the margin of the text, near the word. Then enter them in the chart below.

Key Word	Paragraph	Meaning

GUIDE QUESTIONS

Directions: Develop a list of questions that elicit the important ideas in the reading selection. Start at the beginning and work your way sequentially through the text until you have addressed all of the author's major ideas.

APPLICATION

Directions: When you have a list of guide questions, read through the selection again. This time, write one or more questions that require the application of the information in the text to a situation in the real world.

WRITING

Directions: Your last task is to prepare a writing assignment. For example, you might ask for a paragraph in which the writer comments on the ideas in the reading selection. You might also ask for a summary of the selection.

BIBLIOGRAPHY

FOR FURTHER READING ON THE
THEME OF EDUCATION

Mortimer Adler	*Six Great Ideas,*
	How to Read a Book,
	and many others
Russell Baker	*Growing Up*
	So This Is Depravity
Ray Bradbury	*Fahrenheit 451*
E. R. Braithwaite	*To Sir with Love*
Pat Conroy	*The River Is Wide* (The movie *Conrack* is based on this book)
Frederick Douglass	*Narrative of the Life of Frederick Douglass*
Nicholas Gage	*Eleni*
	A Place for Us
James Herndon	*The Way It Spozed to Be*
Barbara Jordan	*Barbara Jordan: A Self-Portrait*
Jerzy Kosinski	*Being There*
Gary Soto	*Living up the Street*
Muriel Spark	*The Pride of Miss Jean Brodie*
Malcolm X	*The Autobiography of Malcolm X*

UNIT TWO

READING AND THINKING ABOUT CULTURE

As the traveler who has once been from home is wiser than he who has never left his own doorstep, so a knowledge of one other culture should sharpen our ability to scrutinize more steadily, to appreciate more lovingly, our own.

—Margaret Mead

Culture regulates our lives at every turn. From the moment we are born until we die there is, whether we are conscious of it or not, constant pressure upon us to follow certain types of behavior that other men have created for us.

—Clyde Kluckhohn

THINKING ABOUT CULTURE

Before you begin this part of the textbook, think about the brief descriptions below. Then answer the question at the end.

A small group of people called *hijras* live in India. *Hijras* are men who live as women. They wear female clothing and jewelry and their body language is feminine. They earn their living by asking for alms and receiving pay for blessing newborn babies. They believe in a goddess named Bahuchara Mata and identify with her totally. They undergo emasculation as a way of expressing their devotion to the goddess.

The Mundugumor people of New Guinea live a life of extreme individualism and hostility. They live in subdivided households and there is little community life. Babies are kept in hard uncomfortable baskets. When they cry, the mothers do not pick them up and hold them. Instead, they make scratching noises on the side of the basket. If the child continues to cry, the mother will feed it, standing up, in an awkward manner. As soon as the child has eaten, it is immediately returned to the basket.

The Wodaabe of West Africa hold a celebration every year before which the unmarried men spend days styling their hair, donning elegant robes, and applying elaborate and enormous amounts of make-up. As a result

they are transformed into very feminine-looking young men. Nevertheless, the young women of the village are enchanted by the sight of these
men, who most Americans would take for women. A beauty contest is
then held to choose the most "beautiful" man. Then, if they agree, the
winner and the most eligible young woman of the village may wed.

These are snapshots of people living in various cultures. Do these people seem
very different from you and your family? Can you imagine that they would find
your customs to be strange indeed? How can we account for the great differences
that exist among human beings all over the world? After all, we are all basically
the same animal, with a few differences in skin color, height, hair texture, eye
shape, and so on. The major differences seem to be in the *culture* each group has
developed. Think about this question:

What is culture?

Now, write your own definition or explanation of culture.

Anthropologist Clifford Geertz says in his book The Interpretation of Cultures, *"There is no such thing as a human nature independent of culture. Men without culture . . . would be unworkable monstrosities with very few useful instincts, fewer recognizable sentiments, and no intellect: mental basket cases."*

In this section, you will be introduced to the basic elements of culture and will take a look at different groups of people to see how they are different from us—and how they are the same.

CULTURE

Clyde Kluckhohn

Why do the Chinese dislike milk and milk products? Why would the Japanese die   1
willingly in a Banzai charge [in World War II] that seemed senseless to Americans?
Why do some nations trace descent through the father, others through the mother,
still others through both parents? Not because different peoples have different instincts, not because they were destined by God or Fate to different habits, not because the weather is different in China and Japan and the United States. Sometimes
shrewd common sense has an answer that is close to that of the anthropologist:
"because they were brought up that way." By *culture,* anthropology means the total
life way of a people, the social legacy the individual acquires from his group. Or *culture*
can be regarded as that part of the environment that is the creation of man.

This technical term has a wider meaning than the *culture* of history and literature.   2
A humble cooking pot is as much a cultural product as is a Beethoven sonata. In ordinary speech a man of culture is a man who can speak languages other than his own,
who is familiar with history, literature, philosophy, or the fine arts. In some cliques
that definition is still narrower. The cultured person is one who can talk about James
Joyce, Scarlatti, and Picasso. To the anthropologist, however, to be human is to be
cultured. There is culture in general, and then there are the specific cultures, such
as Russian, American, British, Hottentot, Inca. The general abstract notion serves to
remind us that we cannot explain acts solely in terms of the biological properties of
the people concerned, their individual past experience, and the immediate situation.
The past experience of other men in the form of culture enters into almost every
event. Each specific culture constitutes a kind of blueprint for all of life's activities.

One of the interesting things about human beings is that they try to understand   3
themselves and their own behavior. While this has been particularly true of Europeans in recent times, there is no group which has not developed a scheme or
schemes to explain man's actions. To the insistent human query "why?" the most
exciting illumination anthropology has to offer is that of the concept of culture. Its
explanatory importance is comparable to categories such as evolution in biology,
gravity in physics, disease in medicine. A good deal of human behavior can be understood and, indeed, predicted, if we know a people's design for living. Many acts
are neither accidental nor due to personal peculiarities nor caused by supernatural
forces nor simply mysterious. Even those of us who pride ourselves on our individualism follow most of the time a pattern not of our own making. We brush our teeth

on arising. We put on pants—not a loincloth or a grass skirt. We eat three meals a day—not four or five or two. We sleep in a bed—not in a hammock or on a sheep pelt. I do not have to know the individual and his life history to be able to predict these and countless other regularities, including many in the thinking process, of all Americans who are not incarcerated in jails or hospitals for the insane.

4   To the American woman a system of plural wives seems "instinctively" abhorrent. She cannot understand how any woman can fail to be jealous and uncomfortable if she must share her husband with other women. She feels it "unnatural" to accept such a situation. On the other hand, a Koryak woman of Siberia, for example, would find it hard to understand how a woman could be so selfish and so undesirous of feminine companionship in the home as to wish to restrict her husband to one mate.

5   Some years ago I met in New York City a young man who did not speak a word of English and was obviously bewildered by American ways. By "blood" he was American, for his parents had gone from Indiana to China as missionaries. Orphaned in infancy, he was reared in a remote village. All who met him found him more Chinese than American. The facts of his blue eyes and light hair were less impressive than a Chinese style of gait, Chinese arm and hand movements, Chinese facial expression, and Chinese modes of thought. The biological heritage was American, but the cultural training had been Chinese. He returned to China.

6   Another example of another kind: I once knew a trader's wife in Arizona who took a somewhat devilish interest in producing a cultural reaction. Guests who came her way were often served delicious sandwiches filled with a meat that seemed to be neither chicken nor tuna fish yet was reminiscent of both. To queries she gave no reply until each had eaten his fill. She then explained that what they had eaten was not chicken, not tuna fish, but the rich, white flesh of freshly killed rattlesnakes. The response was instantaneous—vomiting, often violent vomiting. A biological process is caught in a cultural web.

7   A highly intelligent teacher with long and successful experience in the public schools of Chicago was finishing her first year in a [North American] Indian school. When asked how her Navaho pupils compared in intelligence with Chicago youngsters, she replied, "Well, I just don't know. Sometimes the Indians seem just as bright. At other times they just act like dumb animals. The other night we had a dance in the high school. I saw a boy who is one of the best students in my English class standing off by himself. So I took him over to a pretty girl and told them to dance. But they just stood there with their heads down. They wouldn't even say anything." I inquired if she knew whether or not they were members of the same clan. "What difference would that make?"

8   "How would you feel about getting into bed with your brother?" The teacher walked off in a huff, but, actually, the two cases were quite comparable in principle. To the Indian, the type of bodily contact involved in our social dancing has a directly sexual connotation. The incest taboos between members of the same clan are as severe as between true brothers and sisters. The shame of the Indians at the suggestion that a clan brother and sister should dance and the indignation of the white teacher at the idea that she should share a bed with an adult brother represent equally nonrational responses, culturally standardized unreason.

All this does not mean that there is no such thing as raw human nature. The   9
very fact that certain of the same institutions are found in all known societies indicates that, at bottom, all human beings are very much alike. The files of the Cross-
Cultural Survey at Yale University are organized according to categories, such as
"marriage ceremonies," "life crisis rites," "incest taboos." At least seventy-five of
these categories are represented in every single one of the hundreds of cultures an-
alyzed. This is hardly surprising. The members of all human groups have about the
same biological equipment. All men undergo the same poignant life experiences, such
as birth, helplessness, illness, old age, and death. The biological potentialities of the
species are the blocks with which cultures are built. Some patterns of every culture
crystallize around focuses provided by the inevitables of biology: the difference between the sexes, the presence of persons of different ages, the varying physical
strength and skill of individuals. The facts of nature also limit culture forms. No culture provides patterns for jumping over trees or for eating iron ore.

VOCABULARY

Directions: Find each of the key words in the reading selection. Study the word in
its context and try to determine its meaning. Write your guess in the margin of
the text, near the word. Then read over the sentence, mentally substituting your
guess for the key word. Does the sentence still make sense? Does it retain its original meaning? If it does, you've probably figured out the meaning of the key word
correctly. In any case, confirm your guess by checking a dictionary or thesaurus.

If you take your meaning from a dictionary or thesaurus, be sure the definition includes words you already know and feel comfortable using. If it doesn't,
you will be worse off than when you started—you will have begun with one
word you didn't know and ended with *two* words you don't know!

Record the new words you've learned below.

Key Word	Paragraph	Meaning
1. legacy	1	
2. cliques	2	
3. insistent	3	
4. abhorrent	4	
5. gait	5	
6. instantaneous	6	
7. poignant	9	
Others?		

GUIDE QUESTIONS

Directions: The purpose of guide questions is to "guide" your analysis of the text. Your thoughtful answers will ensure that you have understood the main ideas the author wanted to convey. Some of the questions require that you simply find the stated facts in the reading selection; others will ask you to do more difficult tasks, such as paraphrasing information (putting the author's ideas into your own words), synthesizing several ideas into one complex thought, evaluating (making judgments about) an idea, or taking information from the reading and applying it to a new situation or to your own life.

Write answers to the questions in your notebook or on a separate sheet of paper if your instructor wishes to collect it. Your answers will form the basis of class discussion.

1. Kluckhohn states that the term *culture* can have two different meanings, depending on the context. What does *culture* mean in ordinary speech? What does *culture* mean to an anthropologist?
2. a. Many people feel that the way we eat, drink, marry, walk, and talk are somehow "instinctual" or "natural." Give some examples from the text that contradict this.
   b. Explain what Kluckhohn means by his description of people's reaction to eating rattlesnake: "A biological process is caught in a cultural web."
3. Kluckhohn cites many institutions that have been found in every single one of the hundreds of cultures that have been studied. How does he explain the presence of so many similarities among the peoples of the world?

APPLICATION

Directions: Consider each of the little stories below, which describe the traditional behavior of a group of people in a certain situation. Compare and contrast these with how you and the members of your culture would act in the same situation.

Work in small groups to complete this assignment. First, choose a *group leader,* who will be responsible for directing the conversation and ensuring that every member participates. Next, choose a *reader,* who will read each of the stories out loud before the group discusses it. Next, choose a *secretary,* who will record the group's answers to the questions below. Finally, choose a *timekeeper,* whose job is to "keep the ball rolling" and make sure the group works efficiently. When you finish, your instructor may want you to hand in your answers.

1. *Finding a Wife.* A Chiricahua man, young and unmarried, goes to visit an old woman, the grandmother of an unmarried girl:

   > I went to her place that night. I had heard the old lady had some *tiswin* (a fermented liquor made of corn). When I got there she told me to have a drink. As we talked she told me that I was single and needed a wife. She mentioned this girl (her grandchild) and said it was worth two horses to get her. I had never seen the girl before. When I got home I started to think about it seriously. I talked it over with my relatives. An uncle of mine gave me a mule, and a cousin gave me a horse.

The next day I went to the home of a certain woman, a middle-aged woman. She was eating when I arrived. I called her outside and hired her to speak for me to this girl's grandmother. This woman lived just on the other side of a stream from the girl and her grandmother. The next day my go-between demanded two good horses. My go-between thanked the grandmother and came to tell me what had been said. I gave her the horse and the mule to lead to the old woman, and the next day I went to the girl.

Morris E. Opler, An Apache Life-Way, p. 157

Describe how a member of your culture finds a wife. List the similarities and differences between the way you would do it and the way the Chiricahua did it. (The Chiricahua are North American Indians.)

2. *A Husband Discovers His Wife Has Been Unfaithful.* A Chiricahua man is expected to take drastic action:

> A wronged husband who does not show some rancor is considered unmanly. . . . The woman, since she is close at hand, is likely to be the first to feel the husband's wrath. A beating is the least punishment she suffers. If there is no one to intercede for her, her very life may be forfeit, or she may be subjected to mutilation. . . . The husband is just as insistent that the man who has disrupted his home be punished. After the husband has punished or killed his wife, he will go after the man and kill him.

An Apache Life-Way, p. 410

List the similarities and differences between how a member of your culture would handle this situation and how the Chiricahua behaved.

3. *A Wedding in Tahiti.*

> Tahitian weddings generally last two days, the law allowing two days off from work, with pay. The civil ceremony takes place at the mayor's office. If there is a religious ceremony, it takes place later at the church. The reception is usually at the home of a family member. The decorations include a temporary covered terrace (in case of rain), posts wrapped in coconut leaves with flowers inserted into them; flowers and greenery everywhere. The bride and groom are welcomed to the reception with flower garlands and leis. Tahitians do not serve a wedding cake or throw a wedding bouquet or the garter. The festivities include eating, storytelling, singing, spoontapping, and dancing. At the reception the couple is given their new name, the "marriage name" by which they will henceforth be called. Usually the name is selected by the family and is the name of an ancestor or a name from the Bible. The names of the couple's first and second children are also selected.

Describe the similarities and differences between a wedding in Tahiti and a wedding in your culture.

4. *A Funeral among the Teton-Dakota Indians.*

> At the death of an individual, his relatives and friends gathered at his tepee to mourn. The women spent four days in intermittent wailing. Parents often gashed themselves or severed a finger to express their grief. A bereaved father might wander from camp, singing a death song, to shoot down the first person whom he met and then kill himself. A give-away of the family's property to the mourners was part of the funeral ceremony, and another give-away ended the year of mourning.
>
> Gordon MacGregor, *Warriors without Weapons: Society and Personality Development of the Pine Ridge Sioux,* p. 94

Describe a funeral ritual in your society. How is it similar and different from a funeral among the Teton-Dakota Indians? (The Teton-Dakotas are North American Indians.)

5. *A Boy Becomes a Man—The Ndembu of Africa.*

> The ritual lasts four months. After a night of feasting, singing, and sexual freedom, the boys receive a last meal from their mothers. Then they are marched to another camp known as the "place of dying," where they remain in seclusion under the supervision of a group of male guardians. Here they are circumcised, hazed, harangued, and lectured on the rules of manhood. Finally, covered in white clay that symbolizes rebirth, the initiates are taken back to their families. At first their mothers greet them with songs of mourning, but as each realizes that her son is safe, these turn to songs of jubilation. After the novices are washed and given new clothes, each performs the dance of war to signify his new status as a man.
>
> Plog, Jolly, and Bates, *Anthropology, The Forest of Symbols,* quoting Turner, pp. 402–03

Does your culture have a ceremony to mark a boy's passage into manhood? Compare and contrast it to that of the Ndembu.

WRITING

Directions: Return to the definition of culture that you were asked to write on page 44, "Thinking about Culture." Evaluate your definition in light of what you learned from this selection. Compare your definition to Kluckhohn's explanation of *culture.* Is your definition sufficient? Is it accurate? How would you rewrite it? Write a few sentences in response to these questions.

In Japan, when two businessmen meet, they automatically bow to one another; in the United States, two men in the same situation would shake hands. In Iran, men and women eat separately, while in most Western countries, men and women have their meals together. Fish is used as a food by most American Indian tribes, but some, including the Navajos and Apaches of New Mexico, consider it nauseating and unfit for human consumption. The aboriginal tribes of Australia and the Indians of Tierra del Fuego wear almost no clothing at all; the Baganda people of East Africa must be fully clothed from neck to ankles. Among the Navajos of the American Southwest, a man was not supposed to speak to or even look at his wife's mother. In northwestern India, married older brothers were not expected to show jealousy when younger brothers slept with their brides. Countless other cultural differences exist among human societies. When asked, for example, why they eat with knives and forks rather than with chopsticks, most Americans would reply, "Because that's the way we do it," or perhaps "Because it's the 'right' way to eat," or even "I don't know." Such answers are not very informative. Most people don't think about these common patterns of social behavior—they simply obey the rules. As anthropologist Clyde Kluckhohn says, "Culture regulates our lives at every turn. From the moment we are born until we die there is, whether we are conscious of it or not, constant pressure on us to follow certain types of behavior that other men have created for us."

In this selection we learn about the rules—imposed by culture—called norms.

NORMS

Mary C. Fjeldstad

Why do we behave in controlled and predictable ways? Because we are members   1
of a society of human beings, our actions are controlled by *norms*—shared guidelines that prescribe the appropriate behavior in a particular situation. Norms define how we are expected to behave in specific circumstances in a specific society. Many norms are unwritten rules that regulate even the smallest details of social life. Usually, we are not even aware that we are obeying norms; they are simply a part of us. Such norms include knowing when to speak, how to address other people (Sir, Mr. Jones, or Bobby), when to sit or stand and when to leave. We learn these norms through the process of *socialization*—the education of individuals in society's customs and beliefs through the family, the school, professional organizations, and so on.

We generally only think about a norm when someone departs from it. For ex-   2
ample, if, in a restaurant, someone were to suddenly begin eating with his hands, we would all be surprised, or distressed, or even amused by this departure from the American norm of using silverware to eat. Our criticism of the person, or ridicule, or even request for him to leave would be our way of applying sanctions to him. When we visit people from other cultures, we quickly become aware that they do things according to their own set of rules, which may be very different from ours. If we were to visit a village in Burkina Faso in Africa, for example, we would probably find ourselves the victim of sanctions if we did not use our hands to eat, as is the custom there.

This selection is based in part on information in Ian Robertson, *Sociology*.

3   What is the purpose of norms? Norms help society to function smoothly. They give guidelines to follow in our own behavior and help us anticipate how others will behave. Imagine how difficult life would be if we had no norms! Each time you encountered a novel situation, you'd have to figure out anew how you were going to act. Take a job interview, for example: should you wear a T-shirt or a jacket? Should you stand or sit? Or why not kneel down or lie on the floor? How can you expect the interviewer to act? Will he or she speak first? Or wait for you to begin? Will the interviewer direct the conversation? Shake your hand or bow? Or perhaps kiss your cheek? All of these questions are answered by our knowledge of the rules of our society. Life would indeed be stressful if we could not rely on norms.

4   The function of norms—regulating social behavior—is so crucial to day-to-day life that there is always pressure on people to conform.

5   There are two major types of norms. The first, *folkways,* are the ordinary rules of everyday life. We expect conformity to folkways, but accept a great deal of nonconformity. For example, in the United States, we expect people to bathe frequently, speak quietly in a library, wait for their turn in line. If people do not follow such rules, they are sanctioned, or "punished," by being criticized, or laughed at, but they are not considered criminal or depraved. Society is generally not outraged when someone violates a folkway.

6   On the other hand, *mores,* much more powerful norms, are treated more seriously. Rules against theft, murder, and rape are examples of mores. People believe that their mores are crucial to the decent and orderly functioning of society and are deeply outraged by violations of them. Penalties for those who disobey mores are serious and can range from monetary fines to physical attack to imprisonment or commitment to a mental institution.

7   One special type of more is the *taboo*—a powerful prohibition against acts that society considers loathsome. In most cultures, for example, the eating of human flesh is a taboo, one that is rarely broken.

8   Most mores are formally encoded and thus are also laws. A *law* is simply a rule of conduct that a society has officially recorded and that is enforced by the power of the state. Laws are written to codify existing norms, to specify the requirements and the exact penalties for violations of them. Penalties can vary widely both within a culture and from one culture to another. For example, in Iran, adultery may be punished by death, while in the United States violations of this law are usually ignored by the authorities. Within the United States the penalties for violations of laws vary from state to state. For example, drug abuse in certain states, such as Texas, is punished more severely than in many other states. The penalty for speeding while driving in New York is a heavy fine, as much as $500, while in the state of Montana the fine is only $5, no matter how fast the driver was going. The penalty for drunk driving can be as severe as a $1,000 fine plus a year in jail (in South Dakota) or as light as a $100 fine and ten days in jail (in Oklahoma).

9   Sometimes legislators introduce new laws in an attempt to alter existing norms. For example, in 1919 a constitutional amendment outlawing the manufacture and sale of alcoholic beverages was passed. Such laws are often ineffective if they run counter to a society's norms. In this case, the prohibition law was routinely violated

until it was repealed fourteen years later. Other examples of ineffective laws are those prohibiting stores from being open on Sunday and those forbidding the personal use of certain drugs.

Norms are not fixed, however. Social protest and political movements may bring   10
about changes in social norms—for example, abortion-law reform, treatment of homosexuals by society, and changes in the roles of women. Unlike Prohibition, certain laws that oppose social norms have survived. A notable example is the civil-rights laws passed in the 1960s and 1970s, which were aimed at changing the traditional behaviors of white-dominated society, especially in the South. Laws that required equal access to public facilities for people of all races ran counter to traditional norms and provoked great resistance. Eventually, however, the norms began to change to conform to the civil rights laws and great differences in folkways and mores have occurred in the past few decades. Traditional modes of behavior in the South, such as requiring blacks to sit at the rear of public buses, use separate public toilet facilities, or eat at lunch counters reserved for "colored," have changed through the strict enforcement of new laws as well as the efforts of civil rights groups.

VOCABULARY

Directions: Find each of the key words in the reading selection. Study the word in its context and try to determine its meaning. Write your guess in the margin of the text, near the word. Then read over the sentence, mentally substituting your guess for the key word. Does the sentence still make sense? Does it retain its original meaning? If it does, you've probably figured out the meaning of the key word correctly. In any case, confirm your guess by checking a dictionary or thesaurus.

If you take your meaning from a dictionary or thesaurus, be sure the definition includes words you already know and feel comfortable using. If it doesn't, you will be worse off than when you started—you will have begun with one word you didn't know and ended with *two* words you don't know!

Record the new words you've learned below and on the next page.

Key Word	Paragraph	Meaning
1. sanctions	2	
2. novel	3	
3. conform	4	
4. depraved	5	
5. crucial	6	
6. loathsome	7	
7. run counter to	9	

Key Word	Paragraph	Meaning	

Others?

_____

_____

_____

_____

GUIDE QUESTIONS

Directions: The purpose of guide questions is to "guide" your analysis of the text. Your thoughtful answers will ensure that you have understood the main ideas the author wanted to convey. Some of the questions require that you simply find the stated facts in the reading selection; others will ask you to do more difficult tasks, such as paraphrasing information (putting the author's ideas into your own words), synthesizing several ideas into one complex thought, evaluating (making judgments about) an idea, or taking information from the reading and applying it to a new situation or to your own life.

Write answers to the questions in your notebook or on a separate sheet of paper if your instructor wishes to collect them. Your answers will form the basis of class discussion.

1. Define the term *norms.*
2. It is a norm in American society for men to shake hands upon meeting one another. Give an example of a different norm in some other society that regulates the same situation.
3. How do we learn the norms of our society?
4. Explain the purpose of norms.
5. Give some examples of what your day-to-day life would be like if we did not have norms.
6. List the two major types of norms discussed in the text.
7. a. Give an example of a folkway mentioned in the text.
   b. Give an example of a folkway not mentioned in the text.
8. Describe the type of pressure that is put on people to conform to folkways.
9. How do mores differ from folkways?
10. Give some examples of mores in American society.
11. Describe the type of pressure that society puts on people to conform to mores.
12. What are taboos?
13. Define the term *laws.*
14. a. Explain why the Prohibition amendment was not effective.
    b. Can you think of any laws in force right now that are not effective because they go against societal norms?
15. What can cause the norms of a society to change?

APPLICATION

1. Norms vary from society to society (as you probably already know if you are from another country or if you know people from other countries). One example of this variation in norms is that, in the United States, marriage is thought of as a private arrangement between a man and a woman who are motivated by romantic love. Do you know of other cultures where marriage is *not* a product of romantic love? Where the bride and groom have no control over whom or when they marry? If you do, write a paragraph describing this different kind of marriage. Be sure to name the society you are describing. You may need to visit the library and research marriage customs in the culture you choose.

2. Choose a social situation (other than marriage), and in two paragraphs describe how it is articulated in two different societies: the United States and some other society. In the first paragraph, describe the situation and the norm that regulates it in the United States; in the second paragraph, describe how the situation is regulated in some other society. For example, you might write one paragraph describing how Americans eat dinner using plates, knives, forks, and spoons, and a second paragraph describing how the Chinese use different utensils for their meals.

3. Write at least one paragraph in response to the following statement: Norms are constantly changing, especially in a dynamic society such as the United States. List as many norms as you can that have changed in your lifetime, or since your parents' youth. Then explain *how* each norm has changed. For example, you might consider how norms regarding premarital sex, smoking, or dress have changed in the past several years.

4. Underlining and annotating the important ideas in a textbook chapter are important skills for college students. Marking your text in this way helps you to be an active rather than a passive reader, forces you to focus on the main ideas in the chapter, and is a study aid when it comes time to review for an exam. Turn to Appendix B to review and practice *underlining* and *annotating*. Then underline and annotate the selection "Norms."

WRITING

Directions: Write a summary of the selection "Norms." Remember, a summary should include the main points of the selection with few examples. To review summary writing, turn to Appendix B.

Which is more important to you—winning that tennis game or making sure your friend has a good time playing? Both reflect values important to most Americans—winning and friendship. Sometimes we must decide between two equally desirable things, and it can be tough!

Most Americans would say they value honesty very highly. But what if it comes into conflict with some other value, like friendship? For example, if you saw your friend cheating on an exam, and he begged you not to tell, would you? You are caught in a conflict of two important values. What would you do?

Many Americans expect to work hard, overtime if necessary, to make decisions fast, and implement them quickly. If Americans try to work "as usual" in another culture where a long, relaxed lunch is the norm, and speedy implementation of decisions is unknown, they may become upset and frustrated because their values conflict with those of their new culture. Which values are at work here?

In this excerpt from a textbook chapter we learn about values, the principles that underlie a society's ideas and behavior.

VALUES

Ian Robertson

1   The norms of a society are ultimately an expression of its values—socially shared ideas about what is good, right, and desirable. The difference between values and norms is that values are abstract, general concepts, whereas norms are specific guidelines for people in particular kinds of situations.

Importance of Values

2   The values of a society are important because they influence the content of its norms. If a society values education highly, its norms will make provision for mass schooling. If it values a large population, its norms will encourage big families. In principle at least, all norms can be traced to a basic social value. For example, the norms that require a student to be more polite and formal to a professor than to other students express the value our society places on respect for authority and learning. The mid-century norms that insisted on short hair for men reflected the high value placed on men's "masculinity" in American culture—a value that was threatened by long hair because it was regarded as "effeminate."

3   Although all norms express social values, many norms persist long after the conditions that gave rise to them have been forgotten. The folkway that requires us to shake hands, especially when greeting a stranger, seems to have originated long ago in the desire to show that no weapon was concealed in the right hand. The folkway of throwing rice or confetti over a bride and groom may seem rather meaningless, but it actually stems from an ancient practice of showering newlyweds with nuts, fruits, and seeds as symbols of fertility.

American Values

4   Unlike norms, whose existence can easily be observed in everyday behavior, values are often more difficult to identify. The values of a society have to be inferred from

its norms, so that any analysis of social values relies heavily on the interpretations of the observer. The United States presents a particular problem, for it has a heterogeneous culture drawn from many different racial, ethnic, religious, and regional traditions, and so lacks the unquestioned consensus on values that smaller, traditional communities tend to display. Sociologists have therefore concentrated on detecting "core" values that appear to be shared by the majority of Americans. The most influential of these attempts is that of Robin Williams, who found fifteen basic value orientations in the United States:

1. *Achievement and success.* The society is highly competitive, and great value is placed on the achievement of power, wealth, and prestige.
2. *Activity and work.* Regular, disciplined work is highly valued for its own sake; those who do not work are considered lazy and even immoral.
3. *Moral orientation.* Americans tend to be moralists, seeing the world in terms of right and wrong and constantly evaluating the moral behavior of others.
4. *Humanitarianism.* Americans regard themselves as a kindly, charitable people, always ready to come to the aid of the less fortunate or the underdog.
5. *Efficiency and practicality.* Americans believe that problems have solutions, and they are an intensely practical people; the ability to "get things done" is widely admired.
6. *Progress.* Americans look to the future rather than the past, sharing a conviction that things can and should get better; their outlook is fundamentally optimistic.
7. *Material comfort.* Americans value the "good life," which they define in terms of a high standard of living and the possession of material goods.
8. *Equality.* Americans claim to believe in human equality, particularly in equality of opportunity; they generally relate to one another in an informal, egalitarian way.
9. *Freedom.* The freedom of the individual is regarded as one of the most important values in American life; Americans believe devoutly that they are and should remain "free."
10. *External conformity.* Despite their expressed belief in "rugged individualism," Americans tend to be conformist and are suspicious of those who are not.
11. *Science and rationality.* Americans believe deeply in a scientific rational approach to the world and in the use of applied science to gain mastery over the environment.
12. *Nationalism—patriotism.* Americans are proud of their country and its achievements; the "American way of life" is highly valued and assumed to be the best in the world.
13. *Democracy.* Americans regard their form of government as highly democratic, and believe that every citizen should have the right of political participation.
14. *Individual personality.* To be a responsible, self-respecting individual is very important, and Americans are reluctant to give the group priority over the individual.

15. *Group-superiority themes.* A strong countervalue to that of individual personality is the one that places a higher value on some racial, ethnic, class, or religious groups than on others.

6   It is obvious that some of these values are not entirely consistent with one another. Many of them, too, are accepted by some Americans but rejected by others. Also, Williams's list does not exhaust all the possibilities, and other writers have identified rather different values. James Henslin, for example, includes several items on Williams's list but adds others, such as education, religiosity, male supremacy, romantic love, monogamy, and heterosexuality. Moreover, values change over time, and some of those listed by Williams may be eroding. Questions have been raised, for example, about the meaning of "progress," and about new problems posed by science and technology, such as pollution of the environment. There is perhaps less insistence now on the value of conformity, and certainly less emphasis on group superiority, than there was a few decades ago.

VOCABULARY

Directions: Locate each of the key words in the reading selection. Then read and study each word in its context and try to determine its meaning. Use a dictionary or thesaurus to check your guess. Write the meanings of the words in the margin of the text.

Record the new words you've learned.

Key Word	Paragraph	Meaning
1. inferred	4	
2. heterogeneous	4	
3. consensus	4	
4. conformity	6	
Others?		

GUIDE QUESTIONS

Directions: The purpose of these guide questions is to ensure your understanding of what you have read. They also will help you to analyze and evaluate the author's ideas and apply them to the real world and your own life.

Write answers to the questions in your notebook or on a separate sheet of paper if your instructor wishes to collect them. Your answers will form the basis of class discussion.

1. Contrast the definitions of *values* and *norms* according to the information given in the first paragraph.
2. Give two examples of values that you personally hold.
3. a. Cite a few of the examples of values from the selection and the norms that result from them.
   b. Based on your understanding of question 3a, how would you describe the *relationship* between values and norms?
4. In paragraph 3 of the selection, the author states that some norms persist despite the fact that the conditions that produced them have disappeared. Give one of the examples from the paragraph. Then think of another example from your own knowledge and experience.
5. Discuss the point made in paragraph 4 of the selection: "The United States presents a particular problem, for it has a heterogeneous culture . . ." What does the author mean by "a heterogeneous culture"? How can we account for the fact that the United States is so heterogeneous?
6. Study Robin Williams's list of "value orientations." Do you agree that these are all American values? Can you think of any that Williams omitted?
7. In the introduction and in paragraph 6, you read that we often must choose between two values in the same situation—for example, between honesty and friendship when your friend asks you to help her cheat on an exam. Can you think of some other situations in which two values are in conflict?
8. It is important to remember that values are different in different societies. The Tangu, a group of people who live in New Guinea, play a game called *taketak,* which is similar to bowling. The goal of the game is not for one team to score more points than the other, but rather for both sides to score the *same* number of points. The Tangu place a high value on *equivalence* and think that winning generates ill will. In fact, when the Europeans introduced soccer to New Guinea, the Tangu changed the rules so that the object of the game was for the two teams to score the same number of goals. Sometimes their soccer games went on for days! Americans, of course, value competition and winning and insist on winners and losers. Living among the Tangu would certainly be very different from living in the United States. What might be some of the *advantages* of living in a society where equivalence is valued and winning is disapproved of? What might the *disadvantages* be?
9. A major distinction between values and norms is that values are abstract concepts and norms are concrete rules for behavior. Using the chart below, give several examples of abstract values and some of the concrete norms that are derived from them. Some information is already filled in to get you started.

The Value	The Norm
Honesty	*I pay my taxes.*
	I will not cheat on Tuesday's exam.
Efficiency	*I make a list of "things to do" every day.*
Thrift	

APPLICATION

Directions: Choose one of the following exercises.

1. Did you know that in Mexico clocks do not "run," they "walk"? And that Mexicans do not say they "missed" the bus, but rather the bus "left" them? In three or four sentences, explain what you think these two examples tell us about the differing values of the United States and Mexico.

2. An American is visiting Copenhagen, Denmark. It is three o'clock in the morning. Not a car is in sight but a small crowd of pedestrians has gathered because a music club has just closed for the night. The traffic light turns red. All the people stop and wait patiently at the curb, despite the fact that a car has not passed for an hour. The American hesitates, then crosses the empty street against the red light. The Danes waiting at the curb are shocked; some even call out "tsk tsk" and "shame!" The American is surprised and confused. In a few sentences, explain the conflict of values between the United States and Denmark illustrated by this incident.

3. Work in small groups to complete this exercise. Below are brief descriptions of people in specific situations. Read the descriptions out loud, then discuss with your group members which American value is reflected in each little story.

   a. A mother says angrily to her young child, "You march right back to that bathroom—and this time use soap!"

   b. A boss looks at the clock as an employee arrives at work. The clock says 9:25 A.M. The boss says, "Well, good *afternoon!*"

c. A girl wins an essay-writing contest sponsored by a nearby university. When told of her prize, she smiles and says, "Oh, it was nothing—anyone could have done it."

d. A father takes his young daughter outside to practice baseball every night, rain or shine. When the girl is beaten by another child in a ballgame, they increase the length of their practice sessions. When the girl is chosen "Most Valuable Player" of her league, the father and daughter are happy and proud.

e. A male executive hears there may be layoffs in his company, so he decides to look for another job. Before going on his first interview, he visits a hair-styling salon to have his gray hair dyed back to its original brown color.

4. Underlining and annotating the important ideas in a textbook chapter are important skills for college students. Marking your text in this way helps you to be an active rather than a passive reader, forces you to focus on the main ideas in the chapter, and provides a study aid when it comes time to review for an exam. Turn to Appendix B to review and practice *underlining* and *annotating*. Then underline and annotate Robertson's "Values."

WRITING

Directions: Write a summary of the selection "Values." Remember that a summary should be a restatement of the main ideas of the selection with few examples. To review how to write a summary, read Appendix B.

The diversity of behavior among the peoples of the world is tremendous. For example, in some societies, bending your finger toward your body means "come here," while in other cultures, it means "go away." In India, cows wander freely through the streets, something Americans find offensive; in the United States, dogs run freely in homes, something visitors from India would find disgusting. Most Americans teach their children not to fight. "Solve your problems with words, not fists," they counsel. Among the Yanomamo of South America, a father deliberately teases and goads his son until the child, in desperation, strikes him in the face. The father cries out in approval. Why have humans all over the world, who are so similar physically, developed such different ways of living? Cultural anthropologists try to discover why people behave as they do. In this chapter we learn that our culture is only one alternative among the many designs for living. No one group of people has developed the "right" way of living. "Other fields, other grasshoppers," say the Javanese.

UNITY IN DIVERSITY

Donald Light and Suzanne Keller

1   What is more basic, more "natural" than love between a man and woman? Eskimo men offer their wives to guests and friends as a gesture of hospitality; both husband and wife feel extremely offended if the guest declines. The Banaro of New Guinea believe it would be disastrous for a woman to conceive her first child by her husband and not by one of her father's close friends, as is their custom.

2   The real father is a close friend of the bride's father. . . . Nevertheless the first-born child inherits the name and possessions of the husband. An American would deem such a custom immoral, but Banaro tribesmen would be equally shocked to discover that the first-born child of an American couple is the offspring of the husband.

3   The Yanomamo of northern Brazil, whom anthropologist Napoleon A. Chagnon named "the fierce people," encourage what we would consider extreme disrespect. Small boys are applauded for striking their mothers and fathers in the face. Yanomamo parents would laugh at our efforts to curb aggression in children, much as they laughed at Chagnon's naiveté when he first came to live with them. To be officially considered a man, a Yanomamo boy must compile a record of successful battles, and if he is to be taken seriously, by the time he reaches puberty his body must be covered with scars. Older men, hardened to injury, duel with each other constantly in an effort to prove which man has the greater capacity to bear pain. Even women do not escape tribal savagery since men will frequently prove just how fierce they are by beating, mutilating, or wounding their wives. A wife cannot even escape to her family because, to the family, the husband's behavior is simply part of a long tradition.

4   The variations among cultures are startling, yet all peoples have customs and beliefs about marriage, the bearing and raising of children, sex, and hospitality—to name just a few of the universals anthropologists have discovered in their cross-cultural explorations. But the details of cultures do indeed vary: in this country, not so many years ago, when a girl was serious about a boy and he about her, she wore

his fraternity pin over her heart; in the Fiji Islands, girls put hibiscus flowers behind their ears when they are in love. The specific gestures are different but the impulse to symbolize feelings, to dress courtship in ceremonies, is the same. How do we explain this unity in diversity?

Cultural Universals

Cultural universals are all of the behavior patterns and institutions that have been found in all known cultures. Anthropologist George Peter Murdock identified over sixty cultural universals, including a system of social status, marriage, body adornments, dancing, myths and legends, cooking, incest taboos, inheritance rules, puberty customs, and religious rituals.   5

The universals of culture may derive from the fact that all societies must perform the same essential functions if they are to survive—including organization, motivation, communication, protection, the socialization of new members, and the replacement of those who die. In meeting these prerequisites for group life, people inevitably design similar—though not identical—patterns for living. As Clyde Kluckhohn wrote, "All cultures constitute somewhat distinct answers to essentially the same questions posed by human biology and by the generalities of the human situation."   6

The way in which a people articulate cultural universals depends in large part on their physical and social environment—that is, on the climate in which they live, the materials they have at hand, and the peoples with whom they establish contact. For example, the wheel has long been considered one of humankind's greatest inventions, and anthropologists were baffled for a long time by the fact that the great civilizations of South America never discovered it. Then researchers uncovered a number of toys with wheels. Apparently the Aztecs and their neighbors did know about the wheel; they simply didn't find them useful in their mountainous environment.   7

Adaptation, Ethnocentrism, and Cultural Relativity

Taken out of context, almost any custom will seem bizarre, perhaps cruel, or just plain ridiculous. To understand why the Yanomamo encourage aggressive behavior in their sons, for example, you have to see things through their eyes. The Yanomamo live in a state of chronic warfare; they spend much of their time planning for and defending against raids with neighboring tribes. If Yanomamo parents did not encourage aggression in a boy, he would be ill-equipped for life in their society. Socializing boys to be aggressive is **adaptive** for the Yanomamo because it enhances their capacity for survival. "In general, culture is . . . adaptive because it often provides people with a means of adjusting to the physiological needs of their own bodies, to their physical–geographical environment and to their social environments as well."   8

In many tropical societies, there are strong taboos against a mother having sexual intercourse with a man until her child is at least two years old. As a Hausa woman explains,   9

> A mother should not go to her husband while she has a child she is suckling. . . . [I]f she only sleeps with her husband and does not become pregnant,

it will not hurt her child, it will not spoil her milk. But if another child enters in, her milk will make the first one ill.

10   Undoubtedly, people would smirk at a woman who nursed a two-year-old child in our society and abstained from having sex with her husband. Why do Hausa women behave in a way that seems so overprotective and overindulgent to us? In tropical climates protein is scarce. If a mother were to nurse more than one child at a time, or if she were to wean a child before it reached the age of two, the youngster would be prone to kwashiorkor, an often fatal disease resulting from protein deficiency. Thus, long post-partum sex taboos are adaptive. In a tropical environment a post-partum sex taboo and a long period of breast-feeding solve a serious problem.

11   **Ethnocentrism** is the tendency to see one's own way of life, including behaviors, beliefs, values, and norms as the only right way of living. Robin Fox points out that "any human group is ever ready to consign another recognizably different human group to the other side of the boundary. It is not enough to possess culture to be fully human, you have to possess our culture." Although the error of this way of thinking about culture may seem self-evident today, it is a lesson that anthropologists and the missionaries who often preceded them to remote areas learned the hard way, by observing the effects their best intentions had on peoples whose way of life was quite different from their own. In an article on the pitfalls of trying to "uplift" peoples whose ways seem backward and inefficient, Don Adams quotes an old Oriental story:

> Once upon a time there was a great flood, and involved in this flood were two creatures, a monkey and a fish. The monkey, being agile and experienced, was lucky enough to scramble up a tree and escape the raging waters. As he looked down from his safe perch, he saw the poor fish struggling against the swift current. With the very best intentions, he reached down and lifted the fish from the water. The result was inevitable.

12   No custom is good or bad, right or wrong in itself; each one must be examined in light of the culture as a whole and evaluated in terms of how it works in the context of the entire culture. Anthropologists and sociologists call this **cultural relativity.**

13   The Tangu, who live in a remote part of New Guinea, play a game called *taketak,* which, in many ways, resembles bowling. The game is played with a top that has been fashioned from a dried fruit and with two groups of coconut stakes that are driven into the ground (more or less like bowling pins). The players divide into two teams. Members of the first team take turns throwing the top into the batch of stakes; every stake the top hits is removed. Then the second team steps to the line and tosses the top into their batch of stakes. The object of the game, surprisingly, is not to knock over as many stakes as possible. Rather, the game continues until both teams have removed the same number of stakes. Winning is completely irrelevant.

14   In a sense, games are practice for "real life"; they reflect the values of the culture in which they are played. **Values** are the criteria people use in assessing their daily lives, arranging their priorities, measuring their pleasures and pains, choosing between

alternative courses of action. The Tangu value equivalence: the idea of one individual or group winning and another losing bothers them, for they believe winning generates ill will. In fact, when Europeans brought soccer to the Tangu, they altered the rules so that the object of the game was for two teams to score the same number of goals. Sometimes their soccer games went on for days! American games, in contrast, are highly competitive; there are always winners and losers. Many rule books include provisions for overtime and "sudden death" to prevent ties, which leave Americans dissatisfied. World Series, Superbowls, championships in basketball and hockey, Olympic Gold Medals are front-page news in this country. In the words of the late football coach Vince Lombardi, "Winning isn't everything, it's the only thing."

Norms

Norms, the rules that guide behavior in everyday situations, are derived from values, but norms and values can conflict, as we have seen. You may recall a news item that appeared in American newspapers in December 1972, describing the discovery of survivors of a plane crash twelve thousand feet high in the Andes. The crash had occurred on October 13; sixteen of the passengers (a rugby team and their supporters) managed to survive for sixty-nine days in near-zero temperatures. The story made headlines because, to stay alive, the survivors had eaten parts of their dead companions. Officials, speaking for the group, stressed how valiantly the survivors had tried to save the lives of the injured people and how they had held religious services regularly. The survivors' explanations are quite interesting, for they reveal how important it is to people to justify their actions, to resolve conflicts in norms and values (here, the positive value of survival versus the taboo against cannibalism). Some of the survivors compared their action to a heart transplant, using parts of a dead person's body to save another person's life. Others equated their act with the sacrament of communion. In the words of one religious survivor, "If we would have died, it would have been suicide, which is condemned by the Roman Catholic faith."

15

VOCABULARY

Directions: Locate each of the key words in the reading selection. Then read and study each word in its context and try to determine its meaning. Use a dictionary or thesaurus to check your guess. Write the meanings of the words in the margin of the text.

Record the new words you've learned below and on the next page.

Key Word	Paragraph	Meaning
1. naiveté	3	
2. adornments	5	
3. derive	6	

Key Word	Paragraph	Meaning
4. baffled	7	
5. chronic	8	
6. wean	10	
7. pitfalls	11	
Others?		

GUIDE QUESTIONS

Directions: The purpose of these guide questions is to ensure your understanding of what you have read. They also will help you to analyze and evaluate the authors' ideas and apply them to the real world and your own life.

Write answers to the questions in your notebook or on a separate sheet of paper if your instructor wishes to collect them. Your answers will form the basis of class discussion.

1. Define *cultural universal.*
2. Cite several examples of cultural universals.
3. The authors state that the *details* of cultural universals may vary from society to society. Give examples of cultural universals that are acted out differently in different cultures.
4. Explain why cultural universals exist.
5. According to the authors of the selection, what determines the way people articulate cultural universals?
6. Define or describe the concept of *adaptation.*
7. Explain why the Hausa post-partum sex taboo is *adaptive.*
8. Define *ethnocentrism.*
9. What moral or lesson can we learn from the Oriental story quoted in the selection?
10. Define *cultural relativity.*
11. Explain the conflict of values and norms cited in the story of the Andes plane-crash survivors.

APPLICATION

Directions: Read the following excerpt from the essay "Body Ritual among the Nacirema" by anthropologist Horace Miner:

1   The Nacirema have an almost pathological horror of and fascination with the mouth, the condition of which is believed to have a supernatural influence on all social relationships. Were it not for the ritual of the mouth, they believe that their teeth would fall out, their gums bleed, their jaws shrink, their friends desert them, and their lovers reject them. They also

believe that a strong relationship exists between oral and moral characteristics. For example, there is a ritual ablution of the mouth for children which is supposed to improve their moral fiber.

The daily body ritual performed by everyone includes a mouth-rite. Despite the fact that these people are so punctilious about care of the mouth, this rite involves a practice which strikes the uninitiated stranger as revolting. It was reported to me that the ritual consists of inserting a small bundle of hog hairs into the mouth, along with certain magical powders, and then moving the bundle in a highly formalized series of gestures.   2

In addition to the private mouth-rite, the people seek out a holy mouth-man twice a year. These practitioners have an impressive set of paraphernalia, consisting of a variety of augers, awls, probes, and prods. The use of these objects in the exorcism of the evils of the mouth involves almost unbelievable ritual torture of the client. The holy mouth-man opens the client's mouth and, using the above-mentioned tools, enlarges any holes which decay may have created in the teeth. Magical materials are put into these holes. If there are not naturally occurring holes in the teeth, large sections of one or more teeth are gouged out so that the supernatural substance can be applied. In the client's view, the purpose of these ministrations is to arrest decay and to draw friends. The extremely sacred and traditional character of the rite is evidenced by the fact that the natives return to the holy mouth-man year after year, despite the fact that their teeth continue to decay.   3

If you feel that living among the people who practice such bizarre customs would be strange and horrifying, then reexamine the excerpt *after* you read the name of the tribe—Nacirema—backwards!

Note the formal, highly technical language used to describe ordinary, everyday things. In order to understand the passage, "translate" the following phrases into everyday language.

1. In paragraph 2:
    mouth-rite—
    small bundle of hog hairs—
    magical powders—
    moving the bundle in a highly formalized series of gestures—
2. In paragraph 3:
    holy mouth-man—
    exorcism of the evils of the mouth—
    magical materials are put into these holes—
    large sections . . . are gouged out—
3. In paragraph 1:
    What is Miner referring to at the end of paragraph 1 when he says "there is a ritual ablution of the mouth for children which is supposed to improve their moral fiber"?

Why does Miner describe our dental habits in such a "foreign" way? What point is he making here? Discuss these questions with your classmates.

WRITING

1. a. Consider this custom of the Thompson Indians (a North American Indian tribe): Their puberty ritual includes a long period of fasting, sweating, and beating of the teenaged boys to prepare them to take on the responsibilities of manhood. Write a few sentences describing the reactions of ethnocentric individuals upon learning of this ritual. How would they feel about it? What would they say? What might they do about it?

   b. Now write a similar short paragraph from the perspective of a person who believes in the concept of cultural relativity.

2. The authors tell us in paragraph 6 that cultural universals developed from the requirements for survival in group life. Why do they specify *group* life? Why would these concepts not apply to *individual* life—say, to a hermit living alone on a deserted island?

3. In order to fully understand the important concepts presented in "Unity in Diversity," you must make the ideas your own. In your own words, write definitions of the key concepts: cultural universals, adaptation, ethnocentrism, cultural relativity, norms, and values.

While Japanese strength in the global economy ebbs and flows, America's interest in its rival remains constant. We are fascinated by the history and culture of this Asian nation that seems so different from ours, but at the same time seems so much the same. This article is one of a series published by The New York Times *in 1995 and 1996.*

WHO NEEDS LOVE!

In Japan, Many Married Couples Survive without It

Nicholas D. Kristof

Yuri Uemura sat on the straw *tatami* mat of her living room and chatted cheerfully   1
about her forty-year marriage to a man whom, she mused, she never particularly
liked.

"There was never any love between me and my husband," she said blithely, re-   2
calling how he used to beat her. "But, well, we survived."

A seventy-two-year-old midwife, her face as weathered as an old baseball and   3
etched with a thousand seams, Mrs. Uemura said that her husband had never told
her that he liked her, never complimented her on a meal, never told her "thank you,"
never held her hand, never given her a present, never shown her affection in any way.
He never called her by her name, but summoned her with the equivalent of a grunt
or a "Hey, you."

"Even with animals, the males cooperate to bring the females some food,"   4
Mrs. Uemura said sadly, noting the contrast to her own marriage. "When I see that,
it brings tears to my eyes."

In short, the Uemuras have a marriage that is as durable as it is unhappy, one   5
couple's tribute to the Japanese sanctity of family.

The divorce rate in Japan is at a record high but still less than half that of the   6
United States, and Japan arguably has one of the strongest family structures in the
industrialized world. As the United States and Europe fret about the disintegration
of the traditional family, most Japanese families remain as solid as the small red table
on which Mrs. Uemura rested her tea.

A study published last year by the Population Council, an international nonprofit   7
group based in New York, suggested that the traditional two-parent household is
on the wane not only in America but throughout most of the world. There was one
prominent exception: Japan.

In Japan, for example, only 1.1 percent of births are to unwed mothers—virtu-   8
ally unchanged from twenty-five years ago. In the United States, the figure is 30.1
percent and rising rapidly.

Yet if one comes to a little Japanese town like Omiya to learn the secrets of the   9
Japanese family, the people are not as happy as the statistics.

"I haven't lived for myself," Mrs. Uemura said, with a touch of melancholy, "but   10
for my kids, and for my family, and for society."

Mrs. Uemura's marriage does not seem exceptional in Japan, whether in the big   11
cities or here in Omiya. The people of Omiya, a community of 5,700 nestled in the

rain-drenched hills of the Kii Peninsula in Mie Prefecture, nearly 200 miles south-west of Tokyo, have spoken periodically to a reporter about various aspects of their daily lives. On this visit they talked about their families.

Survival Secrets—Often, the Couples Expect Little

12 Osamu Torida furrowed his brow and looked perplexed when he was asked if he loved his wife of thirty-three years.

13 "Yeah, so-so, I guess," said Mr. Torida, a cattle farmer. "She's like air or water. You couldn't live without it, but most of the time, you're not conscious of its existence."

14 The secret to the survival of the marriage, Mr. Torida acknowledged, was not mutual passion.

15 "Sure, we had fights about our work," he explained as he stood beside his barn. "But we were preoccupied by work and our debts, so we had no time to fool around."

16 That is a common theme in Omiya. It does not seem that Japanese families sur-vive because husbands and wives love each other more than American couples, but rather because they perhaps love each other less.

17 "I think love marriages are more fragile than arranged marriages," said Tomika Kusukawa, forty-nine, who married her high-school sweetheart and now runs a car-repair shop with him. "In love marriages, when something happens or if the couple falls out of love, they split up."

18 If there is a secret to the strength of the Japanese family, it consists of three in-gredients: low expectations, patience, and shame.

19 The advantage of marriages based on low expectations is that they have built-in shock absorbers. If the couple discovers that they have nothing in common, that they do not even like each other, then that is not so much a reason for divorce as it is par for the course.

20 Even the discovery that one's spouse is having an affair is often not as traumatic in a Japanese marriage as it is in the West. A little sexual infidelity on the part of a man (though not on the part of his wife) was traditionally tolerated, so long as he did not become so besotted as to pay his mistress more than he could afford.

21 Tsuzuya Fukuyama, who runs a convenience store and will mark her fiftieth wed-ding anniversary this year, toasted her hands on an electric heater in the front of the store and declared that a woman would be wrong to get angry if her husband had an affair.

22 "It's never just one side that's at fault," Mrs. Fukuyama said sternly. "Maybe the husband had an affair because his wife wasn't so hot herself. So she should look at her own faults."

23 Mrs. Fukuyama's daughter came to her a few years ago, suspecting that her hus-band was having an affair and asking what to do.

24 "I told her, 'Once you left this house, you can only come back if you divorce; if you're not prepared to get a divorce, then you'd better be patient,'" Mrs. Fukuyama recalled. "And so she was patient. And then she got pregnant and had a kid, and now they're close again."

The word that Mrs. Fukuyama used for patience is *gaman,* a term that comes up 25
whenever marriage is discussed in Japan. It means "toughing it out, enduring hardship," and many Japanese regard *gaman* with pride as a national trait.

Many people complain that younger folks divorce because they do not have 26
enough *gaman,* and the frequency with which the term is used suggests a rather
bleak understanding of marriage.

"I didn't know my husband very well when we married, and afterward we used 27
to get into bitter fights," said Yoshiko Hirowaki, fifty-six, a store owner. "But then
we had children, and I got very busy with the kids and with this shop. Time passed."

Now Mrs. Hirowaki has been married thirty-four years, and she complains about 28
young people who do not stick to their vows.

"In the old days, wives had more *gaman,*" she said. "Now kids just don't have 29
enough *gaman.*"

The durability of the Japanese family is particularly wondrous because couples 30
are, by international standards, exceptionally incompatible.

One survey asked married men and their wives in thirty-seven countries how 31
they felt about politics, sex, religion, ethics, and social issues. Japanese couples ranked
dead last in compatibility of views, by a huge margin. Indeed, another survey found
that if they were doing it over again, only about one-third of Japanese would marry
the same person.

Incompatibility might not matter so much, however, because Japanese husbands 32
and wives spend very little time talking to each other.

"I kind of feel there's nothing new to say to her," said Masayuki Ogita, an egg 33
farmer, explaining his reticence.

In a small town like Omiya, couples usually have dinner together, but in Japan- 34
ese cities there are many "7–11 husbands," so called because they leave at 7 A.M.
and return after 11 P.M.

Masahiko Kondo now lives in Omiya, working in the chamber of commerce, 35
but he used to be a salesman in several big cities. He would leave for work each
morning at 7, and about four nights a week would go out for after-work drinking or
mah-jongg sessions with buddies.

"I only saw my baby on Saturdays or Sundays," said Mr. Kondo, a lanky good- 36
natured man of thirty-seven. "But in fact, I really enjoyed that life. It didn't bother
me that I never spent time with my kid on weekdays."

Mr. Kondo's wife, Keiko, had her own life, spent with her child and the wives of 37
other workaholic husbands.

"We had birthday parties, but they were with the kids and the mothers," she 38
remembers. "No fathers ever came."

A national survey found that 30 percent of fathers spend less than 15 minutes 39
a day on weekdays talking with or playing with their children. Among eighth graders,
51 percent reported that they never spoke with their fathers on weekdays.

As a result, the figures in Japan for single-parent households can be deceptive. 40
The father is often more a theoretical presence than a homework-helping reality.

Still, younger people sometimes want to see the spouses in daylight, and a result 41
is a gradual change in the focus of lives from work to family. Two decades ago,

nearly half of young people said in surveys that they wanted their fathers to put priority on work rather than family. Now only one-quarter say that.

Social Pressures—Shame Is Keeping Bonds in Place

42 For those who find themselves desperately unhappy, one source of pressure to keep plugging is shame.

43 "If you divorce, you lose face in society," said Tatsumi Kinoshita, a tea farmer. "People say, 'His wife escaped.' So folks remain married because they hate to be gossiped about."

44 Shame is a powerful social sanction in Japan, and it is not just a matter of gossip. Traditionally, many companies were reluctant to promote employees who had divorced or who had major problems at home.

45 "If you divorce, it weakens your position at work," said Akihiko Kanda, twenty-seven, who works in a local government office. "Your bosses won't give you such good ratings, and it'll always be a negative factor."

46 The idea, Mr. Kanda noted, is that if an employee cannot manage his own life properly, he should not be entrusted with important corporate matters.

47 Financial sanctions are also a major disincentive for divorce. The mother gets the children in three-quarters of divorces, but most mothers in Japan do not have careers and have few financial resources. Fathers pay child support in only 15 percent of all divorces with children, partly because women often hesitate to go to court to demand payments and partly because men often fail to pay even when the court orders it.

48 "The main reason for lack of divorce is that women can't support themselves," said Mizuko Kanda, a fifty-one-year-old housewife. "My friends complain about their husbands and say that they'd divorce if they could, but they can't afford to.

49 The result of these social and economic pressures is clear.

50 Even in Japan, there are about twenty-four divorces for every one hundred marriages, but that compares with thirty-two in France, forty-two in England, and fifty-five in the United States.

The Outlook—Change Creeps in, Imperiling Family

51 But society is changing in Japan, and it is an open question whether these changes will undermine the traditional family as they have elsewhere around the globe.

52 The nuclear family has already largely replaced the extended family in Japan, and shame is eroding as a sanction. Haruko Okumura, for example, runs a kindergarten and speaks openly about her divorce.

53 "My mom was uneasy about it, but I never had an inferiority complex about being divorced," said Mrs. Okumura, as dozens of children played in the next room. "And people accepted me easily."

54 Mrs. Okumura sees evidence of the changes in family patterns every day: fathers are playing more of a role in the kindergarten. At Christmas parties and sports contests, fathers have started to show up along with mothers. And Mrs. Okumura believes that divorce is on the upswing.

55 "If there's a weakening of the economic and social pressures to stay married," she said, "surely divorce rates will soar."

Already divorce rates are rising, approximately doubling over the last twenty-five years. But couples are very reluctant to divorce when they have children, and so single-parent households account for exactly the same proportion today as in 1965.

56

Shinsuke Kawaguchi, a young tea farmer, is one of the men for whom life is changing. Americans are not likely to be impressed by Mr. Kawaguchi's open-mindedness, but he is.

57

"I take good care of my wife," he said. "I may not say 'I love you,' but I do hold her hand. And I might say, after she makes dinner, 'This tastes good.'"

58

"Of course," Mr. Kawaguchi quickly added, "I wouldn't say that unless I'd just done something really bad."

59

Even Mrs. Uemura, the elderly woman whose husband used to beat her, said that her husband was treating her better.

60

"The other day, he tried to pour me a cup of tea," Mrs. Uemura recalled excitedly. "It was a big change. I told all my friends."

61

VOCABULARY

Directions: Locate each of the key words in the reading selection. Try to figure out each word's meaning by using the context. Confirm your guess by checking the dictionary or thesaurus. Write the meanings of the words in the margin of the text. Then record the meanings in the chart below.

Key Word	Paragraph	Meaning
1. blithely	2	
2. fret	6	
3. on the wane	7	
4. par for the course	19	
5. traumatic	20	
6. trait	25	
7. bleak	26	
8. disincentive	47	
Others?		

GUIDE QUESTIONS

Directions: These questions will guide your understanding of what you have read. Write your answers in your notebook or on a separate sheet of paper if your instructor wishes to collect it. Your answers to these questions will be the basis of class discussion.

1. Compare and contrast the divorce rate, the existence of the two-parent household, and births to unwed mothers in the United States and Japan.
2. What is the author's purpose in describing the marriage of Yuri Uemura and her husband?
3. What are some of the "survival secrets" of Japanese marriages, according to the article?
4. Compare and contrast the attitude toward infidelity in marriage in your family and that of the Japanese as described in the article.
5. Explain the term *gaman* and its relevance to marriage in Japan.
6. In the United States, many people divorce, citing "incompatibility" as the reason. How would the Japanese probably react to this?
7. Discuss the role of *shame* in keeping marriages together in Japan.
8. According to Mizudo Kanda, what is the main reason for the lack of divorce in Japan?
9. According to the article, change is occurring in Japan; cite some of the changes that Japanese society is experiencing.

APPLICATION

Directions: Complete one of the following assignments.

1. Do some research on marriage in another culture. Use your school library or local public library to find information on the following statistics: 1) divorce rates from twenty-five years ago; 2) the number of single-parent households twenty-five years ago; 3) the number of births to unwed mothers twenty-five years ago. Then find the same statistics for today. (The most recent statistics for the United States are from the 1990 census.) Summarize the similarities and differences in the statistics of the country you investigated with those of the United States and Japan.
2. Work in small groups to complete this assignment. Think about the differences in marriage in Japan and in the United States. What are the *advantages* and *disadvantages* of each? Use the table below and on the next page to list as many as you can.

MARRIAGE

	Japan	United States
Advantages		

MARRIAGE

	Japan	United States
Disadvantages		

WRITING

Directions: Choose one of the assignments below.

1. Use the information in the table in Application assignment 2 to write a brief essay. Compare and contrast marriage in the United States and Japan. Discuss the advantages and disadvantages of each society.

2. Write a summary of the article "Who Needs Love! In Japan Many Married Couples Survive without It." Review the steps for writing summaries in Appendix B.

Most Americans (if they think about it at all) think of monogamy as "natural" and are surprised to learn that many other societies practice different forms of marriage. Problems can arise when people leave their home countries and immigrate to new lands with different values and norms. Should immigrants be allowed to bring their customs with them? What if those customs are illegal in their new countries? This article appeared in the international section of The New York Times *in January 1996.*

AFRICAN WOMEN IN FRANCE BATTLE POLYGAMY

Marlise Simons

1   Khadi Keita shifted in her chair in a Paris cafe as she described the day she became a stranger in her own home. That was the day in 1985 when her husband suddenly arrived here with a new wife.

2   He hung a curtain in the middle of the cramped bedroom and announced that, from now on, the two women would have to share him, the kitchen, the closets, everything.

3   The next four years became a nightmare of pregnancies, babies, nasty fights, and long, hostile silences, Mrs. Keita said. Then her husband, a Muslim, went home to his African village, married again and brought wife no. 3.

4   Mrs. Keita, who has since divorced—a rarity in polygamous marriages—and become a social worker, is an immigrant from Senegal. She is one of the African women in France who are now willing to speak openly about the secrets of polygamy and about the strains, the anger, and the humiliations of their marriages.

5   Long overshadowed by other immigrant problems of poverty and discrimination, the widespread practice of polygamy in France is coming to light because African women here are fighting the tradition. In the current anti-immigrant mood, the government has also decided to take a stand.

6   After quietly tolerating the Muslim male right to have up to four wives, the government has said France will recognize only one spouse and consider other marriages annulled.

7   The discussion of polygamy has raised anew the question of how a society should deal with immigrant customs that are unacceptable or against the law in a new land. There have already been heated debates about whether girls may wear Muslim headscarves, a religious symbol, in France's secular schools, and French prosecutors have gone to court to forbid the tradition of sexually mutilating Muslim girls.

A Custom Tolerated in the Homeland Turns Sour Abroad

8   "Polygamy may be as old as Africa, but it doesn't work in France," said Mrs. Keita, whose former husband could not be located.

9   "It's unbearable because there is no room for two or three wives and fifteen children in one small place. The women are rivals. The husband is never fair. He has a favorite, so there are horrible fights."

There is the wrenching lack of privacy. "You hear everything, your husband and   10
the other wives," she said. "You hear how he behaves with his favorite, usually the
new one. The women end up hating the man. Everyone feels bad inside."

The politics of polygamy is no less charged. Ivry, a Paris suburb, has some fifteen   11
hundred African immigrants, and two out of three families are polygamous. "Consider the costs," a town official said. "One husband with three wives and a team of
children may need government health care, education, and subsidies for up to twenty
people. Is this fair?"

He said this question weighs heavily at a time when France's social welfare sys-   12
tem is in the midst of an enormous debt crisis. In December, government plans to
cut benefits caused three weeks of strikes and protests.

Polygamy has come to France with the tens of thousands of African immigrants   13
from countries like Senegal, Mali, and Mauritania. The French Interior Ministry says
there are no firm statistics because foreign wives are often in the country clandes-
tinely and immigrants keep other wives back in Africa.

In the United States, the law bars polygamous immigrants and the authorities   14
say they believe that such cases are rare.

In the Paris area alone, it is estimated that 200,000 people live in polygamous   15
families. They live in the rickety neighborhoods behind Montmartre and in glum
suburbs like Bobigny, St. Denis, and Creteil.

Moustafa Djaara, a construction worker from Mali, lives in Bobigny with his two   16
wives and nine children. Both wives are pregnant. He wants to bring his young, third
wife to France. His modest income is more than doubled by the generous benefits
the French state pays to children and pregnant women, regardless of their status.

Mr. Djaara asserts that polygamy is hardest for the husband because his wives   17
fight a lot, he has his job, and does all the shopping. He shops because he must control all the money, he said.

Given his complaints, why does he want more than one wife? "My father did,   18
my grandfather did, so why shouldn't I?" Mr. Djaara said.

"When my wife is sick and I don't have another, who will care for me?" Besides,   19
he said, "one wife on her own is trouble. When there are several, they are forced
to be polite and well behaved. If they misbehave, you threaten that you'll take another wife."

Ruling at home may be one thing, but living with the neighbors is another.   20

Town officials and building owners have refused large tribal families on their   21
premises. In St. Denis last year, a welfare office allocated a small apartment to a
Mauritanian family of six. Two months later, thirty members of the same family had
moved in. The French neighbors, outraged at the noise, pressed the town hall until
the group was moved.

It was mainly the Socialist government in the 1980s that quietly admitted more   22
than one wife per husband as part of its family-reunification policy. The argument was
that immigrants had the right to a "normal" family life.

As a result, many immigrants brought not just their wives but, as their income   23
improved, they went home to buy new, young brides, often still teenagers. Once
the women gave birth in France, mother and child were allowed to stay.

24   "We've been telling the French for ten years that this was wrong, that polygamy couldn't work here because we saw the problems," said Madine Diallo, who was born in Mali and now heads an African women's health and family-planning group.

25   "In Africa there is space. Even if co-wives live around the same courtyard, at least each wife has her own room or her house. The man visits her there, in her own bed. Here two, three families are packed into two rooms."

26   It is a myth that African women like polygamy, she continued. "Our mothers and grandmothers and every woman before them would go to the witch doctor to get a potion or cast a spell if she knew her husband was going to take another wife. Many still do. And women do it even here."

27   Fatima Traoré, who came from Mali, said she sometimes feels she will lose her mind. Sometimes she and her two co-wives do not talk to each other for days. She and her husband had been in Paris for four years when he went "on holiday" and came back with another wife.

28   "From one day to the next, another wife comes and does what you do," Mrs. Traoré said. "She meddles in the house. She gets pregnant. You still get your turn with your husband, your nights with him. But he pays no attention to you. Just two, three minutes to satisfy himself. That's it. Whatever you do makes no difference. You can cry all you want. He doesn't care."

29   Women in polygamous marriages describe the marital routine like this: The husband spends two nights with one wife, then two nights with the next. The wife who has her turn in the marital bed does the cooking for the family. "If a woman says 'It's my turn in the kitchen,' then you know," Mrs. Traoré said.

30   Health workers say the feelings boiling in close quarters can make the women ill or violent.

31   "Sometimes the women go crazy, they attack each other," said Catherine Rixain, a family counselor who works in the suburbs. "Or they take it out on each other's children. We have seen children beaten by a desperate co-wife."

32   Hawa Koulibali is one of the women who feel trapped. She came as a young bride from Mali twenty years ago and now lives with her two co-wives and their fourteen children in Marne-la-Vallée, half an hour's train ride east of Paris. But she and the co-wives have never seen Paris. They cannot read. They speak no French.

33   Although their husband goes home every two years, he says a trip for all of them would be too expensive. Cut off from France and cut off from Mali, Mrs. Koulibali feels lost. She and the co-wives try to get along. But being friends is too difficult, she said.

34   Beyond the strains and rivalry at home, immigrant women can find moments of solidarity in the support groups formed by French and African social workers. One group met recently in a day-care center at Emerainville, east of Paris.

35   The center is a cheerful, airy place, festooned with toys and drawings. But in a back room, sixteen women, all in polygamous marriages, met around a small table. Ostensibly they met to discuss child care. But other questions seemed more haunting.

36   They denied that anyone liked polygamy. "We have no choice!" a woman in her thirties shouted. The consensus was that the immigrant women here had lost their dignity.

"If you don't get along with your co-wife in Africa, you do not pass by her door   37
and she does not pass yours," a woman from Mauritania said. Another participant
whispered: "An African woman will not sleep with her husband in a bed that another
woman uses. Here we must take turns."

The anger quickly focused on the men. The women complained of injustices: 38
husbands gave money to their favorite wife, usually the new one; husbands had used
money a wife had earned in France in order to go to Africa and buy another wife. As
humiliating, the women said, was when a husband took the wife's identity card to
Africa and used it to bring in a new wife.

In the support groups, counselors have been prodding women to warn their   39
husbands that they will denounce them if they beat their wives or if they seize their
cards.

"We try to stop some of the dirty tricks," said Kani Sidibe, who used to work for   40
Air Afrique and is now a social worker. "Some women are losing their fear. They
come and talk to us. But we have a long way to go."

Some signs of change have appeared; for example, in the life of Moustafa Diop,   41
an immigrant from Senegal who lives near Charles de Gaulle Airport. He does odd
jobs driving a truck. One wife works as a part-time cleaner and one as a seamstress.
The third does the home work. At night they look after the eighteen children.

He concedes that "the women are not content," but now outright rebellion   42
looms. Two years ago Mr. Diop went back to Senegal and used the family savings to
buy another bride. He paid for a dowry and a big wedding. "It gives a man great standing," he said.

While he prepared to bring his young bride from Dakar, his three wives in Paris   43
banded together. They are furious because he wasted their hard-earned money on
another wife.

"They say if the new one comes, they will all leave," Mr. Diop said. With three   44
wives in France and one in Dakar, Mr. Diop said he has great prestige in his village,
but he is unsure how to deal with the rebellion at home. The French government
may settle that. The Interior Ministry has already said it will not give a residence
permit to more than one wife.

VOCABULARY

Directions: Locate each of the key words in the article. Try to figure out each word's
meaning by using the context. Confirm your guess by checking the dictionary or
thesaurus. Write the meanings of the words in the margin of the text. Then record
the meanings in the chart below and on the next page.

Key Word	Paragraph	Meaning
1. annulled	6	
2. wrenching	10	
3. rickety	15	

Key Word	Paragraph	Meaning
4. glum	15	
5. meddles	28	
6. prodding	39	
Others?		

GUIDE QUESTIONS

Directions: These questions will guide your understanding of what you have read. Write your answers in your notebook or on a separate sheet of paper if your instructor wishes to collect it. Your answers to these questions will be the basis of class discussion.

1. Define the word *polygamy* and try to recall anything you may know about it.
2. According to the author, why is the practice of polygamy in France coming to the attention of the public at this time?
3. Explain the relationship between the practice of polygamy and the question of how a society should deal with immigrant customs that are unacceptable or illegal in a new land.
4. Cite some of the statistics on polygamy (and the difficulty of acquiring good statistics).
5. In paragraph 16, Moustafa Djaara gives the polygamous man's side of the story. What are the pros and cons of polygamy for Mr. Djaara?
6. Why do town officials, landlords, and neighbors oppose having polygamous families in their neighborhoods?
7. Describe some of the complaints voiced by the women in polygamous marriages in the article.
8. What are some strategies that African women in France are using to combat polygamy?

APPLICATION

Directions: We learned in the article that polygamy is practiced in Senegal, Mali, and Mauritania. Use the library to research the issue further. In what other countries is polygamy practiced? Is it legal or is it practiced illegally? Was polygamy ever practiced in the United States? Use the information you gather as a basis for a class discussion.

WRITING

Directions: Imagine you are the husband of one of the women in the article "African Women in France Battle Polygamy." Write a letter to *The New York Times* reacting to the information in the article.

THE FORMS OF MARRIAGE

Marriage can take many different forms throughout the world:

Monogamy: From the Greek word part *mono,* meaning "one" and *gamy,* meaning "marriage." In this type of marriage, there is one husband and one wife. Only about 20 percent of societies in the world are strictly monogamous.

Polygyny: From the Greek word part *poly,* meaning "many" and *gyny,* meaning "female." In this form of marriage there is one husband and two or more wives. Approximately four-fifths of the world's societies permit polygyny. However, even where polygyny is permitted, few men actually do take more than one wife. Usually only wealthy men can afford to marry two or more wives.

Polyandry: From the Greek word part *poly,* meaning "many" and *andr,* meaning "male." This form of marriage includes one wife and two or more husbands. Polyandry is very rare, found in less than 1 percent of societies. The most frequent form of polyandry is fraternal, where one wife considers two or more men who are brothers as her husbands. Polyandry is most often found in economically depressed societies. Since a woman can have only one child per year, this form of marriage keeps the birth rate down, but allows the women many sexual partners.

Group marriage: This structure allows two or more men to be married to two or more wives. Group marriage is rare.

In the 1970s, as its population soared toward one billion, China began the implementation of strict family-planning measures. Over the next two decades the average number of babies per woman dropped from five or six to two or three. Without the controls, officials say, 240 million more babies would have been born. The goal of one child per family is now accepted in the cities and, even in the countryside, most people are having fewer children than their parents did. But an unforeseen problem has arisen: millions of children are growing up without siblings, and are the sole object of their parents' affection. As a result, many Chinese say the children are growing up spoiled, selfish, and lazy. This article appeared in The New York Times *in 1996.*

AS A PAMPERED GENERATION GROWS UP, CHINESE WORRY

Patrick E. Tyler

1   It was just another school day for Liu Huamin when the father of one of her students burst through the classroom door and said his teen-age son was threatening to commit suicide by jumping off the fourth-floor balcony of the family's apartment building.

2   Why? asked Mrs. Liu, a chemistry teacher at Waluji Middle School here.

3   Because, the man replied, the boy's mother would not cook his favorite meat dumplings for breakfast.

4   He did not jump, but the story of his breathtaking display of willfulness incites a look of instant recognition across the faces of many Chinese teachers today.

5   Indeed, it seems at times as if the willfulness of China's generation of "little emperors"—children growing up without siblings under China's one-child population control policy—knows no bounds.

6   In Guangdong Province a power failure prevented a housewife from cooking dinner for her fourteen-year-old son, who flew into a rage and went out to watch television with a friend. When the boy returned, there was still no dinner, so he seized a meat cleaver and killed his mother with ten blows to the head. Then he hanged himself.

7   An extreme case, but the fact that China's government-run news organization gave it prominent display last year also illustrates the concern of many Chinese that its first generation of only children is rapidly maturing into a generation of spoiled, self-absorbed tyrants.

8   After decades of famine and political turmoil in China, parents who grew up in troubled and often violent times under Mao, suffering long periods of deprivation in the countryside and interrupted schooling, are now rearing—in many cases doting on—a generation of only children.

9   And these new parents are filled with anxiety about whether they are doing it right.

10   "This is a fixation," said James L. Watson, an anthropologist at Harvard University who has studied the Chinese family. "I would call it kind of a compensation com-

plex. The generation of parents that we are dealing with now, many of them are Cultural Revolution veterans who themselves did not have much of a childhood, and I think that many of them are trying hard to make sure that their own children get all the benefits and more that they missed out on."

But they are doing it with little cultural guidance. The current generation of parents has been cut adrift from both the traditional Confucian values emphasizing reverence for elders that were once the foundation of China's extended families and from the Communist values imposed for three decades under Mao.   11

Neither has much credibility in China today.   12

Specialists say it is too early to say whether China's "little emperors" are growing up to be a generation of self-centered autocrats, whose politics may be more aggressive than the generation that grew up under Mao, or whether they are so overindulged at home that they will be ill prepared for the competitive pressures and harsh realities of China's market economy.   13

Off to Bad Start, Teachers Say

"Seems like it could go either way," said David Y. H. Wu, an anthropologist at Chinese University of Hong Kong. "You could either raise a generation of rebels against the controls of the Communist party or you could raise a generation that would feel more nationalistic and assertive as Chinese.   14

"Talking about personality traits and trying to project to the whole nation is very difficult, but I can see a whole generation perhaps more independent and willing to challenge authority, or simply more authoritative because of their intensified relationships with their parents, and the symbol of parents is government."   15

Either way, if today's teachers are any judge, the "little emperor" generation is off to an inauspicious start.   16

"As life and economic conditions get better and better, the moral principles of students and their sense of responsibility to society and family get worse and worse," said Mrs. Liu, the chemistry teacher, who has an eighteen-year-old son. "We teachers often wonder how these students can take up their social responsibility when they get older."   17

Teachers around the world have long complained about the quality of the next generation. But in China, a generation of children is growing up in the midst of a profound economic revolution, where social and political values seem suspended in time as the country waits for the death of Deng Xiaoping,* the ninety-one-year-old paramount leader, not knowing whether that event will usher in a new era with a new value system.   18

"My most terrifying concern," said Zhang Xiaoyun, thirty-three, who teaches literature at the China Youth Political College in Beijing, a former Communist party school, "is that you must raise a child within some system of beliefs, but our generation has no beliefs, so how can we educate our children?"   19

---

* Deng Xiaoping died on February 19, 1997.

20   The demographic shift from multi-child families under strong patriarchs to small, nuclear families centered on only children "is going to have a profound effect" on Chinese society, Professor Watson said.

Increased Spending on Toys and Books

21   One of the ways that Chinese are overcompensating in bringing up the country's only children is by spending the greatest portion of family income ever on toys, books, educational materials, personal computers, and food.

22   The national obsession with children is fostering multibillion-dollar opportunities for business.

23   Baby food, which barely existed in China a decade ago, is now a staple of family life and a major item in family budgets.

24   China's "little emperors" are the single greatest force in determining consumer decisions today, experts say.

25   "I met a woman who took her daughter to McDonald's in Beijing twice a week to give her modern nutrition," said Yan Yunxiang, a Chinese-born anthropologist at Johns Hopkins University, who frequently returns to examine the culture he grew up in.

26   When he asked the woman why she was spending as much as half a normal worker's income each month on McDonald's, she replied: "I want my daughter to learn more about American culture. She is taking English typing classes now, and next year I will buy her a computer."

27   Professor Watson said: "It turns out that most Chinese don't even like the food, but what they are buying is culture. They are buying connectedness to the world system.

28   "The idea is that if these kids can connect with McDonald's, they are going to end up at Harvard Law School."

29   One of China's most popular amusement parks, Window on the World in Shenzhen, has no rides and no arcades. Chinese come from all over the country to pay, in some cases a week's wages, to show their children miniatures of Manhattan Island, the Statue of Liberty, the Eiffel Tower, and the Taj Mahal.

A Generation Driven by Rewards

30   "Most of our time and money are spent on this child," said Wen Geli, the mother of a two-year-old boy who seems less attentive to the park's attractions than to gorging himself on ice cream. "We want to give him an introduction to the world and expand his outlook."

31   "My generation grew up with hardship," said her husband, Zhang Xinwen, a communications officer in the Chinese Army. "We were born in the 1960s, and that was a period of bitter shortage, but this generation is growing up in richer times and we want to take advantage of this better environment."

32   Not far away, a retired sports teacher, Cai Kunling, fifty-nine, was squiring his five-year-old granddaughter, Fu Hua, past the wonders of the world. "She should be in kindergarten today," he said, "but she wanted to take me to this place," he added in a tone that reflected who was in charge.

The two of them sat for their photo in front of a miniature of Niagara Falls and   33
then strolled over to the little Manhattan.

To Mr. Cai, who lived through the Mao period, it was like a dream world.   34

"My generation made a lot of sacrifices and had a lot of devotion to the coun-   35
try," he said. "But this generation needs a reward if you want them to do something. If there is no compensation, they don't want to do it."

Free-for-All Future Worries the Parents

Sitting around a dinner of baked carp with three other teachers one evening, Mrs. Liu   36
and some of her colleagues vented their anxieties.

Li Shunmei, thirty-one, a high-school teacher with a three-year-old daughter,   37
said: "I worry a lot about my daughter's future, because I have doubts about whether
she can survive under the harsher and harsher competition of Chinese society.

"Nowadays, there are many children who commit suicide. I think it is because   38
parents obey their children's every demand, so they are not able to endure any re-
versals or hard times."

This strain of anxiety is very prominent in Chinese families.   39

The old "iron rice bowl" society of cradle-to-grave social welfare protection is   40
giving way year by year to the new market economy, where life is beginning to look
like a terrifying free-for-all to many Chinese used to something more secure.

"The home can be very sweet and gentle for these toddlers, but the world out   41
there is a cruel world," said Jing Jun, a Beijing native who now teaches anthropology
at City College in New York. "When we were growing up, the state arranged everything for you, but now parents know the state is not going to do anything for them
and the job market is pretty grim."

Mr. Jing said he believed that China's "little emperors" would have to pass   42
through a tough period of adjustment. "They are under so much pressure," he said,
"and their parents have such great expectations for them. Whether they are psy-
chologically prepared for that, I cannot say."

Professor Watson said, "A lot of people, including Chinese psychologists, are   43
concerned whether the next generation is going to be able to 'eat bitterness,'
whether they are going to be able to work hard or whether they will be willing to
sacrifice themselves as was true under socialism."

Some Chinese feel that the "little emperors" will adjust.   44

"I'm optimistic," said Wang Xujin, a teacher at Beijing Business College with a   45
nine-year-old son.

But, he confessed, "although the students each year are smarter and smarter,   46
I like them less and less."

VOCABULARY

Directions: Locate each of the key words in the article. Try to figure out each word's
meaning by using the context. Confirm your guess by checking the dictionary or
thesaurus. Write the meanings of the words in the margin of the text. Then
record the meanings in the chart on the next page.

Key Word	Paragraph	Meaning
1. willfulness	4, 5	
2. fixation	10	
3. autocrats	13	
4. traits	15	
5. inauspicious	16	
6. overcompensating	21	
7. staple	23	
8. gorging	30	
Others?		

GUIDE QUESTIONS

Directions: These questions will guide your understanding of what you have read. Write your answers in your notebook or on a separate sheet of paper if your instructor wishes to collect it. Your answers to these questions will be the basis of class discussion.

1. Here, as in many news feature stories, the author begins with an example to illustrate his main point. Summarize the example and the point it illustrates.
2. Why are the children in the article described as "little emperors"?
3. Describe the differences in living conditions now and during the childhood of the parents of the "little emperors."
4. According to anthropologist James Watson, why are Chinese parents "doting on" their children now?
5. Explain the author's point in paragraph 11: "But they are doing it with little cultural guidance."
6. Anthropologist David Y. H. Wu says, "Seems like it could go either way." What does he mean?
7. Adults throughout history have complained about "the next generation." Judging from the information in this article and anything else

you may know about the topic, do you think the next generation of Chinese children will have special problems? Explain.

8. React to the comments of the mother described in paragraph 25 who, among other things, took her child to McDonald's to give her "modern nutrition."

9. Do you see similarities between the treatment of Chinese children as described in the article and American children?

10. a. Explain what is meant by the old "iron rice bowl" society of China.
    b. Contrast the "iron rice bowl" society with the situation in China today.

APPLICATION

Directions: Choose one of the assignments below.

1. China's one-child policy was established in the 1970s. Investigate the reasons for the policy and what the results have been. Use the school library or the public library to get the information.

2. If you read the selections "Norms" (page 51) and "Values" (page 56), try to make connections between what you learned from those selections and the problems facing the parents of China's current generation of children. Be sure to consider the information in paragraphs 10 through 12 here.

WRITING

Directions: Write a summary of the article. To review summary writing, turn to Appendix B.

For centuries they lived undisturbed in the lush jungles of northern Brazil, carrying on traditions nearly as old as the forest they lived in. Today only about nine thousand members of the Yanomamo tribe survive. Now their entire way of life is threatened—by gold prospectors hoping to gain great wealth from Yanomamo land. They invaded the territory and extracted tons of gold, leaving behind them disease, prostitution, weapons, alcohol, ruined forests, and polluted rivers. Will the Yanomamo Indians survive the twentieth century? This report from Newsweek *magazine tells a grim story.*

THE LAST DAYS OF EDEN

Spencer Reiss

1   Doshamosha-teri sits on a little hill near a bend in the clear black Siapa River, just north of the equator, in one of the least traveled regions of the Amazonian rain forest. Two dozen extended families of Yanomamo Indians—149 broad-chested men, painted women, and their children—live there, in one roughly circular thatch-roofed dwelling furnished only with bark hammocks. They cultivate small plots of plantains, gourds, and bananas on the hillside. Beyond that, the great wall of the emerald rain forest rises, enclosing a dazzling bazaar of wild pigs, monkeys, and plumed birds. Most people in Doshamosha-teri ("Maggot-of-the-Gumba-Tree Place") have never heard of Venezuela, though they happen to live there. They have yet to invent the wheel. Their entire number system consists of "one," "two," and "many." Ask about abstractions such as work and leisure, poverty or wealth, and you get a blank stare. Life consists of survival.

2   Survival has never been ensured; everyone knows that evil charms can carry death through the air, that tiny gremlins race over the treetops hunting for souls, that jaguars and enemy bowmen crouch in ambush. But these days there is talk of another danger. *Garimpeiros,* the grizzled prospectors on the front lines of Brazil's Amazonian gold rush, are pushing relentlessly toward and, in a few places now, into the pristine Venezuelan rain forest. No one in Doshamosha-teri has ever seen a *garimpeiro,* but everyone associates the Portuguese word with trouble. "They put poison in the water and the fish die," says a man named Amoahiwa. "Where the *garimpeiros* go," adds Reriwa, the local headman's son, "the Yanomamo die."

3   Until recently, the Yanomamo had the good fortune to live their Stone Age lives on land that no one else wanted. Today, their world, sixty thousand square miles of rain forest straddling the Venezuelan–Brazilian border, sits in the path of the onrushing juggernaut of development. The nine thousand Yanomamo in Brazil have dwindled by one-sixth since the gold rush began three years ago, luring tens of thousands of prospectors—and the malaria and other diseases they carry. The dazed survivors are scattered among nineteen reserves, gold-hungry miners pressing in from all sides. "The dangers to the Yanomamo twenty years ago were minuscule compared to what they are now," anthropologist Napoleon Chagnon said during a recent three-day visit to Doshamosha-teri and other Yanomamo settlements in Venezuela's remote Siapa River valley. "The best we can hope for is a respite, long enough for them to consider their choices."

As the world's largest remaining group of unacculturated tribal people, the 4
Yanomamo represent a last chance for the modern world to atone for the savage
obliteration of so many of the original Americans, North and South alike. Without
fast action, the Yanomamo will suffer the same fate—or, perhaps worse, give up their
independent ways and join the modern world's long list of pathetic misfits. Governments, Indian activists, and scientists agree on the need to save them. The question
is, how?

Part of the answer can be found by observing how not, and nowhere is that les- 5
son more acute than in Brazil. There, until the mid-1980s, the Yanomamo's contact
with outsiders was fleeting. "Missionaries and anthropologists brought things they
wanted, like axes and machetes," says Father Giovanni Saffirio, who heads a mission
in Yanomamo territory. "The Yanomamo never understood that outsiders could
be dangerous." Apocalypse arrived with the 1987 gold rush in Roraima state, with a
jackpot reaching $1 billion a year. Miners poured in as bewildered Indians looked on
helplessly. In an effort to protect the Yanomamo, Brazil reaffirmed the tribes' rights
to eight thousand square miles of land. But it was chopped into small parcels—reserves whose borders government agents have been totally unable to defend. Now,
whole Yanomamo villages hover on the edge of starvation, the women too ill to
tend gardens, the men too wasted by white men's disease to pursue game already
decimated by miners' rifles. Malaria rates are as high as 90 percent in some villages;
of 1,682 Yanomamo in one Health Ministry survey, 243 died this year. The plain fact
is that there is little hope for the Brazilian Yanomamo. As anthropologist Orlando
Villas Boas said, "All we can do is . . . marvel that we lived to witness the last days
of Eden."

The Venezuelan Yanomamo, in contrast, do have some hope of survival, if the 6
term is broadly defined. Their virtually impenetrable "green hell," as early explorers
called the Amazonian rain forest, seems to contain nothing that anyone in oil-rich
Venezuela wants badly enough to come in and haul out. Outsiders would be lucky
to even find the place. A vast and trackless expanse of public lands, Caracas barely
administers it; the closest thing to an outside presence is half a dozen tiny Roman
Catholic and Protestant missions. Anthropologists may have been too late to save
Brazil's Yanomamo; but now, as scientists lobby hard to save indigenous peoples, the
Venezuelan tribes may benefit. Says Chagnon, "To simply go out and study a people
to advance a theory is tantamount to professional irresponsibility." (Ironically,
Chagnon's celebrated description of the Yanomamo as "the fierce people," 44 percent of whose adult males have participated in killing another human, has been seized
on by some to advocate bringing the Yanomamo into "civilized" society where they
can be pacified.)

Physical Survival

The first task is to ensure the Yanomamo's basic physical survival. Historically, dis- 7
ease brought by Europeans killed more Indians in North and South America than
bullets ever did. Now, the near certainty of greater contact with the outside world
and its germs means that Venezuela's Yanomamo need to be vaccinated against
mumps, measles, polio, and tuberculosis. That is not easy. The Indians are isolated

and their settlements are spread over thousands of square miles. The national government is supposed to assign a doctor to one mission on the Orinoco, but the job has been open for six months because no one will take it.

8   To survive in more than body, the Yanomamo need rights to their land. Only then can they maintain the hunting grounds and trading networks that define their way of life. Deciding which rights, however, gets tricky. The most radical scheme, advanced by Indian-rights advocates, would give the Yanomamo total sovereignty. That's a non-starter in Caracas. There is more hope for creating a protected ecological park run by the tribes with advice from anthropologists and others. Under one proposal, three-quarters of the area would remain pristine, 10 percent (bordering Brazil) would become a security zone, and the rest would be open to tourism and benign development. Venezuelan President Carlos Andres Perez, who is being advised by the Caracas-based aid group FUNDAFACI, has hinted that some such "biosphere" plan will be approved early next year, but with the government retaining fundamental control.

9   Can land rights be cast in a way that also protects the environment? What if the Yanomamo decide to raze the forest and peddle hardwoods to Japan? Some Yanomamo headmen in Brazil are already talking about selling mining rights. Perhaps autonomy includes the right to self-destruct. But many global environmental problems depend for their solution on the rain forest; some voice in the use of the jungle would seem to belong to the Argentine farmer losing his lands to global warming, and to the Chilean cancer patient whose survival depends on a rare rain-forest flower, no less than to the Yanomamo who live there.

Land Rights

10   Protection from disease and guaranteed land rights would buy the Yanomamo time to choose their own future. Today they are aware dimly, if at all, of the inconceivably powerful and unforgiving world that is about to come crashing in on them. There is no question that civilization will reach them. "The question is whether it will be on their terms or someone else's," says Venezuelan anthropologist Roberto Lizaraldi. Adds David Maybury-Lewis, president of Cultural Survival, a group that works to protect indigenous peoples, "They don't have the option to not change at all. But I've never seen a society whose desire for change is zero." The point is to allow the Yanomamo to choose the pace of that change. Is that possible? To decide how much of the twentieth century they wish to adopt, the Yanomamo will have to see it. Having done so, can they ever regain their innocence? Can the Yanomamo engage the Western world without joining it?

11   There is something astonishing in the fact that the Yanomamo even exist, five centuries after Columbus launched the bloody conquest of the New World's great civilizations. Chagnon calls them "our contemporary ancestors," their cultural development diverging from ours ten thousand years ago. If we lose them, we lose part of ourselves. Or, if that's too sentimental, consider that they may be the only ones who know how to use the rain forest without killing it. Throughout history, people meeting a more powerful culture have had to adapt or die. The tragedy is that, for the Yanomamo, adaptation may be death itself.

VOCABULARY

Directions: Locate each of the key words in the reading selection. Then read and study each word in its context and try to determine its meaning. Use a dictionary or thesaurus to check your guess. Write the meanings of the words in the margin of the text.

Record the new words you've learned.

Key Word	Paragraph	Meaning
1. relentlessly	2	*Persistent Determined Tenacious*
2. minuscule	3	*extremely small microscopic*
3. obliteration	4	*total distruction*
4. apocalypse	5	*revelation*
5. decimated	5	*destroyed*
6. lobby	6	*group of people with a similar interest* *to lobby / to pressure / to influence*
7. tantamount to	6	*equal to the same as*
8. sovereignty	8	
9. pristine	8	
10. benign	8	
Others?		

GUIDE QUESTIONS

Directions: The purpose of these guide questions is to ensure your understanding of what you have read. They also will help you to analyze and evaluate the author's ideas and apply them to the real world and your own life.

Write answers to the questions in your notebook or on a separate sheet of paper if your instructor wishes to collect them. Your answers will form the basis of class discussion.

1. Describe the Yanomamo: Who are they? Where and how do they live?
2. Survival has never been an easy thing for the Yanomamo, but now they face a new danger. Describe this new danger.
3. Explain how the Yanomamo have managed to avoid twentieth-century civilization until now.
4. In paragraph 4, the author refers to the fact that other original North and South American peoples have been obliterated. Can you name some of the groups that have been wiped out or have lost their cultures?
5. According to the author, how can the Yanomamo be saved?
6. Is there any chance the Yanomamo can avoid the change that twentieth-century civilization will bring to their tribe?
7. Explain Chagnon's phrase describing the Yanomamo: "our contemporary ancestors."
8. What is your opinion of the title of the article, "The Last Days of Eden"? Explain your answer.

APPLICATION

Directions: On a map of Brazil and Venezuela, locate the region where Yanomamo live. Do some research to learn more about the Amazon rain forest. What is the importance of rain forests to the entire world? What are the threats to their existence?

WRITING

Directions: React to the view of some people (described in paragraph 6) that the Yanomamo, "the fierce people," should be brought into the twentieth century so that they can be "civilized."

SHORT TAKE

AT PLAY IN THE FIELDS OF THE STONE AGE

Spencer Reiss

The little bull of a man with brushcut hair and only a bark string around his waist was studying our Venezuela Air Force Super Puma helicopter like a scientist. Once before he had seen something similar and he drew his arm high across the sky in an arc, "I kept calling him to come down, but no luck." What about the chopper, we asked, what was it? He paused for a moment then tentatively offered, "It's an animal, a *hashimo*"—a smooth-feathered green grouse—and by way of explanation waved his arms and made the thrashing sound of a big bird exploding from the underbrush. What kept it here? "It's a pet." Did he want to go for a ride? "I don't think so," he said, suddenly getting nervous. "Maybe later. A long time from now. A really long time."

We learned only later that his name was Yokokoma, a fact divulged by one of the "informants" that field anthropologists like Napoleon Chagnon, who led our visit, depend on to construct accurate genealogies from behind the fog of Yanomamo taboos. To us he was simply Shoriwa, literally "brother-in-law," the same honorific he used for us. Seemingly in his late forties, and roughly five foot one—about average for a grown Yanomamo man—he was only visiting Doshamosha-teri; his own *shabano* was Shokoburuba-teri, about a day's walk away. Typically, too, he had four children: two girls ("one ripe, one not ripe") and two boys ("one who ties his penis up, and one who will soon"). His wife, Wiyami, looked a few years younger—an earlier one died, Chagnon's informant told us—and seemed cheerful about the indignities of an utterly sexist life. "She's a very good worker— I don't have to get angry," Yokokoma proudly told us. "Just look at her head—she has hardly any scars."

Yokokoma's hair was cut short because he had recently been sick with what was probably malaria—he mimicked chills when we asked, but blamed them on an enemy from another village "blowing charms." While most of the men and boys were satisfied just to touch our clothes, Yokokoma examined the helicopter and toyed with the shortwave radio. He quickly mastered an auto-focus camera, and borrowed a pad and pen to "take notes"—row after row of snakelike squiggles across the page. But there were definitely communication limits. When I gestured to him—I thought—to take a note to *Newsweek* photographer Bill Gentile back at the *shabano,* he tore it in half and cheerfully stuck it in his ears like little ice-cream cones.

On the final morning, when the rest of our group had already left for the chopper, Yokokoma stood gravely and asked me for some good-bye gifts. First he pantomimed what he called "the bottom part of clothes." He also wanted some soap, which he indicated by rubbing his hair and smiling like he had with some shampoo we had given him in the river the day before. I gave him the soap, but not the shorts. When I finally left, I had the feeling of watching a movie you know will end badly. I hoped he wouldn't go for a ride for a long time, a really long time.

In 1972, anthropologist Colin Turnbull published a book, The Mountain People, *in which he described the two years he spent living among a small tribe called the Ik in northern Uganda. Expecting to find a small society of nomadic hunters, and to be welcomed by a warm, friendly people, Turnbull was astonished to discover a society of humans in which all goodness and love seemed to have disappeared. Deprived by the government of their ancestral hunting lands, the Iks had been forced to give up their traditional way of life and become farmers. The Iks had neither agricultural skills nor equipment and the lands they were allowed to use were too poor to support the population. The result? The Iks were starving.*

Turnbull's book offers a look at the depths to which humans can sink when every day brings the possibility of death. Confronted with the constant threat of starvation, the Iks have lost all interest in their spouses, parents, children, and friends. Children are forced out of the home by the age of three to fend for themselves. Some of the children manage to survive by forming groups that hunt for food. These children quite naturally reject their parents when they become old and beg their children for help or food. Sex is of little interest to the Iks, as it requires too much energy—energy that could be better devoted to finding food. Prostitution, however, does flourish among young girls who use it as a way to get food from men in neighboring villages. Friendship is almost unheard of among the Iks, who view others mainly as competitors for what little food is available.

Listen to Turnbull's conclusions about the Iks, and, by extension, about us all. "The people were as unfriendly, uncharitable, inhospitable, and generally mean as any people can be. For those positive qualities [kindness, generosity, consideration, affection, honesty, hospitality, compassion, charity, etc.] we value so highly are no longer functional for the Iks; even more than in our own society, they spell ruin and disaster. It seems that, far from being basic human qualities, they are superficial luxuries we can afford in times of plenty, or mere mechanisms for survival and security." The anthropologist has described his experience with the Iks as a shocking challenge to his belief in the inherent goodness of mankind— would we all behave in the same cruel and loveless way if we were in a similarly desperate situation?

In the following essay, Lewis Thomas takes another look at the Iks and what they may have to say about the nature of man and society.

A SPECIAL CASE—THE IK

Lewis Thomas

1   The small tribe of Iks, formerly nomadic hunters and gatherers in the mountain valleys of northern Uganda, have become celebrities, literary symbols for the ultimate fate of disheartened, heartless mankind at large. Two disastrously conclusive things happened to them: the government decided to have a national park, so they were compelled by law to give up hunting in the valleys and become farmers on poor hillside soil, and then they were visited for two years by an anthropologist who detested them and wrote a book about them.

2   The message of the book is that the Iks have transformed themselves into an irreversibly disagreeable collection of unattached, brutish creatures, totally selfish and loveless, in response to the dismantling of their traditional culture. Moreover,

this is what the rest of us are like in our inner selves, and we will all turn into Iks when the structure of our society comes all unhinged.

The argument rests, of course, on certain assumptions about the core of human beings, and is necessarily speculative. You have to agree in advance that man is fundamentally a bad lot, out for himself alone, displaying such graces as affection and compassion only as learned habits. If you take this view, the story of the Iks can be used to confirm it. These people seem to be living together, clustered in small, dense villages, but they are really solitary, unrelated individuals with no evident use for each other. They talk, but only to make ill-tempered demands and cold refusals. They share nothing. They never sing. They turn the children out to forage as soon as they can walk, and desert the elders to starve whenever they can, and the foraging children snatch food from the mouths of the helpless elders. It is a mean society.   3

They breed without love or even casual regard. They defecate on each other's doorsteps. They watch their neighbors for signs of misfortune, and only then do they laugh. In the book, they do a lot of laughing, having so much bad luck. Several times they even laughed at the anthropologist, who found this especially repellent (one senses, between the lines, that the scholar is not himself the world's luckiest man). Worse, they took him into the family, snatched his food, defecated on his doorstep, and hooted dislike at him. They gave him a bad two years.   4

It is a depressing book. If, as he suggests, there is only Ikness at the center of each of us, our sole hope for hanging on to the name of humanity will be endlessly mending the structure of our society, and it is changing so quickly and completely that we may never find the threads in time. Meanwhile, left to ourselves, alone, solitary, we will become the same joyless, zestless, untouching, lone animals.   5

But this may be too narrow a view. For one thing, the Iks are extraordinary. They are absolutely astonishing, in fact. The anthropologist had never seen people like them anywhere, nor have I. You'd think, if they were simply examples of the common essence of mankind, they'd seem more recognizable. Instead, they are bizarre, anomalous. I have known my share of peculiar, difficult, nervous, grabby people, but I've never encountered any genuinely, consistently detestable human beings in all my life. The Iks sound more like abnormalities, maladies.   6

I cannot accept it. I do not believe that the Iks are representative of isolated, revealed man, unobscured by social habits. I believe their behavior is something extra, something laid on. This unremitting, compulsive repellence is a kind of complicated ritual. They must have learned to act this way; they copied it, somehow.   7

I have a theory, then. The Iks have gone crazy.   8

The solitary Ik, isolated in the ruins of an exploded culture, has built a new defense for himself. If you live in an unworkable society you can make up one of your own, and this is what the Iks have done. Each Ik has become a group, a one-man tribe on its own, a constituency.   9

Now everything falls into place. This is why they do seem, after all, vaguely familiar to all of us. We've seen them before. This is precisely the way groups of one size or another, ranging from committees to nations, behave. It is, of course, this aspect of humanity that has lagged behind the rest of evolution, and this is why the Ik seems so primitive. In his absolute selfishness, his incapacity to give anything away,   10 no matter what, he is a successful committee. When he stands at the door of his hut, shouting insults at his neighbors in a loud harangue, he is one city addressing another city.

11   Cities have all the Ik characteristics. They defecate on doorsteps, in rivers and lakes, their own or anyone else's. They leave rubbish. They detest all neighboring cities, give nothing away. They even build institutions for deserting elders out of sight.

12   Nations are the most Iklike of all. No wonder the Iks seem familiar. For total greed, rapacity, heartlessness, and irresponsibility there is nothing to match a nation. Nations, by law, are solitary, self-centered, withdrawn into themselves. There is no such thing as affection between nations, and certainly no nation ever loved another. They bawl insults from their doorsteps, defecate into whole oceans, snatch all the food, survive by detestation, take joy in the bad luck of others, celebrate the death of others, live for the death of others.

13   That's it, and I shall stop worrying about the book. It does not signify that man is a sparse, inhuman thing at his center. He's all right. It only says what we've always known and never had enough time to worry about, that we haven't yet learned how to stay human when assembled in masses. The Ik, in his despair, is acting out this failure, and perhaps we should pay closer attention. Nations have themselves become too frightening to think about, but we might learn some things by watching these people.

VOCABULARY

Directions: Locate each of the key words in the reading selection. Then read and study each word in its context and try to determine its meaning. Use a dictionary or thesaurus to check your guess. Write the meanings of the words in the margin of the text.

Record the new words you've learned.

Key Word	Paragraph	Meaning
1. dismantling	2	
2. forage	3	
3. repellent	4	
4. anomalous	6	
5. harangue	10	
6. rapacity	12	
Others?		

GUIDE QUESTIONS

Directions: The purpose of these guide questions is to ensure your understanding of what you have read. They also will help you to analyze and evaluate the author's ideas and apply them to the real world and your own life.

Write answers to the questions in your notebook or on a separate sheet of paper if your instructor wishes to collect them. Your answers will form the basis of class discussion.

1. Cite the two things that happened to the Iks that Thomas calls "disastrous" and "conclusive."
2. According to Thomas, what is the message of the book about the Iks?
3. According to Thomas, what assumptions must we make about the nature of human beings in order to accept this message?
4. What do you think is Thomas's opinion of Colin Turnbull, the anthropologist who lived among the Ik? Not much hard evidence appears in the essay, but you may be able to draw a few inferences.
5. Summarize the main point of paragraph 5.
6. Why do you think Thomas says that the Ik are "bizarre" and "abnormalities"?
7. In paragraph 6, Thomas says he has never known any genuinely, consistently detestable human being in his entire life. Does this surprise you? Have you ever met or heard of such a person?
8. Paragraph 7 summarizes the contrasting views of the Ik held by Turnbull and Thomas.
   a. It first presents Turnbull's theory that the Iks are representatives of men "unobscured by social habits." What does he mean by this?
   b. Thomas says the Iks "must have learned to act this way." What does this imply?
9. What does Thomas mean when he says, in paragraph 11, that cities also "defecate on doorsteps"?
10. In paragraphs 9 through 12, Thomas explains his view of the Iks' behavior. Summarize his ideas.

APPLICATION/WRITING

Directions: In small groups, discuss the following questions. What is your view of the significance of the Iks? Do you agree with Turnbull that the Iks show what individuals are really like deep down inside? That we would all become loveless, cruel, and joyless if we had to confront death every day? Or do you support Thomas's view that the Ik are small examples of humans living in society? That people in groups, such as cities, behave in loveless, cruel, and joyless ways?

Then, in one paragraph, explain why you agree with one or the other (or neither, if that's the case). In a second paragraph, state what you think we can learn from the story of the Ik.

COLLABORATIVE LEARNING

WORKING IN GROUPS TO GUIDE YOUR OWN READING

Along with each of the reading selections in this unit, you were provided with questions and exercises to guide your understanding of the text. However, in most of your college reading, you will not be given exercises to help you understand vocabulary or questions that guide your understanding of a textbook chapter. You will be expected to master the material on your own.

Research has shown that one of the most effective ways to study is in groups— working with classmates to master the material of a college course. The give-and-take that comes naturally when working with other people helps us to avoid falling into bad habits like passive reading. (We have all had this experience: reading a whole chapter, then realizing that we don't remember one single thing we read.) Working with other students will help you to avoid such problems. For this assignment, form groups of four to six students. In your group you will consider the two following reading selections, "On Friendship" by Margaret Mead and Rhoda Metraux and "Crack and the Box" by Pete Hamill. You will create your own vocabulary chart, guide questions, an application exercise, and a writing assignment for the reading selections.

Follow these steps to complete this assignment.

1. Preview the selection before you read—look at and think about the title, the headings, the first paragraph, the last paragraph, and the first sentence of each paragraph.
2. Read through the selection one time quickly.
3. Read the selection carefully a second time; this time mark the pages. Underline words you want to look up and ideas you think are important. Put a question mark next to things you don't understand and want to discuss with your group members or your instructor. Ask yourself questions as you read along and try to find the answers to your questions.
4. Brainstorm with your group. Ask yourselves: What important issues is the author discussing? What new information did you learn? Can the issues discussed in the selection be connected to those you have studied in earlier lessons? Can any of the information here be applied to situations in your own life?
5. Now, *create* a set of exercises similar to those you have *completed* in previous chapters:
   a. *Vocabulary.* Make a list of key vocabulary words from the text. Set them up in chart format as on page 47.
   b. *Guide questions.* Write questions that will guide understanding of the major ideas in the reading.
   c. *Application.* Prepare an application exercise that takes one or more of the important ideas in the reading and relates them to real life.
   d. *Writing.* Prepare a writing assignment to conclude the chapter.

Before you begin, it would be a good idea to review the questions and exercises included in the previous reading selections for reference.

When you are finished, submit your work to your instructor for review. Your instructor may review and combine the work of all the groups and return the exercises to the class. You will then have the opportunity to *answer* the questions you and your classmates have developed.

Now, use your skills as an active independent reader to tackle the following reading selections. Good luck!

Make a list of people you consider "friends." How did you become friends? Were you in elementary or high school together? Were you neighbors? Or co-workers? Have you ever lost a good friend? What happened?

Write your own definition of a friend.

Do you believe friendship is basically the same all over the world? Or does it vary from culture to culture?

In this essay, two anthropologists consider the meaning of friendship in the United States, France, Germany, and England.

ON FRIENDSHIP

Margaret Mead and Rhoda Metraux

1   Few Americans stay put for a lifetime. We move from town to city to suburb, from high school to college in a different state, from a job in one region to a better job elsewhere, from the home where we raise our children to the home where we plan to live in retirement. With each move we are forever making new friends, who become part of our new life at that time.

2   For many of us the summer is a special time for forming new friendships. Today millions of Americans vacation abroad, and they go not only to see new sights but also—in those places where they do not feel too strange—with the hope of meeting new people. No one really expects a vacation trip to produce a close friend. But surely the beginning of a friendship is possible? Surely in every country people value friendship?

3   They do. The difficulty when strangers from two countries meet is not a lack of appreciation of friendship, but different expectations about what constitutes friendship and how it comes into being. In those European countries that Americans are most likely to visit, friendship is quite sharply distinguished from other, more casual relations, and is differently related to family life. For a Frenchman, a German, or an Englishman friendship is usually more particularized and carries a heavier burden of commitment.

4   But as we use the word, *friend* can be applied to a wide range of relationships—to someone one has known for a few weeks in a new place, to a close business associate, to a childhood playmate, to a man or woman, to a trusted confidant. There are real differences among these relations for Americans—a friendship may be superficial, casual, situational, or deep and enduring. But to a European, who sees only our surface behavior, the differences are not clear.

5   As they see it, people known and accepted temporarily, casually, flow in and out of Americans' homes with little ceremony and often with little personal commitment. They may be parents of the children's friends, house guests of neighbors, members of a committee, business associates from another town or even another country. Coming as a guest into an American home, the European visitor finds no visible landmarks. The atmosphere is relaxed. Most people, old and young, are called by first names.

Who, then, is a friend?   6

Even simple translation from one language to another is difficult. "You see," a   7
Frenchman explains, "if I were to say to you in France, 'This is my good friend,' that
person would not be as close to me as someone about whom I said only, 'This is my
friend.' Anyone about whom I have to say more is really less."

In France, as in many European countries, friends generally are of the same sex,   8
and friendship is seen as basically a relationship between men. Frenchwomen laugh
at the idea that "women can't be friends," but they also admit sometimes that for
women "It's a different thing." And many French people doubt the possibility of a
friendship between a man and a woman. There is also the kind of relationship within
a group—men and women who have worked together for a long time, who may be
very close, sharing great loyalty and warmth of feeling. They may call one another *copains*—a word that, in English, becomes "friends" but has more the feeling of "pals"
or "buddies." In French eyes this is not friendship, although two members of such a
group may well be friends.

For the French, friendship is a one-to-one relationship that demands a keen   9
awareness of the other person's intellect, temperament, and particular interests. A
friend is someone who draws out your own best qualities, with whom you sparkle
and become more of whatever the friendship draws upon. Your political philosophy
assumes more depth, appreciation of a play becomes sharper, taste in food or wine
Emphasize is accentuated, enjoyment of a sport is intensified.

And French friendships are compartmentalized. A man may play chess with a   10
friend for thirty years without knowing his political opinions, or he may talk politics
with him for as long a time without knowing about his personal life. Different friends
fill different niches in each person's life. These friendships are not made part of family life. A friend is not expected to spend evenings being nice to children or courteous
to a deaf grandmother. These duties, also serious and enjoined, are primarily for relatives. Men who are friends may meet in a cafe. Intellectual friends may meet in larger
groups for evenings of conversation. Working people may meet at the little bistro
where they drink and talk, far from the family. Marriage does not affect such friendships; wives do not have to be taken into account.

In the past in France, friendships of this kind seldom were open to any but in-   11
tellectual women. Since most women's lives centered on their homes, their warmest
relations with other women often went back to their girlhood. The special relationship of friendship is based on what the French value most—on the mind, on compatibility of outlook, on vivid awareness of some chosen area of life.

Friendship heightens the sense of each person's individuality. Other relation-   12
ships commanding as great loyalty and devotion have a different meaning. In World
War II the first resistance groups formed in Paris were built on the foundation of *les
copains*. But significantly, as time went on, these little groups, whose lives rested in
one another's hands, called themselves "families." Where each had a total responsibility for all, it was kinship ties that provided the model. And even today such ties,
crossing every line of class and personal interest, remain binding on the survivors of
these small, secret bands.

13   In Germany, in contrast with France, friendship is much more articulately a matter of feeling. Adolescents, boys and girls, form deeply sentimental attachments, walk and talk together—not so much to polish their wits as to share their hopes and fears and dreams, to form a common front against the world of school and family and to join in a kind of mutual discovery of each other's and their own inner life. Within the family, the closest relationship over a lifetime is between brothers and sisters. Outside the family, men and women find in their closest friends of the same sex the devotion of a sister, the loyalty of a brother. Appropriately, in Germany friends usually are brought into the family. Children call their father's and their mother's friends "uncle" and "aunt." Between French friends, who have chosen each other for the congeniality of their point of view, lively disagreement and sharpness of argument are the breath of life. But for Germans, whose friendships are based on mutuality of feeling, deep disagreement on any subject that matters to both is regarded as a tragedy. Like ties of kinship, ties of friendship are meant to be irrevocably binding. Young Germans who come to the United States have great difficulty in establishing such friendships with Americans. We view friendship more tentatively, subject to changes in intensity as people move, change their jobs, marry, or discover new interests.

14   English friendships follow still a different pattern. Their basis is shared activity. Activities at different stages of life may be of very different kinds—discovering a common interest in school, serving together in the armed forces, taking part in a foreign mission, staying in the same country house during a crisis. In the midst of the activity, whatever it may be, people fall into step—sometimes two men or two women, sometimes two couples, sometimes three people—and find that they walk or play a game or tell stories or serve on a tiresome and exacting committee with the same easy anticipation of what each will do day by day or in some critical situation. Americans who have made English friends comment that, even years later, "you can take up just where you left off." Meeting after a long interval, friends are like a couple who begin to dance again when the orchestra strikes up after a pause. English friendships are formed outside the family circle, but they are not, as in Germany, contrapuntal to the family nor are they, as in France, separated from the family. And a break in an English friendship comes not necessarily as a result of some irreconcilable difference of viewpoint or feeling but instead as a result of misjudgment, where one friend seriously misjudges how the other will think or feel or act, so that suddenly they are out of step.

15   What, then, is friendship? Looking at these different styles, including our own, each of which is related to a whole way of life, are there common elements? There is the recognition that friendship, in contrast with kinship, invokes freedom of choice. A friend is someone who chooses and is chosen. Related to this is the sense each friend gives the other of being a special individual, on whatever grounds this recognition is based. And between friends there is inevitably a kind of equality of give-and-take. These similarities make the bridge between societies possible, and the American's characteristic openness to different styles of relationship makes it possible for him to find new friends abroad with whom he feels at home.

VOCABULARY

Directions: Mark any important words in the reading selection that you don't know. Then list them in the following chart along with their paragraph numbers. Try to figure out each word's meaning by reading over the context carefully for clues to help you guess the meaning of the unfamiliar word. Check your dictionary or thesaurus to confirm your guess. After you discuss the words with your group members, write the meanings in the margin of the text, near the word. Then enter them in the chart.

Key Word   Paragraph   Meaning

_____

_____

_____

_____

_____

_____

GUIDE QUESTIONS

Directions: Develop a list of questions that elicit the important ideas in the reading selection. Start at the beginning and work your way sequentially through the text until you have addressed all of the author's major ideas.

APPLICATION

Directions: When you have a list of guide questions, read through the selection again. This time, write one or more questions that require the application of the information in the text to a situation in the real world.

WRITING

Directions: Your last task is to prepare a writing assignment. For example, you might ask for a paragraph in which the writer comments on the ideas in the reading selection. You might also ask for a summary of the selection.

Why do so many Americans choose to spend their lives stupefied by drugs? Author Pete Hamill thinks he has found the answer: television. In this essay, which appeared in Esquire *magazine in 1990, Hamill describes the startling similarities between drugs and television and their dreadful effect on American society.*

CRACK AND THE BOX

Pete Hamill

1   One sad rainy morning last winter, I talked to a woman who was addicted to crack cocaine. She was twenty-two, stiletto-thin, with eyes as old as tombs. She was living in two rooms in a welfare hotel with her children, who were two, three, and five years of age. Her story was the usual tangle of human woe: early pregnancy, dropping out of school, vanished men, smack and then crack, tricks with johns in parked cars to pay for the dope. I asked her why she did drugs. She shrugged in an empty way and couldn't really answer beyond "makes me feel good." While we talked and she told her tale of squalor, the children ignored us. They were watching television.

2   Walking back to my office in the rain, I brooded about the woman, her zombie-like children, and my own callous indifference. I'd heard so many versions of the same story that I almost never wrote them anymore; the sons of similar women, glimpsed a dozen years ago, are now in Dannemora or Soledad or Joliet: in a hundred cities, their daughters are moving into the same loveless rooms. As I walked, a series of homeless men approached me for change, most of them junkies. Others sat in doorways, staring at nothing. They were additional casualties of our time of plague, demoralized reminders that, although this country holds only 2 percent of the world's population, it consumes 65 percent of the world's supply of hard drugs.

3   *Why,* for God's sake? Why do so many millions of Americans of all ages, races, and classes choose to spend all or part of their lives stupefied? I've talked to hundreds of addicts over the years; some were my friends. But none could give sensible answers. They stutter about the pain of the world, about despair or boredom, the urgent need for magic or pleasure in a society empty of both. But then they just shrug. Americans have the money to buy drugs; the supply is plentiful. But almost nobody in power asks, *Why?* Least of all, [then President] George Bush and his drug warriors.

4   William Bennett [the Bush administration's drug policy director] talks vaguely about the heritage of '60s permissiveness, the collapse of Traditional Values, and all that. But he and Bush offer the traditional American excuse: It Is Somebody Else's Fault. This posture set the stage for the self-righteous invasion of Panama, the bloodiest drug arrest in world history. Bush even accused [former Panamanian leader] Manuel Noriega of "poisoning our children." But he never asked *why* so many Americans demand the poison.

5   And then, on that rainy morning in New York, I saw another one of those ragged men staring out at the rain from a doorway. I suddenly remembered the inert postures of the children in that welfare hotel, and I thought: *television.*

6   Ah, no, I muttered to myself: too simple. Something as complicated as drug addiction can't be blamed on television. Come on. . . . But I remembered all those desperate places I'd visited as a reporter, where there were no books and a TV set was

always playing and the older kids had gone off somewhere to shoot smack, except for the kid who was at the mortuary in a coffin. I also remembered when I was a boy in the '40s and early '50s, and drugs were a minor sideshow, a kind of dark little rumor. And there was one major difference between that time and this: television.

We had unemployment then; illiteracy, poor living conditions, racism, govern- 7
mental stupidity, a gap between rich and poor. We didn't have the all-consuming presence of television in our lives. Now two generations of Americans have grown up with television from their earliest moments of consciousness. Those same American generations are afflicted by the pox of drug addiction.

Only thirty-five years ago. drug addiction was not a major problem in this coun- 8
try. There were drug addicts. We had some at the end of the nineteenth century, hooked on the cocaine in patent medicines. During the placid '50s, Commissioner Harry Anslinger pumped up the budget of the old Bureau of Narcotics with fantasies of reefer madness. Heroin was sold and used in most major American cities, while the bebop generation of jazz musicians got jammed up with horse.

But until the early '60s, narcotics were still marginal to American life; they 9
weren't the $120 billion market they make up today. If anything, those years have an eerie innocence. In 1955 there were 31,700,000 TV sets in use in the country (the number is now past 184 million). But the majority of the audience had grown up without the dazzling new medium. They embraced it, were diverted by it, perhaps even loved it, but they weren't *formed* by it. That year, the New York police made a mere 1,234 felony drug arrests; in 1988 it was 43,901. They confiscated ninety-seven *ounces* of cocaine for the entire year; last year it was hundreds of pounds. During each year of the '50s in New York, there were only about a hundred narcotics-related deaths. But by the end of the '60s, when the first generation of children *formed* by television had come to maturity (and thus to the marketplace), the number of such deaths had risen to twelve hundred. The same phenomenon was true in every major American city.

In the last Nielsen survey of American viewers, the average family was watch- 10
ing television seven hours a *day*. This has never happened before in history. No people has ever been entertained for seven hours a day. The Elizabethans didn't go to the theater seven hours a day. The pre-TV generation did not go to the movies seven hours a day. Common sense tells us that this all-pervasive diet of instant imagery, sustained now for forty years, must have changed us in profound ways.

Television, like drugs, dominates the lives of its addicts. And though some lonely 11
Americans leave their sets on without watching them, using them as electronic companions, television usually absorbs its viewers the way drugs absorb their users. Viewers can't work or play while watching television; they can't read; they can't be out on the streets, falling in love with the wrong people, learning how to quarrel and compromise with other human beings. In short, they are asocial. So are drug addicts.

One Michigan State University study in the early '80s offered a group of four- 12
and five-year-olds the choice of giving up television or giving up their fathers. Fully one-third said they would give up Daddy. Given a similar choice (between cocaine or heroin and father, mother, brother, sister, wife, husband, children, job), almost every stone junkie would do the same.

13   There are other disturbing similarities. Television itself is a consciousness-altering instrument. With the touch of a button, it takes you out of the "real" world in which you reside and can place you at a basketball game, the back alleys of Miami, the streets of Bucharest, or the cartoony living rooms of Sitcom Land. Each move from channel to channel alters mood, usually with music or a laugh track. On any given evening, you can laugh, be frightened, feel tension, thump with excitement. You can even tune in *MacNeil/Lehrer* and feel sober.

14   But none of these abrupt shifts in mood is *earned*. They are attained as easily as popping a pill. Getting news from television, for example, is simply not the same experience as reading it in a newspaper. Reading is *active*. The reader must decode little symbols called words, then create images or ideas and make them connect; at its most basic level, reading is an act of the imagination. But the television viewer doesn't go through that process. The words are spoken to him by Dan Rather or Tom Brokaw or Peter Jennings. There isn't much decoding to do when watching television, no time to think or ponder before the next set of images and spoken words appears to displace the present one. The reader, being active, works at his or her own pace: the viewer, being passive, proceeds at a pace determined by the show. Except at the highest levels, television never demands that its audience take part in an act of imagination. Reading always does. In short, television works on the same imaginative and intellectual level as psychoactive drugs. If prolonged television viewing makes the young passive (dozens of studies indicate that it does), then moving to drugs has a certain coherence. Drugs provide an unearned high (in contrast to the earned rush that comes from a feat accomplished, a human breakthrough earned by sweat or thought or love).

15   And because the television addict and the drug addict are alienated from the hard and scary world, they also feel they make no difference in its complicated events. For the junkie, the world is reduced to him and the needle, pipe, or vial; the self is absolutely isolated, with no desire for choice. The television addict lives the same way. Many Americans who fail to vote in presidential elections must believe they have no more control over such a choice than they do over the casting of *L.A. Law*.

16   The drug plague also coincides with the unspoken assumption of most television shows: Life should be easy. The most complicated events are summarized on TV news in a minute or less. Cops confront murder, chase the criminals, and bring them to justice (usually violently) within an hour. In commercials, you drink the right beer and you get the girl. *Easy!* So why should real life be a grind? Why should any American have to spend years mastering a skill or a craft, or work eight hours a day at an unpleasant job, or endure the compromises and crises of a marriage? Nobody *works* on television (except cops, doctors, and lawyers). Love stories on television are about falling in love or breaking up; the long, steady growth of a marriage—its essential *dailiness*—is seldom explored, except as comedy. Life on television is almost always simple: good guys and bad, nice girls and whores, smart guys and dumb. And if life in the real world isn't that simple, well, hey, man, have some dope, man, be happy, feel good.

17   The doper always whines about how he *feels*; drugs are used to enhance his feelings or obliterate them, and in this the doper is very American. No other people on

earth spend so much time talking about their feelings; hundreds of thousands go to shrinks, they buy self-help books by the millions, they pour out intimate confessions to virtual strangers in bars or discos. Our political campaigns are about emotional issues now, stated in the simplicities of adolescence. Even alleged statesmen can start a sentence, "I feel that the Sandinistas should . . ." I'm convinced that this exaltation of cheap emotions over logic and reason is one by-product of hundreds of thousands of hours of television.

18   Most Americans under the age of fifty have now spent their lives absorbing television; that is, they've had the structures of drama pounded into them. Drama is always about conflict. So news shows, politics, and advertising are now all shaped by those structures. Nobody will pay attention to anything as complicated as the part played by Third World debt in the expanding production of cocaine; it's much easier to focus on Manuel Noriega, a character right out of *Miami Vice,* and believe that even in real life there's a Mister Big.

19   What is to be done? Television is certainly not going away, but its addictive qualities can be controlled. It's a lot easier to "just say no" to television than to heroin or crack. As a beginning, parents must take immediate control of the sets, teaching children to watch specific television *programs,* not "television," to get out of the house and play with other kids. Elementary and high schools must begin teaching television as a subject, the way literature is taught, showing children how shows are made, how to distinguish between the true and the false, how to recognize cheap emotional manipulation. All Americans should spend more time reading. And thinking.

20   For years, the defenders of television have argued that the networks are only giving the people what they want. That might be true. But so is the Medellin cartel.

VOCABULARY

Directions: Mark any important words in the reading selection that you don't know. Then list them in the chart below along with their paragraph numbers. Try to figure out each word's meaning by reading over the context carefully for clues to help you guess the meaning of the unfamiliar word. Check your dictionary or thesaurus to confirm your guess. After you discuss the words with your group members, write the meanings in the margin of the text, near the word. Then enter them in the chart.

Key Word	Paragraph	Meaning
SHRUGGED →		
RAGGED —		old clothes — ragged clothes
STAINED —		to achieve
ALLEGED → to say		specially in making a legal statement Not certain
		without giving proof
		He is alleged to be the author But may be it is not true

GUIDE QUESTIONS

Directions: Develop a list of questions that elicit the important ideas in the reading selection. Start at the beginning and work your way sequentially through the text until you have addressed all of the author's major ideas.

APPLICATION

Directions: When you have a list of guide questions, read through the selection again. This time, write one or more questions that require application of the information in the text to a situation in the real world.

WRITING

Directions: Your last task is to prepare a writing assignment. For example, you might ask for a paragraph in which the writer comments on the ideas in the reading selection. You might also ask for a summary of the selection.

SHORT TAKE

TV OR NOT TV?

In 1992, *TV Guide* polled its readers on their TV attitudes. Here are some of the results:

> *When asked this question, "Suppose that, as part of a scientific experiment, you were placed on a deserted island for one full year with just your family. If you could have only one or the other, which would you choose to have—a television set or a telephone?" most people (60 percent) said they would choose the telephone, but one person in three (34 percent) opted to give up contact with anyone outside the family for twelve months in order to have television. When the question was changed to being placed on a deserted island with* either *your family or a television, only 5 percent chose TV, while 93 percent chose their loved ones. Whew!*
>
> *Viewers were asked what they do when they walk into a room in their homes and the television is off. Two in five (42 percent) said they turn it on; half (51 percent) said they leave it off. No other appliance has that kind of grip on its owners. As for that old saying that a man's best friend is his dog, this poll suggests that it may, in fact, be his TV. If a television set is off, nearly half of all men (48 percent) turn it on when they enter a room.*
>
> *Who owns the zapper? Nearly nine out of ten households have a remote-control. Who controls it?*

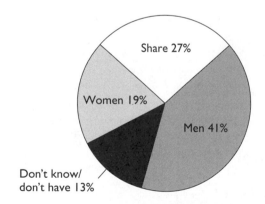

> *When asked if they would agree to "give up watching absolutely all types of television" for the rest of their lives in exchange for $25,000, fewer than one in four (23 percent) said they would take the offer. Almost half (46 percent) said they would refuse to give up TV for anything under a million dollars. One in four (25 percent) would refuse to stop watching TV even for $1 million. Twenty-five percent of those who earn less than $20,000 a year also said they wouldn't give up TV for a million dollars—the equivalent of fifty years' salary!*

SPECIAL PROJECT

EXPLORING YOUR OWN CULTURE

How much do you know about your own culture? As you have seen in the readings in this section of the text, every culture has its own set of traditions and beliefs. Investigate your roots by interviewing older family members and friends and by reading about your culture in the library.

Describe the rituals and traditions associated with:

1. the birth of a child
2. a wedding
3. a funeral
4. a special holiday or event

Visit the library to find materials describing the traditions of your culture. List the books, periodicals, and other references you find at the end of your report.

Your report should consist of four sections. Give a title to each section; for example, you might name your first section "The Birth of a Child in Mexico." Then describe the rituals surrounding this event. For example, you may answer questions such as the following: Is it customary to have a party to celebrate the birth of a baby? Do friends and family bring gifts? Is a special type of gift traditional? Are special foods prepared? How long does the celebration last? Is the baby given a name at this time? How is the name chosen? Is special clothing worn? If there are other features to your culture's celebration, include them. Does your own family have any special customs?

Do the same with the other three sections of your report: a wedding, a funeral, a special holiday or event.

At the end of your report, include a list of references in the library. Think of this list as a resource for someone who would like to learn more about your culture and its traditions.

BIBLIOGRAPHY

For Further Reading on the Theme of Culture

Kobo Abe	*The Woman in the Dunes* (Japanese)
Chinua Achebe	*Things Fall Apart*
	Arrow of God (African)
Isabel Allende	*House of the Spirits*
	Of Love and Shadows
	Eva Luna (Latin American)
Maya Angelou	*I Know Why the Caged Bird Sings* (United States— African American)
Elemore Smith Bowen	*Return to Laughter* (African)
Dee Brown	*Bury My Heart at Wounded Knee*
	Folktales of the Native American (United States— American Indian)
Ina Corrinne Brown	*Understanding Other Cultures* (general)
Chitra Divakaruni	*Arranged Marriage* (Indian)
John Van Druten	*I Remember Mama* (Norwegian-American)
Marian Wright Edelman	*The Measure of Our Success* (United States—African American)
Ralph Ellison	*The Invisible Man* (United States—African American)
Elizabeth Fernea	*Guests of the Sheik* (Middle Eastern)
Carlos Fuentes	*The Good Conscience* (Mexican)
William Golding	*Lord of the Flies* (general)
Nadine Gordimer	*My Son's Story* (South African)
Joanne Greenberg	*In This Sign* (Deaf)
Walt Harrington	*Black Like Me*
	Crossings: A White Man's Journey to Black America (United States—African American)
Tom Humphries	*Deaf in America* (Deaf)
Jamaica Kincaid	*Annie John* (Caribbean)
Barbara Kingsolver	*Pigs in Heaven*
	Animal Dreams (United States—American Indian)

Maxine Hong Kingston	*Woman Warrior* (Chinese-American)
Harlan Lane	*When the Mind Hears*
	Mask of Benevolence (Deaf)
Oscar Lewis	*Five Families* (Mexican)
Elliot Liebow	*Tally's Corner* (United States—"Culture of Poverty")
Cherry and Charles Lindholm	*Generosity and Jealousy: The Swat Pakhtun of Northern Pakistan* (Pakistani)
Gabriel Garcia Marquez	*Chronicle of a Death Foretold*
	Love in the Time of Cholera (Latin American)
Mark Mathabane	*Kaffir Boy* (South African)
Margaret Mead	*People and Places* (general)
N. Scott Momeday	*The Way to Rainy Mountain* (United States—American Indian)
Alan Paton	*Cry, The Beloved Country* (South African)
Nahid Rachlin	*The Foreigner* (Iranian-American)
Marjorie Shostak	*Nisa: The Life and Words of a !Kung Woman* (African)
James Spradley	*Anthropology through Literature*
	Conformity and Conflict (general)
Amy Tan	*The Kitchen God's Wife*
	The Joy Luck Club (Chinese-American)
Elizabeth Marshall Thomas	*The Harmless People*
Colin Turnbull	*The Forest People*
	The Mountain People (African)

UNIT THREE

READING AND THINKING ABOUT LANGUAGE

All words are pegs to hang ideas on.

—Henry Ward Beecher

[It] is only through language that we enter fully into our human estate and culture, communicate freely with our fellows, acquire and share information. If we cannot do this, we will be bizarrely disabled and cut off—whatever our desires, or endeavors, or native capacities.

—Oliver Sacks

THINKING ABOUT LANGUAGE

Before you begin this part of the text, think about and answer the questions below.

1. What is language? Write your own definition.
2. Do animals have language? If so, is it the same as human language? In what ways is it the same? In what ways is it different?
3. Linguists, the people who study language, believe humans began using language about fifty thousand years ago. Before then, they relied on crude gestures and sounds for what communication did go on. Try to imagine that you are a "cave man" or a "cave woman." What are some gestures, signs, or sounds you would use to communicate?
4. How would your life be different if humans had never invented language? Imagine some of the events of a typical day and describe how you would communicate what you need to say, without words.

Everyone has a very personal interest in language. Because it is all around us and within us, too, we all feel that language belongs to us. And all of us, bank presidents, farmers, secretaries, and traffic cops, are language experts even though we don't often stop to think about it.

Before you read this selection, take a moment to think about language—its definition and its meaning in your life.

LANGUAGE

Mary C. Fjeldstad

Defining Language

1   In order to discuss language, we must begin with a definition; to build a definition, let's start by listing the characteristics of language. First, the most basic characteristic is that language is a means of *communication*. Language is what we use to get through the day, to buy a newspaper, order a cup of coffee, ask for directions on the street, or decide on a movie. Language lets us think about our desire for a better life, the love we feel for our family, the vacation we plan to take, and the sadness at the death of a friend. Language lets us dream about things that never were, and perhaps never will be. You can imagine a werewolf or a vampire because you have a *name* for it, even though such a thing never existed. If you see a picture of a handsome or beautiful person of the opposite sex, you can imagine or talk about meeting such a person in your future because you have language. The past and the future can be just as great a part of your reality as the present—because of language.

2   Without language we would be isolated from our fellow humans. Human societies never would have formed without language; cultures never would have developed. Language is essentially what made human civilization possible. It is language that has allowed us to produce literature, music, mathematics, and science. Language has allowed us to transmit knowledge, the sum of our stored experience in spoken or written form, from one generation to the next. Without language, life as we know it would not be possible.

Language Consists of Symbols

3   A second major characteristic of language is that it consists of *symbols*. A symbol is something that represents something else. A person can be a symbol. For example, Martin Luther King, Jr., stood for nonviolent opposition to racial discrimination. The Pope is a symbol of the Catholic church. Gestures, like the clenched fist, or a facial expression like a smile or a frown, can be symbols of attitudes or moods. Objects can be symbols. In the United States a woman may wear a diamond ring on her left hand as a symbol of her engagement to a man; in the Fiji Islands young women wore hibiscus flowers behind their ears to symbolize the fact they were in love.

4   But *words* are also symbols. The word *hamburger* is a symbol for that item of food Americans so love to eat, and while the word may set our mouths to watering, we do not start chewing on the word—we must wait until the thing it symbolizes is cooked and on the plate.

We live in two worlds at the same time: the real (or physical) world—the world   5
we can see and touch and smell and taste—and the verbal (or symbolic) world—
where we use language to name and talk about and think about all the things we experience in the physical world.

Imagine what it would be like if you did not have the ease of words or symbols   6
to communicate with other people. Your conversation would be limited to the objects, or persons, or events, actually present in your physical world at that moment
in the conversation. People have long been fascinated by this notion of language as
symbols. The writer Jonathan Swift, in his famous satire, *Gulliver's Travels,* plays with
the possibility of nonsymbolic words:

> [This] was urged as a great advantage in point of health as well as brevity.
> For it is plain that every word we speak is, in some degree, a diminution of
> our lungs by corrosion, and consequently contributes to the shortening of
> our lives. An expedient was therefore offered that since words are only
> names for things it would be more convenient for all men to carry about
> with them such things as were necessary to express a particular business
> they are to discourse [speak] on. . . . Many of the most learned and wise
> adhere to the new scheme of expressing themselves by things, which has
> only this inconvenience attending it, that, if a man's business be very great,
> and of various kinds, he must be obliged, in proportion, to carry a greater
> bundle of things upon his back unless he can afford one or two strong ser-
> vants to attend him. I have often beheld two of these sages [wise men] al-
> most sinking under the weight of their packs, like peddlers among us; who,
> when they meet in the street, would lay down their loads, open their
> packs, hold conversation for an hour, and then put up their implements,
> help each other to resume their burdens, and take their leave.

Swift's comical description makes the importance of symbols in language clear—   7
just imagine if the people in his story wished to talk about an elephant or the Empire State Building!

Is Language Unique to Humans?

People have long speculated that animals have their own languages and, of course,   8
many animals do communicate with one another. Birds use sounds to warn other
birds of danger or to announce "ownership" of a particular tree. Bees "dance" to
inform other bees of food sources. Velvet monkeys make sounds that signal the
proximity of predators. Certainly many pet owners swear that their dog or cat
"talks" to them and understands them when they talk. But none of these examples
of communication will fit our definition of language because they are not *symbolic;*
that is, none has a one-to-one correlation to a specific object or concept.

Several years ago there was great excitement among language researchers when   9
it was shown that the great apes (especially chimpanzees) could learn language to
some extent. While they do not have the physical apparatus necessary for speech,
apes do have the ability to understand the meanings of words as symbols for things
and relationships. Apes have been taught a limited number of words through sign

language and through the use of typewriters and other devices. A gorilla named Koko was taught more than three hundred words in American Sign Language. To the surprise of most scientists, she also was able to "invent" new words and phrases, a skill that was previously believed to be uniquely human. For example, she invented sign words for *ring* ("finger bracelet") and *mask* ("eye hat"). She was even able to use sign words to refer to abstract ideas, such as pain and fear. Although the success of Koko and other apes encouraged many scientists to believe that these animals are capable of sophisticated human language, it soon became apparent that the apes' abilities are severely limited. No ape has ever progressed beyond the level of that of a two-and-a-half-year-old child. Nor can apes produce sentences of more than two words. Human language, on the other hand, allows us to communicate an infinite number of thoughts and to preserve these thoughts over long periods of time and distance.

10   Language allows us to step out beyond the confinement of the immediate present. It means that people can, for example, talk about food to eat at the present time, and also food tomorrow and food yesterday. If you believe that your dog has a human-like language ability to communicate, try to talk to Spot about "dog food tomorrow." Another example is the important symbol of the personal name. While it seems clear that dogs understand names, their own, their masters', and others, they do not understand them in the same way humans do. If you say to Spot "Sam is at work," how does Spot react? He will look for Sam, understanding *Sam* only as an immediate sign, exactly as he would react to his master's voice or the sound of his footsteps at the door. A human, on the other hand, will probably ask you something like, "When is Sam coming home?" or "How does he like his job?" or any of thousands of other thoughts that were stimulated by the symbol *Sam*. All of these thoughts are forever beyond the capabilities of the dog.

Symbols Are Not the Events They Symbolize

11   When you communicate with another person, you use symbols—words. However, the words you use to refer to objects, persons, events, situations, sensations, and feelings are not those *actual* objects, persons, events, situations, sensations, or feelings. For example, it is one thing to experience a toothache and quite another to comment "I have a toothache." Those words merely refer to your pain, but there is no way the other person can experience your toothache.

12   Have you ever tried to think about something—anything—without using its name? As Peter Farb says, "Try to think about the stars, a grasshopper, love or hate, pain, anything at all—and it must be done in terms of language. There is no other way; thinking is language spoken to oneself. Until language has made sense of experience, that experience is meaningless." Our ability to use the symbol system of language is the main thing that distinguishes us from other animals and makes us human beings.

Language Is Systematic

13   A third characteristic of language is that it is a *system*. That system is called *grammar*. Grammar is a set of rules that defines how words may be combined. For example, because we know the grammar system of English, we understand the sentence *The man bit the dog* to mean one thing and *The dog bit the man* to mean something quite

different. In both examples, the meanings of the five words are exactly the same. But the way they are combined changes the meaning of the sentence completely. Similarly, *The bit dog man the,* although using the same, easy-to-understand words, is meaningless—because it does not follow the rules of grammar we all carry around in our heads.

Language Is Limitless

The final characteristic of language is that it is infinitely creative. In fact, most of the   14
sentences we utter are original, that is, we have never heard or read them before in exactly the same form. As Steven Pinker says in his book *The Language Instinct,*   *cAsuAL*
"Go into the Library of Congress and pick a sentence at random from any volume, and chances are you would fail to find an exact repetition no matter how long you continued to search. Estimates of the number of sentences that an ordinary person is capable of producing are breathtaking."

Definition of Language

To conclude, let's review the characteristics of language we have discussed: Lan-   15
guage is communication. Language is symbolic. Language is systematic. Language is infinitely creative.

Now we can write our definition: *Language is an infinitely creative system of com-*   16
munication, consisting of symbols. Compare this definition to the one you wrote at the beginning of this selection, and think about what you've learned as you study the rest of this unit.

VOCABULARY

Directions: Find each of the key words in the reading selection. Study each word in its context and try to determine its meaning. Write what you think it means in the margin of the text, near the word. Then read over the sentence, mentally substituting your guess for the key word. Does the sentence still make sense? Does it retain its original meaning? If it does, you've probably figured out the meaning of the key word correctly. In any case, confirm your guess by checking a dictionary or thesaurus.

If you take your meaning from a dictionary or thesaurus, be sure the definition includes words you already know and feel comfortable using. If it doesn't, you will be worse off than when you started—you will have begun with *one* word you didn't know and ended with *two* words you don't know!

Record the new words you've learned below and on the next page.

Key Word	Paragraph	Meaning
1. satire	6	WRITING WICH MAKES A PERSON FUNNY
2. adhere	6	REMAIN LOYAL
3. speculated	8	MAKIG GUESSES

Key Word	Paragraph	Meaning
4. predators	8	_Animals that attack others to food_
5. infinitely	14	_extremely_
Others?		

GUIDE QUESTIONS

Directions: The purpose of guide questions is to "guide" your analysis of the text. _to carry_ Your thoughtful answers will ensure that you have understood the main ideas the author wanted to convey. Some of the questions require that you simply find the stated facts in the reading selection; others will ask you to do more difficult tasks, such as paraphrasing information (putting the author's ideas into your own words), synthesizing several ideas into one complex thought, evaluating (making judgments about) an idea, or taking information from the reading and applying it to a new situation or to your own life.

Write answers to the questions in your notebook or on a separate sheet of paper if your instructor wishes to collect them. Your answers will form the basis of class discussion.

1. Define *symbol* and give some examples of symbols.
2. In the excerpt from Jonathan Swift's classic novel *Gulliver's Travels,* people supposedly believed speaking corroded their lungs and shortened their lives. So they decided it would be better for their health to stop using words, the symbols of things, and carry around the things themselves. Assume you did this in school tomorrow. What things would you have to carry with you? Imagine your participation in class, or a conversation with a friend in the cafeteria. What things would you pull out of your bag? How would you communicate your thoughts about those things without using any words? How would you feel about communicating like this? How does Swift's story reinforce the idea that words are symbols?
3. Consider this statement made by a little boy (quoted by the linguist S. I. Hayakawa): "Pigs are called pigs because they are such dirty animals." Explain the mistake the little boy makes in his remark.
4. Following are some strings of words that, while containing easily comprehensible English words, are in some way "not quite right." Consider each example and explain why it does not make sense; that is, explain how it violates the rules of grammar.

This sentence no verb.
This book has contains six units.
Is raining.
The car was put in the.
Where did he put it the car?
Please say those little three words.

APPLICATION

1. *Directions:* Work in groups to complete this exercise. Think of a simple everyday message you would like to convey to the members of another group in the class. Then try to communicate your message without using words.
2. *Directions:* Underline and annotate the selection "Language." To review and practice underlining and annotating, turn to Appendix B.

WRITING

1. *Directions:* Think about the exercise you did in Application question 1. What difficulties did you have communicating your message and understanding the message of the other group? In a paragraph, describe your experience and how you felt about it. Relate your experience to what you learned when you read the selection "Language."
2. *Directions:* Summary writing is an important skill for college students. Writing a summary forces you to be an active reader and thinker because you are identifying and restating ideas yourself, not just responding to clues as you do, for example, when you take a multiple-choice test. Summary writing requires that you truly understand what you are reading and that you express your ideas in clear, concise language. Write a summary of the selection "Language." To learn and practice the steps for writing a good summary, turn to the section "The Summary" in Appendix B.

Helen Keller was born in 1880. At the age of nineteen months, she suffered an illness that left her both blind and deaf. Later she also became unable to speak. Her young years were indeed difficult as she raged against her forced isolation from the world, unable to communicate except by means of gestures and direct physical contact. Nevertheless, by age twenty-four, she had graduated cum laude from Radcliffe College, where, in addition to mastering all her other subjects, she learned many different languages, including Latin and Greek. She went on to write many books and travel the country giving inspirational speeches, many on behalf of the handicapped—all with the help of her dedicated teacher, Anne Sullivan, who came to her when Keller was seven. In this excerpt from her autobiography, Keller takes the first indispensable step to thought and to learning—realizing that words are symbols.

In the Beginning was the Word.

—St. John

THE KEY TO LANGUAGE

Helen Keller

1   The morning after my teacher came she led me into her room and gave me a doll. The little blind children at the Perkins Institution had sent it and Laura Bridgman had dressed it; but I did not know this until afterward.

2   When I had played with it a little while, Miss Sullivan slowly spelled into my hand the word "d-o-l-l." I was at once interested in this finger play and tried to imitate it. When I finally succeeded in making the letters correctly I was flushed with childish pleasure and pride. Running downstairs to my mother I held up my hands and made the letters for doll. I did not know that I was spelling a word or even that words existed; I was simply making my fingers go in monkey-like imitation. In the days that followed I learned to spell in this uncomprehending way a great many words, among them *pin, hat, cup,* and a few verbs like *sit, stand,* and *walk.* But my teacher had been with me several weeks before I understood that everything has a name.

3   One day, while I was playing with my new doll, Miss Sullivan put my big rag doll into my lap also, spelled "d-o-l-l" and tried to make me understand that "d-o-l-l" applied to both. Earlier in the day we had had a tussle over the words "m-u-g" and "w-a-t-e-r." Miss Sullivan had tried to impress it upon me that "m-u-g" is *mug* and "w-a-t-e-r" is *water,* but I persisted in confounding the two. In despair she had dropped the subject for the time only to renew it at the first opportunity. I became impatient at her repeated attempts and, seizing the new doll, I dashed it upon the floor. . . .

4   We walked down the path to the well-house, attracted by the fragrance of the honeysuckle with which it was covered. Someone was drawing water and my teacher placed my hand under the spout. As the cool stream gushed over one hand she spelled into the other the word *water,* first slowly, then rapidly. I stood still, my whole attention fixed upon the motions of her fingers. Suddenly I felt a misty consciousness, as of something forgotten—a thrill of returning thought; and somehow

the mystery of language was revealed to me. I knew then that "w-a-t-e-r" meant the wonderful cool something that was flowing over my hand. That living word awakened my soul, gave it light, hope, joy, set it free. There were barriers still, it is true, but barriers that could, in time, be swept away.

I left the well-house eager to learn. Everything had a name and each name gave   5
birth to a new thought. As we returned to the house every object which I touched seemed to quiver with life. That was because I saw everything with the strange, new sight that had come to me. On entering the door I remembered the doll I had broken. I felt my way to the hearth and picked up the pieces. I vainly tried to put them together. Then my eyes filled with tears; for I realized what I had done, and for the first time I felt repentance and sorrow.

I learned a great many new words that day. I do not remember what they all   6
were; but I do know that *mother, father, sister, teacher* were among them—words that were to make the world blossom for me, "like Aaron's rod, with flowers." It would have been difficult to find a happier child than I was as I lay in my crib at the close of that eventful day and lived over the joys it had brought me, and, for the first time, longed for a new day to come. . . .

I had now the key to all language and I was eager to learn to use it. Children   7
who hear acquire language without any particular effort; the words that fall from others' lips they catch on the wing, as it were, delightedly, while the little deaf child must trap them by a slow and often painful process. But whatever the process, the result is wonderful. Gradually, from naming an object we advance step by step until we have traversed the vast distance between our first stammered syllable and the sweep of thought in a line of Shakespeare.

At first, when my teacher told me about a new thing I asked very few questions.   8
My ideas were vague, and my vocabulary was inadequate, but as my knowledge of things grew, and I learned more and more words, my field of inquiry broadened, and I would return again and again to the same subject, eager for further information. Sometimes a new word revived an image that some earlier experiences had engraved on my brain.

I remember the morning that I first asked the meaning of the word *love*. This   9
was before I knew many words. I had found a few early violets in the garden and brought them to my teacher. She tried to kiss me; but at that time I did not like to have anyone kiss me except my mother. Miss Sullivan put her arm gently around me and spelled into my hand "I love Helen."

"What is love?" I asked.   10

She drew me closer to her and said, "It is here," pointing to my heart, whose   11
beats I was conscious of for the first time. Her words puzzled me very much because I did not then understand anything unless I touched it.

I smelt the violets in her hand and asked, half in words, half in signs, a question   12
which means, "Is love the sweetness of flowers?"

"No," said my teacher.   13

Again I thought. The warm sun was shining on us.   14

"Is this not love?" I asked, pointing in the direction from which the heat came,   15
"Is this not love?"

16   It seemed to me that there could be nothing more beautiful than the sun, whose warmth makes all things grow. But Miss Sullivan shook her head, and I was greatly puzzled and disappointed. I thought it strange that my teacher could not show me love.

17   A day or two afterward I was stringing beads of different sizes in symmetrical groups—two large beads, three small ones, and so on. I had made many mistakes, and Miss Sullivan had pointed them out again and again with gentle patience. Finally I noticed a very obvious error in the sequence and, for an instant, I concentrated my attention on the lesson and tried to think how I should have arranged the beads. Miss Sullivan touched my forehead and spelled with decided emphasis, "Think."

18   In a flash, I knew that the word was the name of the process that was going on in my head. This was my first conscious perception of an abstract idea.

VOCABULARY

Directions: Locate each of the key words in the reading selection. Then read and study each word in its context and try to determine its meaning. Use a dictionary or thesaurus to check your guess. Write the meanings of the words in the margin of the text.

Record the new words you've learned below.

Key Word	Paragraph	Meaning
1. quiver	5	
2. hearth	5	
3. vainly	5	
4. repentance	5	
5. symmetrical	17	
Others?		

GUIDE QUESTIONS

Directions: The purpose of these guide questions is to ensure your understanding of what you have read. They also will help you to analyze and evaluate the author's ideas and apply them to the real world and your own life.

Write answers to the questions in your notebook or on a separate sheet of paper if your instructor wishes to collect them. Your answers will form the basis of class discussion.

1. Because most of us learned language at a very early age, we do not remember, nor were we old enough to comprehend, the power that the use of language gave to us. Describe the process that brought Keller to her exciting discovery that words are symbols.
2. Contrast the way hearing children learn language with the way deaf children learn it, according to Keller.
3. To Keller, was there a difference in learning that the word *doll* was a symbol for a doll and that the word *love* was a symbol for love? Explain why these are different concepts.

APPLICATION

Directions: Keller's discovery of the "key to language" was obviously one of the turning points in her life. Think about the turning points in your own life. What were they? What were their results? Describe one or more of the turning points in your life in a paragraph or two.

WRITING

Directions: React to the fact that, despite her enormous handicaps, Keller managed to graduate cum laude from Radcliffe College and become a world-famous lecturer and scholar. Write at least one paragraph.

Can your name have an effect on your life? Here are some actual names of real people for your consideration. Mrs. Screech was a singing teacher; Mr. Vroom was a motorcycle dealer; Justin Tune was a choir director; Wyre and Tapping were detectives; Groaner Digger was an undertaker; I. C. Shiver was—you guessed it—an iceman; Grecian T. Snooze was a university student, of course. Perhaps while on vacation he met July August September? Mr. Doctor, Mr. Bonecutter, Mr. Paine, and Mr. Butcher all became physicians, naturally. So did Mr. Rash: his speciality is dermatology. Is there a connection between Mr. Vice's name and the fact that he was arrested 890 times and convicted 421 times? What were Rapid Integration's parents thinking when they named their baby? Not to mention Ms. Virginia May Sweat Strong and Buncha Love. We leave without comment Mr. A. Moron, who was a Commissioner of Education in the Virgin Islands.[1]

WHAT'S IN A NAME?

Kiley Armstrong

1   Sticks and stones may break your bones, but the wrong name can land you in an asylum, a language expert says.

2   "You will have a higher chance of being in an asylum or jail if you have an unusual name," warns Leonard R. N. Ashley of Brooklyn College, past president of the American Name Society.

3   But if you are strong enough to overcome the stigma of a wrong name, you also have a higher chance of becoming a college president, a movie star, or even a religious leader, says Ashley.

4   Ashley, who has a doctorate in psychology, studies names as "an aspect of human behavior." He writes articles for professional journals and is working on an anthology of British names.

5   He contends that the "way you perceive people depends on their name. Have you ever met an Episcopal priest named Buck?"

6   And he believes an unusual name will have either a wonderful or a terrible effect on your life.

7   The late Ima Hogg, daughter of Texas Governor James Hogg, overcame an unusual name to become a prominent Houston socialite and philanthropist. Before she died in 1975, fictitious stories abounded about the existence of a sister named Ura.

8   Then there are names like "Oral Roberts or Hubert Humphrey. If you stand up to that, you can become unique instead of peculiar and can do very well," Ashley says.

9   A sense of humor can help, as in the case of Manila's archbishop—Cardinal Jaime Sin.

10   The cardinal often tells in speeches how he enjoys inviting people to "the house of sin," his official residence in a Manila suburb.

11   "When I was little I suppose you could call me a 'Venial Sin,' but after I die people will realize I was a 'Mortal Sin,'" he adds.

---

[1] All these names were taken from John Train, *Remarkable Names of Real People* (New York: Clarkson N. Potter, 1977).

Even ordinary names often imply something about their owners "whether it is   12
true or not," says Ashley.

"Everybody named Leonard wears glasses and is interested in the futures mar-   13
ket," says Leonard Ashley. "*George* means "farmer" in Greek. But now it suggests
someone who is a weak husband."

"Christopher suggests intellectuality and Katherine is determined and strong,"   14
he says.

People's names, product names, place names, and the names of objects all are   15
scrutinized by the American Name Society, a group composed of linguists, psychologists, and other people who study names.

Its scholars have found that the origins of names often are clouded by   16
assimilation.

"Darren is an African name. But the British saw the TV show "Bewitched" and   17
thought it was an American name."

Some name guidelines for parents include: 18

—Pay attention to the initials. "When Arthur S. Sullivan grows up and
gets a briefcase with his initials on it, he's going to be furious."

—Watch for double meanings. "I once had a student named Warren
Peace. He signed his name W. Peace because he was embarrassed."

—Choose names that offer a lot of nicknames—such as Margaret, which
yields Maggy, Peggy, Margie—so the child has an option.

—Keep "family heirloom" names. "If the name is ugly, just give the kid
an extra name or two."

As for Leonard R. N. Ashley, call him Leonard or Tim. But don't ask what the   19
R. N. stands for—he won't tell.

VOCABULARY

Directions: Locate each of the key words in the reading selection. Then read and
study each word in its context and try to determine its meaning. Use a dictionary or thesaurus to check your guess. Write the meanings of the words in the
margin of the text.

Record the new words you've learned.

Key Word	Paragraph	Meaning
1. stigma	3	
2. anthology	4	
3. philanthropist	7	
4. imply	12	
Others?		

GUIDE QUESTIONS

Directions: Answering these guide questions will help ensure that you understand what you have read. They also will help you to analyze and evaluate the author's opinions and apply the ideas contained in the article to the real world and your own life.

Write answers to the questions in your notebook or on a separate sheet of paper if your instructor wishes to collect them. Your answers will form the basis of class discussion.

1. a. Think about your own first name. Do you like it? Hate it? Why?
    b. Do you know the origin of your first name? (That is, where did it come from? Were you named after someone or something?)
2. Think about your surname. Do you know its derivation? What does it mean?
3. If you could change your name, what would you change it to? Why?
4. a. Identify the authority on names who is described in the article.
    b. What are his credentials?
5. State the main idea of the article.
6. How does the example of Ms. Hogg support the main idea of the article?
7. Give two examples from the article of the effect a name can have on a person's life.
8. Do you agree that a person's name can have an effect on his or her life? Clearly, many famous people felt strongly enough about it to actually change their names. Consider the following:[2]

> Alphonse D'Abruzzo became Alan Alda.
> Allen Konigsberg became Woody Allen.
> Marion Morrison became John Wayne.
> Paul Rubenfeld became Pee-Wee Herman.
> Reginald Kenneth Dwight became Elton John.
> Annie Mae Bullock became Tina Turner.
> Pal became Lassie.

Do you know anyone who changed his or her name? What was the reason? What if your parents had named you Pat Fanny? Rhoda Bike? Rock Pile? Robin Droppings? Doris Closed? Isabel Ringing? (All of these are real names of real people.) Would you have changed your name?

APPLICATION

Directions: Investigate your own name. Try to find the origin of your first and last names. Interview your family members. Visit the school library or public library where you will find many helpful reference tools. If you are not able to find information about your own name, investigate the name of a friend or some person who interests you. Discuss your findings with your classmates.

---

[2] Taken from *All Those Wonderful Names* by J. N. Hook (New York: Wiley, 1991).

WRITING

Directions: Write a summary of the selection "What's in a Name?" To review summary writing turn to Appendix B.

SHORT TAKE

UPDATE ON THE NAME GAME

One British couple named Beer chose the first name Bottled for their new son. Then there is the Wall family, who named their baby Stone and Mr. and Mrs. Jordan whose new addition is named River. Don't forget the Waters family: they named their daughter Mineral, or the Castle family and their new son, Windsor. All these come from the Registrar in the British town of Stafford, whose list also includes children named Rheumatism and Fatso. But all these pale when compared to the couple in Sweden who want to name their son the following: Brfxxccxxmnpccclllmmnprxvclmnckssqlbb11116. (They pronounce it Albin.)

You can't spell it. It's hard to pronounce. Its vocabulary is immense; its grammar complex. Learning it as a second language is excruciating. Despite all these obstacles, English seems to be the language of choice for business, technology, and commerce all over the world. The alert traveler encounters English at every turn. Here, language expert Bill Bryson, author of The Mother Tongue: English and How It Got That Way, *reports that the language may be getting a bit jumbled in its foreign travels.*

A TASTE FOR SCRAMBLED ENGLISH

Bill Bryson

1   In Stockholm, there is a chain of fast-food restaurants where you can get, along with a risk of heartburn, what must rank as the ultimate in culinary oxymorons: a hamburger called a Mini Big.

2   If that sounds a trifle too indecisive for you, you may choose from such offerings as a Cheeseburgare, a Baconburgare, a Big Dream, or something called a Big Clock (which is what I plumped for and which is presumably so named because it tells you when it's time to stop eating it—after the second bite). All these names, you will notice, are in English, more or less. It appears that, in Sweden these days, as in the world generally, people not only increasingly speak English but also eat it.

3   And they wear it. Anyone who has traveled almost anywhere in the world in the past couple of years will have noticed that young people everywhere sport T-shirts, sweatshirts, and warm-up jackets bearing messages that are invariably (1) in English and (2) gloriously meaningless.

4   Recently in Hamburg I saw a young man in a bomber jacket that stated on its back: "Ful-O-Pep Laying Mash." In slightly smaller letters it added: "Made by Taverniti Oats Company Chicago USA 1091DS." In Tokyo, a correspondent for *The Economist* magazine sighted a T-shirt proclaiming: "O.D. on Bourgeoisie Milk Boy Milk." The words, one supposes, were chosen from an unabridged dictionary by a parrot with a stick in its mouth.

5   What is perhaps even more alarming is that these bewilderingly vague sentiments have begun appearing in the English-speaking world. In a store on Oxford Street in London, I saw a jacket, made in Britain, that announced in large letters: "Rodeo—100% Boys for Atomic Atlas."

6   What do these strange messages mean? Well, in the literal sense, nothing, of course. But in a more metaphoric way they do underscore the huge, almost compulsive, appeal of English in the world. It is an odd fact that almost everywhere on the planet products are deemed to be more appealing, and sentiments more powerful, if they are expressed in English—even if they make next to no sense.

7   I have before me a Japanese eraser that says: "Mr. Friendly Quality Eraser, Mr. Friendly Arrived!! • He always stay near you, and steals in your mind to lead you a good situation." It is a product made in Japan solely for Japanese consumers, yet there is not a word of Japanese on it. Coca-Cola cans in Japan come with the slogan "I Feel Coke & Sound Special." Until recently, a Japanese company called Cream Soda

marketed a whole range of products with the exquisitely ditzy slogan "Too old to die, too young to happy."

In Naples, there was a sporting goods store called Snoopy's Dribbling (the name becomes fractionally less alarming when you realize that *dribbling* is the British term for moving a soccer ball up and down a field). And two years ago in Brussels I saw a boutique where a sign in the window intriguingly offered "Sweat, 690 francs." Closer inspection revealed this to be merely a Belgian truncation of the English word *sweatshirt.* 8

This practice of taking English words and hacking away at them until they emerge as something more like native products is surprisingly widespread, particularly among the Japanese, who employ the same sort of ingenuity miniaturizing English words as they do in miniaturizing cameras and VCRs. In Japan, "word processor" becomes *wa-pro;* "personal computer" becomes *paso-kon;* "mass communications" metamorphoses into *masu-koml,* and "commercial" is unceremoniously shorn of its troublesome consonant clusters and shrunk to a terse *CM.* 9

Oftentimes this naturalization process leaves the English words all but unrecognizable, at least at first glance. It would take a sharp eye indeed to notice that *ajshrym, erebeta* and *kontaklinser* are, respectively, the Polish for "ice cream," the Japanese for "elevator," and the Swedish for "contact lenses." The champion of this dissembling process must surely be the Italian *schiacchenze,* which is simply a literal rendering of the English "shake hands," although, in Africa, the Swahili word for "traffic island," *kip-leftl* (literally "keep left"), runs a close second. 10

Sometimes English words are given not only new spellings but also entirely new meanings. In the last century, the Russians, for reasons that no one now seems quite sure of, took the name of an obscure London railroad station, Vauxhall, and made it their generic word for all railroad stations: *vokzal.* In much the same way, the Japanese word for a fashionably cut suit, *sebiro,* is a corruption of Savile Row, the London street where the finest suits are made. More recently, the French borrowed the English slang words *jerk* and *egghead,* but gave them largely contrary meanings— namely, an egghead in France is not a brainy person but a dimwit, while *jerk* is a term of praise for an accomplished dancer. 11

Occasionally, borrowers of English words use them to form the basis for entirely new words. The Japanese have lately appropriated the English word *mansion,* respelled it *manshon,* and used it to signify not a large single dwelling but a high-rise apartment building. But because the syllable *man* also means "ten thousand" in Japanese, they have coined a further word, *okushon,* based on the Japanese word for one hundred million (*oku*), because that implies even greater luxury. 12

This practice is more common than you might expect. The Germans, in particular, are adept at taking things a step further than it ever occurred to anyone in English. In Germany, a young person goes from being in his teens to being in his twens; a book that doesn't quite become a best seller is instead *ein steadyseller,* and a person who is more relaxed than another is *relaxter.* 13

A final curiosity of borrowing is that the words sometimes lose their emotional charge when conveyed overseas. The Dutch, most notably, have adopted an English 14 expletive far too coarse to reproduce here (though if I say "hits the fan" I expect you'll be with me again), but use it as a mild and largely meaningless epithet roughly equivalent to our "gosh" or "golly" or even just "hmmmm"—to such an extent, I'm told, that they must now take special care not to shock English-speaking visitors. Oddly enough, a century ago, we did much the same thing with a rude Dutch term, *pappekok,* which we Anglicized into the anodyne *poppycock.*

VOCABULARY

Directions: Locate each of the key words in the reading selection. Then read and study each word in its context and try to determine its meaning. Use a dictionary or thesaurus to check your guess. Write the meanings of the words in the margin of the text.

Record the new words you've learned below.

Key Word	Paragraph	Meaning
1. culinary	1	
2. deemed	6	
3. ditzy	7	
4. truncation	8	
5. obscure	11	
6. generic	11	
7. corruption	11	
8. adept	13	
Others?		

GUIDE QUESTIONS

Directions: The purpose of these guide questions is to ensure your understanding of what you have read. They also will help you to analyze and evaluate the author's ideas and apply them to the real world and your own life.

Write answers to the questions in your notebook or on a separate sheet of paper if your instructor wishes to collect them. Your answers will form the basis of class discussion.

1. Bryson gives several examples of English words and expressions that have popped up around the world. Pick out two or three examples; describe them and their context. Then try to explain their meanings.

2. a. Why do you think Bryson uses the word *gloriously* when he describes the messages on T-shirts, sweatshirts, and warm-up jackets (paragraph 3) as "gloriously meaningless"?
   b. How does Bryson say that the messages were probably chosen?
   c. How do *you* think they were chosen?

3. Why do you think the author says it is perhaps "even more alarming" that these bewilderingly vague messages have begun appearing in English-speaking countries?

4. According to Bryson, what do these strange messages mean in the literal sense? In the metaphoric sense?

5. Bryson describes three major ways English words are "borrowed" by speakers of other languages.
   a. List the three ways.
   b. Give one example of each of the three ways.

6. After reading and thinking about this essay, what conclusion can you draw about what might happen to English in the future?

APPLICATION

Directions: Bryson uses three important linguistic terms in his essay: 1) *oxymoron,* 2) *literal meaning,* 3) *metaphor.* Review the meanings of each of these terms. Prepare a list of several examples of each to share with your classmates to help ensure your understanding of the terms.

WRITING

Directions: Many people believe that English is fast becoming the world's language (if it isn't already). They feel that everyone will eventually speak some variety of English as a first, second, or third language. Based on what you read in the selection "A Taste for Scrambled English" and on your own knowledge and experience, what problems can you foresee with the spread of English as the universal language? Write at least one paragraph.

SHORT TAKE

IS ENGLISH BROKEN HERE?

Consider the English sentences below, written by persons with, to say the least, an imperfect command of the language. Can you "translate" these fractured sentences into comprehensible English?

- A warning to motorists by a Tokyo car-rental agency: "When a passenger of the foot heave in sight, tootle the horn. Trumpet at him melodiously at first, but if he still obstacles your passage, then tootle him with vigor."
- A sign in a Bangkok dry cleaning shop: "Drop your trousers here for best results."
- A sign at an Austrian ski resort: "Do not preambulate the corridors in the hours of repose in the boots of ascension."
- A hotel in Acapulco boasted: "The manager has personally passed all the water served here."
- A notice in a Norwegian cocktail lounge reads: "Ladies are requested not to have children in the bar."
- A doctor in Rome advertised his specialties as: "women and other diseases."
- An airline in Copenhagen promises to: "take your bags and send them in all directions."
- Instructions on a package of convenience food from Italy: "Besmear a backing pan, previously buttered with a good tomato sauce, and after, dispose the cannelloni, lightly distanced between them in a only couch."
- A sign in a Tokyo hotel: "It is forbidden to steal hotel towels please. If you are not a person to do such thing please not to read notice."
- A dentist in Hong Kong advertised tooth extractions: "using the latest Methodists."
- A hotel in Yugoslavia announced heartily: "The flattening of underwear with pleasure is the job of the chambermaid. Turn to her straightaway."
- Beware of a tailor on the Greek island of Rhodes who couldn't guarantee he could finish summer suits ordered by tourists: "Because is big rush we will execute customers in strict rotation."
- A laundry in Rome invites: "Ladies, leave your clothes here and spend the afternoon having a good time."
- A Swiss eatery warns: "Our wines leave you nothing to hope for."

Do you ever go to the rest room to rest? Or to the powder room to powder? And just how often do you take a bath when you make a trip to the bathroom? Did you know that in many parts of the southern United States people don't die? No, they pass away. Some even go to their reward. In other parts of the country, people just buy the farm or experience the end of the ball game. Shakespeare never said "die," his characters shuffled off this mortal coil. People who would be mortally ashamed to discuss being naked feel free to discuss their birthday suit, or being in the altogether. Aware of it or not, we all use euphemisms. Here, the author of Euphemisms and Other Doubletalk *introduces us to these "linguistic fig leaves and verbal flourishes for artful users of the English language."*

EUPHEMISMS

Hugh Rawson

Mr. Milquetoast gets up from the table, explaining that he has to go to the *little boys' room* or to *see a man about a dog;* a young woman announces that she is *enceinte*. A secretary complains that her boss is a pain in the *derriere;* an undertaker or *mortician* asks delicately where to ship the *loved one*. These are euphemisms—mild, agreeable, or roundabout words used in place of coarse, painful, or offensive ones. The term comes from the Greek *eu,* meaning "well" or "sounding good," and *pheme,* "speech."   1

Many euphemisms are so delightfully ridiculous that everyone laughs at them. (Well, almost everyone: The people who call themselves the National Selected Morticians usually manage to keep from smiling.) Yet euphemisms have very serious reasons for being. They conceal the things people fear the most—death, the dead, the supernatural. They cover up the facts of life—of sex and reproduction and excretion—which inevitably remind even the most refined people that they are made of clay, or worse. They are beloved by individuals and institutions (governments, especially) who are anxious to present only the handsomest possible images of themselves to the world. And they are embedded so deeply in our language that few of us, even those who pride themselves on being plain-spoken, ever get through a day without using them.   2

The same sophisticates who look down their noses at *little boys' room* and other euphemisms of that ilk will nevertheless say that they are going to the *bathroom* when no bath is intended; that Mary has been *sleeping* around even though she has been getting precious little shut-eye; that John has *passed away* or even *departed* (as if he'd just made the last train to Darien); and that Sam and Janet are *friends,* which sounds a lot better than "illicit lovers."   3

Thus, euphemisms are society's basic *lingua franca*. As such, they are outward and visible signs of our inward anxieties, conflicts, fears, and shames. They are like radioactive isotopes. By tracing them, it is possible to see what has been (and is) going on in our language, our minds, and our culture.   4

Euphemisms can be divided into two general types—positive and negative. The positive ones inflate and magnify, making the euphemized items seem altogether grander and more important than they really are. The negative euphemisms deflate and diminish. They are defensive in nature, off-setting the power of tabooed terms   5 and otherwise eradicating from the language everything that people prefer not to deal with directly.

6   Positive euphemisms include the many occupational titles, which salve the egos of workers by elevating their job status: *custodian* for janitor (itself a euphemism for caretaker), *counsel* for lawyer, the many kinds of *engineer* (*exterminating engineer, mattress engineer, publicity engineer*, ad infinitum), *help* for servant (itself an old euphemism for slave), *hooker* and *working girl* for whore, and so forth. A common approach is to try to turn one's trade into a profession, usually in imitation of the medical profession. *Beautician* and the aforementioned *mortician* are the classic examples, but the same imitative instinct is responsible for social workers calling welfare recipients *clients*, for football coaches conducting *clinics*, and for undertakers referring to corpses as *cases* or even *patients*.

7   Other kinds of positive euphemisms include personal honorifics such as *colonel*, the *honorable*, and *major*, and the many institutional euphemisms, which convert madhouses into *mental hospitals*, colleges into *universities*, and small business establishments into *emporiums, parlors, salons*, and *shoppes*. The desire to improve one's surroundings also is evident in geographical place names, most prominently in the case of the distinctly non-green *Greenland* (attributed to an early real-estate developer named Eric the Red), but also in the designation of many small burgs as *cities*, and in the names of some cities, such as *Troy*, New York (née Vanderheyden's Ferry, its name-change in 1789 began a fad for adopting classical place names in the United States).

8   Negative, defensive euphemisms are extremely ancient. It was the Greeks, for example, who transformed the Furies into the Eumenides (the "kindly ones"). In many cultures, it is forbidden to pronounce the name of God (hence, pious Jews say Adonai) or of Satan (giving rise to the *deuce*, the *good man*, the *great fellow*, the generalized *Devil*, and many other roundabouts). The names of the dead, and of animals that are hunted or feared, may also be euphemized this way. The bear is called *grandfather* by many peoples and the tiger is alluded to as the *striped one*. The common motivation seems to be a confusion between the names of things and the things themselves: The name is viewed as an extension of the thing. Thus, to know the name is to give one power over the thing (as in the Rumpelstiltskin story). But such power may be dangerous: "Speak of the Devil and he appears." For mere mortals, then, the safest policy is to use another name, usually a flattering, euphemistic one, in place of the supernatural being's true name.

9   As strong as—or stronger than—the taboos against names are the taboos against particular words, especially the infamous *four-letter words*. (According to a recent Supreme Court decision, the set of *four-letter words* actually contains some words with as few as three and as many as twelve letters, but the logic of Supreme Court decisions is not always immediately apparent). These words form part of the vocabulary of everyone above the age of six or seven. They are not slang terms, but legitimate Standard English of the oldest stock, and they are euphemized in many ways, typically by conversion into pseudo-Latin (e.g., *copulation, defecation, urination*) into slang (*make love, number two, pee*), or into socially acceptable dashes (*f—, s—, p—*, etc.). In the electronic media, the function of the dash is fulfilled by the *bleep*

(sometimes pronounced *blip*), which has completed the circle and found its way into print.

The taboo against words frequently degenerates into mere prudery. At least— 10 though the defensive principle is the same—the primitive (or *preliterate*) hunter's use of *grandfather* seems to operate on a more elemental level than the excessive modesty that has produced *abdomen* for belly, *afterpart* for ass, *bosom* for breast, *limb* for leg, *white meat* for breast (of a chicken), and so on.

When carried too far, which is what always seems to happen, positive and neg- 11 ative euphemisms tend finally to coalesce into an unappetizing mush of elegancies and genteelism, in which the underlying terms are hardly worth the trouble of euphemizing, i.e., *ablutions* for washing, *bender* for knee, *dentures* for false teeth, *expectorate* for spit, *home* for house, *honorarium* for fee, *ill* for sick, *libation* for drink, *perspire* for sweat, *position* for job, etc., etc., etc.

VOCABULARY

Directions: Locate each of the key words in the reading selection. Then read and study each word in its context and try to determine its meaning. Use a dictionary or thesaurus to check your guess. Write the meanings of the words in the margin of the text.

Record the new words you've learned.

Key Word	Paragraph	Meaning
1. *enceinte*	1	
2. ilk	3	
3. eradicating	5	
4. honorifics	7	
5. née	7	
6. infamous	9	
7. prudery	10	
8. coalesce	11	
Others?		

GUIDE QUESTIONS

Directions: The purpose of these guide questions is to ensure your understanding of what you have read. They also will help you to analyze and evaluate the author's ideas and apply them to the real world and your own life.

Write answers to the questions in your notebook or on a separate sheet of paper if your instructor wishes to collect them. Your answers will form the basis of class discussion.

1. Explain and give two examples of euphemisms.
2. Contrast the two types of euphemisms Rawson describes.
3. According to Rawson, what happens when the use of euphemisms is "carried too far"?
4. If you read the selection "Language" (p. 114), relate the use of euphemisms to the notion of confusing symbols (in this case, words) with the actual things they symbolize.
5. Rawson gives many examples of euphemisms, but he does not exhaust the subject. Money is one of the subjects we tend to disguise with euphemisms. In many cases it is considered poor taste to ask people about their financial affairs; we don't usually ask casual acquaintances, "How much is your salary?" Bill collectors often use indirect ways of asking for payment: "We beg to call your attention to what might be an oversight on your part," or "We would appreciate your early attention to this matter," instead of "Send us the money you owe!" Can you think of any other topics that we discuss using euphemisms?

APPLICATION

Directions: Working in pairs or in small groups, collect euphemisms. You will find ads from magazines, newspapers, radio, and TV especially rich sources of euphemisms, but you can easily find them in magazine and newspaper articles as well as in day-to-day conversations. Prepare the chart below with your collection of euphemisms.

Cite the source for each euphemism (for example, a real estate ad or a television commercial). Copy the euphemism into the appropriate column. Then write the word you think the euphemism replaces in the last column. An example is done for you.

Source	The Euphemism	The Word(s) the Euphemism Replaces
A memo from the CEO of my company.	It said: "We are forced by a downturn in the economy to downsize our work force."	It meant that they are going to fire a lot of us.

WRITING

Directions: Write a summary of the selection "Euphemisms." To review summary writing, turn to Appendix B. In this summary, you should include one or two examples of each of the key ideas in order to make the summary clear and complete.

SHORT TAKE

BREAK IT TO ME GENTLY. . . .

Writers know when they submit their work to publishers it is very likely to be rejected. Most American publishers simply return the manuscript along with a brief letter saying effectively, "Thanks, but no thanks." A Chinese journal of economics, however, found a way to say NO in an entirely new and marvelous way:

> *We have read your manuscript with boundless delight. If we were to publish your paper it would be impossible for us to publish any work of a lower standard. As it is unthinkable that, in the next thousand years, we shall see its equal, we are, to our regret, compelled to return your divine composition, and to beg you a thousand times to overlook our short sight and timidity.*

—cited in *The Times Diary,* July 9, 1982

Why do people use obscene language? Julianne Malveaux, an editor for Essence *maga-zine, says it is a result of "flabby thinking and speaking habits." And it hurts—not only the people it is used against but the users as well. In this article, Malveaux offers some good language advice for everyone, but especially for African Americans and other minorities who, she says, "suffer most from the use of dirty words."*

EAT THOSE DIRTY WORDS

Julianne Malveaux

1   "Sticks and stones will break my bones, but names will never hurt me," chant the kids on the playground to drown out one anothers' insults. But schoolyard truth is replaced by mother-wit when we move light years and long paces away from child-hood. Words can hurt as well as they can heal. A compliment can give confidence, and a stirring speech can spur us to new heights. "Yes, I can," has always been a powerful motivation.

2   If we acknowledge the power of positive thinking, we can't deny the damage done by negative talk. There are insults that bruise as easily as body blows, verbal attacks that sting as smartly as slaps. A person can flinch from a word as clearly as she recoils from a touch, or have a spirit as thoroughly broken by words as a body is broken by stones.

3   We wouldn't throw punches without second thoughts, but how many of us hurl words at one another without thinking? Some words just aren't fit for consump-tion. They've crept into our vocabularies because we've developed flabby thinking, and speaking, habits. But as we African Americans move into this last decade of the twentieth century, careless thinking and talking are the very last things we need. Maybe we should resolve to improve our vocabularies by following these guidelines:

- *Never say never,* especially when the "never" is used to dampen dreams or set unnecessary limitations. Louisiana State Senator Cleo Fields remembers the teacher who told him he would "never" be more than a mechanic. While he didn't accept her assessment as truth, he struggled to get beyond it. If you say you'll never do something, such as see the world or get a better job, you're probably right.

4   There are a host of other negatives like "never" that are used expressly to limit our possibilities—words such as *can't, don't,* or *won't.* Pay attention and train your language so you can keep your options open.

- *Cut the cussing.* If we want to communicate with others, we have to deal with the jarring force that our words have on them. The thing is, we can often make our point as emphatically by not cursing at all. For instance, you can make someone seem more slimy and dishonest when you call them a pre-varicator than when you call them a m-f-liar.

5   If you have trouble cutting your cussing, think of the literal meaning of your words, and ask yourself if you like what you're saying. Do you really want somebody

you can't stand to kiss any part of your anatomy? Is "f— you" an invitation, wishful thinking, or verbal laziness? Challenge yourself out of using language that makes every other word a curse word. Find a dictionary, a thesaurus, and a better set of adjectives!

- *Don't call me "nigger."* Just between us Black folks, the word *nigger* is often used as a term of endearment. As our society becomes more superficially integrated, others pick up the term because they hear us use it among ourselves. If we want other people to stop using this derisive slur, then we need to make sure we stop using it ourselves.

- *Eliminate "fighting words."* The Supreme Court says that ethnic slurs are fighting words, and with just cause. Just as we bristle at derisive descriptions of Black people, others get steamed about words like *chink, spic, faggot,* and *hymie.* Think about why you are using the word, what your biases are, and how you'd feel with the shoe on the other foot. Your ability to co-exist with other people, especially those of color—who with us will make up one-third of the nation in the next century—is limited by the words you use to describe them.

If we hone our verbal skills, we can say what we want to without saying the wrong thing. We can call it like we see it without saying "shit" or "damn." We don't have to say "nigger" to sound like a homegirl, or curse to get "down and dirty." If we acknowledge to ourselves the enormous power of verbal communications, we'll either learn to watch our mouths or be forced to eat the funky words we speak.

6

VOCABULARY

Directions: Locate each of the key words in the reading selection. Then read and study each word in its context and try to determine its meaning. Use a dictionary or thesaurus to check your guess. Write the meanings of the words in the margin of the text.

Record the new words you've learned here and on the next page.

Key Word	Paragraph	Meaning
1. flinch	2	
2. dampen	3	
3. prevaricator	4	
4. derisive	5	

Key Word	Paragraph	Meaning
5. slur	5	
6. hone	6	
Others?		

GUIDE QUESTIONS

Directions: The purpose of these guide questions is to ensure your understanding of what you have read. They also will help you to analyze and evaluate the author's ideas and apply them to the real world and your own life.

Write answers to the questions in your notebook or on a separate sheet of paper if your instructor wishes to collect them. Your answers will form the basis of class discussion.

1. State the main idea of the article.
2. a. What reason does Malveaux cite for letting bad words creep into our vocabulary?
   b. Do you agree with her? Or do you think there are other reasons?
3. a. List the guidelines Malveaux suggests for improving our vocabulary.
   b. Using your own words, explain each guideline.
4. What does the author mean when she says our society is becoming more "superficially" integrated? Why does she use the word *superficially?*

APPLICATION

Directions: Choose one of the assignments below.

1. In small groups, consider either Kiley Armstrong's "What's in a Name?" (p. 124) or Hugh Rawson's "Euphemisms," (p. 133) and discuss whether the author you chose would agree with Malveaux's thesis. Be sure to use evidence from the readings to support your opinion.
2. In small groups, discuss these questions: Are ethnic slurs and dirty words a serious problem as the author maintains? Do you use such language? Why or why not? How do you feel about other people who use it? Use the ideas you generate in your group to do the writing assignment below.

WRITING

Directions: React to Malveaux's thesis. Write at least 250 words. Your essay should answer the following questions: Do you think ethnic slurs and dirty words are a serious problem? Give some examples or evidence to support your answer. Do you use such language? Why or why not?

Writing is written language. The earliest writing we know of is called cuneiform, *which dates back to about 3500* B.C. *in the valley of the Tigris and Euphrates Rivers. Within the next five hundred years or so the Egyptians developed a picture-writing system called* hiero-glyphics. *Somewhere around 1800* B.C. *it is believed the Phoenicians developed a phonetic alphabet—one based on sounds. All the phonetic alphabets of history, including that of English, are based on this great invention. In the following essay, the author helps us imagine the beginnings of writing.*

Before you read "Symbols of Humankind," try to think of what prompted humans to invent writing.

1. *Why was spoken language insufficient for human needs? Think about the advantages that written language has over spoken language.*
2. *"Non-literate" societies (people who do not have a written language) still exist. Why do you suppose they have not developed writing?*
3. *Imagine how daily life would be if written language had never been developed. List some of the things you do each day that are completely dependent on writing.*

SYMBOLS OF HUMANKIND

Don Lago

Many thousands of years ago, a man quietly resting on a log reached down and picked up a stick and with it began scratching upon the sand at his feet. He moved the stick slowly back and forth and up and down, carefully guiding it through curves and straight lines. He gazed upon what he had made, and a gentle satisfaction lighted his face.   1

Other people noticed this man drawing on the sand. They gazed upon the figures he had made, and though they at once recognized the shapes of familiar things such as fish or birds or humans, they took a bit longer to realize what the man had meant to say by arranging these familiar shapes in this particular way. Understanding what he had done, they nodded or smiled in recognition.   2

This small band of humans didn't realize what they were beginning. The images these people left in the sand would soon be swept away by the wind, but their new idea would slowly grow until it had remade the human species. These people had discovered writing.   3

Writing, early people would learn, could contain much more information than human memory could and contain it more accurately. It could carry thoughts much farther than mere sounds could—farther in distance and in time. Profound thoughts born in a single mind could spread and endure.   4

The first written messages were simply pictures relating familiar objects in some meaningful way—pictographs. Yet there were no images for much that was important in human life. What, for instance, was the image for sorrow or bravery? So from pictographs humans developed ideograms to represent more abstract ideas. An eye flowing with tears could represent sorrow, and a man with the head of a lion might be bravery.   5

6   The next leap occurred when the figures became independent of things or ideas and came to stand for spoken sounds. Written figures were free to lose all resemblance to actual objects. Some societies developed syllabic systems of writing in which several hundred signs corresponded to several hundred spoken sounds. Others discovered the much simpler alphabetic system, in which a handful of signs represented the basic sounds the human voice can make.

7   At first, ideas flowed only slightly faster when written than they had through speech. But as technologies evolved, humans embodied their thoughts in new ways: through the printing press, in Morse code, in electromagnetic waves bouncing through the atmosphere, and in the binary language of computers.

8   Today, when the earth is covered with a swarming interchange of ideas, we are even trying to send our thoughts beyond our planet to other minds in the universe. Our first efforts at sending our thoughts beyond earth have taken a very ancient form: pictographs. The first message, on plaques aboard *Pioneer* spacecraft launched in 1972 and 1973, featured a simple line drawing of two humans, one male and one female, the male holding up his hand in greeting. Behind them was an outline of the *Pioneer* spacecraft, from which the size of the humans could be judged. The plaque also included the "address" of the two human figures: a picture of the solar system, with a spacecraft emerging from the third planet. Most exobiologists believe that when other civilizations attempt to communicate with us they too will use pictures.

9   All the accomplishments since humans first scribbled in the sand have led us back to where we began. Written language only works when two individuals know what the symbols mean. We can only return to the simplest form of symbol available and work from there. In interstellar communication, we are at the same stage our ancestors were when they used sticks to trace a few simple images in the sand.

10   We still hold their sticks in our hands and draw pictures with them. But the stick is no longer made of wood; over the ages that piece of wood has been transformed into a massive radio telescope. And we no longer scratch on sand; now we write our thoughts onto the emptiness of space itself.

VOCABULARY

Directions: Locate each of the key words in the reading selection. Then read and study each word in its context and try to determine its meaning. Use a dictionary or thesaurus to check your guess. Write the meanings of the words in the margin of the text.

Record the new words you've learned below and on the next page.

Key Word	Paragraph	Meaning
1. profound	4	
2. pictographs	5	
3. ideograms	5	

Key Word	Paragraph	Meaning
4. plaques	8	
5. interstellar	9	
Others?		

GUIDE QUESTIONS

Directions: The purpose of these guide questions is to ensure your understanding of what you have read. They also will help you to analyze and evaluate the author's ideas and apply them to the real world and your own life.

Write answers to the questions in your notebook or on a separate sheet of paper if your instructor wishes to collect them. Your answers will form the basis of class discussion.

1. Until humans invented writing, human societies relied upon an oral tradition to pass on their culture from one generation to the next. Older people told stories that explained their world and history to the children. What are some advantages that a system of writing has for humans?
2. Explain what Lago means when he says that the first systems of writing used *pictographs,* whereas more sophisticated writing systems developed *ideograms.* Be sure to explain the distinction the author makes between pictographs and ideograms.
3. Explain the next "leap" that occurred in the development of writing.
4. What kind of alphabetic system does English use: pictograph, ideogram, syllabic, or phonetic?
5. What new systems of writing have developed as technology has advanced?
6. Explain what the author means when he says, "All the accomplishments since humans first scribbled in the sand have led us back to where we began."

APPLICATION

1. Imagine you are the first person to use writing to communicate your thoughts. What would be the first ideas you would try to communicate to your fellow humans? Write the symbols you would use. Then write the same ideas in the writing system you use now.

2. Imagine again that you are one of the first people to use writing to communicate. What would you write to communicate the following ideas:

   a. fire
   b. stars
   c. snow
   d. happy
   e. fear
   f. Run! Danger!
   g. I'm hungry.
   h. I love my children.
   i. Meet me tomorrow at sunset.

   Did you find the last six ideas more difficult to represent than the first three? Explain why it is easier to write about a star than about love.

WRITING

Directions: Return to the questions in the introduction given above "Symbols of Humankind" on page 141. Think again about your answers. Then choose one of the questions and write one or two paragraphs in response.

Can you remember an experience that affected you so strongly that it changed the entire direction of your life? Here a writer describes a turning point in his life, when, he says "at the eleventh hour as it were, I had discovered a calling."

LEARNING TO WRITE

Russell Baker

When our class was assigned to Mr. Fleagle for third-year English I anticipated another grim year in that dreariest of subjects. Mr. Fleagle was notorious among City students for dullness and inability to inspire. He was said to be stuffy, dull, and hopelessly out of date. To me he looked to be sixty or seventy and prim to a fault. He wore primly severe eyeglasses, his wavy hair was primly cut and primly combed. He wore prim vested suits with neckties blocked primly against the collar buttons of his primly starched white shirts. He had a primly pointed jaw, a primly straight nose, and a prim manner of speaking that was so correct, so gentlemanly, that he seemed a comic antique.

I anticipated a listless, unfruitful year with Mr. Fleagle and for a long time was not disappointed. We read *Macbeth*. Mr. Fleagle loved *Macbeth* and wanted us to love it too, but he lacked the gift of infecting others with his own passion. He tried to convey the murderous ferocity of Lady Macbeth one day by reading aloud the passage that concludes

> . . . I have given suck, and know
> How tender 'tis to love the babe that milks me.
> I would, while it was smiling in my face,
> Have plucked my nipple from his boneless gums . . .

The idea of prim Mr. Fleagle plucking his nipple from boneless gums was too much for the class. We burst into gasps of irrepressible snickering. Mr. Fleagle stopped.

"There is nothing funny, boys, about giving suck to a babe. It is the very essence of motherhood, don't you see."

He constantly sprinkled his sentences with "don't you see." It wasn't a question but an exclamation of mild surprise at our ignorance. "Your pronoun needs an antecedent, don't you see," he would say, very primly. "The purpose of the Porter's scene, boys, is to provide comic relief from the horror, don't you see."

Late in the year we tackled the informal essay. "The essay, don't you see, is the . . ." My mind went numb. Of all forms of writing, none seemed so boring as the essay. Naturally we would have to write informal essays. Mr. Fleagle distributed a homework sheet offering us a choice of topics. None was quite so simpleminded as "What I Did on My Summer Vacation," but most seemed to be almost as dull. I took the list home and dawdled until the night before the essay was due. Sprawled on the sofa, I finally faced up to the grim task, took the list out of my notebook, and scanned it. The topic on which my eye stopped was "The Art of Eating Spaghetti."

This title produced an extraordinary sequence of mental images. Surging up out of the depths of memory came a vivid recollection of a night in Belleville when all of us were seated around the supper table—Uncle Allen, my mother, Uncle Charlie, Doris, Uncle Hal—and Aunt Pat served spaghetti for supper. Spaghetti was an exotic treat in those days. Neither Doris nor I had ever eaten spaghetti, and none of the adults had enough experience to be good at it. All the good humor of Uncle Allen's house reawoke in my mind as I recalled the laughing arguments we had that night about the socially respectable method for moving spaghetti from plate to mouth.

8   Suddenly I wanted to write about that, about the warmth and good feeling of it, but I wanted to put it down simply for my own joy, not for Mr. Fleagle. It was a moment I wanted to recapture and hold for myself. I wanted to relive the pleasure of an evening at New Street. To write it as I wanted, however, would violate all the rules of formal composition I'd learned in school, and Mr. Fleagle would surely give it a failing grade. Never mind. I would write something else for Mr. Fleagle after I had written this thing for myself.

9   When I finished it the night was half gone and there was no time left to compose a proper, respectable essay for Mr. Fleagle. There was no choice next morning but to turn in my private reminiscence of Belleville. Two days passed before Mr. Fleagle returned the graded papers, and he returned everyone's but mine. I was bracing myself for a command to report to Mr. Fleagle immediately after school for discipline when I saw him lift my paper from his desk and rap for the class's attention.

10   "Now, boys," he said, "I want to read you an essay. This is titled 'The Art of Eating Spaghetti.'"

11   And he started to read. My words! He was reading my words out loud to the entire class. What's more, the entire class was listening. Listening attentively. Then somebody laughed, then the entire class was laughing, and not in contempt and ridicule, but with openhearted enjoyment. Even Mr. Fleagle stopped two or three times to repress a small prim smile.

12   I did my best to avoid showing pleasure, but what I was feeling was pure ecstasy at this startling demonstration that my words had the power to make people laugh. In the eleventh grade, at the eleventh hour as it were, I had discovered a calling. It was the happiest moment of my entire school career. When Mr. Fleagle finished he put the final seal on my happiness by saying, "Now that, boys, is an essay, don't you see. It's—don't you see—it's the very essence of the essay, don't you see. Congratulations, Mr. Baker."

VOCABULARY

Directions: Locate each of the key words in the reading selection. Then read and study each word in its context and try to determine its meaning. Use a dictionary or thesaurus to check your guess. Write the meanings of the words in the margin of the text.

Record the new words you've learned below and on the next page.

Key Word	Paragraph	Meaning
1. grim		
2. prim		

Key Word	Paragraph	Meaning
3. listless	2	*without interest*
4. dawdled	6	*to waste time*
✱ 5. reminiscence	9	*remembrance memory*
6. ecstasy	12	*a feeling of very great joy*
✱ 7. calling	12	*vocation, professional interest*
Others?		

Dreariest   *+ very gloomy*

✱ *Snickering*

GUIDE QUESTIONS

Directions: The purpose of these guide questions is to ensure your understanding of what you have read. They also will help you to analyze and evaluate the author's ideas and apply them to the real world and your own life.

Write answers to the questions in your notebook or on a separate sheet of paper if your instructor wishes to collect them. Your answers will form the basis of class discussion.

1. a. In describing Mr. Fleagle, Baker uses the word *prim* over and over again. Surely you have been taught by your writing teachers not to constantly repeat words in your essays. Why does Baker do it here? What effect does it have on the reader?
   b. What other words or phrases are repeated in the story?
2. Describe your impression of Mr. Fleagle at the beginning of the story. Does your opinion of him change by the end? Explain.
3. When Mr. Fleagle first assigns the informal essay, Baker dreads having to write it. What makes him change his mind and get excited about writing an essay?
4. What does Baker mean when he says in the last paragraph "In the eleventh grade, at the eleventh hour as it were, I had discovered a calling"? Have you experienced a similar moment?

APPLICATION

Directions: Read the story below about the great Russian writer Anton Chekhov.

Chekhov told the story of a kitten that was given to his uncle. Wanting to make a champion mouse-killer of the kitten, the uncle set out to train it when it was still very young. First he showed the kitten a live mouse in a cage. The kitten inspected the mouse curiously but without any hostility. The uncle, wanting the kitten to know the mouse was its enemy, slapped and scolded the kitten and sent it away in disgrace. The next day the uncle again showed the mouse to the kitten. This time the kitten looked at the mouse fearfully, but still did not show any signs of attack. Again the uncle slapped and scolded the kitten and sent it away. Day after day, the training went on until the kitten would begin to scream and cry the moment it saw the mouse. The uncle became furious and gave away the kitten, saying it would never learn. He did not realize that the kitten had indeed learned exactly what it had been taught. "I can sympathize with that kitten," said Chekhov, "because that same uncle tried to teach me Latin."

Describe your experience learning to write in elementary and high school. Was it similar to Russell Baker's experience? Or more like the experience of the kitten in Chekhov's story? Write one paragraph.

WRITING

Directions: Write one or two paragraphs describing, as Baker does in his story, "the happiest moment of my entire school career."

Do you groan aloud when faced with the prospect of writing a personal letter? Does it seem like a burden and a chore? Or a pleasant opportunity to express yourself to a friend in a relaxed way? Why write a letter these days when it's so easy to pick up the telephone? How are letters and phone calls different? Would you rather have a call from an old friend or receive a letter? Garrison Keillor, the popular radio show host and writer, gives us some delightful insights on the value of letter writing, and some practical hints on how to write a good letter—"to be our own sweet selves, and express the music of our souls."

HOW TO WRITE A PERSONAL LETTER

Garrison Keillor

We shy persons need to write a letter now and then, or else we'll dry up and blow away. It's true. And I speak as one who loves to reach for the phone, dial the number, and talk. I say "Big Bopper here—what's shakin', babes?" The telephone is to shyness what Hawaii is to February, it's a way out of the woods, and yet: a letter is better.   1

Such a sweet gift—a piece of handmade writing, in an envelope that is not a bill, sitting in our friend's path when she trudges home from a long day spent among wahoos and savages, a day our words will help repair. They don't need to be immortal, just sincere. She can read them twice and again tomorrow: *You're someone I care about, Corinne, and think of often and every time I do you make me smile.*   2

We need to write, otherwise nobody will know who we are. They will have only a vague impression of us as A Nice Person, because frankly, we don't shine at conversation, we lack the confidence to thrust our faces forward and say, "Hi, I'm Heather Hooten, let me tell you about my week." Mostly we say "Uh-huh" and "Oh really." People smile and look over our shoulder, looking for someone else to talk to.   3

So a shy person sits down and writes a letter. To be known by another person—to meet and talk freely on the page—to be close despite distance. To escape from anonymity and be our own sweet selves and express the music of our souls.   4

Same thing that moves a giant rock star to sing his heart out in front of 123,000 people moves us to take ballpoint pen in hand and write a few lines to our dear Aunt Eleanor. *We want to be known.* We want her to know that we have fallen in love, that we quit our job, that we're moving to New York, and we want to say a few things that might not get said in casual conversation: *thank you for what you've meant to me, I am very happy right now.*   5

Skip the Guilt

The first step in writing letters is to get over the guilt of *not* writing. You don't "owe" anybody a letter. Letters are a gift. The burning shame you feel when you see unanswered mail makes it harder to pick up a pen and makes for a cheerless letter when you finally do. *I feel bad about not writing, but I've been so busy,* etc. Skip this. Few letters are obligatory, and they are *Thanks for the wonderful gift* and *I am terribly sorry to hear about George's death,* and *Yes, you're welcome to stay with us next month,* and not many more than that. Write those promptly if you want to keep your friends. Don't worry about the others, except love letters, of course. When your   6 true love writes *Dear Light of My Life, Joy of My Heart, O Lovely Pulsating Core of My Sensate Life,* some response is called for.

7   Some of the best letters are tossed off in a burst of inspiration, so keep your writing stuff in one place where you can sit down for a few minutes and *Dear Ray, I am in the middle of an essay for* International Paper *but thought I'd drop you a line. Hi to your sweetie too* dash off a note to a pal. Envelopes, stamps, address book, everything in a drawer so you can write fast when the pen is hot.

8   A blank white 8″ by 11″ sheet can look as big as Montana if the pen's not so hot— try a smaller page and write boldly. Or use a note card with a piece of fine art on the front; if your letter ain't good, at least they get the Matisse. Get a pen that makes a sensuous line, get a comfortable typewriter, a friendly word processor—whichever feels easy to the hand.

9   Sit for a few minutes with the blank sheet in front of you, and meditate on the person you will write to, let your friend come to mind until you can almost see her or him in the room with you. Remember the last time you saw each other and how your friend looked and what you said and what perhaps was unsaid between you, and when your friend becomes real to you, start to write.

Tell Us What You're Doing

10   Write the salutation—*Dear You*—and take a deep breath and plunge in. A simple declarative sentence will do, followed by another and another and another. Tell us what you're doing and tell it like you were talking to us. Don't think about grammar, don't think about lit'ry style, don't try to write dramatically, just give us your news. Where did you go? who did you see, what did they say, what do you think?

11   If you don't know where to begin, start with the present moment: *I'm sitting at the kitchen table on a rainy Saturday morning. Everyone is gone and the house is quiet.* Let your simple description of the present moment lead to something else, let the letter drift gently along.

Take It Easy

12   The toughest letter to crank out is one that is meant to impress, as we all know from writing job applications; if it's hard work to slip off a letter to a friend, maybe you're trying too hard to be terrific. A letter is only a report to someone who already likes you for reasons other than your brilliance. Take it easy.

13   Don't worry about form. It's not a term paper. When you come to the end of one episode, just start a new paragraph. You can go from a few lines about the sad state of rock 'n' roll to the fight with your mother to your fond memories of Mexico to your cat's urinary-tract infection to a few thoughts on personal indebtedness to the kitchen sink and what's in it. The more you write, the easier it gets, and when you have a True True Friend to write to, a *compadre,* a soul sibling, then it's like driving a car down a country road, you just get behind the keyboard and press on the gas.

14   Don't tear up the page and start over when you write a bad line—try to write your way out of it. Make mistakes and plunge on. Let the letter cook along and let yourself be bold. Outrage, confusion, love—whatever is in your mind, let it find a way to the page. Writing is a means of discovery, always, and when you come to the

end and write *Yours ever* or *Hugs and Kisses,* you'll know something you didn't when you wrote *Dear Pal.*

An Object of Art

Probably your friend will put your letter away, and it'll be read again a few years from now—and it will improve with age. 15

And forty years from now, your friend's grandkids will dig it out of the attic and read it, a sweet and precious relic of the ancient Nineties that gives them a sudden clear glimpse of you and her and the world we old-timers knew. You will then have created an object of art. Your simple lines about where you went, who you saw, what they said, will speak to those children and they will feel in their hearts the humanity of our times. 16

You can't pick up a phone and call the future and tell them about our times. You have to pick up a piece of paper. 17

VOCABULARY

Directions: Locate each of the key words in the reading selection. Then read and study each word in its context and try to determine its meaning. Use a dictionary or thesaurus to check your guess. Write the meanings of the words in the margin of the text.

Record the new words you've learned.

Key Word	Paragraph	Meaning
1. trudges	2	
2. anonymity	4	
3. sensuous	8	
4. relic	16	
Others?		

GUIDE QUESTIONS

Directions: These questions will guide your understanding of what you have read. Write your answers in your notebook or on a separate sheet of paper if your instructor wishes to collect it. Your answers to these questions will be the basis of class discussion.

1. Garrison Keillor is probably America's best-known "shy person." Yet it seems that making a phone call or writing a letter is a pleasure for him. Why do you think that is true? If you are also a shy person, do you feel the same way that Keillor does about phoning and writing?
2. What does Keillor mean when he says in paragraph 8, "if your letter ain't good, at least they get the Matisse." Your answer must, of course, identify Matisse.
3. Summarize the hints Keillor gives for writing a good letter.
4. Look back over the selection. Note the many words that are printed in italic type. Italics are often used for emphasis, as in paragraph 5, where Keillor says with feeling, "*We want to be known.*" But why are italics used in other places, for example in paragraph 11, "*I'm sitting at the kitchen table . . .*"?

APPLICATION

Directions: In a small group, compare and contrast writing a letter to making a phone call. Discuss the advantages and disadvantages of each. Use the chart below to organize your ideas.

	Letters	Phone Calls
Advantages		
Disadvantages		

WRITING

Directions: Choose one of the following assignments.

1. Write a letter to a friend you haven't seen for a long time. Use the advice Keillor gives you in this selection. At the end of the letter, write a paragraph describing how the advice helped you.
2. Using the advice Keillor gives in this essay, write a letter to one of your instructors. In your letter ask any questions you may have about any of the topics in the course, the course itself or school in general. You may have some comments you would like to express to the instructor that you prefer to do in writing rather than in person—use this letter as your opportunity to speak your mind. Your letter should be at least one page, preferably typewritten.

Who would believe that a black South African boy so poor his family often had nothing to eat, who did not learn English until he was ten, who attended schools under the poorest possible conditions, would go on to graduate from an American university and write a best-selling novel? Here, Mark Mathabane, the author of Kaffir Boy, *tells how writing helped him to survive and to heal himself.*

KAFFIR BOY AT THE TYPEWRITER
Determination and a Creative Gift Offer a Rescue from Hell

Mark Mathabane

I was born and raised in Alexandra township, a squalid one-square-mile ghetto just outside Johannesburg, South Africa, with a population of more than 150,000 blacks. The eldest of seven children—two boys and five girls—I lived with my parents and siblings in a shack made of crumbling bricks and rusted sheets of metal zinks. The shack measured roughly 15 × 15 feet. Till I was ten, my siblings and I slept on pieces of cardboard under the kitchen table. During the bitterly cold months of June and July my mother reinforced our flimsy blanket with pieces of old newspapers. My father, whose self-taught skills as a carpenter the Job Discrimination Act (an apartheid law) refused to recognize, earned about $10 a week as a menial laborer. He was often arrested for the "crime" of being unemployed.   1

Whenever my father was carted away to prison, the family, to stay alive, scavenged for half-eaten sandwiches thrown away by whites at the garbage dump. Sometimes we ate leech-like worms called *sonjas* or begged at the local abattoir for cattle blood, which we boiled as soup. During good times, our diet consisted mostly of cornmeal, chicken feet and heads, cattle intestines and greens. There were many days when nothing was available to eat, and we would simply stare at each other, at the empty pots, and at the sun going down.   2

My mother attempted to still our pangs of hunger with her mesmerizing storytelling. Her stories about black culture, traditions, magic, and heroes and heroines were the only books we had. By sharpening my sensibilities and firing my curiosity and imagination, these stories, almost Homeric in their vividness, drama, and invention, became the seeds of my own creativity.   3

To force blacks to leave Alexandra and move to their respective homelands—arid and impoverished reservations run by ruthless and corrupt tribal leaders—the government ordered the local *Peri-Urban* police to raid the ghetto frequently, making random arrests for Influx Control infractions. Under these Kafkaesque laws, my parents had to have a permit allowing them to live together as husband and wife under the same roof. They couldn't get it. So as a child I was awakened almost daily by brutal midnight police raids, which were launched amid a pandemonium of blaring sirens, barking dogs, and thumping feet. I would watch in horror as my parents were marched naked out of bed and interrogated in the middle of the shack.   4

Though illiterate, my mother, a woman of indomitable faith, courage, and love,   5
believed that an education might rescue me from the pit of poverty, suffering, and

degradation into which I was born, and for all intents and purposes, into which I was expected to die. The black educational system, known as *Bantu Education,* was designed in the '50s by Dr. H. Verwoerd, a fanatical believer in apartheid. It was meant to reconcile us black children to our subjection and the status quo, to keep us ignorant of our fundamental rights as human beings, and to make us better servants of whites. That is why, on June 16, 1976, black students revolted against it.

6   My father was vehemently opposed to *Bantu Education*—partly because he felt that it strained his meager wages at a time when survival was first priority; partly because he saw many educated blacks working at menial jobs. It was left to my mother to struggle almost singlehandedly to have me educated. Since black education was not free or compulsory, it took her nearly six months to obtain the birth certificate and permits necessary to enroll me in the local tribal school, which I refused to attend. On my first day of school, she and my grandmother had to literally bind me and drag me to school for the boys on the streets had told me horror stories about teachers beating pupils for lacking books, uniforms, or school fees. My mother used food money to purchase me a slate and uniform, and to pay my school fees. This infuriated my father, who then beat my mother. Witnessing my mother's abuse made me pledge to her that I would go to school for as long as she wanted me to, despite the hardships of black education. Through discipline, drive, and respect for teachers, I soon became the top student.

7   I began learning English, my fifth language, when I was about ten. When I was eleven, my grandmother—who worked for a white family that didn't believe in apartheid—took me to the white world for the first time in my life. I remember gaping with amazement at the large, beautiful homes with neat lawns and beds of flowers, the many stores, the paved roads, the many cars, the neatly dressed and happy-looking white schoolchildren, the tennis courts and swimming pools. *Why is life for whites paradisiacal and for blacks hellish?* I began asking. Granny's employer began giving me books that were only read in white schools. These "revolutionary" books—*Treasure Island, David Copperfield,* and other classics—changed my life. They convinced me that there was a world beyond that of the violence, poverty, and suffering in which I was steeped. They helped emancipate me from mental slavery and taught me to believe in my own worth and abilities, despite apartheid's attempts to limit my aspirations and prescribe my place in life.

8   When I was around thirteen, I began working for Granny's employer on weekends. I mowed the lawn, washed cars, cleaned the pool, polished brass and silver and shoes, and swept the driveway. One day I was given a slightly warped tennis racket as extra payment for a day's work well done.

9   I took the racket back to the ghetto and began pounding balls against the wall at the local stadium where there were a couple sand courts. In November 1973, nearly a year after I took up tennis, Arthur Ashe was finally allowed to set foot on South African soil. Before that he had been *persona non grata* because of his harsh criticism of apartheid. Like all black children in South Africa, I idolized black American athletes and entertainers, who, we assumed, were typical of blacks in America. I went to see Ashe play in Johannesburg, and he became my first positive role model. He was the first free black man I had ever seen. His intelligence, brilliant tennis skills, and confidence before whites filled me with a desire to come to America.

I realized that dream in 1977 when I met 1972 Wimbledon champion Stan Smith   10
and his wife, Margie, during a tournament in which I was the only black playing. After listening to my life story, and my desire to attend college in America, Stan and
Margie agreed to help. Upon returning to the States, Stan contacted college tennis
coaches on my behalf. In the fall of 1978, I finally left South Africa on a full tennis
scholarship to Limestone College in South Carolina.

Once in America, I realized how unrealistic my dream of becoming a profes-   11
sional athlete was. I began emphasizing my education. Culture shock, my refusal to allow coaches to exploit my athletic abilities at the expense of my education, and my
desire to express my individuality rather than conform and blindly follow custom and
authority, all combined to force me to transfer colleges three times, during which
time I lost my scholarship and was supported by Stan Smith.

Shortly after transferring to Dowling College, my fourth school, I volunteered   12
to become the first black editor of the college paper, even though I couldn't yet
type properly. In life I have always taken risks. Working on the paper convinced me
that, as my favorite novelist, Joseph Conrad, said, "The right accent and the right
word can move the world." And his incredible story of not learning English until he
was in his twenties, and of not writing a word until he was in his late thirties, inspired me to begin *Kaffir Boy,* especially since, a year earlier, I had become infected
by the fiery eloquence of Richard Wright, and longed to write about black life in
South Africa the way he wrote about black life in the South.

When I began writing *Kaffir Boy* one snowy winter morning during my junior   13
year, when I was twenty-one, I hardly dreamed that my story would become a nationwide bestseller, reaching #1 on *The Washington Post* bestseller list and #3 on *The
New York Times* list. I did not even think it would get published.

Many who heard that I was writing a book dismissed my attempt as futile. Some   14
thought I was crazy. But I was undeterred. I was determined to prove them wrong.
Though there were times when I despaired, when I thought of giving up, writing
down the experiences that had once haunted me—the night I witnessed a grisly
murder, the day I attempted suicide at age ten, the morning my mother and I discovered a dead baby while scavenging for food at the garbage dump (black mothers
were sometimes driven to kill their babies so they would not lose their jobs)—gave
me a feeling of being purged. I was finally able to fully accept who I was and where I
came from. In short, I wrote to heal myself as well as inform others.

After graduating from Dowling College with a degree in economics, I wanted   15
nothing more than to complete writing *Kaffir Boy.* I approached Stan Smith with the
idea and he agreed to support me for a year while I completed the book (under immigration laws, I wasn't allowed to work at the time). During this year of writing con-
tinuously, I was occasionally asked to speak publicly about my years in South Africa.

One day Oprah Winfrey saw the paperback version of *Kaffir Boy* prominently   16
displayed in a bookstore. She bought a copy. She was so moved by the story that
she tracked me down and offered me an appearance on her show. When she
learned that I had been separated from my family for nearly nine years, she helped
bring several members to America. Our reunion on *Oprah* made nationwide headlines. Shortly thereafter the book became a bestseller in paperback, with more than
200,000 copies in print. It is required reading in many high schools across the nation.

Most readers of *Kaffir Boy* wanted to know what happened to me and my family after I left South Africa in 1978. The results of those requests is *Kaffir Boy in America,* which was published in June [1989].

17   My advice to aspiring writers is never lose hope—keep writing and believing in yourself despite the rejection slips, despite what others may say. Something within compelled me to begin writing my book—an inner voice yearning to be heard; a need to understand myself and come to terms with my past; a longing to show the rest of the world the deplorable truths, in human terms, about the system of legalized segregation and racial discrimination in my homeland. Above all, I wanted to record how, through the support of my family, through clinging to the positive values I was taught when a child, through believing that education was a powerful weapon of hope, and through a determination never to give up the struggle to influence my own destiny, I was able to survive the raging hell of the ghetto with my soul and dignity largely intact.

VOCABULARY

Directions: Locate each of the key words in the reading selection. Then read and study each word in its context and try to determine its meaning. Use a dictionary or thesaurus to check your guess. Write the meanings of the words in the margin of the text.

Record the new words you've learned below and on the next page.

Key Word	Paragraph	Meaning
1. squalid	1	
2. scavenged	2	
3. mesmerizing	3	
4. pandemonium	4	
5. indomitable	5	
6. vehemently	6	
7. emancipate	7	
8. warped	8	
9. *persona non grata*	9	
10. eloquence	12	

Key Word	Paragraph	Meaning
11. deplorable	17	

Others?

GUIDE QUESTIONS

Directions: The purpose of these guide questions is to ensure your understanding of what you have read. They also will help you to analyze and evaluate the author's ideas and apply them to the real world and your own life.

Write answers to the questions in your notebook or on a separate sheet of paper if your instructor wishes to collect them. Your answers will form the basis of class discussion.

1. Synthesize the information in the story with what you already know about South Africa and its system of apartheid. Paint a picture in words of life in South Africa for black people in the 1970s when Mathabane was growing up.
2. Describe the factors that helped Mathabane rise above what he describes as the "hell" of life in South Africa to become a success.
3. Mathabane describes such books as *Treasure Island* and *David Copperfield* as "revolutionary." Are these books considered "revolutionary" in the United States? Why do you think South Africa considered them "revolutionary"?
4. Mathabane tells us that entertainers and athletes like tennis star Arthur Ashe were assumed to be "typical of blacks in America." Why do you think he believed this? Was it true? Explain.
5. Mathabane says he wrote "to heal myself as well as to inform others." What does he mean by this?

APPLICATION

Directions: Mathabane makes allusions to several important writers in his story: Homer (in paragraph 3); Franz Kafka (in paragraph 4); Joseph Conrad (in paragraph 12); and Richard Wright (in paragraph 12). If you are not familiar with these men and their work, visit the library to learn about them. In small groups, discuss who they were and the importance of their work.

WRITING

Directions: Does Mathabane's notion of the value of writing ring true to you? Can you imagine using writing to help yourself feel better? One study showed that college students who spent time writing about their thoughts and experiences had more positive feelings about school and fewer visits to the infirmary. Other studies found that writing can help people recover from personal tragedy. James Pennebaker, a professor of psychology at Southern Methodist University says that "The act of writing helps label and organize stressful events, making them seem more manageable." Have you ever tried it? If you have, write a paragraph or two describing the experience and how you benefited from it.

If you have never tried it, try it now. Think about a problem you are currently struggling with. Write it down, describing it in detail. Then write as many possible solutions as you can to the problem. In your last few sentences, state whether this exercise helped you begin to solve the problem or made you feel better.

SHORT TAKE

SPEAKING DIFFERENT LANGUAGES

Deborah Tannen

An American woman set out for a vacation cruise and landed in a Turkish prison. Reading her book *Never Pass This Way Again,* I could see that Gene LePere's ordeal was an extreme example of the disastrous consequences that can result from cross-cultural differences in what I term conversational style—ways of framing how you mean what you say, and what you think you are doing when you say it. LePere's experience also illustrates, in an unusually dramatic way, the dangers of trying to avoid conflict and say "no" in a polite way.

LePere left her cruise ship for a brief tour of ancient ruins in Turkey. At an archeological site, she fell behind her group as she became absorbed in admiring the ruins. Suddenly, her path was blocked by a man selling artifacts she had no interest in buying. Yet she found herself holding a stone head, and when she told him politely that she did not want it, he would not take it back. Instead, he thrust forward another one, which she also automatically accepted. Since the man would not take either head back, the only path to escape she could envision was offering to buy them. She cut his price in half and hoped he'd refuse so she could move on. Instead he agreed to drop the price, and she dropped the two heads into her tote. But as she handed him the money, he handed her a third head. Once more she insisted she did not want it, but he just stepped back to avoid repossessing it. Seeing no alternative, she paid for the third head and stalked off— shaken and angry. When LePere tried to reboard her cruise ship, she showed her purchases to customs officials, who had her arrested and thrown into jail for trying to smuggle out a national treasure. The third head was a genuine antiquity.

Having lived in Greece and observed the verbal art of bargaining, I could see that talking to the vendor and saying she did not want the artifacts would mean to him that she might want them if the price were lower. If she really had no intention of buying, she would not have talked to him at all. She would have pushed her way past him and walked on, never establishing eye contact—and surely not taking possession of any heads, no matter how insistently he proffered them. Each time she accepted a head, he received evidence of her interest and encouragement to offer another. Each step in his increasingly aggressive sales pitch was a response to what likely appeared to him as her bargaining maneuvers. Refusing to look at or talk to him, or, as a last resort, placing the heads on the ground—these were unthinkable alternatives for a polite American woman.

COLLABORATIVE LEARNING

WORKING IN GROUPS TO GUIDE YOUR OWN READING

Along with each of the reading selections in this unit, you were provided with questions and exercises to guide your understanding of the text. However, in most of your college reading you will not be given exercises to help you understand vocabulary or questions that guide your understanding of a textbook chapter. You will be expected to master the material on your own.

Research has shown that one of the most effective ways to study is in groups—working with classmates to master the material of a college course. The give-and-take that comes naturally when working with other people helps us to avoid falling into bad habits like *passive reading*. (We have all had this experience: reading a whole chapter, then realizing that we don't remember one single thing we read.) Working with other students will help you avoid such problems. For this assignment, form groups of four to six students. In your group you will consider the two following reading selections, "Why Spanish Translations?" by Mauricio Molina and "Rx: Translation Please?" by Perri Klass. You will create your own vocabulary chart, guide questions, an application exercise, and a writing assignment for the reading selections.

Follow these steps to complete this assignment.

1. Preview the selection before you read—look at and think about the title, the headings, the first paragraph, the last paragraph, and the first sentence of each paragraph.
2. Read through the selection one time quickly.
3. Read the selection carefully a second time; this time mark the pages. Underline words you want to look up and ideas you think are important. Put a question mark next to things you don't understand and want to discuss with your group members or your instructor. Ask yourself questions as you read along and try to find the answers to your questions.
4. Brainstorm with your group. Ask yourselves: What important issues is the author discussing? What new information did you learn? Can the issues discussed in the selection be connected to those you have studied in earlier lessons? Can any of the information here be applied to situations in your own life?
5. Now, *create* a set of exercises similar to those you have completed in previous chapters:
   a. *Vocabulary*. Make a list of key vocabulary words from the text. Set them up in chart format as on page 117.
   b. *Guide questions*. Write questions that will guide understanding of the major ideas in the reading.
   c. *Application*. Prepare an application exercise that takes one or more of the important ideas in the reading and relates them to real life.
   d. *Writing*. Prepare a writing assignment to conclude the chapter.

Before you begin, it would be a good idea to review the questions and exercises included in the previous reading selections for reference.

When you are finished, submit your work to your instructor for review. Your instructor may review and combine the work of all the groups and return the exercises to the class. You will then have the opportunity to *answer* the questions you and your classmates have developed.

Now, use your skills as an active independent reader to tackle the following reading selections. Good luck!

When Mauricio Molina arrived in the United States in 1960, he immediately set out to learn English and learn it well. He believed he would not "thrive" in his new country if he did not master its language. Now, many years later, he wonders if he was right.

WHY SPANISH TRANSLATIONS?

Mauricio Molina

1   I was naive twenty years ago. I say this because I came here from Central America and readily accepted what my parents told me. What they told me was that if I wanted to thrive here I had better learn English. English, it seems, was the language that people spoke in this country. In my innocence and naiveté, however, it never occurred to me that I really didn't have to. I can see now that I could have refused.

2   Yes, English is the language of the United States. But if it is, why can I take the written part of my driver's license test in Spanish? If it is, why are businesses forced to provide Spanish translations of practically every blank credit application or contract agreement? And not just businesses—government offices must also have quite a number of Spanish translations for those who want them.

3   Clearly, my old language did not get left behind. Don't misunderstand; this is real nice. It allows me to luxuriate in the knowledge, sweet indeed, that I am privileged. Without a doubt this is the land of opportunity. And I know it. But for those of us whom people call "Hispanics," it's a little bit more. It's the land where opportunity itself is served and seasoned as if this were the old country.

4   How stupid you must think me for complaining! Should we not simply take the opportunity and run? Why complain? Complaining may only spoil the fun for those among us who don't want to learn English.

5   But I choose to complain. I do it because questions nag at me. For instance, just who are those people for whom the Spanish translations are provided? It's a good guess that they're not Chinese, or French, or Serbo-Croatian. Of course, we know them already as "Hispanics." But what in the world does this mean?

6   A Hispanic is someone who came, or whose ancestors came, from a region where Spanish is the only language spoken. Nothing more. Racially, a Hispanic may be anything. It's a mistake to say *Hispanic* and mean by the term a black Cuban just as much as it would puzzle a Chilean named O'Hara.

7   As to who precisely among Hispanics has a need for the Spanish translations, I can't tell yet for sure. If you'll follow me a bit, though, we may together unravel this puzzle and learn something.

8   I would divide Hispanics living in the United States into two groups: those who were born in this country and those who came from elsewhere. It is easy to see that a number of individuals in the latter group, people who perhaps knew no English when they arrived, may have linguistic problems here. Logically, some among them may have need of Spanish translations.

9   The first group I mentioned, made up of people born and reared here, should have no need of any translations, right? Well, not exactly. I'm told that many among them know English very poorly, if at all. So of course they need the help. But here I

hope you'll forgive me if I pause to say that I think this is a very strange thing. I mean, isn't it odd in this day and age that people born right here in the United States may not somehow have mastered English?

Who, then, are the translations meant for? Ah, you probably guessed it by now. They're meant for a goodly cross-section of Hispanics—average, reasonably healthy and intelligent children and adults.   10

I regard these translations as a waste of effort and money. To me they consti-   11 tute a largesse of opportunity totally lacking a logical foundation. And what is the "logic" behind them? The answer I get is that these people are favored so that they may not suffer, because of their handicap, a diminution of their constitutional rights. The thing isn't done out of kindness, but simply out of a sense of fair play.

Fair play? I think not. Unfairness would be to deny these people the opportu-   12 nity to learn English. But the question is, are they being denied? From where I live I couldn't throw a rock out the window without risking severe injury to a number of English teachers. And at various places nearby—YMCAs, colleges, high schools, grammar schools, convention halls—English courses are available for the foreign-born or anyone else who needs them. That, ladies and gentlemen, is opportunity. It's there, but it won't pull you by the nose.

This country has been, is, and, I pray, will continue to be, the land of opportu-   13 nity. It has never been a place where the lazy came to be coddled. It has never been a haven for those who would not look out for their needs.

What do I think should be done? I think that no Spanish translations should   14 be made of anything. Except for one. Spanish translations should be made, and distributed widely, detailing the availability of English courses throughout Hispanic communities.

What if people don't bother to attend? Well, it's a free country.   15

VOCABULARY

Directions: Mark any important words in the reading selection that you don't know. Then list them in the chart below along with their paragraph numbers. Try to figure out each word's meaning by reading over the context carefully for clues to help you guess the meaning of the unfamiliar word. Check your dictionary or thesaurus to confirm your guess. After you discuss the words with your group members, write the meanings in the margin of the text, near the word. Then enter them in the chart.

Key Word   **Paragraph**   **Meaning**

_____

_____

_____

_____

GUIDE QUESTIONS

Directions: Develop a list of questions that elicit the important ideas in the reading selection. Start at the beginning and work your way sequentially through the text until you have addressed all of the author's major ideas.

APPLICATION

Directions: When you have a list of guide questions, read through the selection again. This time, write one or more questions that require the application of the information in the text to a situation in the real world.

WRITING

Directions: Your last task is to prepare a writing assignment For example, you might ask for a paragraph in which the writer comments on the ideas in the reading selection. You might also ask for a summary of the selection.

Perri Klass is both a doctor and a writer, so it is only natural she would take an interest in the special language of medicine. Many professions have their own jargon (if you have ever spent an evening with a group of computer specialists you know what true loneliness is), but Klass illustrates that the special idiom of medicine is especially fascinating—as well as confusing, frightening, useful, and . . . seductive.

RX: TRANSLATION, PLEASE?

Perri Klass

"Mrs. Tolstoy is your basic L.O.L. in N.A.D., admitted for a soft rule-out M.I.," the intern announces. I scribble that on my patient list. In other words Mrs. Tolstoy is a Little Old Lady in No Apparent Distress who is in the hospital to make sure she hasn't had a heart attack (rule out a myocardial infarction). And we think it's unlikely that she has had a heart attack (a *soft* rule-out). 1

If I learned nothing else during my first three months of working in the hospital as a medical student, I learned endless jargon and abbreviations. I started out in a state of primeval innocence, in which I didn't even know that "s̄ C.P., S.O.B., N/V" meant "without chest pain, shortness of breath, or nausea and vomiting." By the end I took the abbreviations so for granted that I would complain to my mother the English professor, "And can you believe I had to put down *three* NG tubes last night?" 2

"You'll have to tell me what an NG tube is if you want me to sympathize properly," my mother said. NG, nasogastric—isn't it obvious? 3

I picked up not only the specific expressions but also the patterns of speech and the grammatical conventions; for example, you never say that a patient's blood pressure fell or that his cardiac enzymes rose. Instead, the patient is always the subject of the verb: "He dropped his pressure." "He bumped his enzymes." This sort of construction probably reflects that profound irritation of the intern when the nurses come in the middle of the night to say that Mr. Dickinson has disturbingly low blood pressure. "Oh, he's gonna hurt me bad tonight," the intern may say, inevitably angry at Mr. Dickinson for dropping his pressure and creating a problem. 4

When chemotherapy fails to cure Mrs. Bacon's cancer, what we say is, "Mrs. Bacon failed chemotherapy." 5

"Well, we've already had one hit today, and we're up next, but at least we've got mostly stable players on our team." This means that our team (group of doctors and medical students) has already gotten one new admission today, and it is our turn again, so we'll get whoever is next admitted in emergency, but at least most of the patients we already have are fairly stable, that is, unlikely to drop their pressures or in any other way get suddenly sicker and hurt us bad. Baseball metaphor is pervasive: a no-hitter is a night without any new admissions. A player is always a patient—a nitrate player is a patient on nitrates, a unit player is a patient in the intensive-care unit, and so on, until you reach the terminal player. 6

It is interesting to consider what it means to be winning, or doing well, in this perennial baseball game. When the intern hangs up the phone and announces, "I got a hit," that is not cause for congratulations. The team is not scoring points; rather, it 7 is getting hit, being bombarded with new patients. The object of the game from the point of view of the doctors, considering the players for whom they are already responsible, is to get as few new hits as possible.

8   These special languages contribute to a sense of closeness and professional spirit among people who are under a great deal of stress. As a medical student, it was exciting for me to discover that I'd finally cracked the code, that I could understand what doctors said and wrote and could use the same formulations myself. Some people seem to become enamored of the jargon for its own sake, perhaps because they are so deeply thrilled with the idea of medicine, with the idea of themselves as doctors.

9   I knew a medical student who was referred to by the interns on the team as Mr. Eponym because he was so infatuated with eponymous terminology,* the more obscure the better. He never said "capillary pulsation" if he could say "Quincke's pulses." He would lovingly tell over the multinamed syndromes—Wolff–Parkinson–White, Lown–Ganong–Levine, Henoch–Schonlein—until the temptation to suggest Schleswig–Holstein or Stevenson–Kefauver or Baskin–Robbins became irresistible to his less reverent colleagues.

10   And there is the jargon that you don't ever want to hear yourself using. You know that your training is changing you, but there are certain changes you think would be going a little too far.

11   The resident was describing a man with devastating terminal pancreatic cancer. "Basically he's C.T.D.," the resident concluded. I reminded myself that I had resolved not to be shy about asking when I didn't understand things. "C.T.D.?" I asked timidly.

12   The resident smirked at me. "Circling The Drain."

13   The images are vivid and terrible. "What happened to Mrs. Melville?"

14   "Oh, she boxed last night." To box is to die, of course.

15   Then there are the more pompous locutions that can make the beginning medical student nervous about the effects of medical training. A friend of mine was told by his resident, "A pregnant woman with sickle-cell represents a failure of genetic counseling."

16   Mr. Eponym, who tried hard to talk like the doctors, once explained to me, "An infant is basically a brainstem preparation." A brainstem preparation, as used in neurological research, is an animal whose higher brain functions have been destroyed so that only the most primitive reflexes remain, like the sucking reflex, the startle reflex, and the rooting reflex.

17   The more extreme forms aside, one most important function of medical jargon is to help doctors maintain some distance from their patients. By reformulating a patient's pain and problems into a language that the patient doesn't even speak, I suppose we are in some sense taking those pains and problems under our jurisdiction and also reducing their emotional impact. This linguistic separation between doctors and patients allows conversations to go on at the bedside that are unintelligible

---

* *Eponymous* means "named after"—in this case, diseases or syndromes are named after the scientists who discovered them.

to the patient. "Naturally, we're worried about adeno-C.A.," the intern can say to the medical student, and lung cancer need never be mentioned.

I learned a new language this past summer. At times it thrills me to hear myself 18 using it. It enables me to understand my colleagues, to communicate effectively in the hospital. Yet I am uncomfortably aware that I will never again notice the peculiarities and even atrocities of medical language as keenly as I did this summer. There may be specific expressions I manage to avoid, but even as I remark on them, promising myself I will never use them, I find that this language is becoming my professional speech. It no longer sounds strange in my ears—or coming from my mouth. And I am afraid that, as with any new language, to use it properly you must absorb not only the vocabulary but also the structure, the logic, the attitudes. At first you may notice these new alien assumptions every time you put together a sentence, but with time and increased fluency you stop being aware of them at all. And as you lose that awareness, for better or for worse, you move closer and closer to being a doctor instead of just talking like one.

VOCABULARY

Directions: Mark any important words in the reading selection that you don't know. Then list them in the chart below along with their paragraph numbers. Try to figure out each word's meaning by reading over the context carefully for clues to help you guess the meaning of the unfamiliar word. Check your dictionary or thesaurus to confirm your guess. After you discuss the words with your group members, write the meanings in the margin of the text, near the word. Then enter them in the chart.

Key Word	Paragraph	Meaning

GUIDE QUESTIONS

Directions: Develop a list of questions that elicit the important ideas in the reading selection. Start at the beginning and work your way sequentially through the text until you have addressed all of the author's major ideas.

APPLICATION

Directions: When you have a list of guide questions, read through the selection again. This time, write one or more questions that require the application of the information in the text to a situation in the real world.

WRITING

Directions: Your last task is to prepare a writing assignment. For example, you might ask for a paragraph in which the writer comments on the ideas in the reading selection. You might also ask for a summary of the selection.

SPECIAL PROJECT

LANGUAGE

A Personal Mini-Dictionary

Many of the new words you will encounter in your college reading will not be words used in everyday speaking and writing. Rather, they will be specific to your major field of study, to your future career. For example, terms such as *double-entry system, trial balance,* and *ammortization* are generally used in the accounting field and not by the general public. Science and technology abound with vocabulary unique to their fields. For example, *hardware, software, boot,* and *byte* are words used in the computer field.

For this project you will create a mini-dictionary of words you need to know in your major field. Find the words in newspapers or magazines, not in your textbooks or dictionaries. For example, if you are a business major, you should be reading a periodical such as *The Wall Street Journal* and one of the major business journals. When you come across a technical term you don't know, enter it in your mini-dictionary according to the following format:

WORD:

DEFINITION:

CONTEXT SENTENCE:

SOURCE:

1. Enter the word.
2. Write the definition of the word. Try to figure out the definition by using the context. If you can't, use a dictionary. If the word is not in the dictionary, you will have to consult a professional dictionary or ask a teacher or someone in the field.
3. Copy the context sentence from the newspaper, periodical, or other source.
4. Name the source of the word—that is, the name of the magazine or newspaper where you found the word.

Follow this procedure for at least ten words each week.

BIBLIOGRAPHY

For Further Reading on the Theme of Language

Bill Bryson	*Mother Tongue*
Sandra Cisneros	*The House on Mango Street*
Annie Dillard	*Teaching a Stone to Talk*
Suzette Haden Elgin	*The Gentle Art of Verbal Self-Defense*
Peter Farb	*Word Play*
Garrison Keillor	*Lake Woebegone Days*
Helen Keller	*The Story of My Life*
Richard Lederer	*Crazy English*
Robert McCrum, William Cran, and Robert MacNeil	*The Story of English*
Bernard Malamud	*God's Grace*
Hugh Rawson	*Dictionary of Euphemisms*
Richard Rodriguez	*Hunger of Memory*
Deborah Tannen	*You Just Don't Understand; Women and Men in Conversation;* and *That's Not What I Meant: How Conversational Style Makes or Breaks Your Relations with Others*
Eudora Welty	*One Writer's Beginnings*
FILMS:	*The Miracle Worker* (the Helen Keller story)
	Children of a Lesser God
	Tootsie
	Quest for Fire

UNIT FOUR

READING AND THINKING ABOUT WORK AND THE WORLD OF BUSINESS

Who built the seven towers of Thebes?
The books are filled with the names of kings.
Was it kings who hauled the craggy blocks of stone?

—Bertolt Brecht

THINKING ABOUT WORKING

Before you begin to read about the world of work, take a few minutes to consider your own attitudes toward working. Read the questions below, think about them, then write down answers. Write freely—there are no "right" or "wrong" answers.

1. Write a definition of success.
2. What factors will enable you to achieve success in your career?
3. What factors about a job can make you feel happy and satisfied?
4. What factors about a job can make you feel unhappy or dissatisfied?
5. If you are unhappy or dissatisfied with your job, what can you do to change things (besides quit)?
6. If you had enough money so that you did not need to work, would you work anyway? Why or why not?
7. Imagine it is your retirement day. What would be the one thing you would want to be able to say about your job? About yourself?

The first day on the job can be terrifying, but imagine how very terrifying it would be if another person's life depended on you doing that job, and doing it right, the first time! In this frightening, comical, and touching story, doctor and writer William Nolen tells of his first day on the job—as a surgeon.

THE FIRST APPENDECTOMY

William A. Nolen, M.D.

1   The patient, or better, victim, of my first major surgical venture was a man I'll call Mr. Polansky. He was fat, he weighed one hundred and ninety pounds and was five feet eight inches tall. He spoke only broken English. He had had a sore abdomen with all the classical signs and symptoms of appendicitis for twenty-four hours before he came to Bellevue.

2   After two months of my internship, though I had yet to do anything that could be decently called an "operation," I had had what I thought was a fair amount of operating time. I'd watched the assistant residents work, I'd tied knots, cut sutures, and even, in order to remove a skin lesion, made an occasional incision. Frankly, I didn't think that surgery was going to be too damn difficult. I figured I was ready, and I was chomping at the bit to go, so when Mr. Polansky arrived I greeted him like a long-lost friend. He was overwhelmed at the interest I showed in his case. He probably couldn't understand why any doctor should be so fascinated by a case of appendicitis: wasn't it a common disease? It was just as well that he didn't realize my interest in him was so personal. He might have been frightened, and with good reason.

3   At any rate, I set some sort of record in preparing Mr. Polansky for surgery. He had arrived on the ward at four o'clock. By six I had examined him, checked his blood and urine, taken his chest x-ray and had him ready for the operating room.

4   George Walters, the senior resident on call that night, was to "assist" me during the operation. George was older than the rest of us. I was twenty-five at this time and he was thirty-two. He had taken his surgical training in Europe and was spending one year as a senior resident in an American hospital to establish eligibility for the American College of Surgeons. He had had more experience than the other residents and it took a lot to disturb his equanimity in the operating room. As it turned out, this made him the ideal assistant for me.

5   It was ten o'clock when we wheeled Mr. Polansky to the operating room. At Bellevue, at night, only two operating rooms were kept open—there were six or more going all day—so we had to wait our turn. In the time I had to myself before the operation I had reread the section on appendectomy in the *Atlas of Operative Technique* in our surgical library, and had spent half an hour tying knots on the bedpost in my room. I was, I felt, "ready."

6   I delivered Mr. Polansky to the operating room and started an intravenous going in his arm. Then I left him to the care of the anesthetist. I had ordered a sedative prior to surgery, so Mr. Polansky was drowsy. The anesthetist, after checking his chart, soon had him sleeping.

Once he was asleep I scrubbed the enormous expanse of Mr. Polansky's abdomen for ten minutes. Then, while George placed the sterile drapes, I scrubbed my own hands for another five, mentally reviewing each step of the operation as I did so. Donning gown and gloves I took my place on the right side of the operating-room table. The nurse handed me the scalpel. I was ready to begin. 7

Suddenly my entire attitude changed. A split second earlier I had been supremely confident; now, with the knife finally in my hand, I stared down at Mr. Polansky's abdomen and for the life of me could not decide where to make the incision. The "landmarks" had disappeared. There was too much belly. 8

George waited a few seconds, then looked up at me and said, "'Go ahead." 9
"What?" I asked. 10
"Make the incision," said George. 11
"Where?" I asked. 12
"Where?" 13
"Yes," I answered, "where?" 14
"Why, here, of course," said George and drew an imaginary line on the abdomen with his fingers. 15

I took the scalpel and followed where he had directed. I barely scratched Mr. Polansky. 16

"Press a little harder," George directed. I did. The blade went through the skin to a depth of perhaps one-sixteenth of an inch. 17

"Deeper," said George. 18

There are five layers of tissue in the abdominal wall: skin, fat, fascia (a tough membranous tissue), muscle, and peritoneum (the smooth, glistening, transparent inner lining of the abdomen). I cut down into the fat. Another sixteenth of an inch. 19

"Bill," said George, looking up at me, "this patient is big. There's at least three inches of fat to get through before we even reach the fascia. At the rate you're going we won't be into the abdomen for another four hours. For God's sake, will you cut?" 20

I made up my mind not to be hesitant. I pressed down hard on the knife, and suddenly we were not only through the fat but through the fascia as well. 21

"Not that hard," George shouted, grabbing my right wrist with his left hand while with his other hand he plunged a gauze pack into the wound to stop the bleeding. "Start clamping," he told me. 22

The nurse handed us hemostats and we applied them to the numerous vessels I had so hastily opened. "All right," George said, "start tying." 23

I took the ligature material from the nurse and began to tie off the vessels. Or rather, I tried to tie off the vessels, because suddenly my knot-tying proficiency had melted away. The casual dexterity I had displayed on the bedpost a short hour ago was nowhere in evidence. My fingers, greasy with fat, simply would not perform. My ties slipped off the vessels, the sutures snapped in my fingers, at one point I even managed to tie the end of my rubber glove into the wound. It was, to put it bluntly, a performance in fumbling that would have made Robert Benchley blush. 24

Here I must give my first paean of praise to George. His patience during the entire performance was nothing short of miraculous. The temptation to pick up the 25 catgut and do the tying himself must have been strong. He could have tied off all the vessels in two minutes. It took me twenty.

26   Finally we were ready to proceed. "Now," George directed, "split the muscle. But gently, please."

27   I reverted to my earlier tack. Fiber by fiber I spread the muscle which was the last layer but one that kept us from the inside of the abdomen. Each time I separated the fibers and withdrew my clamp, the fibers rolled together again. After five minutes I was no nearer the appendix than I had been at the start.

28   George could stand it no longer. But he was apparently afraid to suggest I take a more aggressive approach, fearing I would stick the clamp into, or possibly through, the entire abdomen. Instead he suggested that he help me by spreading the muscle in one direction while I spread it in the other. I made my usual infinitesimal attack on the muscle. In one fell swoop George spread the rest.

29   "Very well done," he complimented me. "Now let's get in."

30   We each took a clamp and picked up the tissue-paper-thin peritoneum. After two or three hesitant attacks with the scalpel I finally opened it. We were in the abdomen.

31   "Now," said George, "put your fingers in, feel the cecum (the portion of the bowel to which the appendix is attached) and bring it into the wound."

32   I stuck my right hand into the abdomen. I felt around—but what was I feeling? I had no idea.

33   It had always looked so simple when the senior resident did it. Open the abdomen, reach inside, pull up the appendix. Nothing to it. But apparently there was.

34   Everything felt the same to me. The small intestine, the large intestine, the cecum—how did one tell them apart without seeing them? I grabbed something and pulled it into the wound. Small intestine. No good. Put it back. I grabbed again. This time it was the sigmoid colon. Put it back. On my third try I had the small intestine again.

35   "The appendix must be in an abnormal position," I said to George. "I can't seem to find it."

36   "Mind if I try?" he asked.

37   "Not at all," I answered. "I wish you would."

38   Two of his fingers disappeared into the wound. Five seconds later they emerged, cecum between them, with the appendix flopping from it.

39   "Stuck down a little," he said kindly. "That's probably why you didn't feel it. It's a hot one," he added. "Let's get at it."

40   The nurse handed me the hemostats, and one by one I applied them to the mesentery of the appendix—the veil of tissue in which the blood vessels run. With George holding the veil between his fingers I had no trouble; I took the ligatures and tied the vessels without a single error. My confidence was coming back.

41   "Now," George directed, "put in your purse string." (The cecum is a portion of the bowel which has the shape of half a hemisphere. The appendix projects from its surface like a finger. In an appendectomy the routine procedure is to tie the appendix at its base and cut it off a little beyond the tie. Then the remaining stump is inverted

into the cecum and kept there by tying the purse-string stitch. This was the stitch I was now going to sew.)

It went horribly. The wall of the cecum is not very thick—perhaps one-eighth   42
of an inch. The suture must be placed deeply enough in the wall so that it won't cut through when tied, but not so deep as to pass all the way through the wall. My sutures were alternately too superficial or too deep, but eventually I got the job done.

"All right," said George, "let's get the appendix out of here. Tie off the base."   43
I did.   44
"Now cut off the appendix."   45
At least in this, the definitive act of the operation, I would be decisive. I took   46
the knife and with one quick slash cut through the appendix—too close to the ligature.

"Oh oh, watch it," said George. "That tie is going to slip."   47
It did. The appendiceal stump lay there, open. I felt faint.   48
"Don't panic," said George. "We've still got the purse string. I'll push the stump   49
in—you pull up the stitch and tie. That will take care of it."

I picked up the two ends of the suture and put in the first stitch. George shoved   50
the open stump into the cecum. It disappeared as I snugged my tie. Beautiful.

"Two more knots," said George. "Just to be safe."   51
I tied the first knot and breathed a sigh of relief. The appendiceal stump re-   52
mained out of sight. On the third knot—for the sake of security—I pulled a little tighter. The stitch broke; the open stump popped up; the cecum disappeared into the abdomen. I broke out in a cold sweat and my knees started to crumble.

Even George momentarily lost his composure. "For Christ's sake, Bill," he said,   53
grasping desperately for the bowel, "what did you have to do that for?" The low point of the operation had been reached.

By the time we had retrieved the cecum, Mr. Polansky's peritoneal cavity had   54
been contaminated. My self-confidence was shattered. And still George let me continue. True, he all but held my hand as we retied and resutured, but the instruments were in my hand.

The closure was anticlimactic. Once I had the peritoneum sutured, things went   55
reasonably smoothly. Two hours after we began, the operation was over. "Nice job," George said, doing his best to sound sincere.

"Thanks," I answered, lamely.   56
The scrub nurse laughed.   57
Mr. Polansky recovered, I am happy to report, though not without a long and   58
complicated convalescence. His bowel refused to function normally for two weeks and he became enormously distended. He was referred to at our nightly conferences as "Dr. Nolen's pregnant man." Each time the reference was made, it elicited a shudder from me.

During his convalescence I spent every spare moment I could at Mr. Polansky's   59
bedside. My feelings of guilt and responsibility were overwhelming. If he had died I think I would have given up surgery for good.

VOCABULARY

Directions: Find each of the key words in the reading selection. Study each word in its context and try to determine its meaning. Write what you think it means in the margin of the text, near the word. Then read over the sentence, mentally substituting your guess for the key word. Does the sentence still make sense? Does it retain its original meaning? If it does, you've probably figured out the meaning of the key word correctly. In any case confirm your guess by checking a dictionary or thesaurus.

If you take your meaning from the dictionary or thesaurus, be sure the definition contains words you already know and feel comfortable using. If it doesn't, you will be worse off than when you started—you will have begun with one word you didn't know and ended with *two* words you don't know!

Record the new words you've learned below.

Key Word	Paragraph	Meaning
1. chomping at the bit	2	
2. equanimity	4	
3. donning	7	
4. dexterity	24	
5. infinitesimal	28	
6. contaminated	54	
7. distended	58	
8. convalescence	59	

Others?

GUIDE QUESTIONS

Directions: The purpose of guide questions is to "guide" your analysis of the text. Your thoughtful answers will ensure that you have understood the main ideas the author wanted to convey. Some of the questions require that you simply find the stated facts in the reading selection; others will ask you to do more difficult tasks, such as paraphrasing information (putting the author's ideas into your own words), synthesizing several ideas into one complex thought, evaluating (making judgments about) an idea, or taking information from the reading and applying it to a new situation or to your own life.

Write answers to the questions in your notebook or on a separate sheet of paper if your instructor wishes to collect them. Your answers will form the basis of class discussion.

1. Dr. Nolen had studied hard and prepared abundantly for the appendectomy. Why do you think he had so much trouble when the time came to actually do the job?
2. Why do you think George (Dr. Walters) allowed Nolen to continue when he was making such a mess of things?
3. The story of the operation has many elements of humor despite the tone of nervousness, even terror. Cite a few points in the narrative that are funny.
4. How do you think Nolen's next operation went?

APPLICATION

Directions: In small groups, discuss a point in your life when you did something for a terrifying "first time"—your first day on a job, or perhaps the first time you drove a car, or gave a speech.

WRITING

Directions: Choose one of the writing assignments below.

1. Using the ideas you generated in the Application exercise above, write a story describing your first time, using "The First Appendectomy" as a model. Write at least 250 words.
2. Rewrite the story "The First Appendectomy" from the perspective of either the scrub nurse or George. Write at least 250 words.

K. C. Cole is a writer who devotes herself mainly to science and women's issues. In this essay, which first appeared in The New York Times *in 1981, she explores the reasons that very few women choose science as a career.*

WOMEN IN SCIENCE
K. C. Cole

1   I know few other women who do what I do. What I do is write about science, mainly physics. And to do that, I spend a lot of time reading about science, talking to scientists, and struggling to understand physics. In fact, most of the women (and men) I know think me quite queer for actually liking physics. "How can you write about that stuff?" they ask, always somewhat askance. "I could never understand that in a million years." Or more simply, "I hate science."

2   I didn't realize what an odd creature a woman interested in physics was until a few years ago when a science magazine sent me to Johns Hopkins University in Baltimore for a conference on an electrical phenomenon known as the Hall effect. We sat in a huge lecture hall and listened as physicists talked about things engineers didn't understand, and engineers talked about things physicists didn't understand. What *I* didn't understand was why, out of several hundred young students of physics and engineering in the room, less than a handful were women.

3   Sometime later, I found myself at the California Institute of Technology reporting on the search for the origins of the universe. I interviewed physicist after physicist, man after man. I asked one young administrator why none of the physicists were women. And he answered: "I don't know, but I suppose it must be something innate. My seven-year-old daughter doesn't seem to be much interested in science."

4   It was with that experience fresh in my mind that I attended a conference in Cambridge, Massachusetts, on science literacy, or rather the worrisome lack of it in this country today. We three women—a science teacher, a young chemist, and myself—sat surrounded by a company of august men. The chemist, I think, first tentatively raised the issue of science illiteracy in women. It seemed like an obvious point. After all, everyone had agreed over and over again that scientific knowledge these days was a key factor in economic power. But as soon as she made the point, it became clear that we women had committed a grievous social error. Our genders were suddenly showing; we had interrupted the serious talk with a subject unforgivably silly.

5   For the first time, I stopped being puzzled about why there weren't any women in science and began to be angry. Because if science is a search for answers to fundamental questions then it hardly seems frivolous to find out why women are excluded. Never mind the economic consequences.

6   A lot of the reasons women are excluded are spelled out by the Massachusetts Institute of Technology experimental physicist Vera Kistiakowsky in a recent article in *Physics Today* called "Women in Physics: Unnecessary, Injurious, and Out of Place?" The title was taken from a nineteenth-century essay written in opposition to the appointment of a female mathematician to a professorship at the University of

Stockholm. "As decidedly as two and two make four," a woman in mathematics is a "monstrosity," concluded the writer of the essay.

Dr. Kistiakowsky went on to discuss the factors that make women in science   7 today, if not monstrosities, at least oddities. Contrary to much popular opinion, one of those is *not* an innate difference in the scientific ability of boys and girls. But early conditioning does play a stubborn and subtle role. A recent *Nova* program, "The Pinks and the Blues," documented how girls and boys are treated differently from birth—the boys always encouraged in more physical kinds of play, more active explorations of their environments. Sheila Tobias, in her book *Math Anxiety*, showed how the games boys play help them to develop an intuitive understanding of speed, motion, and mass.

The main sorting out of the girls from the boys in science seems to happen in   8 junior high school. As a friend who teaches in a science museum said, "By the time we get to electricity, the boys already have had some experience with it. But it's unfamiliar to the girls." Science books draw on boys' experiences. "The examples are all about throwing a baseball at such and such a speed," said my stepdaughter, who barely escaped being a science drop-out.

The most obvious reason there are not many more women in science is that   9 women are discriminated against as a class, in promotions, salaries, and hirings, a conclusion reached by a recent analysis by the National Academy of Sciences.

Finally, said Dr. Kistiakowsky, women are simply made to feel out of place in   10 science. Her conclusion was supported by a Ford Foundation study by Lynn H. Fox on the problems of women in mathematics. When students were asked to choose among six reasons accounting for girls' lack of interest in math, the girls rated this statement second: "Men do not want girls in the mathematical occupations."

A friend of mine remembers winning a Bronxwide mathematics competition in   11 the second grade. Her friends—both boys and girls—warned her that she shouldn't be good at math: "You'll never find a boy who likes you." My friend continued nevertheless to excel in math and science, won many awards during her years at the Bronx High School of Science, and then earned a full scholarship to Harvard. After one year of Harvard science, she decided to major in English.

When I asked her why, she mentioned what she called the "macho mores" of   12 science. "It would have been O.K. if I'd had someone to talk to," she said. "But the rules of comportment were such that you never admitted you didn't understand. I later realized that even the boys didn't get everything clearly right away. You had to stick with it until it had time to sink in. But for the boys, there was a payoff in suffering through the hard times, and a kind of punishment—a shame—if they didn't. For the girls it was O.K. not to get it, and the only payoff for sticking it out was that you'd be considered a freak."

Science is undeniably hard. Often, it can seem quite boring. It is unfortunately   13 too often presented as laws to be memorized instead of mysteries to be explored. It is too often kept a secret that science, like art, takes a well-developed esthetic sense. Women aren't the only ones who say, "I hate science."

That's why everyone who goes into science needs a little help from friends. For   14 the past ten years, I have been getting more than a little help from a friend who is a physicist. But my stepdaughter—who earned the highest grades ever recorded in her California high school on the math Scholastic Aptitude Test—flunked calculus in her first year at Harvard. When my friend the physicist heard about it, he said, "Harvard should be ashamed of itself."

15   What he meant was that she needed that little extra encouragement that makes all the difference. Instead, she got that little extra discouragement that makes all the difference.

16   "In the first place, all the math teachers are men," she explained. "In the second place, when I met a boy I liked and told him I was taking chemistry, he immediately said: 'Oh, you're one of those science types.' In the third place, it's just a kind of a social thing. The math clubs are full of boys and you don't feel comfortable joining."

17   In other words, she was made to feel unnecessary, injurious, and out of place.

18   A few months ago, I accompanied a male colleague from the science museum where I sometimes work to a lunch of the history of science faculty at the University of California. I was the only woman there, and my presence for the most part was obviously and rudely ignored. I was so surprised and hurt by this that I made an extra effort to speak knowledgeably and well. At the end of the lunch, one of the professors turned to me in all seriousness and said: "Well, K. C., what do the women think of Carl Sagan?" I replied that I had no idea what "the women" thought about anything. But now I know what I should have said: I should have told him that his comment was unnecessary, injurious, and out of place.

VOCABULARY

Directions: Locate each of the key words in the reading selection. Try to figure out each word's meaning by using the context. Confirm your guess by checking the dictionary or thesaurus. Write the meanings of the words in the margin of the text. Then record the meanings in the chart below.

Key Word	Paragraph	Meaning
1. askance	1	
2. innate	3	
3. august	4	
4. frivolous	5	
5. esthetic (often spelled aesthetic)	13	
Others?		

GUIDE QUESTIONS

Directions: These questions will guide your understanding of what you have read. Write your answers in your notebook or on a separate sheet of paper if your instructor wishes to collect it. Your answers to these questions will be the basis of class discussion.

1. What do you think prompted the author to write this article? Would you be surprised to find an article titled "Men in Science" in a magazine or newspaper? Why?
2. According to the essay, what are some of the reasons women are excluded from the field of science?
3. Cole describes a friend who excelled in science but, after studying at Harvard for a year, changed her major to English. What reason does Cole's friend give for dropping science?
4. Cole states that "science is undeniably hard" (paragraph 13) and that men also say "I hate science." If these things are true, what explains the fact that women tend to drop out of science while men are much more likely to continue?

APPLICATION

1. *Directions:* Interview four adults. Try to find one person working in the field of science, one in math, and two from other fields. Ask them if their gender made a difference in which profession they chose and, if so, why. Compare their answers to the ideas in the essay. Use your interviews as a basis for a class discussion.
2. *Directions:* If you read the selection "Sexism in the Schoolhouse" on page 19, imagine that K. C. Cole, the author of "Women in Science," had just read that article. What would her reaction be?

WRITING

Directions: Describe your own experience studying science and math. Were boys and girls treated equally? Were there equal opportunities and encouragement for both boys and girls? Think about why you did or did not continue studying science. Are your experiences similar to those you read about in "Women in Science"? Write a 250- to 350-word essay.

Think back to your elementary school days. If your experience is like most people's, all of your teachers were women. Why do you think this was so? Why don't men go into this profession? Has this situation changed in recent years? In the essay that follows, a male elementary school teacher describes his work days and some of the problems he faces as a man doing "woman's work."

ONE MAN'S KIDS

Daniel Meier

1   I teach first graders. I live in a world of skinned knees, double-knotted shoelaces, riddles that I've heard a dozen times, stale birthday cakes, hurt feelings, wandering stories, and one lost shoe ("and if you don't find it my mother'll kill me"). My work is dominated by six-year-olds.

2   It's 10:45, the middle of snack, and I'm helping Emily open her milk carton. She has already tried the other end without success, and now there's so much paint and ink on the carton from her fingers that I'm not sure she should drink it at all. But I open it. Then I turn to help Scott clean up some milk he has just spilled onto Rebecca's whale crossword puzzle.

3   While I wipe my milk- and paint-covered hands, Jenny wants to know if I've seen that funny book about penguins that I read in class. As I hunt for it in a messy pile of books, Jason wants to know if there is a new seating arrangement for lunch tables. I find the book, turn to answer Jason, then face Maya, who is fast approaching with a new knock-knock joke. After what seems like the tenth "Who's there?" I laugh and Maya is pleased.

4   Then Andrew wants to know how to spell "flukes" for his crossword. As I get to "u," I give a hand signal for Sarah to take away the snack. But just as Sarah is almost out the door, two children complain that "we haven't even had ours yet." I stop the snack mid-flight, complying with their request for graham crackers. I then return to Andrew, noticing that he has put "flu" for 9 Down, rather than 9 Across. It's now 10:50.

5   My work is not traditional male work. It's not a singular pursuit. There is not a large pile of paper to get through or one deal to transact. I don't have one area of expertise or knowledge. I don't have the singular power over language of a lawyer, the physical force of a construction worker, the command over fellow workers of a surgeon, the wheeling and dealing transactions of a businessman. My energy is not spent in pursuing, climbing, achieving, conquering, or cornering some goal or object.

6   My energy is spent in encouraging, supporting, consoling, and praising my children. In teaching, the inner rewards come from without. On any given day, quite apart from teaching reading and spelling, I bandage a cut, dry a tear, erase a frown, tape a torn doll, and locate a long-lost boot. The day is really won through matters of the heart. As my students groan, laugh, shudder, cry, exult, and wonder, I do too. I have to be soft around the edges.

7   A few years ago, when I was interviewing for an elementary school teaching position, every principal told me with confidence that, as a male, I had an advantage

over female applicants because of the lack of male teachers. But in the next breath, they asked with a hint of suspicion why I chose to work with young children. I told them that I wanted to observe and contribute to the intellectual growth of a maturing mind. What I really felt like saying, but didn't, was that I loved helping a child learn to write his name for the first time, finding someone a new friend, or sharing in the hilarity of reading about Winnie the Pooh getting so stuck in a hole that only his head and rear show.

8   I gave that answer to those principals, who were mostly male, because I thought they wanted a "male" response. This meant talking about intellectual matters. If I had taken a different course and talked about my interest in helping children in their emotional development, it would have been seen as closer to a "female" answer. I even altered my language, not once mentioning the word *love* to describe what I do indeed love about teaching. My answer worked; every principal nodded approvingly.

9   Some of the principals also asked what I saw myself doing later in my career. They wanted to know if I eventually wanted to go into educational administration. Becoming a dean of students or a principal has never been one of my goals, but they seemed to expect me, as a male, to want to climb higher on the career stepladder. So I mentioned that, at some point, I would be interested in working with teachers as a curriculum coordinator. Again, they nodded approvingly.

10   If those principals had been female instead of male, I wonder whether their questions, and my answers, would have been different. My guess is that they would have been.

11   At other times, when I'm at a party or a dinner and tell someone that I teach young children, I've found that men and women respond differently. Most men ask about the subjects I teach and the courses I took in my training. Then, unless they bring up an issue such as merit pay, the conversation stops. Most women, on the other hand, begin the conversation on a more immediate and personal level. They say things like "those kids must love having a male teacher" or "that age is just wonderful, you must love it." Then, more often than not, they'll talk about their own kids or ask me specific questions about what I do. We're then off and talking shop.

12   Possibly, men would have more to say to me, and I to them, if my job had more of the trappings and benefits of more traditional male jobs. But my job has no bonuses or promotions. No complimentary box seats at the ball park. No cab fare home. No drinking buddies after work. No briefcase. No suit. (Ties get stuck in paint jars.) No power lunches. (I eat peanut butter and jelly, chips, milk, and cookies with the kids.) No taking clients out for cocktails. The only place I take my kids is to the playground.

13   Although I could have pursued a career in law or business, as several of my friends did, I chose teaching instead. My job has benefits all its own. I'm able to bake cookies without getting them stuck together as they cool, buy cheap sewing materials, take out splinters, and search just the right trash cans for useful odds and ends. I'm sometimes called "Daddy" and even "Mommy" by my students, and if there's ever a lull in the conversation at a dinner party, I can always ask those assembled if they've heard the latest riddle about why the turkey crossed the road. (He thought he was a chicken.)

VOCABULARY

Directions: Locate each of the key words in the reading selection. Try to figure out each word's meaning by using the context. Confirm your guess by checking the dictionary or thesaurus. Write the meanings of the words in the margin of the text. Then record the meanings in the chart below.

Key Word	Paragraph	Meaning
1. exult	6	
2. hilarity	7	
3. trappings	12	
4. lull	13	
Others?		

GUIDE QUESTIONS

Directions: These questions will guide your understanding of what you have read. Write your answers in your notebook or on a separate sheet of paper if your instructor wishes to collect it. Your answers to these questions will be the basis of class discussion.

1. Describe what the author does for a living. Then describe your reaction to his profession when you first read the article.
2. What does Meier mean when he says in paragraph 5 that his work is not a "singular pursuit"?
3. Why did Meier think he could not give truly honest answers to the principals who interviewed him for jobs as a teacher?
4. Contrast the types of conversations Meier has with women and with men at social occasions.
5. If you know someone who has held a job typically performed by the opposite sex, describe their experience. Would they recommend such a job to you?

APPLICATION

Directions: Think back to the previous essay, "Women in Science" (page 178). In small groups, discuss the similarities and differences between Daniel Meier's and K. C. Cole's experiences in careers dominated by the opposite sex.

WRITING

Directions: Reflect on what you have read and on the discussion you had in the Application exercise above. Now, think about and answer this question: Would you take a job in a field dominated by the opposite sex? For example, if you are a woman, would you work as a truck driver, construction worker, firefighter? If you are a man, would you work as a nurse, elementary school teacher, or secretary? Consider the advantages and disadvantages of such a job. Write your response and supporting reasons for your response in two or three paragraphs.

Most young people say they would rather be white-collar than blue-collar workers. The image of a fancy office, a secretary, and clean hands at the end of the day is appealing to most of us. But is there a downside to the white-collar life? Because of the downturn in so-called "smokestack" industries, many blue-collar workers are being retrained for white-collar jobs—and some are finding the change to be a stressful one.

CULTURE SHOCK AFFECTS STEELWORKER WHO SWITCHED TO WHITE-COLLAR JOB

Carol Hymowitz

1   When Frank LaRosa was laid off twenty-one months ago, he knew the layoff would never end.

2   He had grown up in the shadow of National Steel Corporation's giant Weirton works in Weirton, West Virginia, and witnessed downturns before. But this time mills like Weirton were threatened with permanent closings. (National Steel is trying to sell its Weirton works to the employees there.) "There isn't a future here," Mr. LaRosa concluded.

3   Today, the twenty-three-year-old former steelworker has traded his work shirt and heavy work boots for a dress shirt and tie—and a new identity as a white-collar worker. He has retrained himself and found a new job as a computer programmer at a Pittsburgh management and personnel consulting company. He is, he says, as capable of writing programs in half a dozen computer languages as he used to be working in a rolling mill.

4   But some days he feels like a refugee trying to adjust to a new country. "In the mill you put in your eight hours, said whatever you felt like saying, and then went out with your buddies for a beer," he says. "But if you're white collar and trying to get ahead, you've got to present yourself just so. And your work is always on your mind, even after work."

5   Many blue-collar workers displaced by industrial restructuring are now trying to fit into the expanding white-collar job market. In the process, they often suffer culture shock. Sales-office and technical jobs are commonly considered more prestigious, but the pay is often a lot lower, at least initially. Usually there aren't any unions to spell out job duties, and seniority doesn't count much either. Relationships with co-workers and supervisors are markedly different, too.

6   "If you're blue collar, you belong to a brotherhood of workers and you're protected by that group," says Joseph Giordano, director of the Louis Caplan Center on Group Identity and Mental Health in New York. "Suddenly to find yourself in a job where you're on your own and are expected to get ahead of the next guy can be very jolting," he adds. "The fact that you've found a job will be uplifting but the transition is bound to be stressful."

7   The transition also is likely to be costly, time-consuming, and risky. Ron Hively, a thirty-five-year-old unemployed steelworker in Pittsburgh, took out a $6,000 student loan to pay for a two-year course in computer programming. He completed the training last summer but still hasn't found a job. He and his family now are on welfare.

Frank LaRosa had to wean himself from a family tradition of work in the steel 8
mills when he made the shift to a white-collar job. His father, uncles, and cousins all
work at the Weirton mill and hope to spend their whole working lives there.

Mr. LaRosa made the break by obtaining a $5,000 student loan, adding $2,000 9
of his own money and enrolling in a fourteen-month course at the Computer Systems Institute in Pittsburgh. As he was only four years out of high school, he says he
"hadn't forgotten how to study like some of the older guys who were trying to re-
train." He graduated last winter with a straight-A average and an associate degree
in computer programming.

The difficult transition began when he obtained a three-month internship at 10
Development Dimensions International, the company where he still works. On his
first day at work, his boss told him that he would prefer to hire a college graduate
and Mr. LaRosa would have to prove himself. "I felt lower than most everybody else
here," he says.

When he was assigned his first programming project, he couldn't sleep for 11
three nights. He pushed himself to finish the assignment a week ahead of schedule.

In February, the company offered Mr. LaRosa a permanent job—and another 12
adjustment problem. The job pays two-thirds the amount Mr. LaRosa earned as a
steelworker.

"Better than Unemployment"

At home in Weirton, where he still lives with his parents, "guys ask me what I'm mak- 13
ing, and when I tell them they turn away," Mr. LaRosa says. He figures that "it's just a
beginning and better than unemployment." He can make do with less because he is
single. Still, he misses the second auto (a sports car) he could afford as a steelworker.

The biggest change is the work itself. As a steelworker, Mr. LaRosa worked in a 14
section of the Weirton works called "the hole." He and three other workers banded
hot strips of steel onto "a fifty-four-inch hot-strip rolling machine. The hole was so
hot that workers wore cotton long johns under their clothes to keep from burning.
"Polyester would melt on you," he recalls.

His new modern office cubicle is temperature-controlled, but it has far more 15
tension. Mr. LaRosa spends hours each day sitting in front of a computer terminal,
trying to block out the noise of telephones ringing in adjacent cubicles, and writing
a variety of accounting and data-management programs. He says the work is "challenging," but it also requires intense concentration, and he is under pressure to
"move, move, move from one thing to the next."

But Mr. LaRosa is developing a new understanding of the management point of 16
view. As a steelworker, he used to hope that machines would break down so that he
would have time off. Now he says he understands what downtime costs the company
and "why they get so upset when it happened." He himself tries to save costs by writing programs quickly and making efficient use of computer time.

A Door and a Window

He is also learning about white-collar status symbols. If he were higher up in the 17
ranks of management he would have an office with a door and a window, he's learned,

and he would exchange his shirt and slacks for a suit. "Until I buy some silk ties I'm really just gray collar," he says.

18   Unfortunately, his colleagues have him labeled, he fears. "They think, 'Once a laborer, always a laborer.' I'm going to have to show them how smart I am."

19   He isn't impressed by college graduates "who have never dirtied their hands and don't know the first thing about working very hard with people of all different ages." He also isn't impressed by office colleagues who try to impress him. When one co-worker boasted that he preferred reading to watching television, Mr. LaRosa thought to himself, "he doesn't have to impress me, I'm just a mill rat."

What's Actually Produced?

20   Sometimes he also misses the satisfaction of making a product as basic and essential as steel. "Lots of times I've questioned what is actually being produced here," he says, gesturing around his office.

21   He is, however, glad to have found "a job with future" and to be out from under the blue-collar system where jobs are assigned on the basis of seniority. "In the mill, all you do is wait in line," he says. "It may take you thirty years to get to be a rolling-mill operator," the worker who controls computerized steel-rolling equipment.

22   But as a computer programmer, "someone may have more seniority than me, but maybe they're just making lateral moves and I can jump around them. As a programmer, nobody is stopping me but me."

VOCABULARY

Directions: Locate each of the key words in the reading selection. Then read and study each word in its context and try to determine its meaning. Use a dictionary or thesaurus to check your guess. Write the meanings of the words in the margin of the text.

Record the new words you've learned below.

Key Word	Paragraph	Meaning
1. seniority	5	
2. transition	6, 7	
3. wean	8	
4. adjacent	15	
Others?		

GUIDE QUESTIONS

Directions: The purpose of these guide questions is to ensure your understanding of what you have read. They will also help you to analyze and evaluate the author's ideas and apply them to the real world and your own life.

Write answers to the questions in your notebook or on a separate sheet of paper if your instructor wishes to collect them. Your answers will form the basis of class discussion.

1. a. Describe the career change that Frank LaRosa made.
   b. Why did he make the change?
2. Throughout this selection, people refer to jobs as "white collar" or "blue collar" or even "gray collar" (paragraph 17).
   a. What is the difference between a blue-collar job and a white-collar job?
   b. List at least five examples of blue-collar jobs.
   c. List at least five examples of white-collar jobs.
3. Explain why the author says LaRosa has "a new identity" as a white-collar worker. What does a job change like this have to do with a person's identity?
4. In the selection LaRosa says he sometimes feels "like a refugee." The author of the article describes the change from blue-collar to white-collar work as resulting in "culture shock." Explain the use of these phrases.
5. List the problems Ron Hively had to face in changing from blue- to white-collar employment.
6. List and explain the career-change difficulties Mr. LaRosa describes.
7. What do you think LaRosa means when he says, "Until I buy some silk ties, I'm really just gray collar"?

APPLICATION

Using the chart below and on the next page, compare blue- and white-collar jobs. List the advantages and disadvantages of each type of job. Use your own experience and knowledge as well as the information in the reading selection to help you.

	Blue-Collar Jobs	White-Collar Jobs
Advantages		

	Blue-Collar Jobs	**White-Collar Jobs**
Disadvantages		

WRITING

If you were Frank LaRosa, would you do the same things he has done? Investing borrowed money and a significant amount of time—and facing the danger of losing both—is a very scary proposition, especially for a career neither you nor any of your family or friends has ever had. Would you risk it? Write one paragraph stating your answer and explaining your reasons.

In the 1970s, Studs Terkel embarked upon a journey around America to discover what people do all day and how they feel about what they do. In the course of his travels he interviewed everyone from newsboys and farmers to famous sports figures and top business executives. Through interviews, Terkel compiled an astonishing portrait of work and workers in America. In this excerpt from his book, Working, *two interviews are presented: in one, a steel-mill worker describes himself as "a mule. A monkey can do what I do." In the second, a stonemason says, "It's a pretty good day laying stone or brick. Not tiring. Anything you like to do isn't tiresome. . . . You usually fight the clock. . . . You're not lookin' for quittin'."*

In the introduction to Working, *Terkel says:*

> *This book, being about work, is, by its very nature, about violence—to the spirit as well as to the body. It is about ulcers as well as accidents, about shouting matches as well as fistfights, about nervous breakdowns as well as kicking the dog around. It is, above all (or beneath all), about daily humiliations. To survive the day is triumph enough for the walking wounded among the great many of us.*

What inferences can you draw from this about Terkel's attitudes toward work? How does his attitude compare to yours? Think about these questions as you read the interviews.

WHO BUILT THE PYRAMIDS?

Studs Terkel

The Steel Mill Worker: Mike Lefevre

It is a two-flat dwelling, somewhere in Cicero, on the outskirts of Chicago. He is thirty-seven. He works in a steel mill. On occasion, his wife, Carol, works as a waitress in a neighborhood restaurant; otherwise, she is at home, caring for their two small children, a girl and a boy.   1

At the time of my first visit, a sculpted statuette of Mother and Child was on the floor, head severed from body. He laughed softly as he indicated his three-year-old daughter: "She Doctor Spock'd it."

I'm a dying breed. A laborer. Strictly muscle work . . . pick it up, put it down, pick it up, put it down. We handle between forty and fifty thousand pounds of steel a day. (Laughs.) I know this is hard to believe—from four hundred pounds to three-and-four-pound pieces. It's dying.   2

You can't take pride any more. You remember when a guy could point to a house he built, how many logs he stacked. He built it and he was proud of it. I don't really think I could be proud if a contractor built a home for me. I would be tempted to get in there and kick the carpenter in the . . . (laughs), and take the saw away from him. 'Cause I would have to be part of it, you know.   3

It's hard to take pride in a bridge you're never gonna cross, in a door you're never gonna open. You're mass-producing things and you never see the end result of it. (Muses.) I worked for a trucker one time. And I got this tiny satisfaction when   4

I loaded a truck. At least I could see the truck depart loaded. In a steel mill, forget it. You don't see where nothing goes.

5   I got chewed out by my foreman once. He said, "Mike, you're a good worker but you have a bad attitude." My attitude is that I don't get excited about my job. I do my work but I don't say whoopee-doo. The day I get excited about my job is the day I go to a head shrinker. How are you gonna get excited about pullin' steel? How are you gonna get excited when you're tired and want to sit down?

6   It's not just the work. Somebody built the pyramids. Somebody's going to build something. Pyramids, Empire State Building—these things just don't happen. There's hard work behind it. I would like to see a building, say, the Empire State, I would like to see on one side of it a foot-wide strip from top to bottom with the name of every bricklayer, the name of every electrician, with all the names. So when a guy walked by, he could take his son and say, "See, that's me over there on the forty-fifth floor. I put the steel beam in." Picasso can point to a painting. What can I point to? A writer can point to a book. Everybody should have something to point to.

7   It's the not-recognition by other people. To say a woman is *just* a housewife is degrading, right? Okay. *Just* a housewife. It's also degrading to say *just* a laborer. The difference is that a man goes out and maybe gets smashed.

8   When I was single, I could quit, just split. I wandered all over the country. You worked just enough to get a poke, money in your pocket. Now I'm married and I got two kids . . . (trails off). I worked on a truck dock one time and I was single. The foreman came over and he grabbed my shoulder, kind of gave me a shove. I punched him and knocked him off the dock. I said, "Leave me alone. I'm doing my work, just stay away from me, just don't give me the with-the-hands business."

9   Hell, if you whip a damn mule he might kick you. Stay out of my way, that's all. Working is bad enough, don't bug me. I would rather work my . . . off for eight hours a day with nobody watching me than five minutes with a guy watching me. Who you gonna sock? You can't sock General Motors, you can't sock anybody in Washington, you can't sock a system.

10   A mule, an old mule, that's the way I feel. Oh yeah. See. (Shows black and blue marks on arms and legs, burns.) You know what I heard from more than one guy at work? "If my kid wants to work in a factory, I am going to kick the hell out of him." I want my kid to be an effete snob. Yeah, mm-hmm. (Laughs.) I want him to be able to quote Walt Whitman, to be proud of it.

11   If you can't improve yourself, you improve your posterity. Otherwise life isn't worth nothing. You might as well go back to the cave and stay there. I'm sure the first caveman who went over the hill to see what was on the other side—I don't think he went there wholly out of curiosity. He went there because he wanted to get his son out of the cave. Just the same way I want to send my kid to college.

* * *

12   If I had a twenty-hour workweek, I'd get to know my kids better, my wife better. Some kid invited me to go on a college campus. On a Saturday. It was summertime. Hell, if I have a choice of taking my wife and kids to a picnic or going to a college

campus, it's gonna be the picnic. But if I worked a twenty-hour week, I could go do both. Don't you think with that extra twenty hours people could really expand? Who's to say? . . .

The twenty-hour week is a possibility today. The intellectuals, they always say 13 there are potential Lord Byrons, Walt Whitmans, Roosevelts, Picassos working in construction or steel mills or factories. But I don't think they believe it. I think what they're afraid of is the potential Hitlers and Stalins that are there too. The people in power fear the leisure man.

* * *

It isn't that the average working guy is dumb. He's tired, that's all. I picked up a book 14 on chess one time. That thing laid in the drawer for two or three weeks, you're too tired. During the weekends you want to take your kids out. You don't want to sit there and the kid comes up: "Daddy, can I go to the park?" You got your nose in a book? Forget it.

I know a guy fifty-seven years old. Know what he tells me? "Mike, I'm old and 15 tired *all* the time." The first thing happens at work: when the arms start moving, the brain stops. I punch in about ten minutes to seven in the morning. I say hello to a couple of guys I like, I kid around with them. . . .

I put on my hard hat, change into my safety shoes, put on my safety glasses, go 16 to the bonderizer. It's the thing I work on. They rake the metal, they wash it, they dip it in a paint solution, and we take it off. Put it on, take it off, put it on, take it off, put it on, take it off. . . .

I say hello to everybody but my boss. At seven it starts. My arms get tired 17 about the first half-hour. After that, they don't get tired any more, until maybe the last half-hour at the end of the day. I work from seven to three thirty. My arms are tired at seven thirty and they're tired at three o'clock. I hope to God I never get broke in, because I always want my arms to be tired at seven thirty and three o'clock. (Laughs.) 'Cause that's when I know that there's a beginning and there's an end. That I'm not brainwashed. In between, I don't even try to think.

If I were to put you in front of a dock and I pulled up a skid in front of you with 18 fifty hundred-pound sacks of potatoes and there are fifty more skids just like it, and this is what you're gonna do all day, what would you think about—potatoes? Unless a guy's a nut, he never thinks about work or talks about it. Maybe about baseball or about getting drunk the other night or he got laid or he didn't get laid. I'd say one out of a hundred will actually get excited about work.

* * *

Oh yeah, I daydream. I fantasize about a sexy blonde in Miami who's got my union 19 dues. (Laughs.) I think of the head of the union the way I think of the head of my company. Living it up. I think of February in Miami. Warm weather, a place to lay in. When I hear a college kid say, "I'm oppressed," I don't believe him. You know what I'd like to do for one year? Live like a college kid. Just for one year. I'd love to. Wow!

(Whispers.) Wow! Sports car! Marijuana! (Laughs.) Wild, sexy broads. I'd love that, hell yes, I would.

* * *

20   After work I usually stop off at a tavern. Cold beer. Cold beer right away. When I was single, I used to go into hillbilly bars, get in a lot of brawls. Just to explode. I got a thing on my arm here (indicates scar). I got slapped with a bicycle chain. O, wow! (Softly.) Mmmm. I'm getting older. (Laughs.) I don't explode as much. You might say I'm broken in. (Quickly.) No, I'll never be broken in. (Sighs.) When you get a little older, you exchange the words. When you're younger, you exchange the blows.

21   When I get home, I argue with my wife a little bit. Turn on TV, get mad at the news. (Laughs.) I don't even watch the news that much. I don't want to go to bed angry. Don't hit a man with anything heavy at five o'clock. He just can't be bothered. This is his time to relax. The heaviest thing he wants is what his wife has to tell him.

22   When I come home, know what I do for the first twenty minutes? Fake it. I put on a smile. I got a kid three years old. Sometimes she says, "Daddy, where've you been?" I say "Work." I could have told her I'd been in Disneyland. What's work to a three-year-old kid? If I feel bad, I can't take it out on the kids. Kids are born innocent of everything but birth. You can't take it out on your wife, either. This is why you go to a tavern. You want to release it there rather than do it at home. What does an actor do when he's got a bad movie? I got a bad movie every day.

23   I don't even need the alarm to get up in the morning. I can go out drinking all night, fall asleep at four, and bam! I'm up at six—no matter what I do. (Laughs.) It's a pseudo-death, more or less. Your whole system is paralyzed and you give all the appearance of death. It's an in-grown clock. It's a thing you just get used to. The hours differ. It depends. Sometimes my wife wants to do something crazy like play five hundred rummy or put a puzzle together. It could be midnight, could be ten o'clock, could be nine thirty.

24   *What do you do weekends?*

25   Drink beer, read a book. See that one? *Violence in America.* It's one of them studies from Washington. One of them committees they're always appointing. A thing like that I read on a weekend. But during the weekdays, gee . . . I just thought about it. I don't do that much reading from Monday through Friday. Unless it's a horny book. . . . I'll read it at work and go home and do my homework. (Laughs.) That's what the guys at the plant call it—homework. (Laughs.) Sometimes my wife works on Saturday and I drink beer at the tavern.

* * *

26   If I were hiring people to work, I'd try naturally to pay them a decent wage. I'd try to find out their first names, their last names, keep the company as small as possible, so I could personalize the whole thing. All I would ask a man is a handshake, see you in the morning. No applications, nothing. I wouldn't be interested in the guy's past. Nobody ever checks the pedigree on a mule, do they? But they do on a

man. . . . Can you picture walking up to a mule and saying, "I'd like to know who his granddaddy was?"

I'd like to run a combination bookstore and tavern. (Laughs.) I would like to   27
have a place where college kids came and a steelworker could sit down and talk. Where a workingman could not be ashamed of Walt Whitman and where a college professor could not be ashamed that he painted his house over the weekend.

If a carpenter built a cabin for poets, I think the least the poets owe the car-   28
penter is just three or four one-liners on the wall. A little plaque. Though we labor with our minds, this place we can relax in was built by someone who can work with his hands. And his work is as noble as ours. I think the poet owes something to the guy who builds the cabin for him.

I don't think of Monday. You know what I'm thinking about on Sunday night?   29
Next Sunday. If you work real hard, you think of a perpetual vacation. Not perpetual sleep. . . . What do I think of on a Sunday night? Lord, I wish . . . I could do something else for a living.

I don't know who the guy is who said there is nothing sweeter than an unfinished   30
symphony. Like an unfinished painting and an unfinished poem. If he creates this thing one day—let's say, Michelangelo's Sistine Chapel. It took him a long time to do this, this beautiful work of art. But what if he had to create this Sistine Chapel a thousand times a year? Don't you think that would even dull Michelangelo's mind? Or if da Vinci had to draw his anatomical charts thirty, forty, fifty, sixty, eighty, ninety, a hundred times a day? Don't you think that would even bore da Vinci?

Way back, you spoke of the guys who built the pyramids, not the pharaohs, the un-   31
knowns. You put yourself in their category?

Yes. I want my signature on 'em, too. Sometimes, out of pure meanness, when   32
I make something, I put a little dent in it. I like to do something to make it really unique. Hit it with a hammer. I deliberately [mess] it up to see if it'll get by just so I can say I did it. It could be anything. Let me put it this way: I think God invented the dodo bird so when we get up there we could tell Him, "Don't you ever make mistakes?" and He'd say "Sure, look." (Laughs.) I'd like to make my imprint. My dodo bird. A mistake, mine. Let's say the whole building is nothing but red bricks. I'd like to have just the black one or the white one or the purple one. Deliberately [mess] up.

This is gonna sound square, but my kid is my imprint. He's my freedom. There's   33
a line in one of Hemingway's books. I think it's from *For Whom the Bell Tolls*. They're behind the enemy lines, somewhere in Spain, and she's pregnant. She wants to stay with him. He tells her no. He says, "If you die, I die," knowing he's gonna die. But if you go, I go. Know what I mean? The mystics call it the brass bowl. Continuum. You know what I mean? This is why I work. Every time I see a young guy walk by with a shirt and tie and dressed up real sharp, I'm lookin' at my kid, you know? That's it.

The Stonemason: Carl Murray Bates

We're in a tavern no more than thirty yards from the banks of the Ohio.   34
Toward the far side of the river, Alcoa smokestacks belch forth: an uneasy coupling of a bucolic past and an industrial present. The waters are polluted, yet the jobs out there offer the townspeople their daily bread.

He is fifty-seven years old. He's a stonemason who has pursued his craft since he was seventeen. None of his three sons is in his trade.

35   As far as I know, masonry is older than carpentry, which goes clear back to Bible times. Stone mason goes back way before Bible time: the pyramids of Egypt, things of that sort. Anybody that starts to build anything, stone, rock, or brick, start on the northeast corner. Because when they built King Solomon's Temple, they started on the northeast corner. To this day, you look at your courthouses, your big public buildings, you look at the cornerstone, when it was created, what year, it will be on the northeast corner. (Laughs.) Superstition, I suppose.

36   With stone we build just about anything. Stone is the oldest and best building material that ever was. Stone was being used even by the cavemen that put it together with mud. They built out of stone before they even used logs. He got him a cave, he built stone across the front. And he learned to use dirt, mud, to make the stones lay there without sliding around—which was the beginnings of mortar, which we still call mud. The Romans used mortar that's almost as good as we have today.

37   Everyone hears these things, they just don't remember 'em. But me being in the profession, when I hear something in that line, I remember it. Stone's my business. I, oh, sometimes talk to architects and engineers that have made a study and I pick up the stuff here and there.

38   Every piece of stone you pick up is different, the grain's a little different and this and that. It'll split one way and break the other. You pick up your stone and look at it and make an educated guess. It's a pretty good day layin' stone or brick. Not tiring. Anything you like to do isn't tiresome. It's hard work; stone is heavy. At the same time, you get interested in what you're doing and you usually fight the clock the other way. You're not lookin' for quittin'. You're wondering you haven't got enough done and it's almost quittin' time. (Laughs.) I ask the hod carrier what time it is and he says two thirty. I say, "Oh, my Lord, I was gonna get a whole lot more than this."

39   I pretty well work by myself. On houses, usually just one works. I've got the hod carrier there, but most of the time I talk to myself, "I'll get my hammer and I'll knock the chip off there." (Laughs.) A good hod carrier is half your day. He won't work as hard as a poor one. He knows what to do and make every move count makin' the mortar. It has to be so much water, so much sand. His skill is to see that you don't run out of anything. The hod carrier, he's above the laborer. He has a certain amount of prestige.

40   I think a laborer feels that he's the low man. Not so much that he works with his hands, it's that he's at the bottom of the scale. He always wants to get up to a skilled trade. Of course he'd make more money. The main thing is the common laborer—even the word common laborer—just sounds so common, he's at the bottom. Man that works with his hands takes pride in his work.

41   I get a lot of phone calls when I get home: how about showin' me how and I'll do it myself? I always wind up doin' it for 'em. (Laughs.) So I take a lot of pride in it and I do get, oh, I'd say, a lot of praise or whatever you want to call it. I don't suppose anybody, however much he's recognized, wouldn't like to be recognized a little more. I think I'm pretty well recognized.

One of my sons is an accountant and the other two are bankers. They're math-   42
ematicians, I suppose you'd call 'em that. Air-conditioned offices and all that. They
always look at the house I build. They stop by and see me when I'm aworkin'. Always want me to come down and fix somethin' on their house, too. (Laughs.) They
don't buy a house that I don't have to look at it first. Oh sure, I've got to crawl under it and look on the roof, you know. . . .

I can't seem to think of any young masons. So many of 'em before, the man lays   43
stone and his son follows his footsteps. Right now the only one of these sons I can
think of is about forty, fifty years old. I started back in the Depression times when
there wasn't any apprenticeships. You just go out and if you could hold your job, that's
it. I was just a kid then. Now I worked real hard and carried all the blocks I could.
Then I'd get my trowel and I'd lay one or two. The second day the boss told me: I
think you could lay enough blocks to earn your wages. So I guess I had only one day
of apprenticeship. Usually it takes about three years of being a hod carrier to start.
And it takes another ten or fifteen years to learn the skill. I admired the men that we
had at that time that were stonemasons. They knew their trade. So naturally I tried
to pattern after them. There's been very little change in the work. Stone is still stone,
mortar is still the same as it was fifty years ago. The style of stone has changed a little.
We use a lot more, we call it golf. A stone as big as a baseball up to as big as a basketball. Just round balls and whatnot. We just fit 'em in the wall that way.

Automation has tried to get in the bricklayer. Set 'em with a crane. I've seen   44
several put up that way. But you've always got in-between the windows and this and
that. It just doesn't seem to pan out. We do have a power saw. We do have an electric power mix to mix the mortar, but the rest of it's done by hand as it always was.

In the old days they all seemed to want it cut out and smoothed. It's harder   45
now because you have no way to use your tools. You have no way to use a string,
you have no way to use a level or a plumb. You just have to look at it because it's so
rough and many irregularities. You have to just back up and look at it.

All construction, there's always a certain amount of injuries. A scaffold will break   46
and so on. But practically no real danger. All I ever did do was work on houses, so
we don't get up very high—maybe two stories. Very seldom that any more. Most of
'em are one story. And so many of 'em use stone for a trim. They may go up four,
five feet and then paneling or something. There's a lot of skinned fingers or you hit
your finger with a hammer. Practically all stone is worked with hammers and chis-
els. I wouldn't call it dangerous at all.

Stone's my life. I daydream all the time, most times it's on stone. Oh, I'm gonna   47
build me a stone cabin down on the Green River. I'm gonna build stone cabinets in
the kitchen. That stone door's gonna be awful heavy and I don't know how to attach
the hinges. I've got to figure out how to make a stone roof. That's the kind of thing.
All my dreams, it seems like it's got to have a piece of rock mixed in it.

If I got some problem that's bothering me, I'll actually wake up in the night and   48
think of it. I'll sit at the table and get a pencil and paper and go over it, makin' marks
on paper or drawin' or however . . . this way or that way. Now I've got to work this
and I've only got so much. Or they decided they want it that way when you already
got it fixed this way. Anyone hates tearing his work down. It's all the same price but
you still don't like to do it.

49   These fireplaces, you've got to figure how they'll throw out heat, the way you curve the fireboxes inside. You have to draw a line so they reflect heat. But if you throw out too much of a curve, you'll have them smoke. People in these fine houses don't want a puff of smoke coming out of the house.

50   The architect draws the picture and the plans, and the draftsman and the engineer, they help him. They figure the strength and so on. But when it comes to actually makin' the curves and doin' the work, you've got to do it with your hands. It comes right back to your hands.

51   When you get into stone, you're gettin' away from the prefabs, you're gettin' into the better homes. Usually at this day and age they'll start into sixty to seventy thousand and run up to about half a million. We've got one goin' now that's mighty close, three or four hundred thousand. That type of house is what we build.

52   The lumber is not near as good as it used to be. We have better fabricating material, such as plywood and sheet rock and things of that sort, but the lumber itself is definitely inferior. Thirty, forty years ago a house was almost entirely made of lumber, wood floors. . . . Now they have vinyl, they have carpet, everything, and so on. The framework wood is getting to be of very poor quality.

53   But stone is still stone and the bricks are actually more uniform than they used to be. Originally they took a clay bank . . . I know a church been built that way. Went right on location, dug a hole in the ground and formed bricks with their hands. They made the bricks that built the building on the spot.

54   Now we've got modern kilns, modern heat, the temperature don't vary. They got better bricks now than they used to have. We've got machines that make brick, so they're made true. Where they used to, they were pretty rough. I'm buildin' a big fireplace now out of old brick. They run wide, long, and it's a headache. I've been two weeks on that one fireplace.

55   The toughest job I ever done was this house, a hundred years old plus. The lady wanted one room left just that way. And this doorway had to be closed. It had deteriorated and weathered for over a hundred years. The bricks was made out of broken pieces, none of 'em were straight. If you lay 'em crooked, it gets awful hard right there. You spend a lifetime tryin' to learn to lay bricks straight. And it took a half-day to measure with a spoon, to try to get the mortar to match. I'd have so much dirt, so much soot, so much lime, so when I got the recipe right I could make it in bigger quantity. Then I made it with a coffee cup. Half a cup of this, half a cup of that . . . I even used soot out of a chimney and sweepin's off the floor. I was two days layin' up a little doorway, mixin' the mortar and all. The boss told the lady it couldn't be done. I said, "Give me the time, I believe I can do it." I defy you to find where that door is right now. That's the best job I ever done.

56   There's not a house in this country that I haven't built that I don't look at every time I go by. (Laughs.) I can set here now and actually in my mind see so many that you wouldn't believe. If there's one stone in there crooked, I know where it's at and I'll never forget it. Maybe thirty years, I'll know a place where I should have took that stone out and redone it but I didn't. I still notice it. The people who live there might not notice it, but I notice it. I never pass that house that I don't think of it. I've got one house in mind right now. (Laughs.) That's the work of my hands. 'Cause you

see, stone, you don't prepaint it, you don't camouflage it. It's there, just like I left it forty years ago.

I can't imagine a job where you go home and maybe go by a year later and you   57
don't know what you've done. My work, I can see what I did the first day I started. All my work is set right out there in the open and I can look at it as I go by. It's something I can see the rest of my life. Forty years ago, the first blocks I ever laid in my life, when I was seventeen years old. I never go through Eureka—a little town down there on the river—that I don't look thataway. It's always there.

Immortality as far as we're concerned. Nothin' in this world lasts forever,   58
but did you know that stone—Bedford limestone, they claim—deteriorates one-sixteenth of an inch every hundred years? And it's around four or five inches for a house. So that's gettin' awful close. (Laughs.)

VOCABULARY

Directions: Locate each of the key words in the reading selection. Then read and study each word in its context and try to determine its meaning. Use a dictionary or thesaurus to check your guess. Write the meanings of the words in the margin of the text.

Record the new words you've learned below.

Key Word	Paragraph	Meaning
1. muses	4	
2. posterity	11	
3. pseudo-death	23	
4. masonry	35	
5. prefabs	51	
6. kilns	54	
Others?		

GUIDE QUESTIONS

Directions: The purpose of guide questions is to ensure your understanding of what you have read. They will also help you to analyze and evaluate the author's ideas and apply them to the real world and your own life.

Write answers to the questions in your notebook or on a separate sheet of paper if your instructor wishes to collect them. Your answers will form the basis of class discussion.

1. Why do you think this selection is titled "Who Built the Pyramids?"
2. Describe Mike Lefevre's attitude toward his job.
3. Why do you think Mike feels the way he does? Support your answer with quotes from the passage.
4. Why do you think Mike says he got "a tiny satisfaction" when he loaded a truck in a previous job?
5. Mike says he would like to run a combination tavern and bookstore. Why do you think this idea appeals to him?
6. Mike calls himself "dumb." Do you think he is dumb? Support your opinion with quotes from the text.
7. In your opinion, what could be done to make Mike more satisfied with his life?
8. Discuss Mike's attitude with some of your friends and relatives; think about your own work experiences. Do you believe Mike is typical of most workers? Explain.
9. Describe Carl Murray Bates's job. What does he do all day?
10. Describe Carl's attitude toward his job. Go through the interview and find evidence to support your answer.
11. Carl discusses the problems of laborers in paragraph 40. What does he think is the common laborer's worst problem? Would Mike agree with him?
12. In the last paragraph Carl discusses immortality. What is immortality as far as Carl is concerned? What is immortality for Mike?

APPLICATION

Directions: Based on all the reading and thinking you have done about jobs and job satisfaction, compile a list of the things you feel are necessary for satisfaction on the job. Then list the jobs you think would fulfill the requirements on your list.

My requirements for job satisfaction:

1. _____

2. _____

3. _____

4. _____

5. _____

6. _____

Examples of jobs that would satisfy my requirements:

1. _____

2. _____

3. _____

4. _____

5. _____

6. _____

When you have completed your lists, compare them to the lists of your classmates. Are there differences in your lists? Discuss the differences and the possible reasons for them.

WRITING

Directions: Return to question 6 in "Thinking about Working" on page 171. "If you had enough money so that you did not need to work, would you work anyway? Why or why not?" Write three paragraphs discussing 1) what you think Mike's answer would be, 2) what you think Carl's answer would be, and 3) your answer. Be sure to explain each of your answers.

SHORT TAKE

THE COURTSHIP OF ARTHUR AND AL

James Thurber

Once upon a time there was a young beaver named Al and an older beaver named Arthur. They were both in love with a pretty little female. She looked with disfavor upon the young beaver's suit because he was a harum-scarum and a ne'er-do-well. He had never done a single gnaw of work in his life, for he preferred to eat and sleep and to swim lazily in the streams and to play Now-I'll-Chase-You with the girls. The older beaver had never done anything but work from the time he got his first teeth. He had never played anything with anybody.

When the young beaver asked the female to marry him she said she wouldn't think of it unless he amounted to something. She reminded him that Arthur had built thirty-two dams and was working on three others, whereas he, Al, had never even made a bread-board or a pin tray in his life. Al was very sorry, but he said he would never go to work just because a woman wanted him to. Thereupon she offered to be a sister to him, but he pointed out that he already had seventeen sisters. So he went back to eating and sleeping and swimming in the streams and playing Spider-in-the-Parlor with the girls. The female married Arthur one day at the lunch hour—he could never get away from work for more than one hour at a time. They had seven children and Arthur worked so hard supporting them he wore his teeth down to the gum line. His health broke in two before long and he died without ever having had a vacation in his life. The young beaver continued to eat and sleep and swim in the streams and play Unbutton-Your-Shoe with the girls. He never Got Anywhere, but he had a long life and a Wonderful Time.

Moral: It is better to have loafed and lost than never to have loafed at all.

As we move toward the twenty-first century, American business faces many challenges. Among them is what some call "the changing American work force." Due to the civil rights movement, increased immigration, and progress toward equality for women, the make-up of the work force is changing from one dominated by white males to one of enormous diversity. As always, change brings problems as well as joys. Business executives have learned that, just as everyone does not look alike, neither do they always think alike or act alike. In this article from Working Woman *magazine, we are told that, if America is to recover its premier place in the world economy, business will have to learn to manage this new diverse work force—and that the manager of the future who can do so successfully will be indispensable.*

CULTURAL DIVERSITY

Audrey Edwards

The second-grade schoolteacher posed a simple-enough problem to the class: "There are four blackbirds sitting in a tree. You take a slingshot and shoot one of them. How many are left?"   1

"Three," answered the seven-year-old European with certainty. "One subtracted from four leaves three."   2

"Zero," answered the seven-year-old African with equal certainty. "If you shoot one bird, the others will fly away."   3

The problem, as it turns out, was not so simple after all. Indeed, in some ways it gets to the very heart of what the fuss is all about regarding cultural diversity and the need to recognize it, understand it, value it, and, finally, manage it. Like it or not, the American work place (like the American classroom) is changing—in gender, color, nationality, and cultural points of view. By the year 2000, according to the Bureau of Labor Statistics, women will make up about 47 percent of workers, and minorities and immigrants will hold 26 percent of all jobs, up from 22 percent in 1990. It is clearly no longer a man's world, and certainly not a white man's world, given that he is expected to account for only 32 percent of the entering work force by 2000.   4

The implications are profound. The ability of American business to recover lost productivity, regain its competitive edge, and move into the twenty-first century with a renewed sense of preeminence will depend precisely on its ability to effectively attract and manage the diverse talent that will characterize its new work force. Many companies find themselves already employing a diverse work force, and those who anticipate trends rather than follow them are taking steps to get a handle on just who these new workers are, how they differ from the old workers and how they can be best utilized.   5

The new focus on managing diversity is partially a reaction to what most human-resource specialists agree have been the shortcomings of affirmative action. "There's always been a discomfort with affirmative action," says Iris Randall, president of New Beginnings, a New York consulting firm that runs corporate seminars on managing diversity. "Those who come in under it always feel there's a suspicion that they wouldn't be there were it not for affirmative action."   6

7   Cultural diversity, on the other hand, describes reality, not quotas or minority hires. But like affirmative action, it also means opportunity. The labor market is going to look and be different. The challenge, then, is in learning how to manage this difference. And the manager who can successfully do so will be as indispensable to corporate management as working capital.

What a Difference Difference Makes

8   Ironically, one major obstacle to managing diversity is embedded in the very principles upon which America was founded: the notion that "all men are created equal." Our nation's character and culture have been built on such concepts as "One nation under God, indivisible . . ." and on the idea of newcomers assimilating into an American mainstream. Equality has always been a guiding principle in American life, yet it has also resulted in a tendency to be uncomfortable with difference. "One of the hidden rules in American culture is that you don't comment on differences, because it's assumed differences mean a deficiency," contends Jo Vanderkloot, a social worker of British ancestry who works with an African-American partner, Myrtle Parnell, in training managers to lead diverse staffs.

9   This discomfort with difference is manifest in subtle and sometimes disturbing ways. A black walks into a room full of whites and everybody ignores his arrival—although it's the only thing on their minds. A polio victim with leg braces laboriously tries to climb a flight of steps, and only one person offers to help. In each of these instances, to comment or otherwise make note of differences would be considered impolite, insensitive, intolerant.

10   Such hidden rules can be catastrophic in the work place. "A major mistake is having a multicultural work force and pretending you don't," says Parnell.

11   She and Vanderkloot started working together in 1982 at a mental-health center in New York's South Bronx—where a third of the staff was black, a third Hispanic, and a third white. They found that the major differences between the three cultural groups lie in how each communicates. "You can really divide the world into two communication styles," says Parnell. "One is a style that connects to people through doing things together and revolves around task, structure, and time." This tends to be the Anglo-American approach to work. "In Hispanic and African-American cultures, the relationship is what's important. There is a need to have some idea of who that other person is in order to work together—what is your common ground? The whole issue of time—get it done now, be here by four o'clock—is so Anglo-American. In other cultures you have an obligation to honor the relationship first."

12   "You can see what happens in the work force when these issues are not understood, when managers assume everybody is the same," adds Vanderkloot. Indeed, when the two seven-year-olds from different cultures were asked to solve the same math problem, each gave a different answer. Who was right and who was wrong? Both and neither, depending on your cultural point of view. For the first seven-year-old, the birds represented a hypothetical situation (structure) that required a literal answer (task). For the second seven-year-old, the birds had a relationship to each other with known behavior that could be expected to occur if one was shot. The

organizations that learn to respect and value the perspectives both cultures bring to problem solving will be ahead in the twenty-first century.

Recognizing the Face of Diversity

It is one thing to recognize that the work force is changing. It is very different, and sometimes difficult, however, to know exactly how to manage people who not only look but also think differently than you do. As Myrtle Parnell and Jo Vanderkloot maintain, it is crucial that we first understand how we have been shaped by our own culture and begin to recognize some of the biases and stereotypes we often bring to our interactions with others who are unlike us. One such stereotype is the belief that it is largely white men who are insensitive to culturally different groups. 13

For Judy Martinez, a thirty-four-year-old career counselor in Orlando, Florida, the black male director at the community-service agency she worked for was the cause of what she terms "the worst day of my career." Martinez, who had been nursing a cold, was seated at her desk sipping from a twelve-ounce bottle of malta, a non-alcoholic barley beverage popular in the Spanish-speaking Caribbean. "The director kept going back and forth past my office and looking in. The next day I received a memo from him that said, 'Alcoholic beverages are not allowed on the premises, and this is an official reprimand. . . .' I was in shock. But then, when I tried to talk to him about his memo to get the reprimand removed from my file, he refused to meet with me. To this day, the man had never admitted he was wrong. He has said nothing to me. *Nada.*" 14

Martinez had to go over the director's head to the executive director, a Panamanian, who personally removed the reprimand from her otherwise unblemished file. Yet Martinez, who is no longer with the agency, still feels hurt by the sting of that cultural misunderstanding. "It was defamation of character," she says angrily. "Why did the director automatically assume that Martinez, a Puerto Rican, was sitting at her desk drinking beer all day? Would he have made the same assumption about an American white man or woman or an African-American person?" "Cross-cultural glitches like this can lead to what's come to be known as an 'apathetic work force,'" says Vanderkloot. 15

"The problem with assumptions and stereotypes is that they are often the only way we have of processing information," says consultant Iris Randall. "If the only Asians you've seen are on *Kung Fu,* then that's your understanding of Asians." What Randall does in her seminars with corporate managers (her clients include Mobil and Avon) is focus on getting managers to see past their assumptions and stereotypes. "When you're working in a corporation, if you're going to empower someone different from you in order to get the best out of them, you've got to look at and understand their behavior." 16

The way managers and employees behave is, of course, largely a function of personal style, but it is influenced by culture. "We start out our seminars by asking everyone to say what it is about themselves that makes them different from everyone else in the room," Randall says. "Everyone brings an individual culture to the work place and it starts being shaped the day they're born. We look at things like birth rank and gender and the region of the country they're from. We ask them: 'What 17 was valued in your family?' 'Did you have multicultural friends, or did you grow up in a small, provincial town?'"

18   Randall then has managers fill out a personal-profile questionnaire used by human-resource trainers to help employees assess their behavioral styles. The Personal Profile System, developed by Performax Systems International, identifies four styles of behavior. Randall explains the four styles and the differences between them, then tells managers which category they fit into.

19   The first style is the D, or dominant, behavior. "People with high D, Donald Trump-type dominant behavior," says Randall, "make decisions rapidly. They're interested in results, the bottom line." Of course, individuals from all cultural backgrounds fall into this category, but Randall says most often it's people with a Euro-American background, particularly white males, who exhibit it.

20   The second style is I, for influencers. "African Americans, Hispanics, and women in general exhibit more I behavior," contends Randall. "These types are very verbal. They are good at influencing and persuading. They are the cheerleaders: 'I can, you can, we can make a difference.' They like people, and they like applause."

21   C is the cautious style, more frequently seen among Asians, believes Randall. "They are taught not to shoot from the hip, not to be confrontational, always to think before they speak, to make sure they are right." And S, or steady, behavior is, Randall feels, more often found among Native Americans. "For the most part, they show the high S behavior of a person who will hang in there. They are good team players and have no trouble recognizing the person in charge, whereas D-behavior types all act as if they are the boss."

22   Of course, to assume that all people from these respective cultures will exhibit these behaviors is to perpetuate more stereotypes. Focusing on culture and behavior—your own as well as those of people different from you—simply helps you develop insight into different mindsets, which is crucial for managing cultural diversity. "If you're a manager and you're looking for higher productivity out of your people, and if you realize that you can get it by understanding how they tend to behave and by talking their language, hopefully you will learn to do it," says Randall. Once you do, the payoff will be increased productivity and decreased conflict.

How to Manage the New Work Force

23   Paul Nolan represents what used to be the typical middle manager in American business: white, male, thirty-something. As director of corporate training for the Lincoln Savings Bank in New York, he is not only observing firsthand the changing face of the American work force but also learning how to value and manage the change. "I've never seen an ethnic make-up like the one here," Nolan says. The bank's employee mix includes Hispanics, Chinese, East Indians, black and Italian-Americans. Over a year ago Lincoln retained the services of Myrtle Parnell and Jo Vanderkloot to teach its employees how to understand and better manage such diversity.

24   Nolan, who does all of the employee training for Lincoln, has been through a number of the multicultural-training sessions conducted for the bank and believes he is a better manager for it. "I've always seen life through white, male eyes," he admits, explaining that, before the training, he tended to bring a classic dominant style to his employee-training sessions. "Even now, when I speak in front of all white males, I'm

very structured, very aggressive, succinct. But if I had the same discussion before a partly, say, Chinese group, I'd ask open-ended questions, such as 'Tell me what you think about this' instead of 'This is what I think.' I've learned that others can perceive me as 'this white man telling me what to do.'"

Nolan says that, before the diversity seminars, his usual approach to training classes was to say what he thought and then expect to be challenged. He would stand over participants and say, "Come on—tell me, tell me what you think. . . ." The Asians on his staff, in particular, would just sit there silently. Now, Nolan says, he understands that they simply weren't comfortable challenging authority that way. So he poses questions differently.   25

Nolan also listens for answers differently. "It used to be that I always knew the question I was going to ask and what I wanted in terms of a response," he says. "But I found that, by structuring the classes that way, I could be alienating some participants. Latinos, for instance, respond to a style that's a little less structured. If I say 1, 2, 3, someone might say 8, 9, 10 instead of 4, 5, 6, but I've got to allow for that. I still like structure and I still want to get a certain answer, but now I also want to know why people think the way they do. I've learned to view problem solving in a new way because of the different perspectives other cultures bring to it."   26

Nolan's new approach to training has shown results. "The participation rate among the minorities on staff has risen dramatically," he says. "It almost matches that of the other employees."   27

In the new information era, communication is the most valuable business tool. Understanding different mindsets and cultural perspectives is more crucial than ever to effective management. That doesn't mean it's easy: To effectively deal with diversity, we will have to change how we do just about everything, assert Vanderkloot and Parnell. "Nobody's cultural rules will prevail intact," says Parnell. "Institutions that were designed around a common culture aren't working anymore."   28

What we must have to make our institutions work again and to be effective as managers is a new respect for cultural differences. As R. Roosevelt Thomas, Jr., executive director of the American Institute for Managing Diversity at Atlanta's Morehouse College, wrote recently in the *Harvard Business Review:* "This is no longer simply a question of common decency. It is a question of business survival."   29

VOCABULARY

Directions: Locate each of the key words in the reading selection. Then read and study each word in its context and try to determine its meaning. Use a dictionary or thesaurus to check your guess. Write the meanings of the words in the margin of the text.

Record the new words you've learned below and on the next page.

Key Word	Paragraph	Meaning
1. implications	5	
2. indispensable	7	

Key Word	Paragraph	Meaning
3. embedded	8	
4. assimilating	8	
5. manifest	9	
6. biases	13	
7. apathetic	15	
8. intact	28	
Others?		

GUIDE QUESTIONS

Directions: The purpose of these guide questions is to ensure your understanding of what you have read. They will also help you to analyze and evaluate the author's ideas and apply them to the real world and your own life.

Write answers to the questions in your notebook or on a separate sheet of paper if your instructor wishes to collect them. Your answers will form the basis of class discussion.

1. How would you have answered the question posed in paragraph 1 of the selection? Compare your answer to those of the two seven-year-olds.
2. Describe some of the changes the author says will occur in the American work place by the year 2000.
3. Cite the "major obstacle to managing diversity" given in the selection. Why does the author call it "ironic"?
4. Do the examples in paragraph 9 of "discomfort with difference" ring true to you? Can you supply other similar examples from your own experience?
5. Discuss the two communication styles cited by Myrtle Parnell.
6. React to the experience Judy Martinez had with her director. Why does the author describe this as a "cultural misunderstanding"?
7. React to the statement made in paragraph 16 by consultant Iris Randall: "If the only Asians you've seen are on *Kung Fu*, then that's your understanding of Asians."

8. List and describe the four behavioral styles identified in the Personal Profile System. Do you fit into any of the four styles?

9. Summarize the things Paul Nolan learned from multicultural training sessions.

10. Explain R. Roosevelt Thomas's conclusion that "This is no longer simply a question of common decency. It is a question of business survival."

APPLICATION

Directions: Look at each of the pictures below and guess what each pair of individuals is discussing.

© Janette Beckman

"A stereotypical first reaction to the frames is to assume that the white men are discussing business-related papers, the women are cooing over baby pictures, and the black men are joking about something sports-related," says Lewis Griggs of Copeland Griggs Productions, which produced a video, Valuing Diversity, from which these pictures are taken. Griggs has observed hundreds of reactions to such scenes. Rather than "What are they looking at?" perhaps the question should be "What are you looking at when you see them?"

© Janette Beckman

WRITING

Directions: With your classmates, discuss your reactions to the pictures on page 209. Then write an essay discussing how stereotypes and assumptions can be harmful to people at work and in school. Write at least two paragraphs.

IT GOT LOST IN THE TRANSLATION

Even experts in business can fall flat on their faces when they forget the importance of language in human affairs. Here are some examples of language goofs by companies involved in international marketing:

—Several years ago Estée Lauder introduced a new foundation make-up in Germany called Country Mist. In the nick of time, a local manager called U.S. headquarters with a linguistic SOS: *Mist* means "manure" in German. The name was changed to Country Moist.

—An ad for Nitto Koygo Company, a golf course designer in Tokyo, goes like this: "Preparing for you club-life of luxurious relaxation always there. Feel and Taste it at any one of our golf clubs both in Japan and overseas as well, please."

—The slogan "Come Alive with Pepsi" almost appeared in the Chinese version of *Reader's Digest* as "Pepsi Brings Your Ancestors Back from the Grave."

—"Body by Fisher" was translated into "Corpse by Fisher" in Flemish.

—The French government published an English-language catalog promoting local CAD/CAM products. Referring to one software program, it read: "Different versions are available for educational institutes for symbolic prices."

—Tokyo Gas Company's slogan in English reads "My Life, My Gas."

—When Totes Inc. bought the German company Jagra-Haus, it announced the company would be renamed Totes Deutschland. Executives retreated when they learned the new corporate name meant "dead Germany."

Mary Madden. a nurse with experience in both the United States and England, compares the practice of her profession in the two societies. Most readers will be surprised to find sharp differences between the two countries and their attitudes toward nurses and nursing.

NURSING PRACTICES—ENGLAND AND AMERICA

Mary Madden

1   I left my native Ireland after I had completed a high-school education. I studied to become a nurse and midwife in England, and I eventually came to the United States of America. Because I have worked five years in hospitals in England and the United States, my friends frequently ask about differences, as I see them, in the practice of nursing on both sides of the Atlantic.

2   Until I realized how different the licensing laws of Great Britain are from those in the United States, I was surprised at the number of restrictions placed on a nurse's actions in this country. A nurse licensed in Britain may practice anywhere in the British Isles and in some countries abroad; in the United States, the nurse must apply in every state in which she hopes to work.

3   In Britain, a nurse is a deeply respected, devoted woman, entrusted with a vast amount of responsibility. The patients place unquestioned confidence in her judgment and advice. The doctor relies on her report of her observations, and he seldom interferes in what is considered a nursing duty.

4   The nurse decides when the patient is allowed out of bed or what type of bath he may have. I do not recall ever seeing an order on a physician's chart such as "OOR in 24 hours" or "may take a shower." The nurse judges when a wound is healed and when sutures may be removed. She is always consulted about the patient's requirements and his progress. And because of the structure of most hospitals in England, the nurse is in view of the patient constantly. Whenever he needs attention, the nurse is there in the ward, and she may observe him, too, unobtrusively.

5   Furthermore, the nurse is a member of the health team who sees the patient most frequently. To the patient she is the most familiar person in the strange hospital world.

6   In the United States, the patient is likely to be under the care of the same doctor in and out of the hospital, so the doctor is the person the patient knows best and the one in whom he confides most easily. But though the patient's treatment and care are discussed with the nursing staff, a nurse is not allowed much freedom to advise a patient. Also, I have seen doctors visit patients without a word of communication to the nurse. Personally I think it difficult to be ignored when a patient's care is concerned and I think it prevents full utilization of the nurse's knowledge and skills.

7   I myself found nursing practice easier, in a way, under the so-called "socialized medicine" of Great Britain than the more individual type of medical care found in the United States. It involved much less writing and left me at the patient's bedside, where I am happiest. There was no need to write several charges and requests for the needs of the patient. Stocks of drugs and other medicines were kept on each

ward, so that when medication was ordered, it was at hand. All charges were met by "National Health"—including all supplies and equipment used on the ward. The nurse tends a person who is free from much anxiety and hence more easily cared for while he is an inpatient.

On the other hand, I found that my introduction to an American hospital was a happy experience. As a new nurse, I was guided by an orientation program given by another nurse and quickly found my place on the patient-care team. I had never experienced such an orientation in England.   8

Policy, drug reference, and procedure books at the nurses' station provide a ready reference where a nurse may check facts when she is in doubt, and she can instruct a new nurse on the staff without confusion. The active U.S. nurse, while working, can keep informed about new trends, discoveries, and inventions in a rapidly changing world of medicine.   9

Here in the United States the nurse is regarded as an individual person and her personal life outside the hospital is given consideration. She develops interests in arts, sport, or a creative hobby; she is encouraged to further her education. Time and means are available to her to expand her horizons and to enrich her personality. Many nurses combine marriage and a career very ably in this country, but not in England or Ireland. All this tends to involve her more with people other than the sick. She is an interesting, informed, and happy person and at the bedside she can show understanding and perception.   10

In Britain, like most nurses, I lived in a nurses' home on the hospital grounds and was thus isolated in a special hospital community. Theoretically, I worked eight hours each day that I was on duty. But these hours were so arranged that one went to work twice in one day. One might work four hours in the morning, have a few hours free, and then go back to the ward for the evening. This schedule demands most of one's waking hours, and so mingling in the larger community outside the hospital was quite limited. The nurse was expected to find full satisfaction in her vocation, and thoughts of increases in salary were considered unworthy. Now, such attitudes are beginning to change and the winds of unrest are blowing through nursing in England, ruffling many a well-placed cap.   11

VOCABULARY

Directions: Locate each of the key words in the reading selection. Then read and study each word in its context and try to determine its meaning. Use a dictionary or thesaurus to confirm your guess. Write the meanings of the words in the margin of the text.

Record the new words you've learned below and on the next page.

Key Word	Paragraph	Meaning
1. midwife	1	
2. sutures	4	

Key Word	Paragraph	Meaning
3. unobtrusively	4	
4. mingling	11	
Others?		

GUIDE QUESTIONS

Directions: The purpose of these guide questions is to ensure your understanding of what you have read. They will also help you to analyze and evaluate the author's ideas and apply them to the real world and your own life.

Write answers to the questions in your notebook or on a separate sheet of paper if your instructor wishes to collect them. Your answers will form the basis of class discussion.

1. Use the information in the reading selection to compare and contrast the practice of nursing in England and the United States. The chart below gives you several categories, suggested by Madden, to consider.

	England	United States
Licensing of nurses		
Amount of responsibility nurse has for the patient		
Relationship with the doctor		
Orientation/ introduction to hospital		
Personal life and professional development		

2. Do you think Madden implies criticism of either country in her essay? In which country do you think she prefers to work? Why?
3. Note the way pronouns are used in this selection. Reread it to see which pronoun, feminine or masculine, is used for doctors, nurses, and patients. Can you draw any conclusions from this?

APPLICATION

Directions: Choose one of the questions below and write one paragraph in response.

1. Based on the information in this selection, where would you prefer to practice nursing, in England or the United States? Give reasons to support your opinion.
2. Based on the information in this selection, in which country, England or the United States, would you prefer to be a patient? Give reasons to support your opinion.

WRITING

Directions: Use the information you provided in the chart on the previous page to write an essay comparing and contrasting nursing practices in England and America. Write five brief paragraphs, one for each category in the chart. For each category, state the similarities and differences in the way nursing is practiced in the two countries.

This article reports on the findings of a survey of the readers of the magazine Working Woman. *Before you read, try your hand at answering some of the questions from the same survey.*

For each of the situations below, state whether you think it is an ethical problem or not an ethical problem.

1. *Unethical or no problem: Your boss treats clients to cocaine.*
2. *Unethical or no problem: A real estate agent showing a house doesn't say that the basement floods.*
3. *Unethical or no problem: An executive learns that his company is about to be sold, which will send its stock price soaring. He leaks this information to two clients as well as to several friends.*
4. *Unethical or no problem: An administrative assistant routinely makes up excuses for her boss when he takes long lunches with his secretary.*
5. *Unethical or no problem: After a year of poor sales, a sales representative convinces her boss to let her give expensive gifts to prospective clients. The tactic works and sales increase.*
6. *Unethical or no problem: A publisher gives his college-age niece a highly sought-after unpaid summer internship at his company.*
7. *Unethical or no problem: Company policy forbids employees to discuss salaries with each other, but two people trade information to negotiate better with their boss.*
8. *Unethical or no problem: A manager has accumulated sick days. She calls in sick even though she isn't and takes a few days off.*
9. *Unethical or no problem: A job applicant finds out the morning before her job interview that she is pregnant. She decides not to say anything rather than jeopardize her chances.*

HOW ETHICAL IS AMERICAN BUSINESS?

Ronni Sandroff

1   Would you work for a company that was polluting the environment . . . or a boss who lied to customers? Do you think it's unethical to flirt to make a sale? Or to call in sick when you need a "mental health" day? More than fourteen hundred *Working Woman* readers examined their scruples—and those of their colleagues—by responding to "Business Ethics: What Are Your Personal Standards?" published in the February issue. Hundreds went beyond the survey to enclose heartfelt letters. Their conclusion? Fair play is disappearing from the American business scene—and it hurts.

2   The majority of respondents said they personally have witnessed such foul play as lying to employees; expense-account abuses at the highest levels; and in-office jockeying involving favoritism, nepotism, and taking credit for other people's work. Almost half have seen discrimination based on sex and color, more than a third, sexual harassment; and just under a third, lying to make a sale. And they charge that this apparent erosion of the fair-play ethic is not only disheartening but is also harmful to productivity, job stability, and profits in American business.

3   "I worked for a medical-device manufacturer that released a product for humans without implant studies," wrote one reader. Her protests went unheeded and

the product failed in some cases, causing unnecessary surgery in already weakened patients. The same company was sued for sending a maintenance man on an industrial espionage mission to sift through a competitor's garbage and collect information. Are tales like this symptomatic of a decline in American business ethics, or are they just a reflection of business as usual? Fifty-six percent of the respondents in the *Working Woman* ethics survey believe that American business ethics have deteriorated in the past ten years.

Contributing to employees' dismay, perhaps, is the fact that bad deeds seem to go unpunished: The companies or institutions that most respondents have worked for have not gotten into trouble over ethical violations. Part of the reason may be that the violations readers have seen most often, such as lying to employees, expense-account abuses, and so on, are difficult to prosecute.   4

And where is this wrongdoing taking place? When asked which industries were hotbeds of unethical behavior, a startlingly high number of readers—66 percent—pointed the finger at the government. We might dismiss this as simply good old American government-bashing if it weren't for the fact that women who work for the government are among those most likely to bash it: 62 percent of government workers feel the government is most unethical. "The government is the most unethical institution I've ever been associated with," wrote one reader. In contrast, other occupation groups think their ethics are better than the popular perception. For example, only 9 percent of lawyers—compared with 40 percent of all respondents—rated law as the most unethical.   5

How will a concern for ethics affect future career patterns? Ethics-wise, most respondents are willing to put their money where their mouths are: A strong majority of those polled said they would not work for a company with a history of environmental accidents, insider trading or worker accidents, or a law firm that defends known racketeers. Women in the helping professions were most scrupulous about where they'd work. However, more lawyers said they would work for any of these companies. "If all attorneys decided that they were too 'ethical' to defend 'known criminals,'" one reader reminded us, "accused persons would have no rights."   6

Where Do You Draw the Line?
Umpiring the ethics of the work place is not merely a spectator sport. Every worker is a player. What personal decisions do people make—and why do they make them? When it comes to personal scruples, the issues seem less clear-cut. Readers consider stealing time (in the form of phony sick days or personal phone calls) and supplies (computer software, office staples) or sharing company discounts with outsiders only minor violations. And trading competitive information with friends in the same industry is OK with almost half the respondents. More than 60 percent would use a stolen secret report from a competitor's company.   7

"Unethical behavior is quickly becoming acceptable behavior," wrote an information-systems director from St. Louis. "Some of us do little things like [putting] an occasional lunch with a friend on the old expense account. Without proper controls, the occasional lunch becomes the occasional trip or vacation. The result is still the same: Someone else pays for the ride."   8

9   The majority of respondents (53 percent) agreed that most successful business people occasionally have to compromise their principles. In fact, in a number of areas, women who rated themselves as highly successful (and generally had the highest incomes and education levels) were more willing to bend and break rules than less successful women. "Had I taken this survey five years ago while in middle management, my answers would have been much more black-and-white. The more exposed to business I become, the more aware I am of the gray areas. Is this because there are gray areas, or because justification has begun to set in?" one reader wondered.

The Reasons—and Excuses?

10   When asked if it's sometimes necessary to break the rules to get ahead, 42 percent of the respondents said yes and 44 percent said no. Some readers blamed the decline in ethics on the atmosphere created in the executive suite. "A fearful, angry employee will steal to get even for the emotional beating she feels she is taking," wrote one respondent. Another asked: "How ethical is it for large corporations to deny workers a pay raise while upper management still receives ridiculously large bonuses? This type of entrenched corruption at high levels eventually creates dishonest behaviors at the lower levels."

11   Unfair treatment of women managers and workers sometimes is used as a justification for not being completely aboveboard with employers. Take the possibility of pregnancy's having a negative impact on a woman's career. Seventy-six percent of respondents did not have ethical difficulty with a job applicant who doesn't tell a prospective employer that she's pregnant. Women with high incomes and education levels were more likely than others to think this way.

Standing Your Ground—and Yielding It

12   Petty thievery and lies aside, what do people do when confronted with a truly grievous wrong, such as the release of a dangerous product, or theft that is likely to bankrupt a company? About two out of three women over thirty years of age have had some experience in taking an ethical stand at work (though fewer than half of those in the eighteen-to-twenty-five-year-old group have yet been tested).

13   Did their stand get results? Respondents were split. "My attempts at 'correcting' ethical wrongs never engendered lasting change," wrote one discouraged reader who has worked for years in both the public and private sectors and ended up with a "great feeling of futility."

14   Another reader learned the hard way that fighting the good fight is worthwhile. "I had a good job that I quit rather than make the tough decision," she wrote. Six months later a male co-worker took the risk and informed one owner that the owner's partner was a cheat. The partner was forced out and the co-worker was rewarded with his job. "I would have been in line for the position if I had stayed and tattled," she wrote. She's since learned to speak out. "I have found that you can usually get the ethical point across and still get the job done."

15   Of women who have taken an ethical stand that has affected their careers, 37 percent said it had a positive effect and 30 percent said it had a negative effect.

Some of the women who took a stand with negative results—like getting fired—have learned, with bitterness, to keep their mouths and eyes shut. "In the two years I have worked full-time, I have seen numerous unethical situations. More often than not, I have decided to make it 'someone else's problem' so as not to jeopardize my career or my peace of mind."

This sort of detached cynicism can be painful for the individual. "While work-   16 ing on this survey I faced a very unsettling fact about myself," wrote one reader. "I find that I choose the path of least resistance more often than not [even though] I believe in honesty. It is scary to see how easily and subtly unethical behavior has become a pattern in my working life, as though one can be one person at work and a totally different creature at home."

What's the answer? Do written codes of ethics help? Should the government   17 step in? Overwhelmingly respondents said the ethical decisions they make on the job were learned at their parents' knees, and those values continue to be the most influential, along with religious teachings and the influences of friends, business colleagues, superiors, and books. Eleven percent had taken a special course in ethics, but only a few of these (1 percent) found that it made a difference.

Since many areas of confusion—such as pirating computer software and ac-   18 cepting gifts from suppliers—are not covered in the Ten Commandments, business ethics specific to the contemporary scene are clearly needed. Yet according to our respondents, these issues tend to be discussed only when a problem arises. Of readers whose work places do not have a formal code of ethics, almost 60 percent think it would be helpful. However, fewer than a third want government regulation of ethics.

The traditional American idea put forth by James Madison that free institutions   19 should not depend on virtue but be fueled by selfish impulses, properly balanced—is echoed by one reader: "There must be a way to teach ethics as self-interest rather than sacrifice: to emphasize that right action is the best way to build community values, trust, and long-term business relationships."

Is this possible in the real world? "I work for a corporation in which the com-   20 pany's standards of conduct are an everyday topic of conversation," wrote one reader. Her company insists on honest business dealings with customers and will not allow stealing confidential information from competitors. "My guess is that we are considered too principled for our own good. But when organizations within the company stray from company values, the results are always bad: low profits, high turnover, poor product quality—and hell to pay with the executive committee." This reader is thrilled to be out of the ethical mire of her previous jobs and to find that, at least in some places, fair play can be a winning strategy.

VOCABULARY

Directions: Locate each of the key words in the reading selection. Then read and study each word in its context and try to determine its meaning. Use a dictionary or thesaurus to check your guess. Write the meanings of the words in the margin of the text.

Record the new words you've learned on the next page.

Key Word	Paragraph	Meaning
1. scruples	1	
2. nepotism	2	
3. erosion	2	
4. unheeded	3	
5. deteriorated	3	
6. hotbeds	5	
7. entrenched	10	
8. engendered	13	
9. cynicism	16	
Others?		

GUIDE QUESTIONS

Directions: The purpose of these guide questions is to ensure your understanding of what you have read. They also will help you to analyze and evaluate the author's ideas and apply them to the real world and your own life.

Write answers to the questions in your notebook or on a separate sheet of paper if your instructor wishes to collect them. Your answers will form the basis of class discussion.

1. Describe the survey, its source, and its purpose.
2. The author of the article states her conclusion at the very beginning of the article; paraphrase it here.
3. Summarize some of the most important findings of the survey.
4. The author asks if the personal stories told by respondents to the survey are "symptomatic of a decline in American business ethics, or are they just a reflection of business as usual?" What does she mean by this question? What answer does she give?
5. According to the selection, where is the "hotbed" of unethical behavior? Does the answer surprise you? Why or why not?
6. Which group listed its own profession as the least unethical?

7. How did most people respond when asked if they would work for a company that allowed unethical situations to persist?

8. The author makes it clear that making ethical decisions is something that every worker must do. Give a few examples from your own knowledge and experience of the personal decisions employees have to make.

9. True or false: According to the article, the more successful and highly paid an employee is, the more likely he or she is to bend and break ethical rules.

10. a. Answer this question from your own perspective: Is it sometimes necessary to break the rules to get ahead?

    b. How did the respondents to the survey answer that same question?

11. Paragraph 16 begins, "This sort of detached cynicism can be painful for the individual." What is the author referring to here?

12. According to the respondents to the survey, where did they learn the values they used in making ethical decisions at work?

13. List some possible solutions to the problems of making ethical decisions at work.

APPLICATION

Here are some further results of the survey. A list of ethical violations is followed by the percentage of respondents who have personally observed them.

VIOLATIONS	PERCENT WHO HAVE WITNESSED VIOLATION
Fairness violations	
Favoritism or nepotism	70%
Taking credit for others' work	67%
Doing business with sexist clients	52%
Discrimination	47%
Sexual harassment	41%
Dishonesty	
Lying to employees	62%
Violating confidentiality	64%
Lying to make a sale	31%
Stealing	
Expense-account abuses	52%
Bribery	5%
Sexual trading	
Flirting to make a sale	43%
Sexual intimacy with boss	29%
Sex with co-worker on company time	19%
Sex with client to make a sale	10%

Have you personally observed any of these violations? Which ones? What did you do about it? Why? Discuss these questions with your classmates.

WRITING

Directions: Return to the answers you gave to the survey questions in the introduction to the selection. Below are the actual results of the survey. Compare your answers to the ones respondents gave.

1. Your boss treats clients to cocaine.
   Unethical   99%
   No problem   1%
2. A real estate agent showing a house doesn't say that the basement floods.
   Unethical   92%
   No problem   8%
3. An executive learns that his company is about to be sold, which will send its stock price soaring. He leaks this information to two clients as well as to several friends.
   Unethical   91%
   No problem   9%
4. An administrative assistant routinely makes up excuses for her boss when he takes long lunches with his secretary.
   Unethical   56%
   No problem   44%
5. After a year of poor sales, a sales representative convinces her boss to let her give expensive gifts to prospective clients. The tactic works and sales increase.
   Unethical   46%
   No problem   54%
6. A publisher gives his college-age niece a highly sought-after unpaid summer internship at his company.
   Unethical   42%
   No problem   58%
7. Company policy forbids employees to discuss salaries with each other, but two people trade information to negotiate better with their boss.
   Unethical   40%
   No problem   60%
8. A manager has accumulated sick days. She calls in sick even though she isn't and takes a few days off.
   Unethical   34%
   No problem   66%
9. A job applicant finds out the morning before her job interview that she is pregnant. She decides not to say anything rather than jeopardize her chances.
   Unethical   24%
   No problem   76%

Choose one of the questions from the list above. State your answer and then explain why you answered it the way you did. Write one paragraph.

Looking for a job is hard under the best of circumstances, but for a person with a handicap, the search is infinitely more difficult. In this selection, a lawyer who graduated with honors from Harvard University is rejected by employers, not because of a lack of ability but because of a disability.

DARKNESS AT NOON

Harold Krents

Blind from birth, I have never had the opportunity to see myself and have been completely dependent on the image I create in the eye of the observer. To date it has not been narcissistic. 1

There are those who assume that since I can't see, I obviously also cannot hear. Very often people will converse with me at the top of their lungs, enunciating each word very carefully. Conversely, people will also often whisper, assuming that since my eyes don't work, my ears don't either. 2

For example, when I go to the airport and ask the ticket agent for assistance to the plane, he or she will invariably pick up the phone, call a ground hostess and whisper: "Hi, Jane, we've got a seventy here." I have concluded that the word *blind* is not used for one of two reasons: Either they fear that if the dread word is spoken, the ticket agent's retina will immediately detach, or they are reluctant to inform me of my condition of which I may not have been previously aware. 3

On the other hand, others know that, of course, I can hear, but believe that I can't talk. Often, therefore, when my wife and I go out to dinner, a waiter or waitress will ask Kit if "he would like a drink" to which I respond that "indeed he would." 4

This point was graphically driven home to me while we were in England. I had been given a year's leave of absence from my Washington law firm to study for a diploma in law degree at Oxford University. During the year I became ill and was hospitalized. Immediately after admission, I was wheeled down to the X-ray room. Just at the door sat an elderly woman—elderly I would judge from the sound of her voice. "What is his name?" the woman asked the orderly who had been wheeling me. 5

"What's your name?" the orderly repeated to me. 6
"Harold Krents," I replied. 7
"Harold Krents," he repeated. 8
"When was he born?" 9
"When were you born?" 10
"November 5, 1944," I responded. 11
"November 5, 1944," the orderly intoned. 12

This procedure continued for approximately five minutes, at which point even my saint-like disposition deserted me. "Look," I finally blurted out, "this is absolutely ridiculous. Okay, granted I can't see, but it's got to have become pretty clear to both of you that I don't need an interpreter." 13

"He says he doesn't need an interpreter," the orderly reported to the woman. 14

The toughest misconception of all is the view that because I can't see, I can't work. I was turned down by over forty law firms because of my blindness, even 15 though my qualifications included a cum laude degree from Harvard College and a good ranking in my Harvard Law School class.

16   The attempt to find employment, the continuous frustration of being told that it was impossible for a blind person to practice law, the rejection letters, not based on my lack of ability but rather on my disability, will always remain one of the most disillusioning experiences of my life.

17   Fortunately, this view of limitation and exclusion is beginning to change. On April 16, the Department of Labor issued regulations that mandate equal-employment opportunities for the handicapped. By and large, the business community's response to offering employment to the disabled has been enthusiastic.

18   I therefore look forward to the day, with the expectation that it is certain to come, when employers will view their handicapped workers as a little child did me years ago when my family still lived in Scarsdale.

19   I was playing basketball with my father in our backyard according to procedures we had developed. My father would stand beneath the hoop, shout, and I would shoot over his head at the basket attached to our garage. Our next-door neighbor, aged five, wandered over into our yard with a playmate. "He's blind," our neighbor whispered to her friend in a voice that could be heard distinctly by Dad and me. Dad shot and missed; I did the same. Dad hit the rim; I missed entirely; Dad shot and missed the garage entirely. "Which one is blind?" whispered back the little friend.

20   I would hope that, in the near future, when a plant manager is touring the factory with the foreman and comes upon a handicapped and nonhandicapped person working together, his comment after watching them work will be, "Which one is disabled?"

VOCABULARY

Directions: Locate each of the key words in the reading selection. Then read and study each word in its context and try to determine its meaning. Use a dictionary or thesaurus to check your guess. Write the meanings of the words in the margin of the text.

Record the new words you've learned.

Key Word	Paragraph	Meaning
1. narcissistic	1	
2. enunciating	2	
3. retina	3	
4. disillusioning	16	When the dreams doesn't come true /where you cannot reach something
Others?		

GUIDE QUESTIONS

Directions: These guide questions will help to ensure your understanding of what you have read. They will also help you to analyze and evaluate the author's ideas and apply them to the real world and your own life.

Write answers to the questions in your notebook or on a separate sheet of paper if your instructor wishes to collect them. Your answers will form the basis of class discussion.

1. Describe Harold Krents: state all the facts and inferences you can draw from the selection.
2. What are some of the problems Krents has encountered because of his blindness?
3. What does Krents say was the most "disillusioning experience" of his life? Why does he feel this way?
4. What is Krents's main purpose in writing this essay?

APPLICATION

Directions: Discuss the question of whether a blind person can be an effective lawyer. What are some problems he or she would face? In which areas would blindness make no difference at all?

WRITING

Directions: Choose one of the people Krents describes—either the airport ticket agent, the waiter in the restaurant, or the woman at the hospital in England. Write that person a letter, reacting to his or her treatment of Krents.

THE QUESTIONS MOST FREQUENTLY ASKED AT JOB INTERVIEWS

1. What do you see yourself doing five years from now?
2. What are your long-range career goals?
3. How much do you expect to be earning five years from now?
4. Why did you choose the career you are preparing for?
5. What is your greatest strength?
6. What is your greatest weakness?
7. Tell me about yourself.
8. How has your education prepared you for your career?
9. What is your definition of success?
10. In what ways do you think you could make a contribution to our company?
11. What two or three accomplishments in your life are you the most proud of?
12. Why did you choose your college?
13. Why did you choose your major?
14. What changes would you make in your college?
15. Do you think your grades are a good indication of your academic achievement?
16. What extracurricular activities have you participated in? What did you learn from them?
17. Describe your ideal job.
18. Why are you seeking a job with this company?
19. What two or three things are most important to you in a job?
20. Are you willing to relocate? To travel?
21. Choose a serious problem you have faced in your life and tell how you dealt with it.
22. Describe a mistake you have made and what you learned from it.
23. Why should we hire you?

Japan's emergence as an economic superstar since World War II has been nothing short of miraculous. Throughout the 1980s and into the 1990s, the United States viewed Japan as a worrisome competitor. In this article, which first appeared in Esquire *magazine, author Pete Hamill muses over whether the Japanese paid too high a price for their economic boom. He reports that "the Japanese trade their personal lives and eighty-hour weeks for a drop-dead existence."*

DEATH OF A SALARYMAN

Pete Hamill

At dusk I was walking slowly through the dense throngs in the Ginza District when   1
the man fell forward on his face. He was medium-size and thin, but he hit the sidewalk hard, as if someone had smashed him from behind with a baseball bat.

A crowd swiftly gathered, murmuring in Japanese. Someone turned him over,   2
and I could see by the bone-colored skin and vacant eyes that he was already dead. A briefcase was clamped in his left hand. A filter-tipped Mild Seven cigarette lay beside him, smoldering where it fell.

"*Karoshi,*" someone whispered, as a cop arrived to move people back and give   3
the dead man air that he no longer needed. A woman standing beside me nodded in a knowing way and repeated the word, "*Karoshi . . .*"

The word means, roughly, "sudden death because of overwork." The average   4
victim is male, in his forties or fifties, just like the man on the sidewalk. The specific cause of death of a *karoshi* victim is usually heart failure or cerebral hemorrhage, brought on by stress or too many hours on the job. So that small, hushed group of Japanese in the Ginza might have been right. I never found out. A paramedic arrived, searched for a pulse, tried mouth-to-mouth resuscitation, finally shook his head without emotion. The fallen salaryman was lifted by stretcher into the ambulance and then carted off to eternity. The people who'd seen him fall were long gone; it was growing dark, and for most of them, there was still work to do.

Tokyo is a city that always reminds me of the America in which I grew up. The   5
language and faces are different, but the mood, spirit, and lack of menace are like New York in some lost year of the 1950s. Like New York in the old days, Tokyo is structured around some erratically designed imaginary dynamo, its coils wrapped about a central core that functions like a god in a bad science-fiction novel: invisible, mute—but all-powerful. Its presence is almost religious and the pace of the communicants is hurried, even frantic. But there are no armies of predators or scavenging junkies. At night women walk home alone without fear. Businessmen doze on subways, their briefcases safe in overhead racks. The absence of menace is not an illusion, the result of a sentimental *gaijin* who can't read the signs. In 1989, there were 754 murders in all of Japan (population: 150 million); in New York City last year, with a mere 7.5 million residents, there were 2,300 homicides.

Work is the major difference in the two societies now. While the United States,   6
its genius and treasury depleted by decades of hot and cold wars, is falling into a sickening swamp of drug addiction, welfare, self-pity, and paranoia, Japan works

harder than any nation on earth. According to 1989 figures from the Ministry of International Trade and Industry, the Japanese worker put in 2,246.8 hours of work the year before—300 more than the average American, 600 more than the West Germans and the French.

7   "That's too low," one Japanese editor friend said, making calculations with a pencil. "They must be leaving out overtime. If I could work 2,500 hours a year, I'd feel as if I was on vacation."

8   Others agreed. Hiroshi Kawahito, secretary-general for the National Defense Council for Victims of Karoshi, believes the true number is closer to 2,500 hours a year and is even higher in some professions. Those working for large banks, brokerage houses, and money markets have their hours determined by foreign marketplaces and time-zone differences; many work through the night. Some bankers begin their days in Tokyo at distant commuter stations at seven in the morning (driven to the far suburbs by Tokyo's insane land prices and ferocious rents) and lurch home at eleven at night. Everybody works overtime.

9   "What happens if you just refuse to work overtime?" I asked one acquaintance. He looked at me blankly and then laughed. "You can't refuse," he said. "Not if you want to go anywhere with the company."

10   Some people do refuse, of course, but their refusals are entered in work reports, where they might be listed as evidence of a bad attitude. This usually isn't necessary. The Japanese don't need lessons in the work ethic, and there is a long—and deep—Japanese tradition of self-sacrifice. Traditional Japanese literature, folktales, history, even gangster movies about the *yakuza,* are full of heroes who persevere in the face of extraordinary obstacles—up to and including death. And the group (beginning with the family) is the basic building block of Japanese society. And when the group wins, so do its individual members. If a worker fails to do his part in the group enterprise, he usually plunges into a deep pool of personal agony and shame. And this is a culture of shame.

11   "If you lose face once," a journalist friend said, "You lose face forever."

12   So the Japanese worker usually feels that if he calls in sick, someone else will have to do his job that day. That is, some fellow member of the group, already burdened with overtime, will have to add even more hours to the day, and that is shameful. It has been a long time since the average American worker gave much of a rat's ass to such considerations. In some ways, inventing excuses for not working is one of the finer American pastimes. The Japanese simply don't do this; they regard work as an essential part of life, as important as sex or food or sleep. Japanese men could no more imagine spending their lives on welfare than they could believe that there was something grand and macho about abandoning women and children to the care of the state (as millions of American men have done in the past three decades). Too many Americans believe that the difficulties of life are always somebody else's fault; the individual Japanese tends to blame himself. And that attitude, joked about by even the Japanese as the basic code of the samurai businessman, might be contributing to the rise of *karoshi.*

13   Anxiety can kill. And in Tokyo, there's always a slight undercurrent of anxiety. There are many people still alive who remember that the city was twice destroyed in this century: in the great 1923 earthquake and in the fierce American firebombing

of March 9 and 10, 1945. Security is never certain to the resident of Tokyo; if nature doesn't destroy what you've built, then man might do it.

But the usual anxiety deepened when the 1973 Oil Shock changed the nature   14
of Japanese capitalism. The business (and political) leadership decided that, to survive and grow, Japanese industry must be made leaner and more efficient. There were no longer any guarantees of lifetime employment; thousands were laid off, some replaced by robots, the work of others made up by the grateful members of the group who were still working. A thin wire of insecurity entered the lives of millions of Japanese workers. As Japan prospered, the salaryman learned that he would not be allowed to relax; he had to work even harder to keep up with the costs of prosperity. And men learned another terrible lesson, filled with its own ironies: In order to support a family, a man could almost never see them.

"My kids were asleep when I went to work," one man told me, "and they were   15
asleep when I got home. I saw them on Sundays, when I was too exhausted even to play baseball with my son."

No wonder that, around ten years ago, people began to notice *karoshi*.   16

"The sudden death of heavily burdened professional people is the ultimate re-   17
sult of working overtime on weekdays and weekends at the sacrifice of family and personal lives," said Kawahito in an interview with the *Japan Times*. His group has dealt with hundreds of *karoshi* cases, trying to help families get compensation benefits for these deaths in the line of capitalist duty. The group has also established a *karoshi* hot line, which receives thousands of calls for advice and has used publicity, foreign and domestic, to bring attention to the problem.

In addition, such hot lines are being set up overseas, where Japanese business-   18
men are having the same problems. A poll by *U.S. Japan Business News* of New York-based Japanese executives showed that the average work day was eleven hours; one man reported working eighty hours a week. As Japanese businessmen travel the globe these days (usually without the consolation of wife and family), many privately complain that the home office won't allow for recovery from jet lag, expects a rigorous exactitude in work no matter what the time zone, and even turns play hours into work (golf with the visiting boss, drinks with his cousin). But nobody officially complains and nothing changes very drastically.

"Even though people know the dangers," one friend said, "it's hard to get them   19
to change."

This is true. In spite of recent pleas from the government for the Japanese to re-   20
lax and enjoy themselves a little, more than 55 percent give up holidays, and the average worker takes only eight days of his guaranteed fifteen days of annual vacation. In 1987, the government asked for some radical changes in male work habits: Cut down on overtime, take your wife to dinner. The government even designated November 22 as National Couples Day. It's impossible to imagine the American government telling its spoiled, whining, self-centered population to work less. But the Japanese haven't listened to their leaders. They keep working. And dying of *karoshi*.

Or so they say. For all their hard work, the Japanese live longer than anyone else   21
on earth: eighty-one for women, seventy-six for men, on average. Those who die of *karoshi* might actually be falling before fatal combinations of cigarettes, cholesterol, whiskey, the sedentary life of desk and office, and other bad habits. I don't know. I

do wish that there would be a major outbreak of *karoshi* in the cities of the United States. If our people would start dying of overwork instead of gunshot wounds, drug overdoses, and drunken car crashes, we'd be a lot duller as a country. But we'd be safer and more prosperous and perhaps even more just.

VOCABULARY

Directions: Locate each of the key words in the reading selection. Try to figure out each word's meaning by using the context. Confirm your guess by checking the dictionary or thesaurus. Write the meanings of the words in the margin of the text. Then record the meanings in the chart below.

Key Word	Paragraph	Meaning
1. throngs	1	
2. dynamo	5	
3. predators	5	
4. depleted	6	
5. paranoia	6	
6. sedentary	21	
Others?		

GUIDE QUESTIONS

Directions: These questions will guide your understanding of what you have read. Write your answers in your notebook or on a separate sheet of paper if your instructor wishes to collect it. Your answers to these questions will be the basis of class discussion.

1. Pete Hamill begins his story with a description of *karoshi* that he witnessed on the streets of Tokyo. Explain *karoshi*.
2. Why does Hamill say that Tokyo reminds him of "the America in which I grew up"?
3. Unless you know Japanese, the word *gaijin* in paragraph 5 is new to you. Can you figure out its meaning simply by the context?
4. What does Hamill say is the major difference between America and Japan now?
5. a. According to the selection, in Japan "everybody works overtime" whether they want to or not. Why don't Japanese workers simply refuse to work overtime?
   b. Hamill makes some harsh comparisons of Japanese and American workers here. Cite a few of them.
6. Describe some of the anxieties that Hamill says the Japanese suffer from.

7. What has been the effect of the Japanese government's efforts to encourage workers to relax more?
8. In his last paragraph, Hamill cites the average life span of Japanese men and women. Compare the Japanese life expectancy to that of Americans. (You will need to consult a reference book in the library to do this.) What is Hamill's point here?
9. While Hamill does not specifically mention the respective roles of men and women in Japanese society, you should be able to make some inferences from the article. What conclusions can you draw about the typical jobs of men and the typical jobs of women in Japan? How do they compare with the jobs of men and women in the United States?

APPLICATION

Directions: Choose one of the exercises below.

1. Interview some of the workers you know—at least four persons. Find out how many hours per year each works. Then compute the *average* number of hours per year these Americans worked and compare it to the figures for the Japanese in paragraph 6 of the selection.
2. It is clear that neither the American nor the Japanese system is perfect. Work in small groups to analyze each system by picking out the good points or advantages of each. Use the chart below.

ADVANTAGES

Japanese System	American System

WRITING

Directions: React to Hamill's comment in paragraph 20, that it's "impossible to imagine the American government telling its spoiled, whining, self-centered population to work less." Write one paragraph.

The transition from school to the business world can be full of pitfalls. This article from the magazine Black Enterprise *gives some tips on how to make a successful leap from college to career. While it is addressed to African-American graduates, its advice is valuable for everyone.*

MAKING IT ON YOUR FIRST JOB
Rhonda Reynolds

1   So, you are patting yourself on the back now that you have landed that first great job. And you think that you are well on your way to a high-powered career. Yes, you may have won the battle, but the war has just begun. How well you arm yourself and take charge of your career could mean the difference between a promotion or a layoff.

2   In the nineties, such formidable foes as an economic recession and corporate cutbacks made it difficult for workers to keep their jobs, let alone advance in them. By the third quarter of 1991, some 377,979 employees in major corporations had been terminated, says Dan Lacey, editor of the bimonthly newsletter *Workplace Trends*. Undoubtedly, there are more people seeking jobs than there are positions available. By October 1991, the national unemployment rate was 6.8 percent, according to the Bureau of Labor Statistics. Moreover, the rate for blacks was 12.7 percent and increasing steadily.

3   In light of these unstable times, it is now more important than ever for you to take an active role in how your career advances. Making it on your first job means making all the right moves. Today you are not only competing with other recent college graduates but with professionals who were downsized as well as those who are already inside of the company.

4   Those who demonstrate initiative, a positive attitude, strong communication skills, and leadership abilities have a greater chance of staying in the ranks of the upwardly mobile. Acquiring a mentor who can help you maneuver through the trenches is another plus. But ultimately it's your responsibility to develop the skills you need to guide your career to the level you desire.

The Corporate Ladder: Rung One

5   The transition from academia to corporate advancement will initially be difficult. For instance, many graduates find that, despite their degrees, they are often offered bottom-of-the-totem-pole positions, with salary to match. Despite this, it is up to you to map out your career path. Set your sights on job development and progression. You ought to have a realistic outline detailing where you want to be in the next six months to a year. In order to thrive during those first few months, ask yourself two questions. One, what do they say they want from me? Two, what do they really want from me? Make sure you understand your boss's expectations.

6   Even though you may comply with everything in your job description, on a scale from one to ten, your rating is one at best, according to Adele Scheele, Ph.D., a management consultant and career strategist in New York City. You have to work on

making sure that the people in your company who count recognize your value. Because everything is a matter of dollars and cents, your worth is determined by how you impact the company's bottom line. Are you helping it to make or lose money?

Normally, your first assignment is when you're first evaluated. You are graded   7
constantly on every assignment, and each success is relative to *your* performance. The first assignment is critical to your career path, because it will show your superiors and co-workers how you solve problems, interact with others, and rely on your own ideas. Recent graduates often don't take their first work assignments as seriously as they should. When they are in school, a new semester begins every six months. "So, in the same way, they feel that they can keep starting over in the work force," says Scheele. Another mistake new employees commonly make is that they take their textbook with them on the job. "Unfortunately," Scheele explains, "you cannot use textbook answers for real-life problems."

Being one of the lowest on the totem pole requires some grunt work. Using   8
these tasks wisely, however, can increase your responsibilities. The best way for your talents to be noticed and appreciated is to take the initiative.

"Just because you are bright does not mean you will shoot up the corporate   9
ladder," says Karen Trader, director of Human Resources for Network Solutions Inc., No. 17 on the BLACK ENTERPRISE INDUSTRIAL/SERVICE 100 in Herdon, Virginia. "No one will help you unless they see you are willing to help yourself. The boss wants to see that you are indeed able to think and act for yourself."

When Charles Jones was about to graduate from college a year ago, he believed   10
the job market was so bleak that he was ready to skip it altogether. But after attending an engineering seminar, he approached the principal speaker, Lewis Smoot, CEO and president of Sherman R. Smoot Corp., a black-owned engineering firm in Washington, D.C. Jones, a twenty-three-year-old Howard University graduate, spent four years studying civil engineering. After a brief interview, he was hired last year and now serves as a project engineer for the company. Jones, whose salary is in the low thirties, is responsible for overseeing the budget and completion of all of the company's construction projects.

Jones says initiative has been a key to his success thus far. This past summer,   11
Jones's crew was behind schedule while working on the construction of Howard University's E. Just Hall. Instead of taking longer to complete the job or hiring a larger temporary staff, Jones shed his suit and went into the field to labor. "I realize I have to give more than is required of me. If I fail, it's not like I'm failing a test. I do whatever I have to do to get the job done right," he says.

The primary relationship between you and conflict should be resolving it. Your   12
problem-solving skills can help to spotlight your analytical talents and your ability to motivate others. Solving conflicts is also a good way to exhibit corporate commitment. Companies admire people who want to contribute.

The Glass Is Always Half Full

To some degree, making it on your first job follows the guidelines of a strong sales   13
pitch. "Whether you are selling yourself or your ideas, maintaining a positive attitude will enable you to scale the corporate ladder come rain or shine," says Gregory

Jones, twenty-four, a sales representative for the copier division of Lanier World-Wide, Inc., in Washington, D.C.

14   You cannot be productive on your job if you are not positive. "Life is 90 percent attitude and 10 percent what happens to you," says a 1991 Baruch College, City University of New York graduate. "It's all in your attitude, how you present yourself, and what you have to offer."

15   "A company may be able to teach you what you need to know to succeed, but it cannot teach attitude," says Stephen Merman, president of the American Society for Training and Development. "When choosing between a purely competent person without interest, and a less competent person with zeal, I always chose zeal over ability," he says.

16   Jones, who earns in the mid-thirties, says that he not only is positive, but he shows initiative and pays attention to details. Jones handles more than three hundred phone calls a week, yet he often makes the sale by going out into the field. "If brochures are not getting the account, I have to think of something else. Most of the time I just carry the copiers up flights of stairs and show them to a potential client," he adds. He believes that someone who pays his or her dues may not advance the fastest, but that person will at least advance consistently.

Say It Right the First Time

17   Just as it is important to be able to think on your feet; you ought to be able to articulate your ideas. Management consultant Adele Scheele says that mastering the art of communication (written and oral) is paramount. The characteristics of an effective communicator are confidence, clarity, conciseness, and directness. Moreover, you must learn to be respectful of your audience's level of understanding, ideas, motives, and time.

18   Communicating in the work place usually takes on two forms. One, the expression of your ideas about a project, problem, or situation, orally or in writing; and two, interaction with your peers and supervisors. It is important that you remain well-informed, so you can talk about the goings-on within your department, and that you share in the interests of your colleagues.

19   If you ask Michael Benefield what is one of his greatest attributes, he will tell you it's his silver tongue. A 1990 graduate of the University of North Carolina at Chapel Hill with a degree in political science, Benefield says that his communication skills helped him land a higher position than the one he had originally applied for, manager of local government relations. Benefield now works as the manager of state government relations for Delaware's New Castle Chamber of Commerce.

20   For the past eight months, Benefield has served as a liaison between state and local government, earning just under $25,000. At the age of twenty-four, he is the youngest, as well as the only, black lobbyist in the Delaware statehouse. "There is a strong presence of the old-boy network," says Benefield.

21   However, "while I am not a seasoned veteran, I am confident about myself and my capabilities," he says. "And I know how to project this quality, which helps to instill their confidence in me."

22   Benefield adds that he knows the ins and outs of the entire agency, in addition to the projects he is involved in. "As long as I parlay my knowledge into informative

answers and make judgments to help promote the organization," he says, "I ultimately promote myself."

Management consultants warn that being knowledgeable does not mean being   23
arrogant. Never talk down to your co-workers or spew out big words to impress senior management. Whether you are meeting with the entire department or brain-
storming with your boss, time and energy are limited. So, use them wisely.

Another significant form of communication in the work environment is social-   24
izing. "Schmoozing is not an asset—it is a requirement," says Scheele. Mingling with
colleagues and management can open many doors. Your conversations may range
from sports and politics to departmental issues and company objectives. The idea is
to be able to relate on many different levels.

The Leader of the Pack

Boot camp is now over, for you have learned the basic survival skills. You know   25
how to initiate ideas and actions and you can communicate what you need and want
to accomplish. The next order of business in managing your career is to develop
leadership abilities. To be a leader you have to identify, define, design, and implement strategies.

The hard part may be accomplishing these tasks without arousing hostility. Just   26
remember that you are part of a service team. You want to display your leadership
qualities without forging ahead of your boss or blatantly calling attention to the inadequacies of your co-workers. The goal is to spotlight yourself, not to sabotage
others.

In fact, part of assuming the role of leader is also being able to "compensate   27
where others are lacking," says Cheryl Harris, a purchasing specialist for American
Express subsidiary IDS Financial Services Inc., in Minneapolis. Fresh out of college,
Harris's first job offer was actually a temporary position as a budget analyst for IDS.
However, when the Florida A&M University graduate arrived at the company, she
was told that the project was almost completed, and the company did not need her.
Instead of packing her bags and heading back, Harris met with her prospective employer and made some recommendations as to where her services could be uti-
lized. "It was obvious I had potential," she says.

Harris spent the next year as an assistant buyer. With an annual salary of   28
$35,000, she currently procures capital equipment and supplies for the entire
Minneapolis-St. Paul office and the 184 national branches, equaling a total budget of
$3.25 million. Harris says that, for the past two years, she has been advancing
mainly because of her strong leadership abilities, including identifying priorities,
building relationships, and implementing ideas. "Nine out of ten times I am the only
black person in a meeting or on a committee. So, I have to be focused," she says.
"I also want to create a positive impression to make way for the people coming
behind me."

Effective leadership comes from being well-informed, says Cynthia Smith, a   29
twenty-three-year-old Employment Coordinator for the Texas City Refinery Corp.
"Read everything you can about the company. This enables you to contribute amply
and intelligently. Make sure you have all of the information before offering even minor input."

30   Smith, a business administration major who graduated from the University of Alabama last year, is responsible for hiring employees for the entire company. "When you decide to lead and not just follow, you have a lot more proving to do." Explains Smith: "I often go in early and stay late. And when the work is not finished I go in on weekends too. To be a leader, I have to show that I am an ideal employee first."

31   It is also important that you realize "you are part of a network," says Tracy Jackson, an associate brand manager for Chicago-based Kraft General Foods. The 1990 University of Michigan graduate oversees the product and campaign schedules for the advertising and production departments. Jackson says she believes you have to learn how to be a team player first before you can become a leader.

Looking the Part

32 Do not be shortsighted and think that your results alone will speak for you. Getting ahead does not center solely on performance. "Nontangibles are critical, especially for black employees who often have to combat stereotypes of incompetence in the work place," says Sheryl Colyer, regional human resources manager for PepsiCo-KFC in Philadelphia.

33   Like it or not, your ability to fit in and to be accepted as a professional is determined in part by your personality and appearance. Joylette Hairston wore dreadlocks while attending Pennsylvania State University, where she majored in liberal arts and minored in speech communications. Upon graduation in 1990, she decided to pursue a career in finance. She took a crash business course working for free in her uncle's brokerage firm. Within a month she started applying for financial training positions. A few weeks and several contacts later, she became an operations management trainee for Bear Stearns in New York City, with an annual salary of $25,000.

34   "Experience is invaluable, but appearance sells the ticket," says Hairston, twenty-five. Sacrificing style for status, she gave up her dreads and redefined her look to fit a more corporate role. "I did not consider it selling out," she concedes, "but more as an investment. Because black women have to fight racist and sexual stereotypes along with a depressed job market, we can't afford to have any strikes against us."

35   Having the proper look is requisite in a corporate environment says Charles Grevious, vice president of The Johnson Group, a New York City-based executive search firm. You don't want to hinder your career advancement unnecessarily by going against the grain.

36   Each business has its own subculture. It is mandatory that you realize, respect, and adhere to whatever is deemed the professional or proper image in your place of business. Echoing that sentiment is Colyer, who believes "blacks especially have to manage perceptions. We have to control how others see us. They want to know that they can dress you up and take you out." At the same time, Grevious suggests that you can be a chameleon within a corporate culture. "Make sure you are true to yourself. You can compromise your clothing, but you should not compromise yourself."

37   As a new employee you are constantly making first impressions; all of your actions are relative to overall performance. An often overlooked but important career issue is the concept of time.

"You are never on time. You are either early or late," says Juan Menefee, pres-   38
ident and CEO of Juan Menefee & Associates, an executive search consulting firm in
Oak Park, Illinois. "Opt to be early," he concludes.

Acquiring Value-Added Services

Companies are in the business of making profits, not promotions. So, you need to   39
see to it that you are a commodity in your employer's eyes. When devising a career
advancement strategy, keep in mind volunteer projects, networking, and strong
mentor relationships. By taking on such special projects you display professional
commitment.

These projects are usually the ones that no one else wants to do because they   40
are boring or time-consuming. Well, with a little extra effort such tasks could trail-
blaze into an opportunity for you to shine. And they often provide the opportunity
to broadcast unique skills, talents, and accomplishments, making you more visible to
senior management and other influential executives.

Networking inside and outside of the company (i.e., professional organizations)   41
also is important in moving up. Develop and maintain good relationships with others in your profession and with those who are a vital part of your industry.

Seeking out a corporate guru also can help to boost your career. Knowing when   42
to ask for a raise or how to approach the boss are the types of problems entry-level
employees can field to a mentor. When it comes time for a promotion, undeniably,
many positions are filled outside of the boardroom. "A mentor can open up opportunities you would not otherwise have access to," says Perry Borman, a recruiting
manager for Amoco Corp. in Chicago. You want to latch onto someone who can
help lift you as he or she climbs the ladder.

Don't Overlook the Obvious

Even donned with the best advice and guidance, inevitably you will make mistakes.   43
Everyone does. The key is to avoid repeating them, says Borman. "If you get it right
the first time, great. When you fail, learn from the experience. But be sure you learn
the lesson, because there are no make-ups," he adds.

Learning how to accept criticism is equally important. Don't take it personally.   44
Just take into account the merits and demerits of your work when you start your
next project. "Dump the ego and listen attentively," says Scheele. Any display of a
temper tantrum, anger, or complaints are unacceptable and intolerable.

Instead, focus your energy on going above and beyond your assignments—do-   45
ing more than your share—and letting others realize your worth. You must show
them what you can and do contribute to the company. No matter what level you
start at in a company, your career must pick up speed if you want to get anywhere.
Being armed with a degree may guarantee you an entry, but it does not automatically enable you to excel.

VOCABULARY

Directions: Locate each of the key words in the reading selection. Then read and
study each word in its context and try to determine its meaning. Use a dictionary

or thesaurus to check your guess. Write the meanings of the words in the margin of the text.

Record the new words you've learned below.

Key Word	Paragraph	Meaning
1. formidable	2	
2. mentor	4	
3. thrive	5	
4. zeal	15	
5. paramount	17	
6. schmoozing	24	
7. blatantly	26	
8. sabotage	26	
9. chameleon	36	
Others?		

GUIDE QUESTIONS

Directions: The purpose of these guide questions is to ensure your understanding of what you have read. They will also help you to analyze and evaluate the author's ideas and apply them to the real world and your own life.

Write answers to the questions in your notebook or on a separate sheet of paper if your instructor wishes to collect them. Your answers will form the basis of class discussion.

1. Discuss why it is so important to do well on your first job.
2. The author of this article makes much use of metaphor. (If you are unsure of what a metaphor is, figurative language is discussed in Appendix D. You may want to discuss it in class as well.)

   Look at the first paragraph of "Making It on Your First Job" where Reynolds compares getting a job to a battle. She continues the metaphor by comparing keeping the job to a war, but states that you can arm yourself for this war. Writers (and speakers) use metaphors to add spice to their language, to catch their readers' attention, and to help the readers remember what the author has to say. Go through the article and find all the metaphors the author uses. List them in the following chart.

Paragraph	Metaphor Used
4	
5	
8	
13	
35	
36	
39	
43	
45	

3. Summarize the advice the author gives in paragraph 5.
4. According to paragraph 7, how can new employees make mistakes by treating their work in the same way they treated school?
5. Explain the meaning of the subheading before paragraph 13, "The glass is always half full."
6. Agree or disagree with the statement in paragraph 14, "Life is 90 percent attitude and 10 percent what happens to you." Remember to explain your answer.
7. List the two major forms of communication described in paragraph 18. Then use your own experience and knowledge to give some examples of each.
8. In paragraph 20, Michael Benefield refers to "the old-boy network." Here, the author assumes you understand this allusion. What is the old-boy network? (If you don't know, find out by asking someone or looking it up.)
9. Discuss the importance of having a mentor.

APPLICATION

1. *Directions:* In paragraph 2, the author cites statistics to show how tough it has been to get and keep a job. Her figures, however, are from 1991 and may no longer be valid. Find the same statistics for the current year. You may want to check the unemployment rates for other groups—women, Hispanics, Asians, etc.—as well. Has the situation improved or worsened?
2. *Directions:* Underline and annotate the essay. To review underlining and annotating, turn to Appendix B.

WRITING
Directions: Write a summary of the advice given to new employees in this article. To review summary writing, turn to Appendix B.

COLLABORATIVE LEARNING

WORKING IN GROUPS TO GUIDE YOUR OWN READING

Along with each of the reading selections in this unit, you were provided with questions and exercises to guide your understanding of the text. However, in most of your college reading you will not be given exercises to help you understand vocabulary or with questions that guide your understanding of a textbook chapter. You will be expected to master the material on your own.

Research has shown that one of the most effective ways to study is in groups—working with classmates to master the material of a college course. The give-and-take that comes naturally when working with other people helps us to avoid falling into bad habits like *passive* reading. (We have all had this experience: reading a whole chapter, then realizing that we don't remember one single thing we read.) Working with other students will help you avoid such problems. For this assignment, form groups of four to six students. In your group you will consider the two following reading selections, "Hispanic USA: The Conveyor-Belt Ladies" by Rose Del Castillo Guilbault and "Less Is More: A Call for Shorter Work Hours" by Barbara Brandt. You will create your own vocabulary chart, guide questions, an application exercise, and a writing assignment for the reading selections.

Follow these steps to complete this assignment.

1. Preview the selection before you read—look at and think about the title, the headings, the first paragraph, the last paragraph, and the first sentence of each paragraph.
2. Read through the selection one time quickly.
3. Read the selection carefully a second time; this time mark the pages. Underline words you want to look up and ideas you think are important. Put a question mark next to things you don't understand and want to discuss with your group members or your instructor. Ask yourself questions as you read along and try to find the answers to your questions.
4. Brainstorm with your group. Ask yourselves: What important issues is the author discussing? What new information did you learn? Can the issues discussed in the selection be connected to those you have studied in earlier lessons? Can any of the information here be applied to situations in your own life?
5. Now, *create* a set of exercises similar to those you have *completed* in previous chapters:
   a. *Vocabulary.* Make a list of key vocabulary words from the text. Set them up in chart format as on page 176.
   b. *Guide questions.* Write questions that will guide understanding of the major ideas in the reading.
   c. *Application.* Prepare an application exercise that takes one or more of the important ideas in the reading and relates them to real life.
   d. *Writing.* Prepare a writing assignment to conclude the chapter.

Before you begin, it would be a good idea to review the questions and exercises included in the previous selections of this unit for reference.

When you are finished, submit your work to your instructor for review. Your instructor may review and combine the work of all the groups and return the exercises to the class. You will then have the opportunity to *answer* the questions you and your classmates have developed.

Now, use your skills as an active, independent reader to tackle the following reading selections. Good luck!

Most of us have had to suffer through summer jobs—usually low-paying, high-boredom work suitable for a temporary, untrained worker. While we may have dreaded the work, the money was welcome and usually essential. In this article, Rose Del Castillo Guilbault describes her last summer job before college. She sorted tomatoes on a conveyor belt, side by side with migrant workers, women who, at first, embarrassed her, but whom she soon came to like and respect.

HISPANIC USA: THE CONVEYOR-BELT LADIES

Rose Del Castillo Guilbault

1   The conveyor-belt ladies were the migrant women, mostly from Texas, I worked with during the summers of my teenage years. I call them conveyor-belt ladies because our entire relationship took place while sorting tomatoes on a conveyor belt.

2   We were like a cast in a play where all the action occurs on one set. We'd return day after day to perform the same roles, only this stage was a vegetable-packing shed, and at the end of the season there was no applause. The players could look forward only to the same uninspiring parts on a string of grim real-life stages.

3   The women and their families arrived in May for the carrot season, spent the summer in the tomato sheds, and stayed through October for the bean harvest. After that, they emptied the town, some returning to their homes in Texas (cities like McAllen, Douglas, Brownsville), while others continued on the migrant trail, picking cotton in the San Joaquin Valley or grapefruits and oranges in the Imperial Valley.

4   Most of these women had started in the fields. The vegetable-packing sheds were a step up, easier than the back-breaking, grueling work the field demanded. The work was more tedious than strenuous, paid better, provided fairly steady hours and clean bathrooms. Best of all, you weren't subjected to the elements.

5   The summer I was sixteen, my mother got jobs for both of us as tomato sorters. That's how I came to be included in the seasonal sorority of the conveyor belt.

6   The work consisted of standing and picking flawed tomatoes off the conveyor belt before they rolled off into the shipping boxes at the end of the line. These boxes were immediately loaded onto waiting delivery trucks, so it was crucial not to let imperfect tomatoes through.

7   The work could be slow or intense, depending on the quality of the tomatoes and how many there were. Work increased when the company's deliveries got backlogged or after rainy weather had delayed picking.

8   During those times, it was not unusual to work from 7 A.M. to midnight, playing catch-up. I never heard anyone complain about the overtime. Overtime meant desperately needed extra money.

9   I was not happy to be part of the agricultural work force. I would have preferred working in a dress shop or baby-sitting, like my friends. But I had a dream that would cost a lot of money—college. And the fact was, this was the highest-paying work I could do.

10   But it wasn't so much the work that bothered me. I was embarrassed because only Mexicans worked at packing sheds. I had heard my schoolmates joke about the

"ugly, fat Mexican women" at the sheds. They ridiculed the way they dressed and laughed at the "funny way" they talked. I feared working with them would irrevocably stigmatize me, setting me further apart from my Anglo classmates.

At sixteen I was more American than Mexican and, with adolescent arrogance, felt superior to these "uneducated" women. I might be one of them, I reasoned, but I was not like them. 11

But it was difficult not to like the women. They were a gregarious, entertaining group, easing the long, monotonous hours with bawdy humor, spicy gossip, and inventive laments. They poked fun at all the male workers and did hysterical impersonations of a dyspeptic Anglo supervisor. Although he didn't speak Spanish (other than *"Mujeres, trabajo, trabajo!"* Women, work, work!), he seemed to sense he was being laughed at. That would account for the sudden rages when he would stamp his foot and forbid us to talk until break time. 12

"I bet he understands Spanish and just pretends so he can hear what we say," I whispered to Rosa. 13

"*Ay, no, hija,* it's all the buzzing in his ears that alerts him that these *viejas* (old women) are bad-mouthing him!" Rosa giggled. 14

But it would have been easier to tie the women's tongues in a knot than to keep them quiet. Eventually the ladies had their way and their fun, and the men learned to ignore them. 15

We were often shifted around, another strategy to keep us quiet. This gave me ample opportunity to get to know everyone, listen to their life stories, and absorb the gossip. 16

Pretty Rosa described her romances and her impending wedding to a handsome field worker. Bertha, a heavy-set, dark-skinned woman, told me that Rosa's marriage would cause nothing but headaches because the man was younger and too handsome. Maria, large, moon-faced, and placid, described the births of each of her nine children, warning me about the horrors of childbirth. Pragmatic Minnie, a tiny woman who always wore printed cotton dresses, scoffed at Maria's stupidity, telling me she wouldn't have so many kids if she had ignored that good-for-nothing priest and gotten her tubes tied! 17

In unexpected moments, they could turn melancholic: recounting the babies who died because their mothers couldn't afford medical care; the alcoholic, abusive husbands who were their "cross to bear"; the racism they experienced in Texas, where they were branded "dirty Mexicans" or "Mexican dogs" and not allowed in certain restaurants. 18

They spoke with the detached fatalism of people with limited choices and alternatives. Their lives were as raw and brutal as ghetto streets—something they accepted with an odd grace and resignation. 19

I was appalled and deeply affected by these confidences. The injustices they endured enraged me; their personal struggles overwhelmed me. I knew I could do little but sympathize. 20

My mother, no stranger to suffering, suggested I was too impressionable when I emotionally told her the women's stories. "That's nothing," she'd say lightly. "If they were in Mexico, life would be even harder. At least there's opportunities here, you can work." 21

22   My icy arrogance quickly thawed, that first summer, as my respect for the conveyor-belt ladies grew.

23   I worked in the packing sheds for several summers. The last season also turned out to be the last time I lived at home. It was the end of a chapter in my life, but I didn't know it then. I had just finished junior college and was transferring to the university. I was already over-educated for seasonal work, but if you counted the overtime, no other jobs came close to paying so well, so I went back one last time.

24   The ladies treated me with warmth and respect. I was a college student, deserving of special treatment.

25   Aguedita, the crew chief, moved me to softer and better-paying jobs within the plant. I went from the conveyor belt to shoving boxes down a chute and finally to weighing boxes of tomatoes on a scale—the highest-paying position for a woman.

26   When the union's dues collector showed up, the women hid me in the bathroom. They had decided it was unfair for me to have to join the union and pay dues, since I worked only during the summer.

27   "Where's the student?" the union rep would ask, opening the door to a barrage of complaints about the union's unfairness.

28   Maria (of the nine children) tried to feed me all summer, bringing extra tortillas, which were delicious. I accepted them guiltily, always wondering if I was taking food away from her children. Others would bring rental contracts or other documents for me to explain and translate.

29   The last day of work was splendidly beautiful, warm and sunny. If this had been a movie, these last scenes would have been shot in soft focus, with a crescendo of music in the background.

30   But real life is anti-climactic. As it was, nothing unusual happened. The conveyor belt's loud humming was turned off, silenced for the season. The women sighed as they removed their aprons. Some of them just walked off, calling *"Hasta la próxima!"* Until next time!

31   But most of the conveyor-belt ladies shook my hand, gave me a blessing or a big hug.

32   "Make us proud!" they said.

33   I hope I have.

VOCABULARY

Directions: Mark any important words in the reading selection that you don't know. Then list them in the chart below along with their paragraph numbers. Try to figure out each word's meaning by reading over the context carefully for clues to help you guess the meaning of the unfamiliar word. Check your dictionary or thesaurus to confirm your guess. After you discuss the words with your group members, write the meanings in the margin of the text, near the word. Then enter them in the chart here and on the next page.

Key Word   **Paragraph**   **Meaning**

Key Word	Paragraph	Meaning

GUIDE QUESTIONS

Directions: Develop a list of questions that elicit the important ideas in the reading selection. Start at the beginning and work your way sequentially through the text until you have addressed all of the author's major ideas.

APPLICATION

Directions: When you have a list of guide questions, read through the selection again. This time, write one or more questions that require the application of the information in the text to a situation in the real world.

WRITING

Directions: Your last task is to prepare a writing assignment. For example, you might ask for a paragraph in which the writer comments on the ideas in the reading selection. You might also ask for a summary of the selection.

Most Americans consider the forty-hour work week to be normal and natural. But many observers think that Americans are working too long and too hard. Here, the author argues that overwork has become a major social problem that has reached crisis proportions. See if you agree with her.

LESS IS MORE: A CALL FOR SHORTER WORK HOURS

Barbara Brandt

1   America is suffering from overwork. Too many of us are too busy, trying to squeeze more into each day while having less to show for it. Although our growing time crunch is often portrayed as a personal dilemma, it is in fact a major social problem that has reached crisis proportions over the past twenty years.

2   The simple fact is that Americans today—both women and men—are spending too much time at work, to the detriment of their homes, their families, their personal lives, and their communities. The American Dream promised that our individual hard work, paired with the advances of modern technology, would bring about the good life for all. Glorious visions of the leisure society were touted throughout the fifties and sixties. But now most people are working more than ever before, while still struggling to meet their economic commitments. Ironically, the many advances in technology, such as computers and fax machines, rather than reducing our work load, seem to have speeded up our lives at work. At the same time, technology has equipped us with "conveniences" like microwave ovens and frozen dinners that merely enable us to adopt a similar frantic pace in our home lives so we can cope with more hours at paid work.

3   A recent spate of articles in the mainstream media has focused on the new problems of overwork and lack of time. Unfortunately, overwork is often portrayed as a special problem of yuppies and professionals on the fast track. In reality, the unequal distribution of work and time in America today reflects the decline in both standard of living and quality of life for most Americans. Families whose members never see each other, women who work a double shift (first on the job, then at home), workers who need more flexible work schedules, and unemployed and underemployed people who need more work are all casualties of the crisis of overwork.

4   Americans often assume that overwork is an inevitable fact of life—like death and taxes. Yet a closer look at other times and other nations offers some startling surprises.

5   Anthropologists have observed that, in pre-industrial (particularly hunting and gathering) societies, people generally spend 3 to 4 hours a day, 15 to 20 hours a week, doing the work necessary to maintain life. The rest of the time is spent in socializing, partying, playing, storytelling, and artistic or religious activities. The ancient Romans celebrated 175 public festivals a year in which everyone participated, and people in the Middle Ages had at least 115.

6   In our era, almost every other industrialized nation (except Japan) has fewer annual working hours and longer vacations than the United States. This includes all of

Western Europe, where many nations enjoy thriving economies and standards of living equal to or higher than ours. Jeremy Brecher and Tim Costello, writing in *Z Magazine* (October 1990), note that "European unions during the 1980s made a powerful and largely successful push to cut working hours. In 1987 German metal-workers struck and won a 37.5-hour week; many are now winning a 35-hour week. In 1990, hundreds of thousands of British workers won a 37-hour week."

7   In an article about work time in the *Boston Globe,* Suzanne Gordon notes that workers in other industrialized countries "enjoy—as a statutory right—longer vacations [than in the United States] from the moment they enter the work force. In Canada, workers are legally entitled to two weeks off their first year on the job. . . . After two or three years of employment, most get three weeks of vacation. After ten years, it's up to four, and by twenty years, Canadian workers are off for five weeks. In Germany, statutes guarantee eighteen days minimum for everyone, but most workers get five or six weeks. The same is true in Scandinavian countries, and in France."

8   In contrast to the extreme American emphasis on productivity and commitment, which results in many workers, especially in professional-level jobs, not taking the vacations coming to them, Gordon notes that "In countries that are America's most successful competitors in the global marketplace, all working people, whether lawyers or teachers, CEOs or janitors, take the vacations to which they are entitled by law. 'No one in West Germany,' a West German embassy's officer explains, 'no matter how high up they are, would ever say they couldn't afford to take a vacation. Everyone takes their vacation.'"

9   And in Japan, where dedication to the job is legendary, Gordon notes that the Japanese themselves are beginning to consider their national workaholism a serious social problem, leading to stress-related illnesses and even death. As a result, the Japanese government recently established a commission whose goal is to promote shorter working hours and more leisure time.

10   Most other industrialized nations also have better family-leave policies than the United States, and in a number of other countries workers benefit from innovative time-scheduling opportunities, such as sabbaticals.

11   While the idea of a shorter workweek and longer vacations sounds appealing to most people, any movement to enact shorter work time as a public policy will encounter surprising pockets of resistance, not just from business leaders but even from some workers. Perhaps the most formidable barrier to more free time for Americans is the widespread mind-set that the forty-hour workweek, eight hours a day, five days a week, fifty weeks a year, is a natural rhythm of the universe. This view is reinforced by the media's complete silence regarding the shorter work-time and more favorable vacation and family-leave policies of other countries. This lack of information, and our leaders' reluctance to suggest that the United States can learn from any other nation (except workaholic Japan) is one reason why more Americans don't identify overwork as a major problem or clamor for fewer hours and more vacation. Monika Bauerlein, a journalist originally from Germany, now living in Minneapolis, exclaims, "I can't believe that people here aren't rioting in the streets over having only two weeks of vacation a year."

12   A second obstacle to launching a powerful shorter work time movement is America's deeply ingrained work ethic, or its modern incarnation, the workaholic syndrome. The work ethic fosters the widely held belief that people's work is their most important activity and that people who do not work long and hard are lazy, unproductive, and worthless.

13   For many Americans today, paid work is not just a way to make money but is a crucial source of their self-worth. Many of us identify ourselves almost entirely by the kind of work we do. Work still has a powerful psychological and spiritual hold over our lives—and talk of shorter work time may seem somehow morally suspicious.

14   Because we are so deeply a work-oriented society, leisure-time activities—such as play, relaxation, engaging in cultural and artistic pursuits, or just quiet contemplation and "doing nothing"—are not looked on as essential and worthwhile components of life. Of course, for the majority of working women who must work a second shift at home, much of the time spent outside of paid work is not leisure anyway. Also, much of our nonwork time is spent not just in personal renewal, but in building and maintaining essential social ties—with family, friends, and the larger community.

15   Today, as mothers and fathers spend more and more time on the job, we are beginning to recognize the deleterious effects—especially on our young people—of the breakdown of social ties and community in American life. But unfortunately, our nation reacts to these problems by calling for more paid professionals—more police, more psychiatrists, more experts—without recognizing the possibility that shorter work hours and more free time could enable us to do much of the necessary rebuilding and healing, with much more gratifying and longer-lasting results.

16   Of course, the stiffest opposition to cutting work hours comes not from citizens but from business. Employers are reluctant to alter the eight-hour day, forty-hour workweek, fifty weeks a year because it seems easier and more profitable for employers to hire fewer employees for longer hours rather than more employees—each of whom would also require health insurance and other benefits—with flexible schedules and work arrangements.

17   Harvard University economist Juliet B. Schor, who has been studying issues of work and leisure in America, reminds us that we cannot ignore the larger relationship between unemployment and overwork: While many of us work too much, others are unable to find paid work at all. Schor points out that "workers who work longer hours lose more income when they lose their jobs. The threat of job loss is an important determinant of management's power on the shop floor." A system that offers only two options—long work hours or unemployment—serves as both a carrot and a stick. Those lucky enough to get full-time jobs are bribed into docile compliance with the boss, while the spectre of unemployment always looms as the ultimate punishment for the unruly.

18   Some observers suggest that keeping people divided into "the employed" and "the unemployed" creates feelings of resentment and inferiority/superiority between the two groups, thus focusing their discontent and blame on each other rather than on the corporations and political figures who actually dictate our nation's economic policies.

19   Our role as consumers contributes to keeping the average workweek from falling. In an economic system in which addictive buying is the basis of corporate

profits, working a full forty hours or more each week for fifty weeks a year gives us just enough time to stumble home and dazedly—almost automatically—shop; but not enough time to think about deeper issues or to work effectively for social change. From the point of view of corporations and policymakers, shorter work time may be bad for the economy, because people with enhanced free time may begin to find other things to do with it besides mindlessly buying products. It takes more free time to grow vegetables, cook meals from scratch, sew clothes, or repair broken items than it does to just buy these things at the mall.

Any serious proposal to give employed Americans a break by cutting into the eight-hour work day is certain to be met with anguished cries about international competitiveness. The United States seems gripped by the fear that our nation has lost its economic dominance, and pundits, policymakers, and business leaders tell us that no sacrifice is too great if it puts America on top again.   20

As arguments like this are put forward (and we can expect them to increase in the years to come), we need to remember two things. First, even if America maintained its dominance (whatever that means) and the economy were booming again, this would be no guarantee that the gains—be they in wages, in employment opportunities, or in leisure—would be distributed equitably between upper management and everyone else. Second, the entire issue of competitiveness is suspect when it pits poorly treated workers in one country against poorly treated workers in another; and when the vast majority of economic power, anyway, is in the control of enormous multinational corporations that have no loyalty to the people of any land.   21

VOCABULARY

Directions: Mark any important words in the reading selection that you don't know. Then list them in the chart below along with their paragraph numbers. Try to figure out each word's meaning by reading over the context carefully for clues to help you guess the meaning of the unfamiliar word. Check your dictionary or thesaurus to confirm your guess. After you discuss the words with your group members, write the meanings in the margin of the text, near the word. Then enter them in the chart.

Key Word	Paragraph	Meaning

GUIDE QUESTIONS

Directions: Develop a list of questions that elicit the important ideas in the reading selection. Start at the beginning and work your way sequentially through the text until you have addressed all of the author's major ideas.

APPLICATION

Directions: When you have a list of guide questions, read through the selection again. This time, write one or more questions that require the application of the information in the text to a situation in the real world.

WRITING

Directions: Your last task is to prepare a writing assignment. For example, you might ask for a paragraph in which the writer comments on the ideas in the reading selection. You might also ask for a summary of the selection.

SPECIAL PROJECT

WORK

Career Exploration

For this project you will do research on the career you hope to have when you finish school. The report should answer the questions below:

1. What is the nature of the work? What does the worker do all day? Describe a typical day.
2. Where does the work take place? Is it in an office, a clinic, a lab, outdoors? Describe the working conditions.
3. What is the typical annual starting salary? What is the typical salary for someone with ten years' experience?
4. What is the employment outlook for this particular career at the present time? Are there jobs available?
5. List some of the major employers in this field in your area.
6. What about this job will make you happy and satisfied? Do you think there will be any negative aspects to the job? If so, how will you cope with them?

Many resources are available to help you complete this project. Visit your school library and your local library. Read magazines that deal with your field. Interview someone who is working in the field. Write a letter to a company or institution you would like to work for, asking them to send you information about requirements and job prospects.

BIBLIOGRAPHY

FOR FURTHER READING ON THE THEME
OF WORK AND BUSINESS

Letitia Baldrige	*The New Complete Guide to Executive Manners*
Karen Bartell	*American Business English*
Heinrich Boll	"The Laugher" (short story)
Ben Carson, M.D.	*Gifted Hands: The Ben Carson Story*
Steven Covey	*The Seven Habits of Highly Effective People, First Things First,* and *Principle-Centered Leadership*
David Halberstam	*The Reckoning*
Carol Kleiman	*The 100 Best Jobs for the 1990s and Beyond*
Michael LeBoeuf	*Working Smart*
Robert Levering, Milton Moskowitz, and Michael Katz	*The 100 Best Companies to Work for in America*
Arthur Miller	*Death of a Salesman* (play)
The New York Times	The New York Times *Special Report: The Downsizing of America*
William Nolen	*The Making of a Surgeon*
Tom Peters and Nancy Austin	*A Passion for Excellence*
Upton Sinclair	*The Jungle*
James Stewart	*Den of Thieves*
Studs Terkel	*Working*
Lester Thurow	*Head to Head: The Coming Economic Battle among Japan, Europe, and America*
James Wallace and Jim Erickson	*Hard Drive: Bill Gates and the Making of the Microsoft Empire*
Sloane Wilson	*The Man in the Gray Flannel Suit*

UNIT FIVE

CRITICAL READING AND THINKING ABOUT CONTROVERSIAL ISSUES

The aim of argument or of discussion should not be victory, but progress.

—Joseph Joubert

THINKING ABOUT CRITICAL READING AND THINKING

Have you ever expressed a strong opinion about a controversial subject, say the death penalty, a political candidate, or the welfare system? Have you ever been challenged to support your view but been unable to explain your position? How did you feel? Embarrassed? Foolish? Many of us go through life with "unexamined" ideas. We accept views of our parents, teachers, and friends without analyzing them, and only discover our ignorance when we are questioned. Socrates, perhaps the greatest philosopher who ever lived, tells us "the unexamined life is not worth living." An important part of our college experience should be the examination of ourselves—taking a look at our values, our opinions and beliefs about our world and why we hold them. In the story below, we see one way of "examining" something. Read the story and decide if you think the blind men's way of looking at the issue of the elephant is a good way to learn about something.

The Blind Men and the Elephant

Once upon a time in a land far away, there was a kingdom of the blind. All of the people were blind, including the king. The king of the land was a very inquisitive man who always wanted to know more about the world. Having heard wondrous tales of an amazing animal called the elephant, he called the three wisest men of the kingdom and ordered them to go and find the elephant so they could come back and tell him what the elephant was like. The three blind wise men went off, and did, indeed, find the elephant. The first blind man went up to the elephant, felt its tail and said, "The elephant is very like a rope!" The second man touched the elephant's trunk and said, "The elephant is very like a snake!" The third man touched the elephant's ear and said "The elephant is very like a fan!"

Now, answer these questions about the story.

1. Which, if any, of the blind men now knows what an elephant is like?
2. When the wise men return and report to the king, will he know what the elephant is like? Why or why not?
3. How could the king find out what the elephant is really like?

Remember that this story is a *fable*. A fable is a story written to teach us a moral or lesson. The characters in them are not real, but are symbols of someone or something in real life. Keep the fable in mind as you read the next selection, "Critical Reading—Critical Thinking." You will see that the elephant is a symbol of any important or controversial issue, while the blind men represent the different single perspectives on the issue. We cannot find out what an elephant is really like—or what an issue is really about—unless we actively seek out and then combine all the different perspectives on it.

CRITICAL READING—CRITICAL THINKING

Mary C. Fjeldstad

One of our greatest challenges as adults is developing a clear understanding about   1
the way things are in the complex, ever-changing world around us. In our lives, many
issues arise that demand our attention, our analysis, and our decision. Unfortunately,
most of us have not been well trained in thinking critically. We tend to accept the
guidance of people whom we respect or are better informed than we are. Thus, we
often reach adulthood still clinging to the attitudes taught us by our parents and
other authority figures from our youth. Educated persons, however, are not satisfied with "borrowing" the opinions and ideas of others—they insist on forming
their own. To do so, they must carefully analyze their beliefs. This is the first step in
developing a responsible opinion. Before we can develop a complete understanding
of an issue, we must consider other viewpoints that may be equally valid. For example, imagine you are looking at a sculpture from one spot, trying to understand
the artist's message. While your view of the sculpture may be *accurate,* it is not *complete.* It is not until you walk around the sculpture and see it from different *perspectives* that you can get a full sense of what it really looks like.

It is the same with most of the important issues and problems in life—one per-   2
spective is not enough to give us the whole picture. It is essential to seek other perspectives on the issues we are trying to understand. What are some ways we can
get information on other perspectives? One way is to use our imaginations. Take,
for example, the emotional issue of abortion. To develop an understanding of the issue, we must examine it from all possible points of view. What are the possible perspectives on this issue? One perspective is that of the pregnant woman, another is
that of the prospective father, another is that of the family of each prospective parent, doctors, religious groups, the fetus itself, and, of course, society as a whole.
We can use our imaginations to inform ourselves by mentally putting ourselves in
the shoes of each of these persons or groups. How would I feel if I were the husband of a pregnant woman who wished to have an abortion? How would I feel as
the doctor? Or the minister? What if the pregnant woman was the victim of a rape?
Or a drug addict who had already given birth to several addicted children or children who were subsequently abused? What is the impact on society of the decision
that will be made?

Other ways of learning about additional perspectives include reading about them   3
in books, magazines, and newspapers, listening to television and radio broadcasts,
and, of course, discussing them with other people.

Learning about each of the perspectives on an issue helps us to see the argu-   4
ments. An *argument* in this context means a *reason*—something that supports the
way a person feels about an issue. For example, when you were considering the issue
of whether to go to college, you probably thought of several different arguments
supporting a decision to go to school; for example:

1. It will help prepare me for a better job.
2. I will earn more money in the long run.

3. I am bored with my life as it is now.
4. It will help me grow as a person.
5. It will help me develop my mind.
6. I will meet new people with similar interests.
7. I will make new friends.

Although some of these arguments may be more important to you than others, all of them are *reasons* to support the decision to go to college. On the other hand, despite all these good arguments, going to school may still not be the right thing for you. You must examine other sides of the issue: what are some arguments *against* attending college?

5   When you learn about developing and analyzing arguments, you will be learning a skill that is important beyond the world of the classroom. You will need to argue many questions in your life. You will, no doubt, argue about political and moral issues. Someone you love may be considering an abortion, or the school in your neighborhood may decide to hand out condoms to students. You may discover a large industry is dumping toxic wastes in the water near your home. You may apply for financial aid or for a scholarship and be turned down unfairly. You may receive a grade in a course that you feel is lower than you deserve. In each of these situations you will need to consider all of the available information and all of the different perspectives before coming to a decision of your own. Once you have developed an opinion you will then be able to present your view to others in a reasonable and effective way. Thus, stating arguments is not limited to the sort of issues reported in newspapers and magazines. When you apply for a job, decide to get married, or give advice to a friend, you need to know how to argue effectively.

6   In order to consider all the perspectives of an issue, we must be open to the viewpoints of other people, and be willing to listen and exchange ideas with them. This process is called a discussion, or *dialogue*. If you felt strongly about the abortion issue, for example, it might make you feel uncomfortable to listen to someone who disagrees with you. But that is the only way you can be sure your own position is supported and strong. Listening to others' points of view should always make us re-examine our own; we may not change our minds, but we will have a more valuable opinion because it has been examined.

7   The selections in this unit will help you clarify your ideas on some of the important issues of the day. By reading, thinking, and writing about them, you will learn to formulate good arguments of your own—and to hold opinions that are mature and valuable. As you read, keep in mind the words of the great French philosopher René Descartes:

> It is now some years since I detected how many were the false beliefs that I had believed to be true since my earliest youth. And since that time, I have been convinced that I must once and for all seriously try to rid myself of all the opinions which I had formerly accepted, and begin to build anew, if I wanted to establish any firm and permanent structure for my beliefs.

VOCABULARY

Directions: Locate each of the key words in the reading selection. Try to figure out each word's meaning by using the context. Confirm your guess by checking the dictionary or thesaurus. Write the meanings of the words in the margin of the text. Then record the meanings in the chart below.

Key Word	Paragraph	Meaning
1. perspective	1	view point
2. prospective	2	potential, possible
3. argument	4	Facts to support what you say
4. dialogue	6	conversation, exchange
Others?		

APPLICATION

1. *Directions:* We experience argumentation all the time in our daily lives—listening to a political candidate trying to persuade us to vote for him or her, a friend trying to convince us to lend him money, classmates trying to convince a teacher to postpone a test, a daughter begging to get her ears pierced, a son to buy the latest fashion.

An important skill in school and in life is to be able to understand the arguments people are making in order to persuade us of something. In the essay below, the writer makes several arguments in favor of polygamy. Read the essay carefully, then in small groups analyze the arguments made by the author. Pull out the arguments the author makes in favor of polygamy—in this case, of allowing men to take two or more wives. Compare your group's list of arguments with the lists of your classmates.

IN DEFENSE OF POLYGAMY

B. Aisha Lemu

Perhaps the aspect of Islam (with respect to women) that is most prominent in the Western mind is that of polygamy. Firstly let me clarify that Islam does not impose polygamy as a universal practice. The Prophet himself was a monogamist for the greater part of his married life, from the age of twenty-five when he married Khadija until he was fifty when she died.

1

One should therefore regard monogamy as the norm and polygamy as the exception.

2

One may observe that, although it has been abused in some times and some places, polygamy has, under certain circumstances, a valuable function. In some

3

situations it may be considered as the lesser of two evils and in other situations it may even be a positively beneficial arrangement.

4   The most obvious example of this occurs in times of war when there are inevitably large numbers of widows and girls whose fiancés and husbands have been killed in the fighting. One has only to recall the figures of the dead in the first and second world wars to be aware that literally millions of women and girls lost their husbands and fiancés and were left alone without any income or care or protection for themselves or their children. If it is still maintained that, under these circumstances, a man may marry only one wife, what options are left to the millions of other women who have no hope of getting a husband? Their choice bluntly stated, is between a chaste and childless old maidenhood, or becoming somebody's mistress—that is, an unofficial second wife with no legal rights for herself or her children. Most women would not welcome either of these since most women have always wanted and still do want the security of a legal husband and family.

5   The compromise, therefore, is for women under these circumstances to face the fact that, if given the alternative, many of them would rather share a husband than have none at all. And there is no doubt that it is easier to share a husband when it is an established and publicly recognized practice than when it is carried on secretly along with attempts to deceive the first wife.

6   And it is no secret that polygamy of a sort is widely carried on in Europe and America. The difference is that, while the Western man has no legal obligations to his second, third, or fourth mistresses and their children, the Muslim husband has complete legal obligations toward his second, third, or fourth wife and their children.

7   There may be other circumstances unrelated to war—individual circumstances where marriage to more than one wife may be preferable to other available alternatives—for example, where the first wife is chronically sick or disabled. There are, of course, some husbands who can manage this situation, but no one would deny its potential hazards. A second marriage, in some cases, could be a solution acceptable to all three parties.

8   Again, there are cases in which a wife is unable to have children while the husband very much wants them. Under Western laws, a man must either accept his wife's childlessness if he can, or, if he cannot, he must find a means of divorce in order to marry again. This could be avoided in some cases if the parties agreed on a second marriage.

9   There are other cases where a marriage has not been very successful and the husband loves another woman. This situation is so familiar that it is known as the Eternal Triangle. Under Western laws the husband cannot marry the second woman without divorcing the first one, but the first wife may not wish to be divorced. She may no longer love her husband, but she may still respect him and wish to stay with him for the security of marriage, for herself and their children. Similarly, the second woman may not wish to break up the man's first family. There are certain cases such as this where both women could accept a polygamous marriage rather than face divorce on the one hand or an extramarital affair on the other.

10   I have mentioned some of these examples because, to the majority of Westerners, polygamy is only thought of in the context of a harem of glamorous young girls, not as a possible solution to some of the problems of Western society itself.

2. *Directions:* Follow the same procedure for the student essay below in which the author argues that the United States should encourage legal immigration.

THE ECONOMICS OF IMMIGRATION

Christopher J. Lovrien and Janelle Anderson

America has long been called a nation of immigrants. It has been said so many times that it has become a cliché. Yet the fact remains, the United States' two-hundred-year rise from newborn to superpower was made possible largely because of the skills and ambitions of immigrants. People such as the Kennedys and the Rockefellers helped lead their new country to world prominence. Immigrants have long brought a vitality to this nation and that is why we should continue to encourage legal immigration.   1

However, more and more Americans seem to want immigration to be restricted. Some have gone so far as to call for a total freeze on immigration for a period of time. As the economy took a downturn in the early 1990s and unemployment rose, some cried out that immigrants were taking jobs from low-skilled Americans. While this may be true in the short term, in the long run immigrants positively affect the economy. More immigrants means not only more workers but also more consumers. In economic terms, this means an increase in demand and the creation of more jobs. Economists will tell you that the number of jobs in an economy is not finite. Also, research shows that native workers' employment opportunities are only slightly reduced when immigrants enter a local labor market.   2

Another concern about the influx of immigrants is that they place an extra burden on the welfare system. This concern is understandable and I share it. Many of the immigrants who seek refuge come having fled their country with very little in the way of economic security. But it might be appropriate to look at welfare to immigrants as an investment. By helping these newcomers out in the beginning, we will enable them to become contributing members of American society. In fact, George Borjas, an economics professor at the University of California at San Diego, calculates that, even though immigrants receive more welfare than they pay in taxes, they actually add $4 billion to the economy by paying for things like food, rent, and clothing. Quite simply, most immigrants are not leeching off the system. In fact, the Urban Institute reports that 74 percent of adult male immigrants are employed, versus 72 percent of the general male population.   3

So what should the U.S. policy on immigration be? We should be conscious that immigration can be a tremendous tool for improving this country. By allowing, and even seeking out skilled immigrants to enter the United States, we can direct immigration to help strengthen our country. In a sense, we could select immigrants to fit our needs. These people would find it easier to acquire work and could be immediate contributors to American economic health.   4

The first step is for the government to ensure it is aware of who is entering the country. To do this, illegal immigration needs to be curbed. We can, of course, increase the number of border patrol officers and erect barriers, both of which amount to throwing money at the problem and may or may not be effective. But the best way to decrease illegal immigration may be to increase legal immigration.   5

Currently, the government allows about 700,000 immigrants to legally enter the country per year. It is estimated that another 300,000 enter illegally. Statistics show that, when legal immigration is cut, illegal immigration generally increases. Increasing the quota of legal immigrants could decrease the number entering illegally. We might have the same number of people entering the country, but we would be in better control of who they are. More legal immigrants would mean we could allow more people with special skills and education to enter the country.

6 Another means to decreasing illegal immigrants is through measures such as NAFTA [North American Free Trade Agreement]. A large percentage of illegal immigrants are Mexicans who cross the border to escape poverty. NAFTA should work to bring the wages in Mexico and the United States closer together. It will also raise the standard of living in Mexico. This would decrease the incentive for Mexicans to sneak into the United States. In fact, University of California at Berkeley economist Sherman Robinson estimates that "each percentage point increase in the value of Mexico's capital stock . . . would be enough stimulus to keep 25,000 of its citizens at home."

7 Looking at the history of opposition to immigration, I see some interesting trends. There seems to always have been those who felt that certain immigrants were going to ruin the country. When the Germans began immigrating to America, some "ethnic" Americans said they would cause the breakdown of America. In fact, the country became stronger. When the potato famine drove a wave of Irish immigrants to America, some Americans (including some of the new German-Americans) said they would ruin the country. They were wrong. The country became stronger and the Irish-Americans eventually flourished, despite prejudice. With history as a precedent, why is there any reason to believe that this new wave of immigrants will be anything but good for America? Unless it is because this new wave is largely non-white. I certainly hope the value of these immigrants is not being judged on the basis of skin color. People like Peter Brimelow, who say that large-scale immigration will cause America to lose its culture, fail to realize that American culture has been immensely enriched by other ethnic cultures.

8 Why are immigrants to America often able to do so well in their new country and add so much to it? In no small part, it's because of their character. Immigrants must be ambitious to leave their native country. Think what a decision that must be. These are people willing to leave everything they know and search for a better life for themselves. They bring this ambition and desire to America. Contrary to what we are led to believe, they are not just the poor and the outcasts of the world. Many are well educated. According to the Urban Institute, 25 percent of the immigrants arriving in the 1980s had college degrees. By increasing legal immigration and selecting skilled people, we can make that ratio even higher.

9 None of what I have suggested means we should restrict immigration only to those who are affluent. We currently accept those who have been politically and economically oppressed. We should continue to do so. For underneath the shackles of poverty might exist an incredible entrepreneur.

10 America has had a long history of talented immigrants. The next great physicist might very well be arriving in New York or San Francisco right now, and whether she is European, Asian, or African, I hope we are bright enough not to send her away.

3. *Directions:* In this last essay, which appeared in *Newsweek* in 1993, the author considers the question of teacher–student dating in colleges and universities. Many schools across the country have adopted policies that forbid any romantic relationship between faculty and students. What are Begley's arguments on the issue? As with the previous essays, read the selection carefully and, working with your group, identify the arguments made by the author. Compare your group's list with the lists of your classmates.

CLIPPING CUPID'S WINGS

Sharon Begley

When "Steve" ran into his foreign-language instructor last April at a cafe near the   1
University of California, Berkeley, where he was a junior, she asked him "to go out sometime." He declined—and later received the second lowest grade in the class, "a grade I didn't deserve," he says. "I don't think that's a coincidence."

Was this sexual harassment going unpunished? Or another crazed P.C.er see-   2
ing evil in every innocent gesture? Colleges aren't waiting for nasty Hill/Thomas-type hearings[1] to sort out the predatory from the friendly. Although the idea that it's dumb to bed someone you teach is implicit in sexual-harassment codes, more and more schools are flat-out prohibiting faculty from dating students in their classes. Harvard, Tufts, and the Universities of Iowa and Pennsylvania, among others, have banned such dating. Amherst College requires faculty who venture into sexual relationships with students to remove themselves from any supervisory role over them. Last week the University of Virginia (UVA) faculty senate prepared to vote on what would have been the most far-reaching ban: a prohibition on sexual relationships and "amorous overtures" between students and *any* faculty member.

Coerced Consent

But in a heated two-hour session, UVA's blanket prohibition never came to a vote;   3
proponents, sensing defeat, instead offered a narrower ban on instructors dating students they teach or supervise. That passed thirty-one to four. But the debate over where to draw the line on campus romances is still resounding in dorms from Cambridge to Palo Alto. It's fueled by the growing belief that many campus relationships deemed "consensual" are not—that (usually female) students get pressured into bed with (usually male) faculty or graduate teaching assistants. Professors' power to determine their students' future, through grades and recommendations, "makes 'consensual' a suspect notion," argued UVA's history professor and Director of Women's Studies Ann Lane. UVA received more than one hundred student complaints last year about romantic feelers from faculty; most believed that spurning the advances would jeopardize their grades.

Even if both student and teacher freely choose romance, others can be ad-   4
versely affected. A grad student living with an assistant professor may get invited to

---

[1] When Clarence Thomas was nominated for the Supreme Court in 1991, his confirmation hearings focused on claims from Anita Hill that she had been sexually harassed by him.

department parties, making other students jealous. Such romances also call into question the objectivity of the grading system. At Harvard, most of the dozen or so complaints received each year about student–instructor affairs come from suspicious undergraduates in the same class as the teacher's love interest. "It would take a Solomon to be entirely fair when you've become romantic with a person you're trying to evaluate," says UVA engineer Thomas Hutchinson.

5   UVA's attempt to clip Cupid's wings failed because it prohibited romances even between faculty and students who have no academic relationship. Many students were outraged over an infringement on their cherished right to date whomever they please. "During four years at UVA, a student will take classes with just 2 percent of the faculty," says Student Council President Matthew Cooper. "[Banning all relationships] denies our autonomy as adults." Stanford University is about to accept that argument: its proposed sexual-harassment policy will not prohibit consensual affairs, but warns of "special risks involved in any sexual or romantic relationship between individuals in inherently unequal positions." (Not all such romances end in disaster. UVA President John T. Casteen, III, is married to a grad student he met when he was a professor at Berkeley in the early 1970s; he won't say whether or not he oversaw her work.) Absolutists, though, reject exceptions for people in different departments. A music student who has an affair with a physics prof may later switch majors and find herself sitting in front of his lectern.

Policing Bedrooms

6   Are blanket prohibitions constitutional? The right to free association is not absolute; a "compelling state interest" can limit it, and some scholars argue that keeping a college free of the problems caused by student–faculty romances is one such interest. Policing a prohibition is another matter. Says Hutchinson, "To regulate the moral behavior of eighteen thousand people puts an unbearable load on the administration." UVA will enforce its ban only if a grievance is brought; Tufts doesn't police bedrooms and no one's been reported for breaking the ban. Few of the prohibitions carry an explicit penalty.

7   In a 1988 survey of eight hundred faculty at a West Coast university, 25 percent of those questioned admitted bedding students, most more than once. Few students actually ask to be protected from lascivious faculty, but surely those who do ought to have some recourse. For schools, the arguments boil down to practicalities. Sexual harassment can require a subjective determination, but a ban on dating draws an unambiguous line. "People have to learn to be decent to each other," says Associate Provost Samuel Jay Keyser of the Massachusetts Institute of Technology. "No policies, no matter how good or complete, can achieve that."

WRITING

Directions: Choose one of the assignments below.

1. Write an essay of at least 350 words that argues one of the following:
   a. Polygamy should be prohibited.
   b. Legal immigration into the United States should be limited.
   c. Student–faculty dating should be allowed.

Consult the list of arguments you developed in the Application exercise above when you write this essay.

2. Explain why learning to think critically is an essential part of higher education. How can the ability to think critically protect a person from advertisers, the mass media, scientists, politicians, dictators, and other tyrants of the mind? Write at least 350 words.

SHORT TAKE

ARGUMENTATION

The word *argumentation* can be confusing. Our first reaction may be to think of the everyday word *argument*—a disagreement, a quarrel. But writing an argumentation paper has nothing to do with anger or unpleasantness. While we may throw dishes and slam doors in an argument with our family, argumentation requires that we think and express ourselves clearly, without letting our feelings interfere. An argumentation paper is an articulate, well-organized statement of our ideas. It attempts to convince others to consider our point of view, and, perhaps, to persuade them to agree with us.

The most important aspect of argumentation, though, is not winning. It is gaining the respect of others, convincing them we are worthy of their attention and consideration. If we can win this, we have won something more valuable than the vote on the issue at hand. It is essential, then, to treat our opponents with respect. No one will listen to us if we treat them as if they were fools. Do not be contemptuous of those who disagree with you. Try not to be narrow-minded. Do not assume you have a monopoly on the truth. And remember, you cannot expect others to listen to you if you do not listen to them.

CONTROVERSIAL ISSUES

Should Adoptive Parents Be Allowed to Return Children They Decide They Don't Want?

In this consumer age, people demand a perfect product and don't hesitate to sue when they feel they've been saddled with "damaged goods." Does an implied warranty cover children as well? If an adopted child turns out to be different from what the parents expected, should they be allowed to return the goods? The following article from Time *magazine discusses this growing problem in an age of demand for designer cars, houses, clothes, and even children.*

WHEN THE LULLABY ENDS

Andrea Sachs

Most eleven-year-olds don't have a lawyer, but Tony is a special case. His adoptive   1
parents decided, five years after his adoption, that Tony had not properly "bonded" with them, and returned him to the state in March. They kept Sam, Tony's natural younger brother. Patrick Murphy, the Chicago public guardian who was appointed to serve as Tony's attorney, says the youngster is an "absolute joy to be around." But there have been scars. Says Murphy: "One of the tragic things is that Tony blames himself."

Tony is one of at least one thousand children adopted in the United States each   2
year who will be returned to agencies by their new parents. Some are sent back because of unmet expectations, others because they have severe emotional problems the parents cannot handle. In a risk-averse age when consumer standards have become more exacting and family commitments seem less binding, there is a danger that adopted children could be viewed as commodities that come with an implied warranty. The problem presents a major challenge for the legal system. "This is not a question of damaged goods; it's a matter of what's in the best interest of the child," says Neil Cogan of Southern Methodist Law School.

Social workers used to believe that all an adopted child needed was a loving   3
home. But now many admit that even the most committed parents may be overwhelmed by unexpected problems. In 1986 Dan and Rhonda Stanton adopted a blond baby girl they named Stacey René. "We thought we had a perfect baby because she didn't cry," says Dan, an insurance agent in suburban Dallas. Their contentment faded as the months passed and Stacey did not develop properly. She didn't babble and laugh like their friends' babies and couldn't pinch with her individual fingers. The tentative diagnosis: Rett's syndrome, a rare genetic disorder in which the brain stops growing. Devastated, the Stantons took Stacey back to the agency and have not seen her since. "We made a commitment to her, but we were not able to live up to that commitment," says Rhonda. "She turned out to be totally different from what we thought we had adopted."

If adoptive parents are saddled with an unforeseen defect, who should shoul-   4
der the load? Most experts put the onus on the adoptive parents. "Families, having

decided to do an adoption, assume a certain risk," says Professor William Winslade of the University of Texas Medical School in Galveston. "If it is an incredibly difficult burden, it seems unfair not to give parents, who have provided the benefit to society by making the adoption, some special help. But I don't think the burden should be totally given back to the state either. Parents adopt because they want the joys—and the sorrows—of having children."

5   About 2 percent of all adoptions in the United States fail. But for older children and children with special needs, the numbers are far higher. For children older than two, 10 percent of the adoptions are dissolved. For ages twelve to seventeen, the rate shoots up to around 24 percent. This poses a special problem, since healthy adoptable babies are increasingly scarce due to the fact that more single women now opt to have abortions or to keep their infants. More families are therefore adopting older or handicapped children. This seems to be a main cause of the growing return-to-sender phenomenon.

6   As the problem of disrupted adoptions spreads, specialists are looking more closely at agency methods. One cause for failure is a practice that Berkeley professor Richard Barth describes as "stretching." In essence, it is a bait-and-switch game: would-be parents are encouraged to adopt a child different from the one they wanted by the withholding of some negative information. For example, a couple who want a baby are persuaded to take an older child and are never told that several earlier placements have not worked out because of emotional problems. Though the motive is benevolent—finding a home for a hard-to-place child—Barth regards the tactic as unethical.

7   Some disappointed parents have begun to fight back in the courts. The notion of "wrongful adoption"—which claims that agencies are liable for damages if they place children without fully disclosing their health backgrounds—is gaining legal recognition. Frank and Jayne Gibbs of Philadelphia are suing two agencies for $6 million, following their adoption of a seven-year-old boy who turned out to be violently disturbed. After the adoption, says the couple, they discovered that he had been horribly abused, including an attempt by his natural mother to cut off his genitals.

8   Many states have passed medical disclosure laws, which make it easier to obtain accurate information about a child. Agencies themselves are attempting to gather more data. The Golden Cradle adoption agency, in Cherry Hill, New Jersey, requires natural mothers to fill out ten-page medical histories that ask about everything from hay fever and heavy drinking to Down's syndrome and blood transfusions. Genetic counselors are often called in as consultants. "We believe an ounce of prevention is worth a pound of cure," says agency supervisor Mary Anne Giello.

9   Still, there are no warranties on adoptions. Those who set out looking for perfect "designer" children are likely to be disappointed. Nor is it possible—or even necessary—to know everything about a child. "People shouldn't get the idea that they can't be parents unless they have a DNA portrait of a kid," says Professor Joan Hollinger of the University of Detroit Law School. Instead, adoptive parents, armed with as much information as possible, should face the inevitable mysteries—just as all parents do.

VOCABULARY

Directions: Locate each of the key words in the reading selection. Try to figure out each word's meaning by using the context. Confirm your guess by checking the dictionary or thesaurus. Write the meanings of the words in the margin of the text. Then record the meanings in the chart below.

Key Word	Paragraph	Meaning
1. risk-averse	2	
2. implied	2	
3. babble	3	
4. onus	4	
5. opt	5	
6. benevolent	6	
7. inevitable	9	
Others?		

GUIDE QUESTIONS

Directions: These questions will guide your understanding of what you have read. Write your answers in your notebook or on a separate sheet of paper if your instructor wishes to collect it. Your answers to these questions will be the basis of class discussion.

1. Eleven-year-old Tony is used as an example in this selection to illustrate a new problem in our society. Explain the problem.
2. Note the use of the word *commodities* in paragraph 2.
   a. Define the word *commodity*.
   b. Look through the selection: what other terms can you find that seem to categorize children as products, rather than as persons?
   c. Why is this view of children as products creating a problem with adopted children?

3. How have social workers' views of the needs of adopted children changed?

4. React to the comment by Ms. Stanton in paragraph 3, "We made a commitment to [the baby], but we were not able to live up to that commitment." If Ms. Stanton had said this to you, how would you have answered her?

5. What is the main cause of the new "return to sender" phenomenon, according to the selection?

6. How have some adoption agencies contributed to the problem of failed adoptions?

7. Explain how other adoption agencies have worked to prevent problems.

8. Put yourself in the place of an adoptive parent who discovers his or her new child has a serious physical or mental disability, that the adoption agency knew about the problem, but never informed you. How would you react? What would you do?

9. What is Professor Hollinger's opinion on adoptive parents returning a child because the child is not exactly what they expected?

APPLICATION/WRITING

Directions: Discuss *all* of the questions below with your classmates. Then write a response to any *one* of the four questions.

1. Remember that to be able to evaluate an issue it is necessary to view it from all possible perspectives. First, take a look at the "return to sender" situation from the viewpoint of adoptive parents. Read the story below:

> After several years of unsuccessfully trying to have a baby, Carol and Jim Field adopt a little girl. At first they are thrilled and happy—she is a beautiful child. Soon, however, it becomes clear that there is something terribly wrong. The baby smiles happily, but never coos or babbles as babies do. She does not respond to colorful toys or to her parents' voices. Fearfully, Carol and Jim consult a doctor who determines that the baby is deaf and blind. Horrified, the Fields seek every kind of treatment that might make their baby hear and see. Finally, they accept that she cannot be helped. Unable to cope with a handicapped child, the Fields decide to return the baby to the adoption agency.

   Imagine that you are Jim or Carol. Write a letter to the agency. In the letter explain, first, that you have decided to return the child. Second, explain your reasons for doing so.

2. Now look at Jim and Carol's situation from the perspective of the agency. Write an answering letter in which you explain to the Fields all the reasons they should not return the baby.

3. Write your own letter to Carol and Jim, explaining to them what *you* think they should do and why.

4. Imagine that it is twenty years in the future. Look at this situation from the perspective of the baby. Pretend you are the child, who is now grown up. Write a letter from her to Carol and Jim reacting to their decision.

CONTROVERSIAL ISSUES

Genetic Testing

Enormous progress in the field of genetic testing over the past decade has led to the identification of genes that underlie heart disease, colon cancer, cystic fibrosis, and a number of other illnesses. Research continues at a frantic pace to identify the genes that carry many ailments and even genes that may play a role in human behavior. These scientific advances may bring great good to society. They may lead to treatments or cures. But is there a downside to these exciting genetic discoveries? Geneticists now offer a test for Huntington's disease, although there is no cure or treatment for it. This article, which appeared in the Chicago Tribune *in 1988, examines the pros and cons of the test.*

A NEW GENETIC TEST CAN FORETELL AGONIZING DEATH: WOULD YOU TAKE IT?

Peter Gorner

Paul and Karen Sweeney, dressed in their finest, kissed in the parking lot and marched resolutely to psychologist Kimberly Quaid's office at the Johns Hopkins Hospital. A lot of lives were on the line. 1

The psychologist greeted the young Virginia couple, and Karen began pacing the room. Paul sat stiffly, breathing deeply, staring straight ahead. 2

"Are you sure you want to know?" 3

Quaid asked the *pro forma* question one last time, doing everything by the book. Maybe they wouldn't want to know, despite months of testing and counseling, particularly about suicide and whether Karen could cope with bad news. 4

She reacted sharply to Quaid's question. She'd spent most of her life wondering and worrying. She never had enjoyed a childhood; never known her mother, except as a twitching, flailing, helpless, and mute victim strapped into a hospital bed before she mercifully died ten years later. Karen's mother had gotten sick at thirty-three, while pregnant with her. Now Karen, twenty-eight, was running out of time. Her emotions welled up, chocking her. 5

"Yes! Please!" she screamed. "Tell us. Please." 6

The news is good, Quaid quietly told them: You beat it. 7

The test showed that there was a 95 percent probability that Karen didn't carry the gene for Huntington's disease, a rare and always fatal hereditary brain disorder. 8

She and Paul had a future after all. And, in that instant, so did their children: Melissa, Jesse, Brenndan, and Shawn. Not to mention *their* children someday. 9

All suddenly, wonderfully, free. 10

The deadly gene that had murdered her grandfather and her mother and had already begun the slow killing of her forty-year-old brother had spared Karen and her new family line. 11

Two years ago, predictive testing for the Huntington's gene began at Hopkins and at Massachusetts General Hospital in Boston, institutions with long histories of caring for Huntington's patients. 12

13   New centers are operating at Columbia Presbyterian Medical Center in New York and at the Universities of Michigan and Minnesota.

14   The new test has produced agonizing dilemmas for the pioneering testers, quandaries that will become increasingly common in coming years as discoveries are made of specific genetic defects that predispose people to future physical and mental illnesses.

15   The idea of a test that can tell a healthy person today that in twenty years he may die of a stroke, cancer, or heart attack, or have his happiness suffocated by a major depressive illness, is altogether new to society.

16   Do people really want that information? Dare society keep it from them? Huntington's disease carries with it a suicide rate four to seven times the national average. Yet the historic DNA test for the lethal gene means the future is already here. It has abruptly shoved medical science to the edge of an ethical abyss.

17   "We know we're all going to die, yes," says Kimberly Quaid. "But most of us don't know how or when.

18   "Many people who come to us don't want to know for themselves; they want to be able to tell their children whether they need to worry. Others, though, say they have an overwhelming need to end the agony of not knowing.

19   "Right now, those of us in this field are becoming the gypsy fortune-tellers of technology. What I see in my job is merely the tip of the iceberg, but it's very distressing. Frankly, I don't think we're ready for this."

20   Karen Sweeney says she vividly remembers the scene last November, when she received the test results on which she had bet her life. Karen recalls the unbelievable high, the hugging, the tears in Kim Quaid's eyes.

21   But Quaid doubts that Karen really remembers. At the moment of truth, people always freeze, regardless of the news. So far, the Hopkins team has told eight people they will get Huntington's disease, twenty-eight people that they won't, and seven people that the test has failed and the results are inconclusive.

22   No matter the news, the brain seizes up in self-defense, denying, refusing to compute. People may act normally; they may sob in grief, sob in relief, or sob in the frustration of no answer. But they're not really processing what's happening to them.

23   That's why researchers insist on the buddy system. There must be an "advocate" present at the disclosure sessions, when healthy young people find out whether they're going to die from a legacy so horrifying that many doctors consider it the worst thing that can happen to a human being.

24   *Escapees* is another term the researchers use. Karen Sweeney is an escapee. All those who come to Hopkins for presymptomatic testing for Huntington's want to be told that they're escapees.

25   But not everyone is. And many others, who could learn, don't want to find out. Some people want to know but don't want other people to know, including their spouses and children.

26   "Every family poses new problems," says Jason Brandt, the cheerful young psychologist who heads the Hopkins testing program.

27   "We thought we were real smart cookies. We thought we had anticipated every possible snafu when we started this. Then the first five patients in the door had us hollering for help."

Quaid says she longed for an ethics hot line, somebody she could call who could tell her what to do.   28

What would you do with identical twins, one of whom wanted the test and the other didn't? The Hopkins team was bewildered. Identical twins share the same genes. If one carries the fatal flaw, the other is doomed as well.   29

"We decided they should work it out," says Brandt, "and if push came to shove, we wouldn't test them. But before they could make a decision, one of them started to show symptoms of the disease. That settled that."   30

What would you do with a doctor (not at Hopkins) who wanted a leukemia victim tested for the Huntington's gene before he considered giving her a life-saving bone-marrow Huntington's transplant? The phone call made Quaid shudder. She icily deflected the doctor.   31

What would you do with the pitiful people—ten so far—who came to Hopkins to be tested and already were showing signs of Huntington's?   32

"They were coming in, ostensibly, to be told that in ten to twenty years, they will get the disease," Quaid says. "They were not prepared to be told: 'I'm sorry, you already have it.'"   33

These are just a few of the issues that the Hopkins team confronts every day. About 25,000 Americans suffer from Huntington's disease, but another 150,000 people live in its shadow, knowing they have a 50–50 chance of getting it. Huntington's, best known as the disease that killed folksinger Woody Guthrie, has been called history's first example of genetically caused insanity. It lies dormant until you reach middle age. Then it strikes, slowly drives you mad, and kills you.   34

The disease is genetic, without doubt. By the time a parent develops it, he or she may already have had children. On average, half of them will die of Huntington's, as well. A sick parent is condemned, but the children don't know if they are too. They oversee the lingering deaths of their parents. They realize what may be in store.   35

So for them, the wait is excruciating, the ambiguity torturous, the anguish almost unimaginable. "There's not one waking hour that you don't think about it," says Karen Sweeney. "It influences everything you do."   36

Should such people get married and have kids? Most of them do and take a chance, knowing that if the gene blazes into action, they've ensured that those they love the most may face the same fate. If they forgo marriage and parenthood and the gene never shows up, they've sacrificed in vain.   37

The first signs of Huntington's disease are diabolically subtle. A twitch. Fidgeting. Clumsiness. A sudden fall. Absentmindedness. Irritability. Depression.   38

Normal people rarely worry about such things, but when someone at risk for Huntington's drops a dish, forgets a name, or trips on the sidewalk, the effect is chilling.   39

Is it starting?   40

Eventually, if someone has the gene, his body starts to work as if by remote control. It starts to move. He can't stop it or control it. The brain has begun to die. The victim develops the distinctive frenzy of aimless twitching, lurching, and jerking. As uncontrolled writhing (choreac movements) gradually increases, the patient must be confined to a bed or wheelchair. Facial expressions may become distorted and grotesque: The eyes roll, the tongue darts in and out, the eyebrows glide up and   41 down. At worst, the entire body becomes a horror of grotesque, involuntary move-ments. Speech is slurred at first, then indistinct, then finally stops altogether as the victim stiffens like a board and loses the ability to swallow.

42   Mental functions similarly deteriorate, and eventually the ability to reason dis-appears. Huntington's can take twenty terrible years to reach full cry. No treatment can slow the inexorable course, let alone halt it. Every afflicted person and his fam-ily must engage in herculean battles against the inevitable, struggling day after day to maintain hope and keep fighting.

43   Usually, victims must be institutionalized. Infection generally ends the story. Families, grieving, say they are amazed to see their loved ones finally stilled. The dev-ilish dancing finally has ceased. Ironically, victims look as they once did, before the long suffering began.

44   For twenty-five years, genetic engineers hoped to find a marker for this obscene disease, some signpost in the complement of forty-six human chromosomes that would predict whether someone carried the gene. Then future victims could make plans for their care. They could do something active, not merely wait in horror. Es-capees would be freed. Affected fetuses could be detected in the womb, and par-ents could decide whether to bring them into the world. The heartbreaking killer might even be wiped out in a generation. It was a possibility; something society could debate.

45   In 1983, Harvard researcher James Gusella found such a marker and electrified science. Nancy Wexler, a Columbia University psychologist who may herself carry the gene, had worked with huge families of rural Venezuelans—nine thousand of them, as of last spring—who have the highest rate of Huntington's in the world. By examining the blood of victims and looking for genetic patterns that escapees didn't have, Gusella was able to isolate the marker.

46   He didn't find the gene. But he pinpointed other genes close to it on its chro-mosome. And suddenly all of science knew where to look for the Huntington's gene: It's out somewhere on the far tip of Chromosome 4. The race to nail it down continues in laboratories every day. "I'm sure they'll find it soon," says Brandt. "Then they can tear it apart and figure out what's wrong. Then they can fix it."

47   Since the breakthrough, sixteen more Huntington's markers have been found, fine-tuning the predictive test to virtually 100 percent—in the right families.

48   Hopkins needs blood from both affected and unaffected relatives to do the test. Sometimes there's not enough material available. Sometimes those who want to be tested are afraid to approach relatives about this ugly family secret. Some-times the markers, the snapshots themselves, are confusing.

49   But in many families, scientists now can identify future victims early, before they have children. No longer do people have to suffer thirty or forty years before the real nightmare begins.

50   The testing procedure, however, is long and involved, requiring months of coun-seling and psychological testing to evaluate inner strengths, family and religious sup-ports, marital relationships, employment situations. (Hopkins advises those who come for testing to buy disability coverage *before* they do.)

51   About a third of those who apply to the program drop out after a few coun-seling sessions.

"The process gives us a unique chance to do research," says Quaid, "to assess   52
the impact of this clinical test before some Dr. Bagodonuts starts using it without
any knowledge of what may happen.

"We don't advocate that anyone take this test. If someone decides they need   53
the information, we will help them in any way we can.

"But the social, financial, and psychological burdens of this disease are staggering.   54
Family breakups and divorce are common. One frightened woman who called me
was an adoptee. She had tracked down her biological parents. She found her natural
father. He was in a nursing home with the terminal stages of Huntington's disease."

Despite polls showing that most Huntington's families wanted to take the test,   55
relatively few have actually applied at the research centers. Living with a 50–50
chance, after all, holds a certain measure of hope. "Regardless of the results," Quaid
says, "this test can completely change someone's self-concept. A lot of people don't
get the family support that they expect. One husband told me he probably wouldn't
be able to handle it if his wife tested positive. He might leave her and would have to
live with the knowledge that he was a coward. When I asked another man what he
would do if his test were positive, he said: 'Well, I wouldn't cheat on my wife.'"

Nancy Wexler, at Columbia Presbyterian, declines to say if she has taken the   56
test. She offers it reluctantly.

"It's not a good test if you can't offer people treatment," she says. She has been   57
struck by those who come in for testing and already are showing signs of the
disease.

"It really indicates how ambivalent people are," she says.   58

"These people say they want to have this information. But they don't really   59
want it, or they would deliver it to themselves. They don't need a fancy DNA test.
If they just looked at their fingers and toes, they'd say: 'Well, that's it, all right.'"

Denial, she notes, is a crucial coping strategy for human beings. How else can   60
those living under a threat like Huntington's be expected to get through the day? All
of us have health fears that we deny all the time.

"But we're cracking people's healthiest defense by making them attend to the   61
fact that they will actually get this disease," Wexler says. "We're opening deep
wounds.

"We spend all our time trying to get them to cope, to come to grips with the   62
fact that it could be really bad news, so they're prepared for the worst. Then, if the
news really is terrible, we instantly have to do a complete turnaround!

"We quickly must tell them: 'Well, you know, the disease isn't really all that bad.   63
It takes a long time to progress, and research is going on like crazy. Surely there'll
be a cure. Now don't get depressed, and please don't go out and kill yourself.'"

No one who has taken the test has tried so far, the centers report.   64

"Jumping out the window is just the most dramatic aspect of it," Wexler says.   65
"People can jump out the window inside. Those might be harder to identify."

Brandt, a fellow psychologist, views the patients differently. "I don't think those   66
who test positive for the gene are dying inside. They are amazingly courageous and
resilient people. These patients who come for testing are unique, I think. They're
highly motivated: They want to know. They're also highly educated: Three years of
college is the norm. Once they learn they carry the gene, they get on with their

lives. They don't come in for regular therapy. They've found out what they needed to know. They don't dwell on it."

67   Nor do the escapees show predictable patterns. "Among those who have tested clear so far," Brandt says, "one got engaged, another had a baby, a third left her husband. So we're seeing different things."

68   The Hopkins program ferociously protects its clients' identities. Yet Quaid worries that such information one day might be used to discriminate against those who carry the gene. Employers might demand screening. Insurers might deny coverage. Then only the wealthy could take the test and learn their futures.

69   Nancy Wexler believes that perhaps now is not the time to volunteer for such a landmark test.

70   "That may be the best outcome after all," she says. Quaid, though, feels that many people really want to know. "I think the potential of this test to do enormous good is there. Half the people will turn out negative. For them it's just an enormous, enormous benefit."

71   Karen Sweeney obviously concurs, "I can't tell anyone to take the test," she says. "But I think we faced death—looked it square in the eye—and are better people for it. I believe many others can find that inner strength, if they try. I know I couldn't have continued to live my life the way it was before.

72   "My family has a future, because of these scientists. Their work may help my brother as well. I feel tremendous guilt that I was spared and he wasn't."

73   And despite the emotional rollercoaster Kimberly Quaid has ridden the last two years, she will keep administering the test.

74   "I can only hope," she says, "that in the future—and I mean the immediate future—we as a society will show compassion to those who, through no fault of their own, are doomed to suffer."

VOCABULARY

Directions: Locate each of the key words in the reading selection. Try to figure out each word's meaning by using the context. Confirm your guess by checking the dictionary or thesaurus. Write the meanings of the words in the margin of the text. Then record the meanings in the chart below and on the next page.

Key Word	Paragraph	Meaning
1. *pro forma*	4	
2. mute	5	
3. quandaries	14	
4. abyss	16	
5. snafu	27	

Key Word	Paragraph	Meaning
6. dormant	34	
7. excruciating	36	
8. inexorable	42	
Others?		

GUIDE QUESTIONS

Directions: These questions will guide your understanding of what you have read. Write your answers in your notebook or on a separate sheet of paper if your instructor wishes to collect it. Your answers to these questions will be the basis of class discussion.

1. While this selection focuses on genetic testing for one particular illness, Huntington's disease, the questions it raises apply to genetic testing in general. Define *genetic testing*.
2. In paragraph 14, the author says the test for Huntington's disease has produced "agonizing dilemmas for the pioneering testers." What are some of the dilemmas the scientists face?
3. Beginning in paragraph 34, the author describes the effects of Huntington's disease. Describe the disease and the effect of "not knowing" if you have it on the people who may have inherited it.
4. Researchers looked for the "marker" for the disease for twenty-five years. What did they hope would happen if the marker was found?
5. James Gusella finally found a marker for Huntington's in 1983 and the search continued for the gene itself. The testing for the marker, however, has had its problems. Describe some of the problems.
6. Nancy Wexler of Columbia Presbyterian Hospital says she offers to do the test "reluctantly." Why does she think "it's not a good test . . ."?
7. The testing program at Johns Hopkins carefully guards the identities of its clients. What could be some of the consequences if these people's identities became known?

APPLICATION

Directions: Divide the class in half or into small groups. Each group will discuss one side of the issue of genetic testing for Huntington's. One half of the class will develop a list of arguments in favor of doing the test. The other half will develop a list of arguments against doing the test. Then use the pro and con arguments to discuss the question: Should the test to determine the presence of Huntington's disease be offered?

WRITING

Directions: Assume that one of your parents suffered from Huntington's disease. Would you want to take the DNA test for the disease? Give reasons to support your decision.

This essay, which appeared in the "My Turn" section of Newsweek *in April 1995, reminds us to consider the impact of genetic testing on the lives of people who are affected. The author says that one of the presumed benefits of the test is that those infected can at least plan for their and their children's future, but, in reality, that is impossible, except for the very wealthy.*

KNOWING ISN'T EVERYTHING

Sally Spaulding

I am one of those people whose life has been drastically altered by the recent advances in genetic testing. In October 1989, shortly after predictive testing became available for Huntington's disease, my doctor told me there was a 92 percent chance I had inherited the gene for it from my father. In July 1994, after breakthroughs in testing, I learned that I have the gene, for sure. 1

Huntington's disease is a progressive, terminal neurological illness that causes mental and physical deterioration over a period of ten to twenty years, usually beginning in a person's thirties or forties. The gene is dominant and thus does not skip generations. Having the gene means I will get the disease. There is no treatment or cure, not even anything experimental. There's no way to stop its onset. I just turned forty. 2

One of the biggest arguments for genetic testing, even when there isn't any cure or treatment to offer the patient, is financial planning. If you know that you're probably going to be disabled and unable to work before reaching fifty, you can plan for it. If you know you'll likely spend several years in a nursing home before you die, you can prepare. But there's a hitch: this sort of financial planning is almost impossible, except for the very wealthy. 3

I fit into a unique niche. Those of us now testing positive for Huntington's are the first to know for sure about future risks. Before testing, there was always hope. Somewhere down the road, there'll be hope again in the form of a cure—or a choice of treatments. However, even armed with knowledge that one has this gene, how can a person plan ahead financially for a devastating illness in this bleak anti-worker economy? Government and big business tell us that the economy continues to improve. But many in the middle and lower classes aren't any better off. What this means to those of us who've tested positive for Huntington's is that we slog along at jobs we don't love but can't leave. We are dependent on employer-provided health, disability, and life insurance. We want to get in as many productive years as possible. We can't return to school to train for a new career because we don't have time. For us, there is no future. 4

We pray that there won't be a gap in our employment—without a paycheck and insurance. Many businesses are converting to long-term temporary employment (sometimes as long as two years) because it means not paying benefits or severance pay. Many of us who have the Huntington's gene don't have savings or investments. People at risk are offered gene tests, and few can resist the lure of knowing the future. But when the results are positive, those who are affected are on their own. There is no more research help. I knew I had to make financial plans for my family. 5

6   In September 1991, I was thirty-six and working as a legal assistant for a two-attorney law office—a successful father-and-son operation. I had a chance at a higher-paying job in the legal department of an insurance company. The man who ran my firm was in his sixties and had no plans to retire. But when I asked, I was told that the firm would probably cease to exist without him if he became disabled or died. I needed to provide my family with health insurance for the first time. Up to that point, my husband, a Presbyterian minister, had provided us with medical benefits. He suffered from depression and changed jobs frequently. He was on the verge of another major breakdown. I knew it was now up to me to make sure we were covered.

7   The insurance company offered a higher salary, excellent benefits, and stability. But one year and nine months after being hired, I was laid off along with others in the department. Despite my extremely diligent efforts at finding work, I was unemployed for the next nine months. My benefits ($305 per week) ran out after six months. I was paying $500 a month to my former employer to continue health-insurance coverage for my family.

8   I finally found a job at another law firm. It lasted seven months before I was fired. I knew I'd done an excellent job. My employer's only complaint was that I couldn't keep up with the workload of the two young attorneys I was assigned to. The attorneys generated too much work for one person—50 percent of their assignments were due the same or next day. But the firm saw it as a personnel problem and let me go. I was shocked. I was also frightened that I was turning into my father, who couldn't hold onto a job after the age of forty-three because of his illness. A long talk with my doctor convinced me that the disease wasn't setting in yet. I'd simply been the victim of a ruthless employer.

9   So I was out of work again for the second time in eighteen months. I was ready to shoot every last perky staffer at the unemployment office who told me losing my job was a new beginning and anything was possible. I felt completely alone and out of place at the unemployment office's happy workshops.

10   This time my unemployment benefits would run out after three months. I didn't have the luxury to spend another nine months looking for a legal-assistant position making $33,000 a year, which was my salary at my last two jobs. I needed to act immediately. Because I can type 65 words a minute, I began looking for a secretarial or administrative-assistant position. I knew I would be lucky to make anything over $20,000. I didn't care. I needed that health insurance.

11   One week before my benefits ran out, I found a new job us a secretary with a national organization of neurologists. The medical benefits are excellent, but I'm earning only $19,200 a year, hardly enough to live on. My now ex-husband lost his job as a pastor and cannot be depended on for financial assistance. The only reason I'm afloat is that my mother is helping out. She went to work to support our family when my father could no longer hold a job. Now seventy, she still works for the same company.

12   Going through predictive testing was supposed to help me gain control of my life, and I'm not sorry I had the test. I am thankful for the knowledge that I have the gene, even if I can't do anything medically about it. But I just wish today's economy would let me do something about it financially.

VOCABULARY

Directions: Locate each of the key words in the essay. Try to figure out each word's meaning by using the context. Confirm your guess by checking the dictionary or thesaurus. Write the meanings of the words in the margin of the text. Then record the meanings in the chart below.

Key Word	Paragraph	Meaning
1. hitch	3	
2. niche	4	
3. on the verge	6	
4. diligent	7	
5. ruthless	8	
Others?		

GUIDE QUESTION

Directions: Write your answer in your notebook or on a separate sheet of paper if your instructor wishes to collect it. Your response will form the basis of class discussion.

1. Sally Spaulding, the author, gives us additional insights into the problems involved in "knowing" if you have an incurable, progressive disease. Summarize the difficulties Spaulding (and others) face once they learn they will get the disease.

APPLICATION

Directions: As science continues to unravel the secrets of DNA, the issue of genetic testing becomes more and more problematic. In small groups, consider the four cases below, which appeared in the journal *Science News* (November 5, 1994). Discuss the pros and cons of each case and try to achieve agreement within your group. Discuss your decisions with the whole class.

A Case of Dwarfism
A husband and his pregnant wife seek genetic counseling. Each carries one flawed copy of the gene responsible for achondroplasia; thus both

are dwarfs. Recently, a California research team described the mutation in a gene on chromosome 4 that causes achondroplasia.

The counselor explains that genetic testing can determine whether the fetus has inherited the achondroplasia mutation. In the discussion, the couple inform the counselor that they will abort any fetus that carries two mutant genes. That's not surprising, since children born with two such genes rarely survive beyond infancy. Indeed, the couple had had such a child.

This time around, they say, they want a baby who is heterozygous for the achondroplasia trait. Such a child inherits a flawed gene from one parent and a healthy gene from the other parent. That genetic combination means the child will be a dwarf—just like the parents.

At the same time, the parents say, they will abort any fetus that does *not* inherit one copy of the mutant gene.

Should the counseling center perform the test, knowing that the couple plans to abort a healthy fetus?

Some things to consider include the fact that achondroplasia is a fairly serious disorder. The bones can be abnormal in structure, sometimes requiring the use of a wheelchair.

Yet many dwarfs live long, healthy lives and don't regard their condition as a disability. In addition, some couples with achondroplasia worry about the problems involved in raising a normal-size child.

Under [the Supreme Court decision] *Roe v. Wade,* women in the United States have the right to obtain an abortion during early pregnancy for a variety of personal reasons.

A Case of Paternity

A husband and wife have a child who suffers from cystic fibrosis (CF), an incurable, fatal hereditary disease that results in frequent infections and difficulty breathing. The couple wants to determine their risk of having another child with this disorder.

Because CF is a recessive disorder, a child usually must inherit the CF gene from both parents to get the disease. A child with just one CF gene is a carrier: Such a person doesn't have the disorder but can pass the trait on to the next generation.

The DNA test revealed that the mother of the child carried the CF trait. However, her husband did not. Indeed, the DNA tests showed that he was not the biological father of the child.

That fact significantly decreased this couple's chance of having another child with CF. But the test has put the counselor in a difficult situation. Should the counselor tell the couple about the nonpaternity findings? Should the mother be told privately? If so, is the center colluding with the mother to withhold information from the husband?

In addition, this case brings up issues concerning the biological father of the child. This man has not contracted with the genetics center for the tests, yet the counselor now knows that this man is probably a carrier of the mutant gene for CF. Should the genetic counselor call this man and tell him about his risk?

A Question of Privacy

A thirty-year-old woman has been diagnosed with familial adenomatous polyposis, an inherited condition that puts her at extremely high risk of colon cancer. Indeed, most people with this condition, if untreated, will develop the cancer by age forty.

The patient's own mother died of colon cancer at age thirty-two. Despite this grim history, the woman refuses to share the diagnosis with her family, including her four siblings and her husband. In addition, she does not want her two children to be tested for the genetic flaw. Researchers know that the mutant gene responsible for this disorder lies on the long arm of chromosome 5. This flaw results in hundreds or thousands of polyps, small wartlike growths, carpeting the lining of the colon. Some of the polyps will become malignant.

The woman's refusal to tell her family puts the genetic counseling center in a quandary. To honor this patient's request might harm the rest of the family. Without appropriate medical intervention, family members with the mutant gene remain at extremely high risk of dying of colon cancer. People who carry this flawed gene undergo frequent screening for suspicious growths in the colon. That aggressive approach slashes their risk of dying of the disease.

Should the counselor disclose the results of the test to the rest of the family despite the woman's objections?

Who "owns" the information encoded in a person's genes? Bear in mind the fact that the rest of the family shares a common heritage with this woman.

A Case of Who Decides

A thirty-seven-year-old pregnant woman worries about her family's history of mental retardation. Genetic testing shows this woman is a carrier of the mutant gene for the fragile X syndrome, an inherited form of mental retardation. U.S. and Dutch researchers have demonstrated that carriers and people with this condition show repetitive DNA segments in a gene called FMR-1.

The woman is offered prenatal testing and says she will abort any affected fetus. She also indicates that she will abort a female fetus that is a carrier of the flawed gene. She states that she wants her legacy of this inherited disorder to end.

This case raises the issue of whether the woman should have the right to abort a healthy fetus that happens to be a carrier of a genetic mutation. In a sense, the mother is making her future daughter's decision for her. By choosing an abortion, the patient has ensured that she will not have grandchildren who carry the flawed gene.

WRITING

Directions: Choose one of the cases you discussed in the Application exercise above. In one or two paragraphs, state your decision and the reasons for it.

CONTROVERSIAL ISSUES

Should English Be the Official Language of the United States?

Most people are surprised to learn that the United States has no official language. In fact, it had never been considered a problem until the early 1980s, when the increased presence of Spanish, Vietnamese, and other languages caused pro-English groups to spring up. Since then, twenty-two states have adopted English as their official language and many legislators are lobbying for a similar law on the national level. This article, which appeared in U.S. News & World Report *in September 1995, asks the question: Would making English the nation's official language unite the country or divide it?*

ONE NATION, ONE LANGUAGE

Susan Headden

For a Sherman Oaks, California, election worker, the last straw was hanging campaign posters in six languages and six alphabets. For a taxpayer in University Park, Texas, it was a requirement that all employees of the local public utility speak Spanish. For a retired schoolteacher from Mount Morris, New York, it was taking her elderly and anxious mother to a Pakistani doctor and understanding only a fraction of what he said.

As immigration, both legal and illegal, brings a new flood of foreign speech into the United States, a campaign to make English the nation's official language is gathering strength. According to a new *U.S. News* poll, 73 percent of Americans think English should be the official language of government. House Speaker Newt Gingrich, [former] Senate Majority Leader Bob Dole, and more than a third of the members of Congress support proposed federal legislation that would make English America's official tongue; twenty-two states and a number of municipalities already have English-only laws on the books.

Like flag burning and the Pledge of Allegiance, the issue is largely symbolic. Without ever being declared official, American English has survived—and enriched itself from—four centuries of immigration. It is not much easier for today's Guatemalan immigrant to get a good education and a good job without learning English than it was for his Italian, Polish, or Chinese predecessors. And at best, eliminating bilingual education might save about a dollar per student per day. But many Americans are feeling threatened by a triple whammy of growing economic uncertainty, some of it caused by foreign competition; rising immigration, much of it illegal; and political pressure to cater to the needs of immigrants rather than letting them sink or swim. "Elevating English as an icon," says author and bilingual expert James Crawford, "has appeal for the insecure and the resentful. It provides a clear answer to the question: Who belongs?"

Nation of Strangers

There is no question that America is undergoing another of its periodic diversity booms. According to the Census Bureau, in 1994 8.7 percent of Americans were born in other countries, the highest percentage since before World War II. More tellingly, at least 31.8 million people in the United States speak a language other than English at home. Of the children returning to urban public schools this fall, a whopping one-third speak a foreign language first. "It blows your mind," says Dade County, Florida, administrator Mercedes Toural, who counts 5,190 new students speaking no fewer than 56 different tongues.

5   English-only advocates, whose ranks include recent immigrants and social liberals, believe that accommodating the more than three hundred languages spoken in the United States undercuts incentives to learning English and, by association, to becoming an American. Massachusetts offers driver's tests in twenty-four foreign languages, including Albanian, Finnish, Farsi, Turkish, and Czech. Federal voting rights laws provide for ballots in multiple translations. Internal Revenue Service forms are printed in Spanish. And in Westminster, California, members of Troop 2194 of the Boy Scouts of America can earn their merit badges in Vietnamese. "It's completely insane," says Mauro Mujica, the chairman of the lobbying group U.S. English and himself an immigrant from Chile. "We are not doing anybody any favors."

Pulling the Plug

6   The proposed official-English laws range from the barely noticeable to the almost xenophobic. A bill introduced by Missouri Republican Representative Bill Emerson would mandate English for government use but provide exceptions for health, safety, and civil and criminal justice. Although it is the most viable of the bunch, it would change the status quo so little that it begs the question of why it is needed at all. The most extreme official-English measures would pull the plug on what their sponsors consider linguistic welfare, ending bilingual education and bilingual ballots.

7   Advocates of official-English proposals deny that their measures are draconian. Says U.S. English's Mujica: "We are simply saying that official documents should be in English and money saved on translations could go to help the people learn English. We're saying you could still take a driver's test in another language, but we suggest it be temporary till you learn English."

8   U.S. English, which reports 600,000 contributors, was founded by the late U.S. Senator S. I. Hayakawa, a Japanese-American linguistics professor, and boasts advisory board members such as Saul Bellow and Alistair Cooke. The group was tarred eight years ago when its founder, John Tanton, wrote a memo suggesting that Hispanics have "greater reproductive powers" than Anglos; two directors quit, Tanton was forced out, and the group has been rebuilding its reputation ever since. Its competitor, English First, whose founder, Larry Pratt, also started Gun Owners of America, is more hard-line.

9   Defenders of bilingual education, multilingual ballots, and other government services ask whether legal immigrants will vote if there are no bilingual ballots. If foreign speakers can't read the street signs, will they be allowed to drive? Such thoughts bring Juanita Morales, a Houston college student, to tears. "This just sets up another barrier for people," she says. "My parents don't know English, and I can hardly speak Spanish anymore and that's painful to me."

10   Go it alone, the hard-liners reply, the way our grandfathers did. But these advocates don't mention that there is little, if any, evidence that earlier German or Italian

immigrants mastered English any faster than the current crop of Asians, Russians, and Central Americans. And it's hard to argue that today's newcomers aren't trying. San Francisco City College teaches English to twenty thousand adults every semester, and the waiting list is huge. In De Kalb County, Georgia, seven thousand adults are studying English; in Brighton Beach, New York, two thousand wait for a chance to learn it.

The economic incentives for learning English seem as clear as ever. Yes, you can   11
earn a good living in an ethnic enclave of Chicago speaking nothing but Polish. But you won't go far. "Mandating English," says Ron Pearlman of Chicago, "is like mandating that the sun is going to come up every day. It just seems to me that it's going to happen."

What worries many Americans are efforts to put other languages on a par with   12
English, which often come across as assaults on American or Western culture. Americans may relish an evening at a Thai restaurant or an afternoon at a Greek festival, but many are less comfortable when their children are celebrating Cinco de Mayo, Kwanzaa, and Chinese New Year along with Christmas in the public schools. In Arlington, Virginia, a classically trained orchestra teacher quit the public school system rather than cave in to demands to teach salsa music.

But diversity carries the day. The U.S. Department of Education policy is not   13
simply to promote learning of English but also to *maintain* immigrants' native tongues. And supporters of that policy make a good case for it. "People ask me if I'm embarrassed I speak Spanish," says Martha Quintanilla Hollowell, a Dallas County, Texas, district attorney. "I tell them I'd be more embarrassed if I spoke only one language."

Language Skills

That may be what's most disturbing about the English-only sentiment: In a global   14
economy, it's the monolingual English speakers who are falling behind. Along with computer skills, a neat appearance, and a work ethic, Americans more and more are finding that a second language is useful in getting a good job. African Americans in Dade County, now more than half Hispanic, routinely lose tourism positions to bilingual Cubans. Schoolteachers cry foul because bilingual teachers earn more money while monolingual teachers are laid off. "There is no way I could get a job in the Los Angeles public schools today," says Lucy Fortney, an elementary school teacher for thirty years.

The proliferation of state and local English-only laws has led to a flurry of   15
language-discrimination lawsuits and a record number of complaints with the U.S. Equal Employment Opportunity Commission. Ed Chen, a lawyer with the San Francisco office of the American Civil Liberties Union, says clients have been denied credit and insurance because they don't speak English. But courts increasingly have endorsed laws that call for exclusive use of English on the job. Officials at New York's Bellevue Hospital, where the vast majority of nurses are Filipino, say an English-only law was necessary because nurses spoke Tagalog among themselves.

Other employers have wielded English-only laws as a license to discriminate, giving rise to fears that a national law would encourage more of the same. A judge in   16
Amarillo, Texas, claimed a mother in a custody case was committing "child abuse" by speaking Spanish to her child at home. Another Texas judge denied probation to

a drunk driver because he couldn't benefit from the all-English Alcoholics Anonymous program. In Monterey Park, California, a citizens' group tried to ban Chinese signs on businesses that served an almost all-Asian clientele. In Dade County, a since-repealed English-only law was so strict that it forbade using public funds to pay for court translations and bilingual signs to warn metrorail riders against electrocution.

17   Though it is not intended as such, the English-first movement is a reminder of a history of prejudice toward speakers of foreign tongues. Many American Indians were prohibited from speaking their own languages. The Louisiana Legislature banned the use of Cajun French in public schools in 1912, but, instead of abandoning their culture, many Cajuns dropped out of school and never learned English. French was finally allowed back in the schools in the 1960s. As recently as 1971, it was illegal to speak Spanish in a public school building in Texas, and, until 1923, it was against the law to teach foreign languages to elementary school pupils in Nebraska. At Ellis Island, psychologists tested thousands of non-English-speaking immigrants exclusively in English and pronounced them retarded.

18   Champions of diversity say it's high time Americans faced the demographic facts. In Miami, with leading trade partners Colombia and Venezuela, businesses would be foolish to restrict themselves to English. If emergency services suffer because of a shortage of foreign-speaking 911 operators, it is downright dangerous not to hire more. As for embattled teachers, Rick Lopez of the National Association of Bilingual Education says: "Why should we expect students to learn a new language if teachers can't do the same? We have to change the product to fit the market. The market wants a Toyota and we're still building Edsels."

19   Many Americans still value the melting pot: General Mills's new Betty Crocker is a digitized, multiethnic composite. But Skokie, Illinois, educator Charlene Cobb, for one, prefers a colorful mosaic. "You don't have to change yourself," she says, "to make a whole thing that's very beautiful." The question is whether the diverse parts of America still make up a whole.

VOCABULARY

Directions: Locate each of the key words in the selection. Try to figure out each word's meaning by using the context. Confirm your guess by checking the dictionary or thesaurus. Write the meanings of the words in the margin of the text. Then record the meanings in the chart below and on the next page.

Key Word	Paragraph	Meaning
1. predecessors	3	
2. advocates	5	
3. incentives	5	
4. status quo	6	
5. draconian	7	

Key Word	Paragraph	Meaning
6. enclave	11	
7. proliferation	15	
Others?		

GUIDE QUESTIONS

Directions: These questions will guide your understanding of what you have read. Write your answers in your notebook or on a separate sheet of paper if your instructor wishes to collect it. Your answers to these questions will be the basis of class discussion.

1. The author indicates that there is significant support for making English the nation's official language. What evidence does she give of this support?
2. Why does the author say (in paragraph 3) that "the issue is largely symbolic"?
3. The author says that many Americans are feeling "threatened"—threatened by what?
4. Summarize the evidence supporting the idea that America is undergoing a "diversity boom."
5. Explain what the author means when she says that many people believe that accommodating the more than three hundred languages spoken in the United States "undercuts incentives to learning English."
6. Describe some of the proposed official-English laws.
7. Name and describe the two major "English-only" organizations.
8. This selection presents much information about the "official English" controversy. It also contains many arguments both pro and con of the issue. In your opinion, does the author present a balanced view of the issue? Or does she lean more to one side than the other? Support your answer with evidence from the selection.

APPLICATION

Directions: A Texas judge ruled recently that a Mexican-American mother who spoke only Spanish to her five-year-old daughter at home was committing a form of child abuse. State District Judge Samuel Kiser ordered Marta Laureano to also speak English with her daughter because not doing so could place the kindergartner at a disadvantage in school.

"If she starts first grade . . . and cannot even speak the language that the teachers and the other children speak, and she's a full-blooded American citizen, you're abusing that child and you're relegating her to the position of a house-maid," the judge said.

But Hispanic groups and the state attorney general criticized the order and said the judge's assumptions are groundless and his comparison to "child abuse" is insulting. "Millions of Americans have grown up speaking the mother tongue of their parents and grandparents," said Attorney General Dan Morales.

The decision arose in a child-custody hearing where the girl's father, who was seeking visitation rights, claimed he was the only person teaching the girl to speak English.

What do you think? Discuss this case in small groups.

WRITING

Directions: Write a brief essay stating the opinion you reached in the Application exercise above. Include all your supporting arguments. Write at least two paragraphs.

SHORT TAKE

ENGLISH-ONLY SPOKEN HERE?

In Los Angeles, Leonor Hernandez, a clerk-typist at a Sears, Roebuck billing office, filed suit against Sears over a rule forbidding her to speak Spanish on the job. A company spokesman defended the English-only rule, saying Spanish-speaking employees were hurting the morale and productivity of those who did not speak Spanish. The rule, which Sears said was informal and had been in effect for years, was restated in 1988 after a Chinese employee complained, saying other workers were talking about her in Spanish during working hours.

In Colorado, the passage of an English-language amendment to the state constitution prompted a school bus driver to require children on the bus to speak only in English.

An English-only constitutional amendment in Arizona was so restrictive that it could have banned zoo signs giving the names of animals in Latin. It was struck down by the courts.

In Monterey Park, a suburb of Los Angeles, which has had a recent influx of Chinese and Vietnamese immigrants, officials tried last year to block a Taiwanese gift of Chinese-language books for the local public library.

T. Euclid Raines, Sr., a member of the state assembly in Alabama, sponsored a state English-only law. "If I go to New York and I buy some cheese, they don't ask me to pay in rupees or pesos," he said. "We have standardization, which serves to unify the country," he continued. "Otherwise things get bemuddled."

Ed Chen of the American Civil Liberties Union said, "For a lot of folks, language becomes a proxy for race or for immigrant status. It becomes a legitimate way of expressing concern about being overrun by hordes of Mexicans and Asians coming into the United States."

This article appeared in the spring 1996 issue of VFW, *the magazine of the Veterans of Foreign Wars organization.*

LET'S MAKE ENGLISH OFFICIAL

Gary Turbak

1   Quick now, what's the official language of the United States of America? French? German? Spanish? No, silly, it's English—right?

2   Wrong. English is not our official language. We don't have an official language, and that shortcoming costs taxpayers a lot of money, drives wedges between Americans, and threatens to turn this country into a modern tower of babble. "America is fast becoming a society divided by language," says Representative Toby Roth (R-Wisconsin), sponsor of legislation to help correct the problem.

3   Although our founding fathers used English to create the Constitution, Bill of Rights, and other seminal American documents, they neglected to make English official. Until recently, this oversight mattered little, as most immigrants traditionally learned—or at least had their children learn—English. English was the glue holding the great melting pot society together, the common denominator of American citizenship.

4   Today, however, 323 different languages are spoken in the United States, and about 32 million Americans speak a language other than English at home. In many cities, immigrants can live, work, and play without ever knowing a word of English, as everything from fast-food menus to telephone books to baseball broadcasts exists in other tongues. Society's melting pot has become a salad bowl of distinctly separate ingredients.

5   A small but vocal minority of immigrants even insists that government provide services to them not in English, but in their native languages. Together with politicians and bureaucrats who benefit from America's continued Balkanization, they are steadily eroding the venerability of our nation's de facto mother tongue.

Bilingual Ed at $8 Billion

6   One taxing (in more ways than one) aspect of language creep is the quagmire of bilingual education. Not to be confused with the traditional study of foreign languages by English-speaking students, bilingual education refers to teaching non-English-speaking children primarily in their native tongues and only partly in English.

7   Every day, hundreds of thousands of American public school students are taught math, history, science, and other subjects in Spanish, Haitian Creole, Bengali, Vietnamese, and a host of other languages. In theory, these youngsters are supposed to move quickly into all-English settings while staying current in their subjects.

8   In practice, however, bilingual education doesn't work. "These programs are proven failures," says Jim Boulet, Jr., executive director of the pro-English group English First. "They are successful merely in creating another generation in need of additional bilingual services." Regardless of their English skills, some children are put in Spanish (or other language) classes simply because of ethnic-sounding surnames.

Many kids remain in these programs for years—both because they don't learn English and because the bilingual bureaucracy needs them there to get more funding. Studies in New York and Texas show that children taught primarily or exclusively in English achieve higher math and reading scores than those instructed in their native language.

Bilingual programs can become language ghettos, dead-end classrooms where   9
kids not only don't learn English but also fail to enter American society. "It used to be that public schools helped immigrants assimilate into their new country," says Boulet.

"Today, the same schools divide American children on the basis of language or   10
ancestry." Mandated by the federal government but generally paid for by state and local taxpayers, bilingual education costs about $8 billion annually.

Multilingualism Run Rampant

Other examples of language creep abound. In 1994, the IRS set up a toll-free Span-   11
ish telephone hotline and spent $113,000 distributing half a million 1040 forms and instruction booklets in Spanish. Despite the return of only 718 of these forms (at a cost to taxpayers of $157 each), the agency is considering similar services for other language groups.

Recently, the Pennsylvania city of Allentown, population 105,000, passed an or-   12
dinance making English the official language of municipal government. Incredibly, the federal Department of Housing and Urban Development (HUD), led by Secretary Henry Cisneros, threatened an investigation and a cutoff of the community's $4 million in federal housing funds. Alerted by English supporters, Congress—led by Representative Joe Knollenberg (R-Michigan)—investigated the issue and forced HUD to cease its attack on Allentown.

U.S. Postal Service materials, Census Bureau questionnaires, and other official   13
publications often appear in other languages. According to the General Accounting Office, the federal government, between 1990 and 1994, printed more than 250 different documents in other tongues.

These included such titles as *Investigation about the Reproductive Behavior of Young*   14
People in the City of Sao Palo (in Portuguese), *The Mint* (in Chinese), and *Nutritive and Dietetic Guide to Wild Animals in Captivity* (in Spanish). Even swearing-in ceremonies for naturalized American citizens have taken place in other languages.

Often, state and local taxpayers are the ones who end up paying the piper   15
of multilingualism. California offers driver's-license exams in thirty-five different tongues (including Tagalog, Hindi, Arabic, and two dialects of Armenian), Michigan in twenty, and Rhode Island in nineteen.

As mandated by federal law, hundreds of jurisdictions must run elections in a   16
host of languages. In 1994, Hawaii spent more than $34,000 preparing voting materials in Japanese. Four people used them—at a cost of $8,500 each. "For that price, the state could have hired a chauffeured limousine and personal interpreter for each voter," says Boulet.

Also, tax dollars are lost and welfare dollars spent whenever workers re-   17
main unemployed because they don't speak English. Ohio University professors of

economics Richard Vedder and Lowell Gallaway estimate this shortfall at $11.3 billion in 1995—between $180 and $500 (depending on the state) for every tax-paying family in America. Is it any wonder that twenty-two states and about forty-five local governments have enacted their own official English statutes? (Few of these are vigorously enforced, however.)

Assuring Full Participation

18 Lately, a national backlash has been building against American polyglotism, with Congress now considering several bills to make English the nation's official language. Two of these, *H.R. 739* (Roth's bill) and *H.R. 1005* sponsored by Representative Pete King (R-New York), also call for the abolition of bilingual ballots, most bilingual education, and citizenship ceremonies in languages other than English.

19 These measures essentially mirror the VFW [Veterans of Foreign Wars] position. "The English language has always been our strongest common bond," says Mike Gormalley, VFW's director of Americanism. "Its erosion and the increased official usage of other languages is a divisive force within our nation."

20 Making English official would let immigrants know they have no right to receive public services in any other language. Most federal government business—documents, meetings, records, legislation, and ceremonies—would be in English.

21 No one, however, would be prohibited from using another language in a nongovernmental setting. After all, freedom of speech is an American cornerstone.

22 "Official English legislation does not infringe on individual rights, nor does it prevent immigrants from preserving their cultures and their languages in their personal lives," says Mauro Mujica, head of the pro-English group U.S. English. "It does, however, encourage immigrants to learn English in order to fully participate in government."

Unifying Thread

23 Lobbying by the bilingual education bureaucracy and other groups has stalled these bills, but public sentiment may get them moving again. A nationwide poll in 1995 by the Lutz Research Companies showed that 86 percent of the American public supports making English official.

24 Most immigrants (81 percent of them, according to the Lutz survey) agree. Mujica, himself an immigrant from Chile, says, "It is particularly galling to me, as a Hispanic, that these government agencies are using *your* tax dollars, claiming to represent *my* interests, to work *against* everything most Spanish-speaking Americans want."

25 Former Senate Majority Leader Bob Dole (R-Kansas) strongly supports official English. "Alternative language education should stop," he says, "and English should be acknowledged once and for all as the official language of the United States."

26 According to Dole, requiring immigrants to learn English "is not an act of hostility, but a welcoming act of inclusion." President Bill Clinton has yet to say whether he would sign an official English bill, but he did so in 1987 when he was governor of Arkansas.

Opponents of official English argue that America thrives on diversity and that   27
language variety adds flavor and texture to our societal mosaic. Logic, however,
suggests just the opposite: It is *because* of our great diversity that we so desperately
need a unifying thread to bind Americans together, to allow us to understand one
another. That thread is English.

VOCABULARY

Directions: Locate each of the key words in the reading selection. Try to figure out
each word's meaning by using the context. Confirm your guess by checking the
dictionary or thesaurus. Write the meanings of the words in the margin of the
text. Then record the meanings in the chart below.

Key Word	Paragraph	Meaning
1. seminal	3	
2. quagmire	6	
3. mandated	10, 16	
4. backlash	18	
5. infringe	22	
6. galling	24	
7. mosaic	27	
Others?		

GUIDE QUESTIONS

Directions: These questions will guide your understanding of what you have read.
Write your answers in your notebook or on a separate sheet of paper if your instructor wishes to collect it. Your answers to these questions will be the basis of
class discussion.

1. Were you surprised when you learned that the United States does not
   have an official language? Why do you think English was never named
   the official language? In your experience, have you ever noticed a problem because of the lack of an official language?

2. The author, Gary Turbak, states that the lack of an official language was not a problem "until recently" since most immigrants or their children learned English anyway. Why does he say the situation has changed?

3. Note that the author uses words like *shortcoming* (paragraph 2), the *problem* (paragraph 2), and *oversight* (paragraph 3), assuming that the reader shares his opinion that the lack of an official language is, indeed, a problem. Why does he do this?

4. In this selection, the author makes imaginative use of metaphor, especially in paragraph 4: "Society's melting pot has become a salad bowl of distinctly separate ingredients." Explain what he means.

5. In paragraph 6, the author introduces a new issue, that of bilingual education. Do you think this issue is so closely related to that of making English the official language that it should be included? Why do you think Turbak does so?

6. In paragraph 11, Turbak uses the phrase "language creep." What does he mean? List some of his examples of "language creep."

7. In paragraph 24, Mauro Mujica, the head of *U.S. English,* is quoted as saying, "It is particularly galling to me, as a Hispanic, that these government agencies are using *your* tax dollars, claiming to represent *my* interests, to work against everything most Spanish-speaking Americans want." What do you think he means when he says "what most Spanish-speaking Americans want"?

APPLICATION

Directions: Reread Turbak's selection carefully. Pull out the arguments he makes in favor of making English the official language of the United States. Working in a small group, compare your list with those of your classmates. Make additions and changes until your group has one complete and accurate list.

WRITING

Directions: Use the list you compiled in the Application exercise above. Write the information in an essay. Begin with the main idea—that English should be made the official language of the United States. Then write the arguments supporting that opinion.

SHORT TAKE

WHERE IS ENGLISH OFFICIAL?

Twenty-three states have declared English their official language. Those states are listed in the table below along with the year in which either the law or amendment to the state constitution was enacted.

STATE	YEAR THE LAW OR AMENDMENT WAS ENACTED
Louisiana	1811
Nebraska	1920
Illinois	1969
Hawaii*	1978
Virginia	1981
Indiana	1984
Kentucky	1984
Tennessee	1984
California	1986
Georgia	1986
North Dakota	1987
Mississippi	1987
North Carolina	1987
South Carolina	1987
Arkansas	1987
Florida	1988
Arizona	1988
Colorado	1988
Alabama	1990
Montana	1995
New Hampshire	1995
South Dakota	1995
Wyoming	1996

* Hawaii has two official languages—English and Hawaiian.

Bill Bryson's book The Mother Tongue *is a joyful celebration of the English language. In this excerpt from the final chapter, Bryson turns his attention to the English-only movement.*

THE FUTURE OF ENGLISH

Bill Bryson

1   In 1787, when representatives of the new United States gathered in Philadelphia to draw up a Constitution that could serve as a blueprint for the American way of life forever, it apparently did not occur to them to consider the matter of what the national language should be. Then, and for the next two centuries, it was assumed that people would speak English. But in the 1980s a growing sense of disquiet among many Americans over the seepage of Spanish, Vietnamese, and other immigrant languages into American society led some of them to begin pressing for laws making English the official language.

2   According to the Census Bureau, 11 percent of people in America speak a language other than English at home. In California alone, nearly one-fifth of the people are Hispanic. In Los Angeles, the proportion of Spanish speakers is more than half. New York City has 1.5 million Hispanics and there are a million more in the surrounding area. Bergenline Avenue in New Jersey runs for ninety blocks and, throughout most of its length, is largely Spanish-speaking. All told, in America there are two hundred Spanish-language newspapers, two hundred radio stations, and three hundred television stations. The television stations alone generated nearly $300 million of Spanish-language advertising in 1987.

3   In many areas, English speakers are fearful of being swamped. Some even see it as a conspiracy, among them the former U.S. Senator S. I. Hayakawa, who wrote in 1987 that he believes that "a very real move is afoot to split the United States into a bilingual and bicultural society." Hayakawa was instrumental in founding U.S. English, a pressure group designed to promote English as the lone official language of the country. Soon, the group had 350,000 members, including such distinguished "advisory supporters" as Saul Bellow, Alistair Cooke, and Norman Cousins, and was receiving annual donations of $7.5 million. By late 1988, it had managed to have English made the official language of seventeen states—among them Arizona, Colorado, Florida, Nebraska, Illinois, Virginia, Indiana, Kentucky, Georgia, and California.

4   It is easy to understand the strength of feeling among many Americans on the matter. A California law requiring that bilingual education must be provided at schools where more than twenty pupils speak a language other than English sometimes led to chaos. At one Hollywood high school, on parents' night every speech had to be translated from English into Korean, Spanish, and Armenian. As of December 1986, California was employing 3,364 state workers proficient in Spanish in order to help non-English speakers in matters concerning courts, social services, and the like. All of this, critics maintain, cossets non-English speakers and provides them with little inducement to move into the American mainstream.

5   U.S. English and other such groups maintain that linguistic divisions have caused unrest in several countries, such as Canada and Belgium—though they generally fail

to note that the countries where strife and violence have been most pronounced, such as Spain, are the ones where minority languages have been most strenuously suppressed. It is interesting to speculate also whether the members of U.S. English would be so enthusiastic about language regulations if they were transferred to Quebec and found their own language effectively outlawed.

U.S. English insists that a national English-language law would apply only to gov-   6
ernment business, and that in unofficial, private, or religious contexts people could use any language they liked. Yet it was U.S. English that tried to take AT&T to court for inserting Spanish advertisements in the Los Angeles Yellow Pages. That would hardly seem to be government business. And many Hispanics feel that there would be further encroachments on their civil liberties—such as the short-lived attempt by Dade County in Florida to require that marriage ceremonies be conducted only in English. U.S. English says that it would not ban bilingual education, but would in-sist that its aim be transitional rather than encouraging entrenchment.

The most unpleasant charge is that all of this is a thinly veiled cover for racism,   7
or at least rampant xenophobia. As an outsider, it is difficult not to conclude some-times that there is a degree of overreaction involved. What purpose, after all, is served by making Nebraska officially English? Nor is it immediately evident how the public good would be served by overturning a New York law that at present stipu-lates that the details of consumer credit transactions be printed in Spanish as well as English. If U.S. English had its way, they would be printed only in English. Would such a change really encourage Hispanics to learn English or would it simply lead to their exploitation by unscrupulous lenders?

There is little evidence to suggest that people are refusing to learn English. Ac-   8
cording to a 1985 study by the Rand Corporation, 95 percent of the children of Mexican immigrants can speak English. By the second generation more than half can speak only English. There is, after all, a huge inducement in terms of convenience, culture, and income to learn the prevailing language. As the Stanford University lin-guist Geoffrey D. Nunberg neatly put it: "The English language needs official protec-tion about as much as the Boston Celtics need elevator shoes."

VOCABULARY

Directions: Locate each of the key words in the reading selection. Then read and study each word in its context and try to determine its meaning. Use a dictio-nary or thesaurus to check your guess. Write the meanings of the words in the margin of the text.

Record the new words you've learned below and on the next page.

Key Word	Paragraph	Meaning
1. seepage	1	
2. chaos	4	
3. cossets	4	

Key Word	Paragraph	Meaning
4. inducement	4	
5. encroachments	6	
6. entrenchment	6	
7. rampant	7	
8. xenophobia	7	
9. unscrupulous	7	
Others?		

GUIDE QUESTIONS

Directions: The purpose of these guide questions is to ensure your understanding of what you have read. They will also help you to analyze and evaluate the author's ideas and apply them to the real world and your own life.

Write answers to the questions in your notebook or on a separate sheet of paper if your instructor wishes to collect them. Your answers will form the basis of class discussion.

1. As Bryson points out, when the United States was founded, it was not considered necessary to establish an official national language. According to Bryson, why was this true? What caused the recent interest in establishing an official language?
2. As always, background knowledge is important in understanding and appreciating what you read. A good example is in paragraph 3, which lists some of the "advisory supporters" of U.S. English. Just as in a political campaign or in a television commercial for a product, endorsements by well-known and respected people are expected to influence the public favorably. Identify the "advisory supporters" and state why their support might be helpful to the U.S. English movement.
3. Bryson admits that accommodating people who speak other languages can sometimes lead to "chaos." Cite one of the examples of chaos he describes.

4. Bryson casts some doubt on U.S. English's claim that a national language law would apply *only* to government affairs. State one of the pieces of evidence that makes him suspicious of this claim.
5. Explain what Bryson says is the "most unpleasant charge" about the whole English-only movement.
6. How does Bryson answer the argument that non-English-speaking people are refusing to learn English?
7. Explain Geoffrey Nunberg's conclusion about the entire U.S. English issue.

APPLICATION

Directions: Work in small groups to complete this assignment. You have now done extensive reading and thinking about making English the official language of the United States. If you had an opinion on the subject before you began reading this part of the text, you should have re-evaluated it, modified it, become more secure with it, or possibly even changed it. Let's retrace *in writing* the process you have just gone through in your mind to form your opinion.

Forming a Valid Opinion   These are the steps we generally follow when we form a good opinion:

1. *First,* we inform ourselves fully about the topic. We read, discuss, listen, think about the issue. We consider all the different perspectives on the issue.
2. *Second,* we formulate a proposal, such as:

   There should be a law making English the official language of the United States.

3. *Third,* we assemble and consider the arguments in favor of the proposal.
4. *Fourth,* we assemble and consider the opposing arguments.
5. *Last,* we arrive at a thoughtful opinion supported by those arguments that convinced us to adopt it.

Now let's implement these steps, *in writing,* for the topic we have just examined. In your group, fill in answers to the questions below:

1. State and give some background information about English as the official language.
2. State the topic in the form of a proposal. (You may use the statement from the second step above if you wish, or write your own.)
3. Using all the information you have read and thought about in this section, list all the arguments in favor of a law making English the official language.
4. Now list all the arguments you can against a law making English the official language.

5. Finally, all the group members should state their opinions and reasons to support their opinions. Discuss and evaluate the supporting arguments to ensure the opinions are valid.

WRITING

Directions: Using the information in the five steps above as an outline, write a composition explaining the issue of making English the official language of the United States, presenting the pro and con arguments and your supported opinion. This composition may be written by the group as a collaborative effort, or your instructor may want each person to write his or her own composition based on the information developed in the group.

CONTROVERSIAL ISSUES

Euthanasia

One of the most controversial and painful issues of our time is that of euthanasia—helping or allowing someone to die by either active or passive methods. As our society ages, and medical science is able to keep people alive who would have died "naturally" in the past, most of us will be confronted with this decision at some point in our lives. As with all important topics, perhaps more so, we must carefully consider the different perspectives and examine the arguments on all sides of the subject of euthanasia before we can form a good opinion. The following article reviews the history of the issue and examines it from various viewpoints.

DECIDING WHEN DEATH IS BETTER THAN LIFE

Gilbert Cant

"I am a broken piece of machinery. I am ready."

—Last words of President Woodrow Wilson, January 31, 1924

1   George Zygmaniak, twenty-six, lacked the former president's rhetorical skills, but as he lay in a hospital bed last month in Neptune, New Jersey, paralyzed from the neck down because of a motorcycle accident, he felt that he was a broken piece of machinery. He was ready to go. He begged his brother Lester, twenty-three, to kill him. According to police, Lester complied—using a sawed-off shotgun at close range. Lester, who had enjoyed an unusually close relationship with his brother, has been charged with first-degree murder.

2   Last December, Eugene Bauer, fifty-nine, was admitted to Nassau County Medical Center on Long Island with cancer of the throat. Five days later, he was in a coma and given only two days to live. Then, charges the district attorney, Dr. Vincent A. Montemarano, thirty-three, injected an overdose of potassium chloride into Bauer's veins. Bauer died within five minutes. Montemarano listed the cause of death as cancer, but prosecutors now say that it was a "mercy killing" and have accused the doctor of murder.

3   The two cases underscore the growing emotional controversy over euthanasia ("mercy killing") and the so-called right to die—that is, the right to slip from life with a minimum of pain for both the patient and his family. No one seriously advocates the impulsive taking of life, as in the Zygmaniak shooting. A person suddenly crippled, no matter how severely, may yet show unpredictable improvement or regain at least a will to live. Whether or not to speed the passage of a fatally ill patient is a far subtler question. The headlong advances of medical science make the issue constantly more complex for patients and their families, for doctors and hospitals, for theologians and lawyers.

4   The doctor's dilemma—how long to prolong life after all hope of recovery has gone—has some of its roots in half-legendary events of 2,400 years ago. When Hippocrates, the "Father of Medicine," sat under his giant plane tree on the Aegean island of Kos, *euthanasia* (from the Greek, meaning "a good death") was widely practiced and took many different forms. But from beneath that plane tree came words that have been immortalized in the physician's Hippocratic oath, part of which reads: "I will neither give a deadly drug to anybody, if asked for, nor will I make a suggestion to this effect."

5   Down the centuries, this has been interpreted by most physicians to mean that they must not give a patient a fatal overdose, no matter how terrible his pain or how hopeless his prospects. Today, many scholars contend that the origin of this item in the oath has been misinterpreted. Most likely it was designed to keep the physician from becoming an accomplice of palace poisoners or of a man seeking to get rid of a wife.

6   The most emphatic opponents of euthanasia have been clergymen of nearly all denominations. Churchmen protest that, if a doctor decides when a patient is to die, he is playing God. Many physicians still share this objection. However much they may enjoy a secret feeling of divinity when dispensing miraculous cures, to play the angel of death is understandably repugnant. Moreover, as psychoanalysts point out, they are chillingly reminded of their own mortality.

7   At a recent conference chaired by the Roman Catholic Archbishop of Westminster, Dr. W. E. Anderson of Glasgow University, a professor of geriatric medicine, called euthanasia "medicated manslaughter." Modern drugs, he argued, can keep a patient sufficiently pain-free to make mercy killing, in effect, obsolete. Perhaps. There is no doubt, however, that a panoply of new techniques and equipment can be and often are used to keep alive people who are both hopelessly ill and cruelly debilitated. Artificial respirators, blood-matching and transfusion systems, a variety of fluids that can safely be given intravenously to medicate, nourish, and maintain electrolyte balance—these and many other lifesavers give doctors astonishing powers.

8   Until about twenty-five years ago, the alternatives facing a doctor treating a terminally ill patient were relatively clear. He could let nature take its sometimes harsh course, or he could administer a fatal dose of some normally beneficent drug. To resort to the drug would be to commit what is called active euthanasia. In virtually all Western countries, that act is still legally considered homicide (though juries rarely convict in such cases).

9   On the record, physicians are all but unanimous in insisting that they never perform active euthanasia, for to do so is a crime. Off the record, some will admit that they have sometimes hastened death by giving an overdose of the medicine they had been administering previously. How many such cases there are can never be known.

10   Now, with wondrous machines for prolonging a sort of life, there is another set of choices. Should the patient's heart or lung function be artificially sustained for weeks or months? Should he be kept technically alive by physico–chemical legerdemain, even if he has become a mere collection of organs and tissues rather than a whole man? If a decision is made not to attempt extraordinary measures, or if, at some point, the life-preserving machinery is shut off, then a previously unknown act

is being committed. It may properly be called *passive euthanasia*. The patient is allowed to die instead of being maintained as a laboratory specimen.

While legal purists complain that euthanasia and the right to die peacefully are   11
separate issues, the fact is that they are converging. With the increasing use of extraordinary measures, the occasions for passive euthanasia are becoming more frequent. The question of whether terminal suffering can be shortened by active or
passive means is often highly technical—depending on the type of ailment. Thus,
the distinctions are becoming blurred, particularly for laymen.

"The idea of not prolonging life unnecessarily has always been more widely ac-   12
cepted outside the medical profession than within it," says a leading Protestant
(United Church of Christ) theologian, University of Chicago's Dr. James Gustafson.
"Now a lot of physicians are rebelling against the triumphalism inherent in the medical profession, against this sustaining of life at all costs. But different doctors bring
different considerations to bear. The research-oriented physician is more concerned
with developing future treatments, while the patient-oriented physician is more
willing to allow patients to make their own choice."

House-staff physicians, says Tufts University's Dr. Melvin J. Krant in *Prism,* an   13
American Medical Association publication, "deal with the fatally ill as if they were
entirely divorced from their own human ecology." The research for absolute biological knowledge precludes a search for existential or symbolic knowledge, and the
patient is deprived of his own singular humanism. "The house staff," Krant says, assumes "that the patient always prefers life over death at any cost, and a patient who
balks at a procedure is often viewed as a psychiatric problem."

Technical wizardry has, in fact, necessitated a new definition of death. For thou-   14
sands of years it had been accepted that death occurred when heart action and
breathing ceased. This was essentially true, because the brain died minutes after the
heart stopped. But, with machines, it is now possible to keep the brain "alive" almost indefinitely. With the machines unplugged, it would soon die. In cases where
the brain ceased to function first, heart and lung activity can be artificially maintained. While legal definitions of death lag far behind medical advances, today's cri-
terion is, in most instances, the absence of brain activity for twenty-four hours.

The question then, in the words of Harvard neurologist Robert Schwab, is   15
"Who decides to pull the plug, and when?" Cutting off the machines—or avoiding
their use at all—is indeed passive euthanasia. But it is an ethical decision—not murder, or any other crime, in any legal code. So stern a guardian of traditional moral-
ity as Pope Pius XII declared that life need not be prolonged by extraordinary
means.

Faced with a painful and tenuous future and an all-too-tangible present crisis,   16
how does the doctor decide what to do? Does he make the decision alone? Dr.
Malcolm Todd, president-elect of the American Medical Association, wants doctors
to have help at least in formulating a general policy. He proposes a commission of
laymen, clergy, lawyers, and physicians. "Society has changed," says Todd. "It's up to
society to decide." The desire to share the responsibility is reasonable, but it is unlikely that any commission could write guidelines to cover adequately all situations.
In individual cases, of course, many doctors consult the patient's relatives. But the

17   family is likely to be heavily influenced by the physician's prognosis. More often than
not, it must be a lonely decision made by one or two doctors.

17   When Sigmund Freud was eighty-three, he had suffered from cancer of the jaw
for sixteen years and undergone thirty-three operations. "Now it is nothing but torture," he concluded, "and makes no sense any more." He had a pact with Max Schur,
his physician. "When he was again in agony," Schur reported, "I gave him two centi-
grams of morphine. I repeated this dose after about twelve hours. He lapsed into a
coma and did not wake up again." Freud died with dignity at his chosen time.

18   Dr. Schur's decision was, in the end, relatively easy. More often, there are un-
avoidable uncertainties in both active and passive euthanasia. Doctors may disagree
over a prognosis. A patient may be so depressed by pain that one day he wants out,
while the next day, with some surcease, he has a renewed will to live. There is the
problem of heirs who may be thinking more of the estate than of the patient when
the time to pull the plug is discussed. Doctors will have to live with these gray areas,
perhaps indefinitely. Attempts to legalize active euthanasia—under severe restrictions—have failed in the United States and Britain, but will doubtless be revived. The
fundamental question, however, is humane rather than legal. To die as Freud died
should be the right of Everyman.

VOCABULARY

Directions: Locate each of the key words in the reading selection. Then read and
study each word in its context and try to determine its meaning. Use a dictionary or thesaurus to check your guess. Write the meanings of the words in the
margin of the text.

Record the new words you've learned.

Key Word	Paragraph	Meaning
1. impulsive	3	
2. repugnant	6	
3. geriatric	7	
4. converging	11	
5. inherent	12	
6. precludes	13	
7. prognosis	18	
Others?		

GUIDE QUESTIONS

Directions: The purpose of these guide questions is to ensure your understanding of what you have read. They will also help you to analyze and evaluate the author's ideas and apply them to the real world and your own life.

Write answers to the questions in your notebook or on a separate sheet of paper if your instructor wishes to collect them. Your answers will form the basis of class discussion.

1. The topic of the reading is euthanasia. Define the term and explain the roots of the word.
2. Consider the case of George Zygmaniak cited in the article. If you had been his brother, would you have agreed to kill him? Explain your position.
3. In the case of Eugene Bauer, do you feel his doctor did the right thing?
4. Discuss the differences in the two cases mentioned in guide questions 2 and 3. Consider, for example, these questions: What were the ages of the persons involved? Did the euthanasia simply speed the death of a person who would have died soon anyway? Who made the decision in each case? What other differences can you see between the two cases? Do the answers to these questions make a difference in how you judge these particular acts of mercy killing?
5. Explain why the controversy over euthanasia is becoming more complex.
6. Who was Hippocrates and what is his relationship to the controversy over euthanasia?
7. Which group of people is most opposed to euthanasia and why?
8. In paragraph 10, why does the author use the phrase "a sort of life"?
9. In your own words, explain why the occasions for passive euthanasia are becoming more frequent.
10. a. What was traditionally considered to be the definition of death?
    b. Why did this definition become inadequate?
11. a. Define active euthanasia.
    b. Define passive euthanasia.
12. Explain the author's use of the term *gray areas* in paragraph 18. Why does the author use this term?
13. Classify the following acts as either *passive* euthanasia or *active* euthanasia:
    a. A family member turns off a machine that is keeping a person alive.
    b. A doctor injects a person with a fatal overdose of a drug.
    c. A kidney patient refuses to submit to dialysis when this decision will surely mean death.
14. As the author of the article points out, the main question has become "who decides?" List the possible persons who should be allowed to make such a decision to perform euthanasia. Then list arguments *against* each of these persons making the decision to perform euthanasia. The first one is done for you on the next page.

Decisionmaker	**Argument against Allowing This Person to Make the Decision**
1. the patient	**A patient may be affected by medication and thus may be unable to make an informed or valid decision.**
2.	
3.	
4.	
5.	
6.	

APPLICATION

Directions: Take a few moments to review all you have read about critical thinking and reading, and about the issue of mercy killing. Here is an opportunity to use your thinking skills in real-life situations. Below are some cases in which life-or-death decisions had to be made by patients, doctors, and family members. Read about each case and ask yourself what your decision would have been. Before you answer, remember to think about the issue from all perspectives. Then, try to imagine all the pro and con arguments. Finally, develop your personal opinion. Write your opinion, then write the supporting arguments that back it up.

Remember. Your goal is to develop a *valid opinion.*

Case 1

Doctors at a university hospital examined a seventeen-year-old boy whose bone cancer of the upper arm had recurred in spite of radiation treatments. The physicians advised amputation of the limb and warned that, without the operation, the boy would probably die. But the boy, a star baseball player who had been scouted by several major league teams, begged his parents and the doctors to let him keep his arm so that he could continue to play baseball.

If you were the parents, what instructions would you give the doctors? Remember to state good, solid reasons for your decision.

Case 2

After the age of eighteen, when she suffered kidney failure, Marilyn Duke had to go to a hospital three times a week for dialysis treatments. (This is a painful procedure in which the patient is hooked up to a machine for several hours while the machine purifies the patient's blood, eliminating wastes. This purification is the normal function of a healthy kidney.)

When she was thirty-three, Marilyn decided she could no longer endure life under these conditions. She told her doctor that she wanted to discontinue the dialysis but, knowing that without medical help she would die in agony, she asked him to ease her pain in her final days. Her

doctor said he could only treat her if she was in a hospital. When she returned to the hospital, doctors tried to put Marilyn on the dialysis machine
again. She refused to go on the machine and the hospital discharged her.
Marilyn died nine days after her last dialysis treatment.

If you were Marilyn, would you have made the same choice? Give arguments
to support your choice.

Case 3
A forty-four-year-old man, a single parent of three children, was hospitalized with brain cancer. Doctors agreed his case was terminal. One night
he suddenly suffered cardiac arrest, but an alert intern got the man's heart
beating again and the patient lived one more month.

Did the doctor do the right thing in resuscitating the man? Why or why not?

WRITING

Directions: Choose one of the three cases in the Application exercise and, in one
paragraph, state your opinion on the issue. Then support your opinion with good,
solid reasons.

In any discussion about euthanasia, one argument is inevitable: We do not have the right to "play God." But what does it mean to "play God"? The answer "to let nature take its course" is not very helpful. After all, if we let nature take its sometimes cruel course, we would not attach the patient to a life-support machine in the first place. If we let nature take its course, we would not rush to resuscitate a person who is dying. Aren't we facing these painful life-and-death decisions because we are, indeed, "playing God" by using medical technology? What, then, is "playing God"? Is it removing life-sustaining equipment (or never using it)? Or is it artificially prolonging a tormented life? This story appeared in Newsweek in 1983.

A CRIME OF COMPASSION

Barbara Huttmann

1   "Murderer," a man shouted. "God help patients who get *you* for a nurse."

2   "What gives you the right to play God?" another one asked.

3   It was *The Phil Donahue Show* where the guest is a fatted calf and the audience a two hundred-strong flock of vultures hungering to pick at the bones. I had told them about Mac, one of my favorite cancer patients. "We resuscitated him fifty-two times in just one month. I refused to resuscitate him again. I simply sat there and held his hand while he died."

4   There wasn't time to explain that Mac was a young, witty, macho cop who walked into the hospital with thirty-two pounds of attack equipment, looking as if he could single-handedly protect the whole city, if not the entire state. "Can't get rid of this cough," he said. Otherwise, he felt great.

5   Before the day was over, tests confirmed that he had lung cancer. And before the year was over, I loved him, his wife, Maura, and their three kids as if they were my own. All the nurses loved him. And we all battled his disease for six months without ever giving death a thought. Six months isn't such a long time in the whole scheme of things, but it was long enough to see him lose his youth, his wit, his macho, his hair, his bowel and bladder control, his sense of taste and smell, and his ability to do the slightest thing for himself. It was also long enough to watch Maura's transformation from a young woman into a haggard, beaten old lady.

6   When Mac had wasted away to a sixty-pound skeleton kept alive by liquid food we poured down a tube, i.v. solutions we dripped into his veins, and oxygen we piped to a mask on his face, he begged us: "Mercy . . . for God's sake, please just let me go."

7   The first time he stopped breathing, the nurse pushed the button that calls a "code blue" throughout the hospital and sends a team rushing to resuscitate the patient. Each time he stopped breathing, sometimes two or three times in one day, the code team came again. The doctors and technicians worked their miracles and walked away. The nurses stayed to wipe the saliva that drooled from his mouth, irrigate the big craters of bedsores that covered his hips, suction the lung fluids that threatened to drown him, clean the feces that burned his skin like lye, pour the liquid food down the tube attached to his stomach, put pillows between his knees

to ease the bone-on-bone pain, turn him every hour to keep the bedsores from getting worse, and change his gown and linen every two hours to keep him from being soaked in perspiration.

At night I went home and tried to scrub away the smell of decaying flesh that   8
seemed woven into the fabric of my uniform. It was in my hair, the upholstery of my car—there was no washing it away. And every night I prayed that Mac would die, that his agonized eyes would never again plead with me to let him die.

Every morning I asked his doctor for a "no-code" order. Without that order,   9
we had to resuscitate every patient who stopped breathing. His doctor was one of several who believe we must extend life as long as we have the means and knowledge to do it. To not do it is to be liable for negligence, at least in the eyes of many people, including some nurses. I thought about what it would be like to stand before a judge, accused of murder, if Mac stopped breathing and I didn't call a code.

And after the fifty-second code, when Mac was still lucid enough to beg for   10
death again, and Maura was crumbled in my arms again, and when no amount of pain medication stilled his moaning and agony, I wondered about a spiritual judge. Was all this misery and suffering supposed to be building character or infusing us all with the sense of humility that comes from impotence?

Had we, the whole medical community, become so arrogant that we believed   11
in the illusion of salvation through science? Had we become so self-righteous that we thought meddling in God's work was our duty, our moral imperative, and our legal obligation? Did we really believe that we had the right to force "life" on a suffering man who had begged for the right to die?

Such questions haunted me more than ever early one morning when Maura   12
went home to change her clothes and I was bathing Mac. He had been still for so long, I thought he at last had the blessed relief of coma. Then he opened his eyes and moaned, "Pain . . . no more . . . Barbara . . . do something . . . God, let me go."

The desperation in his eyes and voice riddled me with guilt. "I'll stop," I told   13
him as I injected the pain medication.

I sat on the bed and held Mac's hands in mine. He pressed his bony fingers   14
against my hand and muttered, "Thanks." Then there was one soft sigh and I felt his hands go cold in mine. "Mac?" I whispered, as I waited for his chest to rise and fall again.

A clutch of panic banded my chest, drew my finger to the code button, urged   15
me to do something, anything . . . but sit there alone with death. I kept one finger on the button, without pressing it, as a waxen pallor slowly transformed his face from person to empty shell. Nothing I've ever done in my forty-seven years has taken so much effort as it took *not* to press that code button.

Eventually, when I was as sure as I could be that the code team would fail to bring   16
him back, I entered the legal twilight zone and pushed the button. The team tried. And while they were trying, Maura walked into the room and shrieked, "No . . . don't let them do this to him . . . for God's sake . . . please, no more."

Cradling her in my arms was like cradling myself, Mac, and all those patients and   17
nurses who had been in this place before, who do the best they can in a death-denying society.

18   So a TV audience accused me of murder. Perhaps I am guilty. If a doctor had written a no-code order, which is the only *legal* alternative, would he have felt any less guilty? Until there is legislation making it a criminal act to code a patient who has requested the right to die, we will all of us risk the same fate as Mac. For whatever reason, we developed the means to prolong life, and now we are forced to use it. We do not have the right to die.

VOCABULARY

Directions: Locate each of the key words in the reading selection. Try to figure out each word's meaning by using the context. Confirm your guess by checking the dictionary or thesaurus. Write the meanings of the words in the margin of the text. Then record the meanings in the chart below.

Key Word	Paragraph	Meaning
1. resuscitated	3	
2. haggard	5	
3. craters	7	
4. negligence	9	
5. lucid	10	
6. impotence	10	
7. meddling	11	
Others?		

GUIDE QUESTIONS

Directions: These questions will guide your understanding of what you have read. Write your answers in your notebook or on a separate sheet of paper if your instructor wishes to collect it. Your answers to these questions will be the basis of class discussion.

1. Although Huttmann has a larger story to tell, she focuses on one man's story. She describes Mac, a young, healthy cop transformed by lung cancer

into a sixty-pound skeleton, barely alive. Why do you think Huttmann describes Mac's physical condition and his suffering in such gruesome detail that it is painful to read?

2. In paragraph 11, Huttmann asks some wrenching questions about the attitude and behavior of the medical community. Why do you think she uses the words *arrogant* and *self-righteous* in her questions? What basic question is she really asking?

3. When Huttmann appears on *The Phil Donahue Show,* she is accused by members of the audience of being a "murderer." In your opinion, is she a murderer? Why?

4. Explain Huttmann's final statement, "We do not have the right to die."

APPLICATION

1. *Directions:* Imagine you are the doctor Huttmann describes in paragraph 9. Write a letter from him to Huttmann explaining your reasons for continuing to resuscitate Mac.

2. *Directions:* Compare Huttmann's position on the right to die with that of Gilbert Cant ("Deciding When Death Is Better than Life," p. 301). Do they agree or disagree? Supply quotes from both articles to support your answer.

WRITING

Directions: Write a response to Barbara Huttmann, agreeing or disagreeing with her actions in allowing Mac to die. Be sure to give good, clear reasons to support your opinion. Write at least 250 words.

Elisabeth Kübler-Ross is a well-known physician and author, best known for her books on the topic of death and dying. In this chapter from her biography, Quest: The Life of Elisabeth Kübler-Ross, *we learn of her distress and grief when she is called upon to make a life-or-death decision about her own mother.*

TO LIVE UNTIL YOU DIE
Derek Gill

1   In the early summer of 1967, Elisabeth and Manny Ross moved for the fifth time. They now felt comfortably settled in Chicago and, assuming they would be living and working there for the foreseeable future, they bought a home a few blocks away from the house they had been renting. The new house was similar to the one they were leaving: a split-level, two-bedroom home with a spacious yard.

2   On a warm Sunday afternoon in June they were enjoying the yard, abloom with flowers. Their visitor was Uncle Anschel, Elisabeth's favorite in-law, now frailer than when she had first met him and suffering from a chronic bronchial ailment. She watched him affectionately as he struggled to breathe while reading a story to Kenneth, who sat astride the elderly man's knees. A few feet away, Barbara was laughing and splashing in a small plastic pool.

3   She and Manny had decided to postpone their annual summer vacation and instead take a holiday at Christmas in order, as they had just explained to their seven-year-old son, Kenneth, to give him and his little sister, Barbara, "a real Swiss Christmas" with sleigh bells and festivals. At Christmastime Elisabeth still felt such a yearning for the country of her birth that it was almost a physical pain, and now that Kenneth was old enough to enjoy it she was especially eager to have him experience the happiest season of her childhood.

4   Suddenly, and apparently without stimulus or prompting, Elisabeth felt a deep and inexplicable concern about her mother's well-being. Before speaking of it to Manny, she tried to rationalize her persistent disquiet. A recent letter from her mother had stated how well and strong she was feeling, although she was in her seventies. Ernst and his family were shortly to fly home from India to vacation in a rented house in the mountain resort of Zermatt. Mrs. Kübler was to join them, as were Eva and her children. She was looking forward to long hikes, and perhaps even a little climbing. But for some reason Elisabeth sensed her mother needed her urgently.

5   She now turned to Manny and told him she had to fly to Switzerland immediately—tomorrow, if they could get plane reservations. Manny threw up his hands. It was she, he reminded her, who had insisted on a Christmas vacation, and he was the one who had been ready to fall in with these plans. Without any valid reason, it would be awkward to make the necessary arrangements at his hospital.

6   Elisabeth admitted that her impulsive decision sounded crazy, but there was some very important reason—a purpose she did not yet understand—why she should be with her mother as quickly as possible. . . . A week later, she and the two children arrived in Zurich, where they boarded the train for Zermatt.

Zermatt was the ideal place for a restful vacation and for what Elisabeth called 7
"a time for old-fashioned happiness." Mrs. Kübler looked in the pink of health and
had, on the day the Ross family arrived, been on an eight-mile hike with Eva [Elisa-
beth's identical triplet] and Ernst [her fraternal triplet]. The family spent the evening
reminiscing while the Kübler, Ross, and Bacher children got to know each other
again. Elisabeth gave no hint of the reason for her unexpected arrival.

The weather remained perfect and the week passed quickly. After a couple of 8
days of aching muscles, Elisabeth rediscovered her mountain legs and did some
climbing. Her children were introduced to the taste of wild berries and of milk still
warm from the cow. Mrs. Kübler hiked each day with her children and grandchildren. Everyone glowed with health.

On the last evening at the resort where they were all staying, when the sun 9
was setting over the peaks, Mrs. Kübler sat with Elisabeth on the balcony of her
bedroom where Kenneth and Barbara, exhausted after the day's outing, were fast
asleep. Mother and daughter sat through a long silence and watched shadows move
like ragged fingers across the green valleys far below. Then Mrs. Kübler turned to
face Elisabeth and said, "I want your solemn promise that you'll do something for
me. I want your promise that, when I become incapable, when I become a human
vegetable, you'll help me to die." She spoke with an uncharacteristic urgency.

Elisabeth was taken aback, both by the appeal and by its timing. She reacted not 10
as an expert on dying, not as a teacher who instructed others to be alert for symbolic language, but as a shocked daughter. She replied too quickly, "What nonsense
is this! A woman who is in her seventies and who can hike miles every day in the
mountains is sure to die very suddenly. Mother, you're the last person to become a
human vegetable."

Mrs. Kübler continued to speak as if she had not heard her. She again asked for 11
a promise that, when she became incapable of caring for herself, Elisabeth would
help her to die.

Elisabeth looked at her mother with astonishment and again protested that the 12
question was purely hypothetical. In any case, she said firmly, she was totally opposed to mercy killing, if that was what her mother was talking about. In her opinion, no physician had the right to give a patient an overdose to relieve suffering. She
could not promise her mother—or for that matter, anyone else—to expedite dying. In the unlikely event that her mother did in fact become physically incapable, all
that she could promise was that she would help her live until she died.

Mrs. Kübler began to cry softly. It was only the second time in her life that Elis- 13
abeth had seen her mother shed tears, the first being when she had gone to be a
housekeeper at Romilly. It was a difficult, awkward moment, and Elisabeth turned the
conversation aside by suggesting that Mrs. Kübler visit them, perhaps in the fall.
Chicago would be cool then. She would love the autumn colors.

Mrs. Kübler rose from her chair and went inside. For a while, Elisabeth sat alone 14
and thought about her mother's request, her own response to it and her attitude
toward euthanasia. It was tempting to avoid the issue. She remembered some lines
of Erich Fromm, the psychiatrist–philosopher. "There is no such thing as medical
ethics. There are only universal human ethics applied to specific human situations."

There were times, she was obliged to admit, when it was wrong to keep someone alive—but such a time would only occur when a patient was clearly beyond medical help, when organs were kept functioning only with machines. So long as there was a meaningful life, so long as a patient could express and receive feelings, it had to be wrong to "play God" and decide arbitrarily whether a patient should live or die.

15   Surely, though, it was not to answer this hypothetical question that she had changed the family's vacation plans and come to Switzerland.

16   Next day, when Mrs. Kübler accompanied Elisabeth and the children to the train station, both women were tense and uncomfortable. However, when the train came in, Elisabeth turned to her mother, hugged her and said, "All I can promise you is that I will do my best to help you live until you die."

17   Mrs. Kübler appeared to understand now what Elisabeth was saying. She nodded, wiped her eyes, smiled and said, "Thank you."

18   Those were the last words Elisabeth heard her mother speak. Hardly had the family arrived back in Chicago when a call came from Eva. It read, "Mother has had a massive stroke."

19   By the weekend, Elisabeth was back in Switzerland. She learned from Eva how the mailman had found her mother paralyzed and sprawled in the passageway of her home. When Mrs. Kübler had not responded to his knock on the door, he had called for help. Later, he accompanied the unconscious woman to the hospital.

20   At the hospital Elisabeth found her mother unable to speak, unable to move anything except her eyelids and, very feebly, her left hand. It was obvious, however, from the expression in her eyes, that Mrs. Kübler understood what was said to her.

21   Elisabeth and her mother devised a method of communicating. Her mother would use her eyelids and her slightly mobile left hand to indicate affirmative or negative answers to questions put to her. One blink of the eyelids or one squeeze of the hand would signify an affirmative and two blinks or two squeezes would mean a negative response.

22   Using this form of communication, Mrs. Kübler made it very clear that she did not want to remain in the hospital. Elisabeth confronted her mother with the impossibility of her returning home, where she would require round-the-clock attention. It was Eva who came up with the solution. She knew of an infirmary, more a rest home than a hospital, in Richen, a few miles outside of Basel. Eva lived in Richen, and Erika too would be within easy range. The infirmary was set in spacious well-tended grounds, it was run by a dedicated group of Protestant nuns. There would be no respirators or other life-prolonging equipment. When the question was put to Mrs. Kübler, her eyes blinked once and her face lit up.

23   On the journey from Zurich to Richen Elisabeth sat with Mrs. Kübler in the ambulance. She had made a complete list of her mother's relatives and friends, and also an inventory of her mother's possessions. During the journey Elisabeth named her mother's possessions one by one and then she ran through the list of friends and kin. By squeezing her left hand, Mrs. Kübler signified her bequests. She indicated, for example, that Eva was to be given her pearl necklace, Erika a ring, a bureau was to go to a certain neighbor, and her mink cape was to be given to the wife of the mailman.

24   By the time the ambulance pulled into the driveway of the infirmary, Elisabeth possessed a detailed list of her mother's bequests. . . .

Immediately after taking her mother to the infirmary, Elisabeth spent a couple   25
of painful days quite alone at the Klosbachstrasse apartment. She sorted clothes,
furniture, and objets d'art; she took down pictures and curtains and labeled everything for subsequent distribution according to her mother's expressed wishes. When
everything was distributed or packed away—including boxes of geraniums from the
balcony which had been her mother's special pride and joy—she walked through
the empty, echoing rooms. She was overwhelmed by feelings that, she realized later,
followed the pattern of feelings she had observed in dying patients.

Her first thought was that the closing of the house was all a bad dream, that it   26
wasn't really happening and that she would always have a home in Switzerland. The
family would surely meet here again—she, her mother, and sisters and brother.

The vision lasted only a few moments before she felt a surge of anger—anger   27
because it was a condition of life that time could not be frozen, that the happiest
moments could not be retrieved and relived.

Her anger grew as she thought how she had been obliged to close down the   28
home alone. None had understood that she was burning the last of the bridges that
linked her to her youth and young womanhood. From now on, when she visited
Switzerland she would come as a visitor. She would have to stay in hotels or, at
best, crowded into her sisters' homes.

The deepest sadness followed an almost desperate sense of loneliness and iso-   29
lation. She walked to the balcony and listened to the rumble of a monorail train
pulling up the hill. It was from this balcony that she had seen the body of her father
taken away. Her heart ached as she thought of the many times she had run down
this street for a trolleybus to take her to the hospital and the university.

Elisabeth remembers too recoiling momentarily from a vision of the work that   30
lay ahead of her—or as she put it, "the higher new mountain peak that I knew I
must climb."

All these feelings coursed through her within a short span, and then came accep-   31
tance of reality. The house was quite empty. A new family would move in shortly. She
would never come home here again. She would no longer have a home in Switzerland. Life did move on. She would have to face the challenge of the new mountain.
No amount of wishful thinking could recapture the past or change the now.

Elisabeth now believes that, in closing down the family home in Zurich, she was   32
given a new and important understanding about life and death. Life, she now sees, is
a series of losses, and every loss is a "little death." In the hour or so before she
finally left the home on Klosbachstrasse she had gone through the five identifiable
stages of dying [denial, anger, bargaining, depression, and acceptance]. Each "little
death"—and this was one of hers—was a salutary and perhaps essential preparation for death itself. But every ending was also a new beginning.

Another lesson, long and difficult, now focused on the infirmary at Richen. Mrs.   33
Kübler, paralyzed and unable to speak, held on to life—not just for the few weeks
that Elisabeth and her sisters had anticipated, not for months, but for four years.
She had clearly foreseen the manner of her dying and, recoiling at the prospect, had
pleaded with Elisabeth for mercy killing.

For Elisabeth, the issue of euthanasia was no longer a hypothetical one, no longer   34
an intellectual debating point, but a question of the heart and conscience. There were

times when she was ready to change her views, moments when she wondered agonizingly whether she should have given her mother the promise she had asked for; but these doubts stalked her only when she was far away from Switzerland. For when she was with her mother—and Elisabeth flew the Atlantic many times to be at her bedside—her conviction remained that neither she nor anyone else had the right to take the life of someone who could still express and receive feelings. Mrs. Kübler was not a human vegetable. She needed no machines to keep her heart beating or her lungs breathing.

35   To every visitor, she expressed gratitude and love through her eyes. Eva visited her every day, and Erika, who was working, came every weekend. The family was especially touched by the number of friends who made the journey from Zurich, including the mailman and milkman, who saved up to buy train tickets and spend an hour or two at her bedside.

36   Following one transatlantic visit to her mother, Elisabeth reflected in her journal:

> I often find it so hard to understand why a good and selfless woman has had to face what she most feared—a long, drawn-out death. When I see her I wonder what meaning such an existence can have? . . . She well knows how much she is loved. . . . Yesterday, when Mr. and Mrs. P. came to see me to talk about their child who has been in a coma for three months, I was truthfully able to say that I understood their feelings. . . . Mother helps me to care more deeply, to understand more readily, helps me to be a better physician, a better teacher, surely a better human being.

VOCABULARY

Directions: Locate each of the key words in the reading selection. Then read and study each word in its context and try to determine its meaning. Use a dictionary or thesaurus to check your guess. Write the meanings of the words in the margin of the text.

Record the new words you've learned below and on the next page.

Key Word	Paragraph	Meaning
1. inexplicable	4	
2. taken aback	10	
3. hypothetical	12	
4. arbitrarily	14	
5. mobile	21	
6. recoiling	30	

Key Word	Paragraph	Meaning
7. salutary	32	
Others?		

GUIDE QUESTIONS

Directions: The purpose of these guide questions is to ensure your understanding of what you have read. They will also help you to analyze and evaluate the issue discussed here and apply your conclusions to the real world and your own life.

Write answers to the questions in your notebook or on a separate sheet of paper if your instructor wishes to collect them. Your answers will form the basis of class discussion.

1. Dr. Kübler-Ross and her mother appeared to have a very close relationship. It came as a surprise, then, when the two women confronted the issue of euthanasia so differently.
   a. In your own words, describe the mother's position on the subject.
   b. Describe Elisabeth's reaction to her mother's request.
2. Why do you think Elisabeth insisted to her mother that her request for help in dying was "purely hypothetical"?
3. a. Summarize Elisabeth's position on mercy killing.
   b. Were there any circumstances under which she would approve mercy killing? Explain.
4. In closing the house after her mother's illness, Elisabeth says she gained an understanding about life and death.
   a. How does she describe life?
   b. Why do you think she says each "little death" is "salutary"?
5. Despite her tragic personal experience, Elisabeth still believed mercy killing was, in general, wrong. She does mention, however, some criteria under which she would approve it. State the criteria.
6. In your opinion, if Elisabeth were to develop an illness like her mother's, how would she react to a suggestion of euthanasia?

APPLICATION

Directions: Work in small groups to complete this assignment. You have now done extensive reading and thinking about euthanasia. If you had an opinion on the subject before you began, you should have re-evaluated it, modified it, become more secure with it, or possibly even rejected it. Let's retrace *in writing* the process you have just gone through in your mind to form your opinion.

Forming a Valid Opinion These are the steps we generally follow when we form a good opinion:

1. *First,* we inform ourselves fully about the topic. We read, discuss, listen, and think about the issue. We consider all the different perspectives on the issue.
2. *Second,* we formulate a proposal, such as:

    Euthanasia should be allowed in the United States.

3. *Third,* we assemble and consider the arguments in favor of the proposal.
4. *Fourth,* we assemble and consider the opposing arguments.
5. *Last,* we arrive at a thoughtful opinion supported by those arguments that convinced us to adopt it.

Now let's implement these steps, in writing, for the topic we have just examined. Fill in answers to the following questions:

1. Define and give some background information about euthanasia.
2. State the topic in the form of a proposal. (You may use the statement from the second step above if you wish, or write your own.)
3. Using all the information you have read and thought about in this section, list all the arguments *in favor of* legalizing euthanasia.
4. Next list all the arguments you can *against* legalizing euthanasia.
5. Finally, all the group members should state their opinions and reasons to support their opinions. Discuss and evaluate the supporting arguments to ensure the opinions are valid.

WRITING

Directions: Now, using the information in the steps above as an outline, write a composition defining euthanasia, presenting the pro and con arguments and your supported opinion. This composition may be written by the group as a collaborative effort or your instructor may want each person to write his or her own composition based on the information developed in the group.

SPECIAL PROJECT

CONTROVERSIAL ISSUES

Research/Writing/Presentation

This assignment has four main goals:

First, to give you experience using the library as a tool for research;

Second, to give you the opportunity to show you can read critically, that you can see viewpoints other than your own, and that you can exchange ideas with others in a systematic and productive way;

Third, to give you experience arranging a large number of facts and presenting them in an organized and graceful way;

Fourth (if your instructor assigns this option), to give you experience presenting your work orally before your classmates.

Teams You will work in teams—four persons per team. Each team will examine a topic of current controversy. (Your instructor may assign you a topic or allow you to choose one yourself.)

With your team, you will research your topic, using your college library or your public library.

Research Look for books, magazines, and newspapers that contain information about your topic. Because you are investigating current topics, books will probably be less useful to you than magazines and newspapers, but if you find one that is helpful, by all means use it.

When you feel you have enough information to write a paper (your instructor will tell you the length expected), divide your team in half: two persons will argue *in favor* of the issue; the other two will argue *against* the issue.

Based on the information you have collected, your paper will present:

1. Your topic and your position on the topic (either for or against);
2. Several paragraphs of clearly stated arguments, examples, and explanations supporting your point of view;
3. A list of references (also called "Works Cited")—the books, magazines, and newspaper articles you used to write your paper.

An example of a student paper follows.

Oral Presentation Finally, if your instructor chooses, you will have the opportunity to present your findings to your classmates. Each team will present the ideas contained in its paper. Fellow students should be invited to comment on, to disagree with, and to discuss the points raised.

An Example of a Student Paper with a List of References

The Drinking Age: Should It Be Lowered to Nineteen in New York State?

For more than twenty years, New York State allowed people to purchase beer, wine, and liquor at the age of eighteen. Then, in the 1980s, the legal drinking age was raised, first to nineteen, then to twenty-one. The change in the age limit was strongly protested by college students, tavern owners, liquor lobbyists, and veterans of the military. I believe that the drinking age should be lowered to nineteen.

At the age of nineteen you are legally considered an adult with given rights. In New York, young adults of nineteen are told they are mature enough to fight a war, vote, marry, incur debts, and sign contracts. But they are not responsible enough to have a glass of beer.

The high age limit discriminates against young adults in the area of employment by eliminating a major source of jobs. If you are too young to drink, then you cannot serve in restaurants that serve alcohol, you cannot work in bars and other places that sell liquor (Tschann 103).

Supporters of the twenty-one-year-old age limit argue it reduces drunken-driving accidents, saying that young drivers have a higher rate of accidents than older ones (Kable 71). But this discriminates against non-drivers, since two-thirds of nineteen- and twenty-year-olds in New York do not possess driver's licenses. Further, the high age limit penalizes young women unjustly, since very few female drivers show up in drunken-driving statistics (Maull 26).

There is much verifiable evidence that proves that a twenty-one-year-old drinking age does not lower the high percentage of drunken-driving accidents. Although young drivers have a relatively high accident rate, 99 percent of eighteen- and

nineteen-year-old drivers were *not* involved in
alcohol-related accidents. Most alcohol-related
accidents involved people over the age of twenty-
one (Hile 118). In the District of Columbia, where
the drinking age was also raised, out of one hundred people killed in alcohol-related traffic accidents during the past year, only one was under
twenty-one (Ward 104). Officials also state that
drunken-driving accidents involving young drivers,
especially eighteen-year-old drivers, had declined sharply before the drinking age was raised
(Ward 105). There is no legitimate proof that raising the drinking age has been responsible for any
decline. There are also some conflicting studies
on the effect of the raised drinking age in other
states. One result from the studies was a 14 percent *increase* in nighttime fatal crashes among
nineteen-year-olds after the drinking age was
raised (Isaacs 112).

Supporters argue that many eighteen-year-olds
are still in high school and tend to encourage even
younger teens to buy and use alcohol. But rather
than maintain the age limit at twenty-one, nineteen
would be the best age limit because by that time
most teenagers are out of high school, and there
would be a reduction in the passing of liquor from
older to younger students.

There are more effective ways of saving lives
and reducing drunken-driving accidents than restricting the rights of young adults. There should
be an increase in the campaign against traffic
deaths and public education programs against drunk-
enness must get wider circulation, including radio
and TV commercials. State laws should be made
tougher, and a convicted drunken-driver's license
should be suspended for a year or two and for more
after second and third offenses. And if a teenager
is guilty of drunken-driving, his license should be
suspended until the age of twenty-one. Other measures to reduce the high risks of accidents include
the instruction in driver training courses, in the
use of alcohol, and making it more difficult for

young adults to regain a license after a conviction. Although some statistics from raising the age have shown a downward trend in deaths, this decline is mainly because of education efforts and stricter traffic laws.

If the goal is to save lives, improving enforcement and taking steps that would not restrict the activities of all young people should be taken. Even if the drinking age remains at twenty-one, young people will continue to find a way to get a drink, whether through parents, older friends, or lenient liquor store or bar owners. Nineteen-year-olds are adults and should be given all the rights of adulthood . . . including the right to drink.

Works Cited

Hile, Mary E. The Teen Years: Passage to
    Adulthood. New York: Keystone Publishers,
    1995.

Isaacs, Beatrice. "Opinions on Teenage Drinking."
    New York Dialogue May 1996: 110-112.

Kable, Margaret. "Rethinking a Rite of Passage."
    The American Story June 6, 1995: 71-72.

Maull, Samuel. "Lower the Drinking Limits? Pros
    and Cons." New York Today March 9, 1997:
    25-26.

Tschann, James. "Full Speed Ahead: Lowering the
    Legal Limit on Drinking." Today's News
    August 1, 1996: 102-103.

Ward, Antoinette. "Minimum Drinking Age: 19?"
    Student News June 24, 1995: 104-105.

BIBLIOGRAPHY

FOR FURTHER READING ON THE THEME
OF CONTROVERSIAL ISSUES

Christiaan Barnard	*Good Life Good Death*
Sylvan Barnet and Hugo Bedau	*Current Issues and Enduring Questions*
Norman Cousins	*Anatomy of an Illness* and *The Celebration of Life*
Ronald Dworkin	*Life's Dominion: An Argument about Abortion, Euthanasia, and Individual Freedom*
Alex Haley	*The Autobiography of Malcolm X*
Derek Humphrey	*Jean's Way*
Elisabeth Kübler-Ross	*On Death and Dying*
Opposing Viewpoints Series	A series of pamphlets presenting contrasting views on current controversial topics
Anna Quindlen	*Thinking out Loud*
Piers Paul Read	*Alive*
Berton Roueche	*The Medical Detectives*
Henry David Thoreau	"Civil Disobedience"

UNIT SIX

READING AND THINKING ABOUT TEXTBOOKS

He that loves reading has everything within his reach.

—William Godwin

Textbook reading is probably the most challenging type of reading you will do in your life. It poses difficulties for a number of reasons. First, you are usually reading about things that are new to you; there is often a great deal of new information to be learned. Second, the typical chapter in a college textbook is longer than what you normally read in, say, the newspaper or a magazine. Third, there are often many new words and concepts you must learn and remember. So, it is important to use all your study skills when attacking your textbooks.

In this unit you will find five chapters taken from five widely used college textbooks. Each chapter is keyed to one of the themes in this book. Thus, you will find a chapter on education (Unit 1), culture (Unit 2), language (Unit 3), work (Unit 4), and critical reading and thinking (Unit 5). Each chapter is accompanied by suggestions on previewing, annotating, and learning important terminology. Following each chapter you will find examples of the actual test questions that students who take the course see on their exams. Working with these sample chapters will give you valuable experience with real college materials.

Steps for Studying Textbook Chapters

Begin by reviewing how to preview: previewing is discussed in Appendix A. Review the four steps for previewing a chapter on page 418.

Next, read, reread, underline, and annotate the chapter. Review the steps for underlining and annotating in Appendix B. Remember, the important first step is to read through the entire chapter one time quickly to get a feel for the information it contains. If the chapter seems very long, divide it up into manageable chunks and attack one chunk at a time. After the first "get-acquainted" reading, go back and read the chapter again. This time, read carefully, underlining and annotating as you go along.

Finally, reflect for a moment on what you have learned. What do you think are the key ideas that you are expected to learn from this chapter? What concepts will you need to remember for the next exam? For the next course in your major? Are there ideas and terms that you will need to know in order to have a successful career? Are there things you would like to remember for the rest of your life?

Remember, *active reading* will help you with the challenging assignments you face in college. *Be active with your textbooks*. While you are underlining and annotating, be sure to mark words you need to look up. Put a question mark next to things you don't understand or want to discuss with a classmate or the instructor. Ask yourself questions as you read along and try to find the answers to your questions.

At the end of each of the chapters in this unit, you will see the exam questions actually used by the instructors who teach the course in which the text is used. Answering these questions will help you to test the effectiveness of your reading and studying.

Now, use your skills as an active independent reader to tackle the following textbook chapters. Good luck!

EDUCATION

A Chapter from the Textbook *Sociology: A Global Perspective,* 2nd ed.

Joan Ferrante

PREVIEWING

Your first step in studying a textbook chapter should always be to preview. If you need to review previewing, turn to Appendix A, beginning on page 417. For this chapter, the most important features to preview are the headings and subheadings. But before you begin, it would be a good idea to think about the meaning of *education* for a moment. What is its definition? What special meanings does the word have for you?

1. Think about the title of the chapter: "Education." It is a very broad topic. List the headings and subheadings of the chapter to discover which aspects of education the chapter will discuss.
2. Skim the first two paragraphs. You will see that the author uses a pessimistic tone. What is she discussing?
3. List any special features, such as bold-face print, tables, lists, etc., that the author uses to highlight important ideas.

EDUCATION

In 1981 the Reagan administration formed The National Commission on Education to study the state of American education. Two years later the commission reported its conclusions in *A Nation at Risk*. The most famous lines in this report are:

> The educational foundations of our society are presently being eroded by a rising tide of mediocrity that threatens our very future as a nation and a people. . . .
>
> If an unfriendly foreign power had attempted to impose on America the mediocre educational performance that exists today, we might well have viewed it as an act of war. . . . We have, in effect, been committing an act of unthinking, unilateral educational disarmament (The National Commission on Excellence in Education, 1983, p. 5).

The dramatic charges in this report, exemplified by the excerpt above, set off a tidal wave of reforms across the fifty states and the more than fifteen hundred school districts. These included lengthening the school year, installing no pass/no play rules for sports, fining parents who failed to comply with attendance laws, extending the school day, enforcing competency testing of teachers and students, and increasing the number of required mathematics, English, foreign-language, and science courses.

Yet, in spite of the many reforms implemented, one phrase captures their basic intent: more of the same. The reforms stipulated more tests, more class time, more home-work, and more courses, but they failed to address the content and the quality of the educational experience. Critics argue that there was a gross disparity between the urgent

tone of *A Nation at Risk* and the superficial nature of the reforms that were enacted.

Apparently the reforms proved ineffective, because in September 1989 at the Governors Conference President Bush announced new educational goals to be achieved by the year 2000. In April 1994 President Clinton signed the Goals 2000 Act, which set aside $700 million in federal funds for states and school districts that implement programs aimed at meeting guidelines related to these goals that include a 90 percent high-school graduation rate and a 100 percent literacy rate. Other goals included:

- Every American child must start school prepared to learn, sound in body and sound in mind.

- All students in grades four, eight, and twelve will be tested for progress in critical subjects.

- American students must rank first in the world in achievements in mathematics and science.

- Every adult must be a skilled, literate worker and citizen, able to compete in a global economy.

- Every school must be drug-free and offer a disciplined environment conducive to learning.

The belief that the inadequacies of the schools threaten the country's well-being is not unique to the 1980s and 1990s. Neither is the call for a restructuring of the American educational system. Indeed, the recommendation that the educational system be more inclusive dates back to the mid-1800s when educational leaders debated whether to establish universal public education. Although the problems and recommendations have remained essentially unchanged over the past two hundred years, various events throughout this period have placed them in a different context and have given them a seemingly new sense of urgency. Between 1880 and 1920, for example, the public was concerned about whether the schools were producing qualified workers for the growing number of factories and businesses and whether they were instilling a sense of national identity (that is, patriotism) in the ethnically diverse student population. When the United States was involved in major wars—World War I, World War II, Korea, and Vietnam—the public was concerned about whether the schools were turning out recruits physically and mentally capable of defending the American way of life. When the Soviet *Sputnik* satellites were launched in the mid-1950s, Americans were forced to consider the possibility that the public schools were not educating their students as well as the Soviets were in mathematics and the sciences. In the 1960s civil rights events forced Americans to question whether the public schools were offering children from less advantaged ethnic groups and social classes the knowledge and skills to compete economically with children in more advantaged groups. During the late 1970s, throughout the 1980s, and now into the 1990s, as multinational corporations draw from a worldwide labor pool, Americans confront the possibility that their schools are educating an inferior work force, one that will be unable to compete in a global labor market.

The ongoing nature of the so-called education crisis in the United States and the corresponding criticisms aimed at the American system of education suggest that the schools are very visible and highly vulnerable, that "they are the stage on which a lot of cultural crises get played out." Inequality, poverty, chronic boredom, family breakdown, unemployment, illiteracy, drug abuse, child abuse, and ethnocentrism are crises that transcend the school environment. Yet, we confront them whenever we go into the schools. Consequently, the schools seem to be, in some way, both a source of problems and a solution for our problems.

In this chapter we give special emphasis to public education, the system in which 89 percent of students are enrolled in the United States, for two reasons. First, many critics, at home and abroad, maintain that the U.S. system of education is not adequate for meeting the challenges associated with global interdependence. Many employees claim that they are unable to find enough workers with a level of reading, writing, mathematical, and critical-thinking skills needed to function adequately in the work place. Such a human capital deficit weakens U.S. competitiveness in the global marketplace (U.S. Department of Education 1993a). Second, the research that compares the performance of American students with that of students in other countries (particularly in Asian and European countries) points to two clear trends. "First, compared with their peers in Asian and European countries, American students stand out for how little they work . . . [and] for how poorly they do."

WHAT IS EDUCATION?

In the broadest sense, education includes those experiences that stimulate thought and interpretation or that train, discipline, and develop the mental and physical potentials of the maturing person. An experience that educates may be as commonplace as reading a sweater label and noticing that it was made in Taiwan or as intentional as performing a scientific experiment to learn how genetic make-up can be altered deliberately through the use of viruses. In view of this definition and the wide range of experiences it encompasses, we can say that education begins when people are born and ends when they die.

Sociologists make a distinction, however, between formal and informal education. **Informal education** occurs in a spontaneous, unplanned way. Experiences that educate informally occur naturally: they are not designed by someone to stimulate specific thoughts or interpretations or to impart specific skills. Informal education takes place when a child puts her hand inside a puppet, then works to perfect the timing between the words she speaks for the puppet and the movement of the puppet's mouth. **Formal education** is a purposeful, planned effort intended to impart specific skills and modes of thought. Formal education, then, is a systematic process (for example, military boot camp, on-the-job training, programs to stop smoking, classes to overcome fear of flying) in which someone designs the educating experiences. We tend to think of formal education as consisting of enriching, liberating, or positive experiences, but it can include impoverishing and narrowing occurrences (such as indoctrination or brainwashing) as well. In any case, formal education is considered a success when the people instructed internalize (or take as their own) the skills and modes of thought that those who design the experiences seek to impart. This chapter is concerned with a specific kind of formal education—schooling.

Schooling is a program of formal and systematic instruction that takes place primarily in classrooms but also includes extracurricular activities and out-of-classroom assignments. In its ideal sense: "Education must make the child cover in a few years the enormous distance traveled by mankind in many centuries." More realistically, schooling is the means by which those who design and implement programs of instruction seek to pass on the values, knowledge, and skills they define as important for success in the world.

This latter conception implies that what is taught in schools is only a part of the knowledge accumulated and stored throughout human history. This point, of course, raises questions about who has the power to select, from the vast amounts of material available, what students should study. Moreover, what constitutes an ideal education—the goals that should be achieved, the material that should be covered, the best techniques of instruction—is elusive and debatable. Conceptions vary according to time and place; they differ according to whether schools are viewed primarily as mechanisms by which the needs of a society are met or the means by which students learn to think independently, thus becoming free from the constraints on thought imposed by family, culture, and nation.

SOCIAL FUNCTIONS OF EDUCATION

Sociologist Emile Durkheim believed that education functions to serve the needs of society. In particular, schools function to teach children the things they need to adapt to their environment. To ensure this end, the state (or other collectivity) reminds teachers "constantly of the ideas, the sentiments that must be impressed" upon children if they are to adjust to the milieu in which they must live. Otherwise, "the whole nation would be divided and would break down into an incoherent multitude of little fragments in conflict with one another." Educators must achieve a sufficient "community of ideas and sentiments without which there is no society." Such logic underscores efforts to use the schools as mechanisms for meeting the needs of society, whether they be to strip away identities of ethnicity and social origin in order to implant a common national identity, to transmit values, to train a labor force, to take care of children while their parents work, or to teach young people to drive.

According to another quite different conception, education is a liberating experience that releases students from the blinders imposed by the accident of birth into a particular family, culture, religion, society, and time in history. Schools therefore should be designed to broaden students' horizons so they will become aware of the conditioning influences around them and will learn to think independently of any authority. When schools are designed to achieve these goals, they can function as agents of change and progress.

These aims are not necessarily contradictory if what benefits the group also liberates the individual. For example, democracies and the free-market system require an informed public that is capable of independent thought. Most sociological research, however, suggests that schools are more likely to be designed to meet the perceived needs of society rather than to liberate minds. (This point raises a question: Who defines the needs of society?) In spite of this intention, however, a significant percentage of the population in every country seems to be functionally illiterate—that is, they do not possess the level of reading, writing, and calculating skills needed to adapt to the society in which they live. In fact, to many critics of the U.S. educational system, illiteracy in America has reached crisis proportions. In order to evaluate the "literacy crisis," we need to define illiteracy, to distinguish among kinds of literacy, and to ask how the United States compares to other countries when it comes to preparing its students to be educated workers and citizens.

ILLITERACY IN THE UNITED STATES

In the most general and basic sense, **illiteracy** is the inability to understand and use a symbol system, whether it is based on sounds, letters, numbers, pictographs, or some other type of character. Although the term *illiteracy* is used traditionally in reference to the inability to understand letters and their use in reading and writing, there are as many kinds of illiteracy as there are symbol systems—computer illiteracy, mathematical illiteracy (or innumeracy), scientific illiteracy, cultural illiteracy, and so on.

If we confine our attention merely to languages, of which there are thought to be between 3,500 and 9,000 (including dialects), we can see that the potential number of literacies is overwhelming and that people cannot possibly be literate in every symbol system. If a person speaks, writes, and reads in only one language, by definition he or she is illiterate in perhaps as many as 8,999 languages. Yet, such a profound level of illiteracy rarely presents a problem because usually people need to know and understand only the language of the environment in which they live.

This point suggests that illiteracy is a product of one's environment—that is, people are considered illiterate when they cannot understand or use the symbol system of the surrounding environment in which they wish to function. Examples include not being able to use a computer, to access information, to read a map in order to find a destination, to make change for a customer, to read traffic signs, to follow the instructions to assemble an appliance, to fill out a job application, or to comprehend the language of those around them.

The contextual nature of illiteracy suggests that it is not "some sort of disease . . . like a viral infection that debilitates an otherwise healthy organism. . . . Illiteracy is a social phenomenon, not a natural one" in that it changes form whenever an environment changes to the point at which old literacy skills are no longer sufficient.

In the United States (and in all countries, for that matter) some degree of illiteracy has always existed, but conceptions of what people needed to know to be considered literate have

DEFINITIONS AND LEVELS OF LITERACY

A society's definition of literacy changes whenever an environment changes to the point at which old definitions of literacy are no longer sufficient to meet the level of reading, writing, critical thinking, and quantitative skills that the new environment demands. In the United States, the most recent definition of literacy identifies three kinds of literacy: prose, document, and quantitative. Each kind of illiteracy is further divided into at least six levels.

PROSE LITERACY	DOCUMENT LITERACY	QUANTITATIVE LITERACY
The knowledge and skills needed to understand and use information from texts that include editorials, news stories, poems, and fiction—for example, finding a piece of information in a newspaper article, interpreting instructions from a warranty, inferring a theme from a poem, or contrasting views expressed in an editorial.	The knowledge and skills required to locate and use information contained in materials that include job applications, payroll forms, transportation schedules, maps, tables, and graphs—for example, locating a particular intersection on a street map, using a schedule to choose the appropriate bus, or entering information on an application form.	The knowledge and skills required to apply arithmetic operations, either alone or sequentially, using numbers embedded in printed materials—for example, balancing a checkbook, figuring out a tip, completing an order form, or determining the amount of interest from a loan advertisement.
1. Identify country in short article	Sign your name	Total a bank deposit entry
2. Underline meaning of a term given in government brochure on supplemental security income	Locate intersection on a street map	Calculate postage and fees for certified mail
3. Write a brief letter explaining error made on a credit card bill	Identify information from bar graph depicting source of energy and year	Using calculator, calculate difference between regular and sale price from an advertisement
4. State in writing an argument made in lengthy newspaper article	Identify the correct percentage meeting specified conditions from a table of such information	Determine correct change using information in a menu
5. Compare approaches stated in narrative on growing up	Use information in table to complete a graph, including labeling axes	Determine shipping and total costs on an order form for items in a catalog
6. Compare two metaphors used in poem	Use table of information to determine pattern in oil exports across years	Using eligibility pamphlet, calculate the yearly amount a couple would receive for basic supplemental security income

Sources: U.S. Department of Education, pp. 3–4, 10 (1993b); U.S. Department of Education (1992a).

varied over time. At one time, people were considered literate if they could sign their names and read the Bible. At other times, a person who had completed the fourth grade was considered literate. The National Literacy Act of 1991 defines literacy as "an individual's ability to read, write, and speak English and compute and solve problems at levels of proficiency necessary to function on the job and in society, to achieve one's goals, and to develop one's knowledge and potential." Today there are various estimates of the number of functionally illiterate adults in the United States. The U.S. Bureau of the Census (1982) estimates that 13 percent of the adult population (or twenty-six million adults) are illiterate. The National Alliance of Business estimates that 30 percent of high school students cannot write a letter seeking employment or information and that one seventeen-year-old in eight cannot read beyond a fifth-grade level.

As the number of low-skill but relatively high-paying manufacturing jobs moved offshore, starting in the 1970s and continuing into the present, ideas of what constituted literacy have become more complex. During this time people who previously had been gainfully employed suddenly came to be defined as functionally illiterate: they lacked the reading, writing, and calculating skills needed to find re-employment in the emerging service and information economy. One of the striking characteristics of this group of functional illiterates is that they are

> *adults who have attended school and have had some contact with reading and writing. They may know the alphabet and even be just capable of deciphering a few words. They may be able to write a little. They may recognize figures and be able to do a few sums, but their knowledge in these fields is rudimentary and insufficient for them to cope easily with everyday life.*

In 1988 the U.S. Congress requested that the Department of Education define literacy in the context of the new economic order and attempt to estimate how many Americans are illiterate. The project involved a representative sample of 26,091 adults (13,600 were interviewed and 1,000 were surveyed in each of 11 states). In addition, 1,100 federal and state prison inmates were interviewed. The project was completed in 1993. The researchers found that 21 to 23 percent of those contacted "demonstrated skills in the lowest level of prose, document, and qualitative proficiencies (level 1)." Approximately 25 to 28 percent of those contacted performed at the next higher level of literacy proficiency. (See "Definitions and Levels of Literacy" box.)

ILLITERACY AND SCHOOLS

The fact that almost a quarter of the adult population could function at the lowest level in a society with mandatory school attendance policies leads social critics, most notably American government officials and business leaders, to point to the schools as one source of the problem. Upon close analysis, we can see that the literacy problem cannot be solved by schools alone. Most Americans seem to believe that if "schools just did their jobs" more skillfully and resolutely, the literacy problem would be solved. Not so, says Lauren B. Resnick, director of the Learning Research and Development Center at the University of Pittsburgh. She argues that policies designed to end illiteracy must consider situations in which people use or value written materials.

Resnick identifies six literacy situations. One of these she terms "the useful situation," which applies to circumstances in which people use printed materials to perform practical activities such as following instructions to install equipment, consulting bus schedules, filling out job applications or other forms, reading receipts, and using computer-software packages. Resnick argues that this "read-do" literacy is acquired primarily outside the classroom. Even before children can read, they observe how adults use texts to carry out tasks. Thus, through observation, they learn general patterns of interacting with texts. Read-do literacy is an important ingredient of work-place literacy. If in fact this literacy is acquired primarily outside the classroom, policies aimed at improving workplace literacy must be designed with this fact in mind.

Despite the complexity of solving the literacy problem, most people are still bothered by the fact that a high-school diploma is no guarantee that one has acquired the skills needed to function in today's economy. The high estimates of illiteracy rates (one person in three), even among those who completed high school, lead people to ask how so many students could attend school for at least twelve years without acquiring enough reading, writing, and problem-solving skills to deal effectively with the work-related problems encountered in the new kinds of entry-level jobs. This question is complicated further by findings that American schoolchildren lag behind their Asian and European counterparts in nearly every subject, especially science and mathematics. This finding holds true even for American students who score in the top 5 to 15 percent on achievement tests compared with their foreign counterparts. "Generally the 'best students' in the United States do less well on the international surveys when compared with the 'best students' from other countries." These findings have prompted many critics to examine the ways in which schools in European and Pacific Rim countries differ from schools in the United States.

INSIGHTS FROM FOREIGN EDUCATION SYSTEMS

At the beginning of the chapter, we noted that, in comparison with their counterparts in Pacific Rim and European countries, American students—even the most able ones—do little school-related work and perform poorly in academic subjects.

> *For example, only 13 percent of a select group of American 17-year-old students achieved algebra scores equal to {those of} 50 percent of 17-year-old Hungarians . . . 25 percent of Canadian 18-year-old students knew as much chemistry as a very select 1 percent of American high-school seniors who had taken an advanced, second-year chemistry course . . . {and} 30 percent of South Korea's 13-year-old students were able to apply "advanced scientific knowledge" compared to 10 percent of American students of the same age.*

A 1993 Department of Education study on gifted children (those who score in the top 3 to 5 percent of achievement and IQ tests) provides insights about why even the best American students perform poorly in the context of the international arena: most report that they study less than one hour a day and that they are bored in class because much of what is taught is a rehash of what they already know. Such results are not meant to imply that Pacific Rim and European schools are operated perfectly or that American schools should emulate their systems. They do suggest, however, that it is important to learn why Americans, as a group, perform so poorly in the international arena.

Amount of Time Spent on Schooling In "The Case for More School Days," Michael Barrett describes how "American children receive hundreds of hours less schooling than many of their European or Asian mates and the resulting harm promises to be cumulative and lasting." This generalization seems to hold no matter how time spent on schooling is measured: by the length of the school year, week, or day; by the amount of time spent doing homework; by the amount of time that parents spend helping their children with homework; by the number of minutes that teachers spend on instruction (as opposed to disciplining or otherwise managing students); by the rate of absenteeism; or by the dropout rate. Barrett maintains that most Americans dismiss suggestions that the amount of time devoted to school-related learning, especially the number of school days, be increased. Instead, most Americans argue that we should learn to use more efficiently the time already allotted. Although Barrett recognizes that increases in time alone cannot improve our ability to compete internationally, he does suggest that Americans need to equalize the time they commit to learning. Barrett also notes the arrogance of thinking that we can accomplish in 180 days what the Europeans and Asians are accomplishing in 200 to 235 days, especially when that 180-day school year includes field trips, schoolwide assemblies, snow days, and teacher in-service days (in-service days count as official school days but only teachers are required to attend school).

One of the most systematic and well-designed studies comparing the time spent on academic activities in three countries was done by Harold W. Stevenson, Shin-ying Lee, and James W. Stigler. They compared mathematics achievement as well as the classroom and home environments of kindergartners, first-graders, and fifth-graders in three cities: Minneapolis (United States), Sendai (Japan), and Taipei (Taiwan). They found that, across all three grades, the Taiwanese, but especially the Japanese, consistently outperformed their American counterparts. At the fifth-grade level, however, the differences in test scores were the most striking:

The highest average score of an American fifth-grade classroom was below that of the Japanese fifth-grade classroom with the lowest average score. In addition, only one Chinese {Taiwanese} classroom showed an average score lower than the American classroom with the highest average score. Equally remarkable is the fact that the lowest average score for a fifth-grade American classroom was only slightly higher than the average score for the best first-grade Chinese classroom.

After thousands of hours of classroom observation and after interviews with both mothers and teachers, Stevenson and his colleagues concluded that Americans devote significantly less time to academic activities either in school or at home and that American parents help their children less with homework. American parents, however, are more likely than their Taiwanese and Japanese counterparts to rate the quality of education at the schools their children attend as good or excellent: 91 percent of American parents, 42 percent of Chinese parents, and 39 percent of Japanese parents rate the quality as good or excellent and are satisfied with the qualities of education (see Table 1). Stevenson maintains that one reason U.S. parents rate quality high is that their school system gives them no clear guidelines about what academic skills children in various grades should possess. Thus they have no baseline by which to judge their child's performance.

Cultural and Economic Incentives   Scott Thomson, executive director of the National Association of Secondary School Principals, argues that the poor international showing by Americans reflects a lack of cultural and economic incentives to do well. He offers the cases of South Korea and Germany as examples. With regard to cultural incentives, American students are less likely than South Korean and German students to receive

	Americans	Taiwanese	Japanese
Table 1 Comparison of Chinese (Taiwanese), Japanese, and American Kindergartners, First-Graders, and Fifth-Graders			

Homework

Minutes per day doing homework*

	Americans	Taiwanese	Japanese
first-graders	14 min.	77 min.	37 min.
fifth-graders	46 min.	114 min.	57 min.

Minutes doing homework (Saturday)

first-graders	7 min.	83 min.	37 min.
fifth-graders	11 min.	73 min.	29 min.

Time parent spent helping with homework

fifth-graders	14 min.	27 min.	19 min.

Percentage who possess a desk at home

fifth-graders	63%	95%	98%

Percentage of parents who purchase workbooks for children to get extra practice

fifth-graders (math)	28%	56%	58%
fifth-graders (science)	1%	51%	29%

Classroom

Percentage of time devoted to academic activities

first-graders	69.8%	85.1%	79.2%
fifth-graders	64.5%	91.5%	87.4%

Hours per week devoted to academic interests

first-graders	19.6 hrs.	40.4 hrs.	32.6 hrs.
fifth-graders	19.6 hrs.	40.4 hrs.	32.6 hrs.

Total hours per week spent in school

first-graders	30.4 hrs.	44.1 hrs.	37.3 hrs.
fifth-graders	30.4 hrs.	44.1 hrs.	37.3 hrs.

Percentage of time a child known to be in school was not in classroom

fifth-graders	18.4%	<0.2%	<0.2%

Proportion of time teacher spends imparting information (all grades)

	21%	58%	33%
	or 6 hrs.	or 26 hrs.	or 12 hrs.

Mother's Perceptions

Evaluation of child's achievement in math on a scale of 1 to 9[†]

	5.9	5.2	5.8

Evaluation of child's intellectual ability[†]	6.3	6.1	5.5

Percentage who believe school is doing a good or excellent job educating children

	91%	42%	39%

Percentage very satisfied with child's academic performance

	40%	<6%	<6%

Evaluation of what is more important to success—ability or effort?

	ability	effort	effort
Percentage who gave child assistance in math	8%	2%	7%

*Mothers' estimates.
[†]With 1 being much below average and 9 being much above average.

Source: Data from "Mathematics Achievement of Chinese, Japanese, and American Children," by Harold W. Stevenson, Shin-ying Lee, and James W. Stigler in *Science*. Copyright © 1986 by the *AAAS*. Reprinted by permission of Harold W. Stevenson and AAAS.

parental assistance with homework and to come from homes where the family value structure is supportive of education. Moreover, in the United States fewer television programs are aimed at educating youth, and the content of the programs and accompanying advertisements aired on American networks encourages students to consume, not to develop the intellect. When school is the backdrop to a television program or commercial, "more often than not, the school principals are portrayed as grumbling misfits, the teachers are blithering incompetents. Students who show the slightest interest in their studies are invariably depicted as wimps. The heroes are those who can best foul up the system."

Economic incentives are another factor in the quality of education. Compared to South Koreans and Germans, Americans devote a smaller percentage of their gross national product to education, they pay their teachers lower salaries, and they make less of a direct connection between academic achievement in high school and the quality of future employment opportunities. Thomson believes that "this tendency to ignore classroom achievement in high school appears to be a peculiarly American phenomenon" and it may help to explain U.S. Secretary of Labor Robert Reich's claim that "America may have the worst school-to-work transition system of any advanced industrial country. Short of a college degree, there is no way someone can signal to an employer that he or she possesses world-class skills." European and Pacific Rim employers, even when hiring clerical and blue-collar workers, express significantly more interest in job applicants' academic achievements. In fact, in many European countries grades and test scores are part of employment resumés. In South Korea, "school is considered too important for students to work . . . students simply do not hold jobs while attending school; their time and energies are directed toward learning." In Japan, "educational credentials and edu-

cated skills are central to employment, to promotion, and to social status in general."

As discouraging as these cross-national findings are for the country as a whole, it is important to acknowledge that students in states such as Iowa, North Dakota, and Minnesota score as high in mathematics, for example, as do students in Japan and Switzerland, countries with the best math scores. Such individual state accomplishments aside, things look bleak when we consider that, within the United States, the average elementary and secondary student misses approximately 20 days of school per year. Moreover, the less advantaged social classes and minority groups have higher dropout rates, higher rates of absenteeism, and lower scores on standardized tests than do those from more advantaged groups. Consider the following facts related to dropout rates:

- Approximately 4,231,000 American students drop out of high school each year.

- The public high-school graduation rate is 71.2 percent. The figure varies by state with a high of 89.5 percent in Minnesota and a low of 54.3 percent in Mississippi.

- The high-school dropout rate for white Americans is 17 percent. The rates for African Americans, Hispanics, and Native Americans are 28 percent, 35 percent, and 45 percent, respectively.

- Young people who live in households with annual incomes of less than $15,000 constitute 60 percent of the high-school dropouts.

The fact that American students spend little time on academic activities compared to their foreign counterparts, in conjunction with the high dropout rate especially among the more disadvantaged groups, suggests that something about the American system of education turns many people away from academic pursuits.

WHAT DID I LEARN FROM PREVIEWING?

Think about what you learned from previewing this chapter. You should have paid special attention to the word *education*. How did the author define education? How did her definition compare with yours? You noted that the author differentiates between informal and formal education—had you ever considered this difference before? Or how the terms *education* and *schooling* can have different meanings? You probably noted the author's frequent use of the word *illiteracy*. This should prepare you for some gloomy news about American education.

Your previewing of the headings and subheadings should have given you a clear picture of the organization of the chapter. Now you are ready to read. Return to the chapter now and give it your first reading.

UNDERLINING AND ANNOTATING

Once you have previewed and read through the chapter, you are ready to do a careful study of the material, underlining and annotating as you read along. The underlining and annotating of your textbooks is your most important study activity. To review these skills, turn to Appendix B. Then underline and annotate this chapter. Discuss your annotation with that of your classmates. This discussion of the text, of what is most important and what is less important, is true *active* studying—the most valuable kind of studying you can do.

VOCABULARY

In this chapter, very few terms are highlighted for you. It is up to you to find and identify any unfamiliar words that you think you'll need to know to comprehend the text. Find and mark each term in the chapter. Put a question mark or some other special symbol next to any term you don't understand. This will remind you to ask a classmate or the instructor for an explanation. If you are keeping a special section of your notebook for important terms and their meanings, write them there also.

EXAM QUESTIONS

Now, to test your understanding of what you've read, consider the following questions. This textbook is used in many introduction to sociology courses around the country. These questions are actual exam questions used by many instructors of the course.

Multiple Choice

_____1. Research comparing the performance of American students with that of students from other countries (especially in Asia and Europe) shows that American students

   a. do less work and poorer work.
   b. attend school more hours.
   c. are more competitive in school.
   d. have more drug problems.

_____ 2. In the broadest sense, education is

     a. purposeful, planned efforts to impart specific skills.
     b. a program of formal and systematic instruction.
     c. those experiences that stimulate thought and interpretation.
     d. spontaneous, unplanned exposure to ideas.

_____ 3. Informal education is defined as experiences that

     a. are designed to stimulate specific thoughts or interpretations.
     b. are designed to teach specific skills.
     c. occur naturally and spontaneously.
     d. are systematic and planned.

_____ 4. Which one of the following words does not describe the process of formal education?

     a. purposeful
     b. systematic
     c. spontaneous
     d. planned

_____ 5. Research suggests that schools are designed to

     a. teach children how to fit into their society.
     b. free students from the constraints of their society.
     c. teach children to become independent thinkers.
     d. broaden students' ideas of the world and its possibilities.

_____ 6. The contextual nature of illiteracy suggests that it is

     a. like a disease.
     b. linked to a lack of desire to want to read and write.
     c. biologically rooted.
     d. a social phenomenon.

_____ 7. The people currently defined as functional illiterates in the United States

     a. do not know the alphabet.
     b. have had no exposure to reading and writing.
     c. do not have sufficient reading and writing skills to cope easily with everyday life.
     d. cannot recognize figures or do sums.

_____ 8. The U.S. Bureau of the Census estimates that approximately _____ million Americans are illiterate.

     a. 16
     b. 2.6
     c. 26
     d. 260

_____ 9. In comparison to students from Pacific Rim and European countries, Americans

    a. do better in science but more poorly in math.
    b. perform more poorly in academic subjects.
    c. do more homework.
    d. study more hours per week.

_____ 10. The tasks of following instructions to install equipment, consulting bus schedules, and filling out job applications fall into the category of

    a. practical literacy.
    b. textbook literacy.
    c. read-do literacy.
    d. task literacy.

True/False

_____ 1. Schooling is instruction that takes place solely in the classroom.

_____ 2. The educational reforms implemented after the release of the report _A Nation at Risk_ were not effective.

_____ 3. The definition of illiteracy changes as the social environment changes.

_____ 4. Americans devote a smaller percentage of their gross national product to education than do South Korea and Germany.

_____ 5. According to sociologist Emile Durkheim, one of education's primary functions is to teach children to adapt to their environment.

_____ 6. A person who cannot understand or use the symbol system of the environment in which he lives is considered illiterate.

_____ 7. The ability to use information in a graph or table is an example of _document literacy._

_____ 8. The state with the highest rate of graduation from high school in the United States is Minnesota.

Short Answer

Describe the differing concerns of the American public regarding the education system during the following periods:

1. between 1880 and 1920
2. during major wars, such as World War I, World War II, the Korean conflict, and the Vietnam War
3. when the _Sputnik_ satellites were launched in the 1950s
4. in the 1960s
5. from the late 1970s to the present

Essay

Based on what you have read, state the major problems affecting education in the United States today. Then choose one of the problems, and, based on your experience and knowledge, propose a solution to the problem.

LANGUAGE AND CULTURE

A Chapter from the Textbook
Looking Out/Looking In, 8th ed.

Ronald B. Adler and Neil Towne

PREVIEWING

The first step in studying a textbook chapter should be previewing. First, to review the benefits and methods of previewing, read Appendix A. The following questions will guide your preview of "Language and Culture."

1. Read the title. What do you think the chapter will be about?
2. Read the first four paragraphs quickly. They will introduce you to the tone and content of the chapter. (If you enjoy the examples of "bungled translations" in the first paragraph, you'll also like reading "It Got Lost in the Translation" in *The Thoughtful Reader* on page 211).
3. Read the subtitles of the chapter. Are there any words or phrases that you don't understand? If so, be sure to mark them so you can ask about them in class.
4. Are any tables or charts included in the chapter? What do they contain?
5. How do the authors indicate the words or terms they feel are important?
6. List the other helpful features (such as a glossary, a summary, margin notes, etc.) that the chapter contains.

▼ LANGUAGE AND CULTURE ▲

▼ INTRODUCTION ▲

Anyone who has tried to translate ideas from one language to another knows that conveying the same meaning isn't always easy. Sometimes the results of a bungled translation can be amusing. For example, the American manufacturers of Pet milk unknowingly introduced their product in French-speaking markets without realizing that the word *pet* in French means "to break wind." Likewise, the English-speaking representative of a U.S. soft-drink manufacturer naively drew laughs from Mexican customers when she offered free samples of Fresca soda pop. In Mexican slang the word *fresca* means "lesbian."

Even choosing the right words during translation won't guarantee that non-native speakers will use an unfamiliar language correctly. For example, Japanese insurance companies warn their policyholders who are visiting the United States to avoid their cultural tendency to say "excuse me" or "I'm sorry" if they are involved in a traffic accident. In Japan, apologizing is a traditional way to express goodwill and maintain social harmony, even if the person offering the apology is not at fault. But in the United States an apology can be taken as an admission of guilt, and result in Japanese tourists being held accountable for accidents in which they may not be responsible.

Difficult as it may be, translation is only a small part of the differences in communication between members of different cultures. Differences in the way language is used and the very world view that a language creates make communicating across cultures a challenging task.

▼ VERBAL COMMUNICATION STYLES ▲

Using language is more than just choosing a particular group of words to convey an idea. Each language has its own unique style that distinguishes it from others. Matters like the amount of formality or informality, precision or vagueness, and brevity or detail are major ingredients in speaking competently. And when a communicator tries to use the verbal style from one culture in a different one, problems are likely to arise.

One way in which verbal styles vary is in their *directness*. Anthropologist Edward Hall identified two distinct cultural ways of using language. **Low-context cultures** use language primarily to express thoughts, feelings, and ideas as clearly and logically as possible. Low-context communicators look for the meaning of a statement in the words spoken. By contrast, **high-context cultures** value

▼ **TABLE I**▲   LOW- AND HIGH-CONTEXT COMMUNICATION STYLES

LOW CONTEXT	HIGH CONTEXT
Majority of information carried in explicit verbal messages, with less focus on the situational context	Important information carried in contextual cues (time, place, relationship, situation); less reliance on explicit verbal messages
Self-expression valued. Communicators state opinions and desires directly and strive to persuade others to accept their own viewpoint	Relational harmony valued and maintained by indirect expression of opinions; communicators abstain from saying "no" directly
Clear, eloquent speech considered praiseworthy; verbal fluency admired	Communicators talk "around" the point, allowing the other to fill in the missing pieces; ambiguity and use of silence admired

language as a way to maintain social harmony. Rather than upset others by speaking clearly, communicators in these societies learn to discover meaning from the context in which a message is delivered: the nonverbal behaviors of the speaker, the history of the relationship, and the general social rules that govern interaction between people. Table 1 summarizes some key differences between the way low- and high-context cultures use language.

North American culture falls toward the low-context end of the scale. Residents of the United States and Canada value straight talk and grow impatient with "beating around the bush." By contrast, most Asian and Middle-Eastern cultures fit the high-context pattern. In many Asian cultures, for example, maintaining harmony is important, and so communicators will avoid speaking clearly if that would threaten another person's face. For this reason, Japanese or Koreans are less likely than Americans to offer a clear "no" to an undesirable request. Instead they would probably use roundabout expressions like "I agree with you in principle, but . . ." or "I sympathize with you. . . ."

The same sort of clash between directness and indirectness can aggravate problems between straight-talking, low-context Israelis who value speaking clearly and Arabs, whose high-context culture stresses smooth interaction. It's easy to imagine how the clash of cultural styles could lead to misunderstandings and conflicts between Israelis and their Palestinian neighbors. Israelis could view their Arab counterparts as evasive, while the Palestinians could perceive the Israelis as insensitive and blunt.

Even within a single country, subcultures can have different notions about the value of direct speech. For example, Puerto Rican language style resembles high-context Japanese or Korean more than low-context English. As a group,

LANGUAGE

Puerto Ricans value social harmony and avoid confrontation, which leads them to systematically speak in an indirect way to avoid giving offense.

Another way in which language styles can vary across cultures is whether they are *elaborate* or *succinct.* Speakers of Arabic, for instance, commonly use language that is much more rich and expressive than most communicators who use English. Strong assertions and exaggerations that would sound ridiculous in English are a common feature of Arabic. This contrast in linguistic style can lead to misunderstandings between people from different backgrounds. As one observer put it,

> First, an Arab feels compelled to overassert in almost all types of communication because others expect him [or her] to. If an Arab says exactly what he [or she] means without the expected assertion, other Arabs may still think that he [or she] means the opposite. For example, a simple "no," by a guest to the host's requests to eat more or drink more will not suffice. To convey the meaning that he [or she] is actually full, the guest must keep repeating "no" several times, coupling it with an oath such as "By God" or "I swear to God." Second, an Arab often fails to realize that others, particularly foreigners, may mean exactly what they say even though their language is simple. To the Arabs, a simple "no" may mean the indirectly expressed consent and encouragement of a coquettish woman. On the other hand, a simple consent may mean the rejection of a hypocritical politician.

Succinctness is most extreme in cultures where silence is valued. In many Native American cultures, for example, the favored way to handle ambiguous social situations is to remain quiet. When you contrast this silent style to the talkativeness that is common in mainstream American cultures when people first meet, it's easy to imagine how the first encounter between an Apache or Navajo and an Anglo might feel uncomfortable to both people.

Along with differences such as directness and indirectness and elaborate and succinct styles, a third way languages differ from one culture to another involves *formality* and *informality.* The informal approach that characterizes relationships in countries like the United States, Canada, and Australia, and the Scandinavian countries is quite different from the great concern for using proper speech in many parts of Asia and Africa. Formality isn't so much a matter of using correct grammar as of defining social position. In Korea, for example, the language reflects the Confucian system of relational hierarchies. It has special vocabularies for different sexes, for different levels of social status, for different degrees of intimacy, and for different types of social occasions. For example, there are different degrees of formality for speaking with old friends, nonacquaintances whose background one knows, and complete strangers. One sign of being a learned person in Korea is the ability to use language that recognizes these relational distinctions. When you contrast these sorts of distinctions with the casual friendliness many North Americans use even when talking with complete strangers, it's easy to see how a Korean might view communicators in the United States as boorish, and how an American might see Koreans as stiff and unfriendly.

▼LANGUAGE AND WORLD VIEW▲

Different linguistic styles are important, but there may be even more fundamental differences that separate speakers of various languages. For almost 150 years, some theorists have put forth the notion of **linguistic determinism:** that the world view of a culture is unavoidably shaped and reflected by the language its members speak. The best-known example of linguistic determinism is the notion that Eskimos have a large number of words (estimated at everything from seventeen to one hundred) for what we simply call "snow." Different terms are used to describe conditions like a driving blizzard, crusty ice, and light powder. This example suggests how linguistic determinism operates. The need to survive in an Arctic environment led Eskimos to make distinctions that would be unimportant to residents of warmer environments, and once the language makes these distinctions, speakers are more likely to see the world in ways that match the broader vocabulary.

Even though there is some doubt that Eskimos really have so many words for snow, other examples do seem to support the principle of linguistic determinism. For instance, bilingual speakers seem to think differently when they change languages. In one study, French-Americans were asked to interpret a series of pictures. When they spoke in French, their descriptions were far more romantic and emotional than when they used English to describe the same kinds of images. Likewise, when students in Hong Kong were asked to complete a values test, they expressed more traditional Chinese values when they answered in Cantonese than when they spoke English. In Israel, both Arab and Jewish students saw bigger distinctions between their group and "outsiders" when using their native language than when they spoke in English, a neutral tongue. Examples like these show the power of language to shape cultural identity . . . sometimes for better, and sometimes for worse.

Linguistic influences start early in life. English-speaking parents often label the mischievous pranks of their children as "bad," implying that there is something immoral about acting wild. "Be good!" they are inclined to say. On the other hand, French adults are more likely to say *"Sois sage!"*—"Be wise." The linguistic implication is that misbehaving is an act of foolishness. Swedes would correct the same action with the words *"Var snall!"*—"Be friendly," "Be kind." By contrast, German adults use the command *"Sei artig!"*—literally "Be of your own kind"—in other words, get back in step, conform to your role as a child.

The best-known declaration of linguistic determinism is the **Sapir–Whorf hypothesis,** formulated by Edward Sapir and Benjamin Whorf. Following Sapir's theory, Whorf observed that the language spoken by Hopi Native Americans represents a view of reality that is dramatically different from more familiar tongues. For example, the Hopi language makes no distinction between nouns and verbs. Therefore the people who speak it describe the entire world as being constantly in process. Whereas we use nouns to characterize people or objects as being fixed or constant, Hopi view them more as verbs, constantly changing. In this sense our language represents much of the world rather like a snapshot camera, whereas Hopi reflects a world view more like a motion picture.

Although there is little support for the extreme linguistically deterministic viewpoint that it is *impossible* for speakers of different languages to view the world identically, the more moderate notion of **linguistic relativism**—that language exerts a strong influence on perceptions—does seem valid. As one scholar put it, "The differences between languages are not so much in what *can* be said, but in what it is *relatively easy* to say." Some languages contain terms that have no English equivalents. For example, consider a few words in other languages that have no English equivalents:

Nemawashi (Japanese): The process of informally feeling out all the people involved with an issue before making a decision

Lagniappe (French/Creole): An extra gift given in a transaction that wasn't expected by the terms of a contract

Lao (Mandarin): A respectful term used for older people, showing their importance in the family and in society

Dharma (Sanskrit): Each person's unique, ideal path in life, and knowledge of how to find it

Koyaanisquatsi (Hopi): Nature out of balance; a way of life so crazy it calls for a new way of living

Once words like these exist and become a part of everyday life, the ideas that they represent are easier to recognize. But even without such terms, each of the concepts above is still possible to imagine. Thus, speakers of a language that includes the notion of *lao* would probably treat its older members respectfully and those who are familiar with *lagniappe* might be more generous. Despite these differences, the words aren't essential to follow these principles. Although language may shape thoughts and behavior, it doesn't dominate them absolutely.

The importance of language as a reflection of world view isn't just a matter of interest for anthropologists and linguists. The labels we use in everyday conversation both reflect and shape the way we view ourselves and others. This explains why businesses often give employees impressive titles, and why a woman's choice of the label "Ms." or "Mrs." can be a statement about her identity.

Relational titles aren't the only linguistic elements that may shape attitudes about men and women. Language reforms like avoiding "he" as a gender-neutral pronoun can lead to less discriminatory thinking. A recent study examined precisely this question. Students were corrected every time they used "he" as a generic pronoun in their writing. At the end of a semester, results showed that the corrections did reduce the use of gender-biased language. However, students did not change their mental images or their attitudes toward language reforms.

Along with **gender labeling, ethnic group labeling** can both affect and reflect the way members of an ethnic group define themselves. Over the years, labels of racial identification have gone through cycles of popularity. In North America, the first freed slaves preferred to be called *Africans*. In the late nineteenth and early twentieth centuries *colored* was the term of choice, but later

THE BILINGUAL WORLD OF THE DEAF

Larry Littleton lost his hearing at age seven after contracting spinal meningitis. He spent the next eight years relying exclusively on lip reading to understand others' speech and using his own voice to express ideas. At age fifteen he learned American Sign Language and finger spelling. Larry has worked for Southern California Edison conducting energy audits, and he volunteers his time speaking to students and community groups.

Most people don't realize that American Sign Language (ASL) is a complete language with its own vocabulary. Some of the symbols we use even have different meanings in ASL than they do in other sign languages. For example, I just came back from Australia, where the sign that we use to mean "sex" means "fun," and the one that means "socks" to us means "learn" to them. You can imagine how confused I was when an Australian used his sign language to ask me, "Are you having fun learning while you're here?" and I thought he was asking, "Are you having sex in socks while you're here?"

Being a bilingual speaker who understands both ASL and English helps me appreciate how different the two languages are. For one thing, I think ASL is a more expressive language. English speakers depend on words to get ideas across. In ASL, a lot more of the meaning comes from how you act out a sign. For example, in ASL the difference between "I'm a little sorry," "I'm sorry" and "I'm terribly sorry" come from your facial expression, your posture, and the way you gesture as you make the sign. I guess you could say that being expressive may be *useful* in spoken language, but it's *essential* in ASL.

Besides being more expressive than English, ASL is more concise. I just read about a study of one elementary-school classroom with a hearing teacher and an ASL interpreter. In one week the speaking teacher used almost eighty-six thousand words; but the interpreter only used forty-three thousand words to get across the same message to the deaf students. Maybe the interpreter missed some ideas, but I also think the difference came because sign language is so concise and expressive.

Let me show you an example. In speaking I could tell you "Sorry, I've lost my train of thought." In ASL, the whole idea gets communicated almost instantly, in one sign [he demonstrates]. Here's another example: I can make one sign [he gestures] that means the same as the seven words: "Don't worry: It's not a big deal."

ASL is good at communicating concepts, but it doesn't work as well when the message contains specific details. When people who are deaf need to get across a precise message—a phone number or somebody's name, for example, they usually fingerspell. Fingerspelling has its own set of symbols for each letter of the alphabet, and you communicate by spelling the word out one letter at a time. Fingerspelling isn't really a different language from English: it's just a different way of "writing."

I think ASL and spoken languages both have strengths. Because they're precise, spoken languages are useful when you need to get across specific details. But when you want to be expressive, I think ASL works much better. I know one ASL interpreter whose translations are beautiful: Almost everything she says comes across like poetry or music. I also think sign languages are more universal. A while ago I was traveling in Europe with a bunch of hearing people. When we got to countries where nobody could speak the local language, my signing got us through a lot of tough situations. I think that's because using sign language develops a communicator's creativity and expressiveness. The same thing happened when I was in Thailand last year. Almost nobody spoke English in the village where I lived, but I got along pretty well because I have had so much practice expressing my ideas with my face and gestures, and also because I spend so much time and energy observing how others act.

I think everybody can benefit from being bilingual, and ASL is a wonderful second language to learn. Besides developing your expressiveness, it can help you appreciate that people who are deaf have the same ideas and feelings that hearing people do.

Negro became the respectable word. Then, in the sixties, the term *Black* grew increasingly popular—first as a label for militants, and later as a term preferred by more moderate citizens of all colors. More recently *African American* has gained popularity. Recent surveys have found that between 60 and 72 percent of Blacks surveyed prefer the term *Black,* while between 15 and 25 percent prefer African American. (The rest either had no opinion or chose other labels.)

Decisions about which name to use reflect a person's attitude. For example, one recent survey revealed that individuals who prefer the label *Black* choose it because it is "acceptable" and "based on consensus" of the larger culture. They describe themselves as patriotic, accepting of the status quo, and attempting to assimilate into the larger culture. By contrast, people who choose the term *Afro-American* derive their identity from their ethnicity and do not want to assimilate into the larger culture, only succeed in it.

▼SUMMARY▲

Different languages often shape and reflect the view of a culture. Low-context cultures, like the United States, use language primarily to express feelings and ideas as clearly and unambiguously as possible. High-context cultures, such as Japan and Saudi Arabia, however, avoid specificity in order to promote social harmony. Some cultures value brevity and the succinct use of language, while others have high regard for elaborate forms of speech. In some societies, formality is important, while others value informality. Beyond these differences, there is evidence to support linguistic relativism—the notion that language exerts a strong influence on the world view of the people who speak it.

▼KEY TERMS▲

ethnic group labeling

high-context cultures

gender labeling

linguistic determinism

linguistic relativism

low-context cultures

Sapir–Whorf hypothesis

WHAT DID I LEARN FROM PREVIEWING?

Reflect for a moment on what you learned by previewing this chapter. First, the title, "Language and Culture" should have triggered many associations in your mind. For example, if you have read any of the selections in Unit 2 or Unit 3 of *The Thoughtful Reader,* try to make connections between them and the information in this textbook excerpt. The subtitles, "Verbal Communication Styles," "Language and World View," serve as an outline to the content of the chapter. The key terms the authors think you should know are written in bold-face type. Two of the key terms, low-context and high-context communication styles, are presented in a table. Finally, a summary repeats the highlights of the chapter.

Now that you have spent a few moments previewing the chapter, you are ready to read and understand the text more easily and thoroughly. Return now to the chapter and read it through.

UNDERLINING AND ANNOTATING

Now that you have previewed this chapter and read it through one time quickly, you are prepared to really study the ideas it contains. The best way to do this is to underline and annotate the chapter. These activities are essential to mastering the ideas in your textbooks. To review these skills, turn to Appendix B. Then underline and annotate the chapter. Compare your marked text with that of your classmates; discuss any differences you find. Remember, your marked text is an invaluable study tool when exam time comes along—there is no need to reread the whole chapter, you only need to review what you underlined and marked.

VOCABULARY

Note that, in this textbook chapter, the authors give you a list of the *Key Terms*—important words they think you should know and remember. Be sure to find and mark each term in the text. Mark any term you don't understand so you'll remember to ask a classmate or the instructor for an explanation. It would be a good idea to keep a special section of your notebook where you write the terms and their meanings.

EXAM QUESTIONS

Each instructor will have his or her own style of testing. Following are several examples of exam questions used by instructors who actually teach the course in which this text is used. Test your understanding of the chapter by answering these questions.

Short Essay Questions
1. Contrast low-context cultures with high-context cultures. Write two to four sentences.
2. Define and explain the concept of linguistic relativism.

3. In *The Thoughtful Reader,* read "Speaking Different Languages," on page 159. Using the information in this chapter, "Language and Culture," explain the problem the American woman had in Turkey. Write one paragraph.

Matching

Match the terms in column 1 with their definitions in column 2.

I	**2**
_____ 1. high-context cultures	a. theory of linguistic determinism in which language is determined by a culture's perceived reality
_____ 2. low-context cultures	b. cultures that avoid direct use of language, relying on the context of a message to convey meaning
_____ 3. linguistic determinism	c. the theory that a culture's world view is unavoidably shaped and reflected by the language its members speak
_____ 4. linguistic relativism	d. cultures that use language primarily to express thoughts, feelings, and ideas as clearly and logically as possible
_____ 5. Sapir–Whorf hypothesis	e. a moderate theory that argues that language exerts a strong influence on the perceptions of the people who speak it

True/False

Mark the statements below as true or false.

_____ 1. According to research, the name you use to describe your ethnic group can reflect your attitude about many aspects of life.

_____ 2. The United States would fall into the category of low-context cultures.

_____ 3. Ambiguity and vagueness are forms of language that are to be avoided at all costs.

_____ 4. A person from the United States is more likely to value direct language than is someone from Japan.

THE FAMILY

A Chapter from the Textbook
Sociology in a Changing World, 3rd ed.

William Kornblum

PREVIEWING

Your first step in studying a textbook should always be a preview of the chapter. Review previewing by reading Appendix A. The following questions will help you preview "The Family."

1. List the subtitles of the chapter "The Family."
2. Does the author use bold-face type, italics, or some other special print to indicate key terms? List a few of the key terms.
3. List the titles of any important charts, tables, or other figures the author uses in the chapter.
4. What other helpful features did you find in the text?

THE FAMILY

DEFINING THE FAMILY

The family is a central institution in all human societies, although it may take many different forms. A **family** is a group of people related by blood, marriage, or adoption. Blood relations are often called *consanguineous attachments* (from the Latin *sanguis,* "blood"). Relations between adult persons living together according to the norms of marriage or other intimate relationships are called conjugal relations. The role relations among people who consider themselves to be related in these ways are termed **kinship.**

The familiar kinship terms—*father, mother, brother, sister, grandfather, grandmother, uncle, aunt, niece, nephew, cousin*—refer to specific sets of role relations that may vary greatly from one culture to another. In many African societies, for example, "mother's brother" is someone to whom the male child becomes closer than he does to his father and from whom he receives more of his day-to-day socialization than he may from his father. Note that biological or "blood" ties are not necessarily stronger than ties of adoption. Adopted children are usually loved with the same intensity as children raised by their biological parents. And many family units in the United States and other societies include "fictive kin"—people who are so close to members of the family that they are considered kin despite the absence of blood ties. Finally, neither blood ties nor marriage nor adoption adequately describes the increasingly common relationship between unmarried people who consider themselves a couple or a family.

The smallest units of family structure are usually called **nuclear families.** This term is usually used to refer to a wife and husband and their children, if any. Nowadays one frequently hears the phrase "the traditional nuclear family" used to refer to a married mother and father and their children living together. But as we will see throughout this chapter, there is no longer a "typical" nuclear family structure. Increasingly, therefore, sociologists use the term *nuclear family* to refer to two or more people related by consanguineous or conjugal ties or by adoption who share a household; it does not require that both husband and wife be present in the household or that there be any specific set of role relations among the members of the household.

The nuclear family in which one is born and socialized is termed one's **family of orientation.** The nuclear family one forms through marriage or cohabitation is known as one's **family of procreation.** The relationship between the two is shown in the figure on the next page.

Kinship terms are often confusing because families, especially large ones, can be rather complex social structures. It may help to devote a little time to

NUCLEAR AND EXTENDED FAMILY RELATIONSHIPS

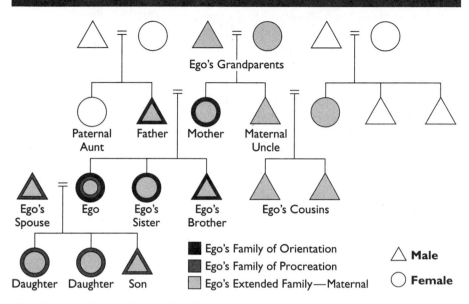

Ego's Grandparents

Paternal Aunt | Father | Mother | Maternal Uncle

Ego's Spouse | Ego | Ego's Sister | Ego's Brother | Ego's Cousins

Daughter | Daughter | Son

■ Ego's Family of Orientation
■ Ego's Family of Procreation
■ Ego's Extended Family—Maternal

△ **Male**
○ **Female**

This diagram shows the family relationships of a hypothetical individual, Ego. Ego was born and socialized into what sociologists call the family of orientation. Ego formed a family of procreation through marriage or cohabitation.

working through the figure above. "Ego" is the person who is taken as the point of reference. You can readily see that Ego has both a family of orientation and a family of procreation. So does Ego's spouse. Ego's parents become the in-laws of the spouse, and the spouse's parents are Ego's in-laws. But like the vast majority of people, Ego also has an **extended family** that includes all the nuclear families of Ego's blood relatives—that is, all of Ego's uncles, aunts, cousins, and grandparents. Ego's spouse also has an extended family, which is not indicated in the figure, nor is it defined as part of Ego's extended family. But relationships with the spouse's extended family are likely to occupy plenty of Ego's time. Indeed, as the figure shows, the marriage bond brings far more than two individuals together. Most married couples have extensive networks of kin to which they must relate in many, varied ways throughout life.

VARIATIONS IN FAMILY STRUCTURE

For the past several years sociologists have been demonstrating that the traditional household consisting of two parents and their children is no longer the typical American family. In the 1940s an American household was about eight times more likely to be headed by a married couple than by unrelated individuals. By 1980 the ratio had declined to about 2.5. Data from Donald Bogue's

FAMILY

analysis of trends in family composition reveal that the proportion of married-couple families declined from 78.2 percent of all households in 1950 to slightly less than 60 percent in 1983. In 1990 the proportion stood at 48 percent.

This trend points to a far greater diversity of family types, including far more people living alone and far more women raising children alone, than ever before. There are also more households composed of unrelated single people who live together not just because they are friends but because only by doing so can they afford to live away from their families of orientation. Thus, when they discuss family norms and roles, sociologists must be careful not to represent the traditional nuclear family, or even the married couple, as typical. These considerations become especially important when they discuss low-income and minority families.

THE CHANGING FAMILY

In his pioneering study of changes in the family, William J. Goode argued that the structure of family units becomes simpler as societies undergo industrialization. Goode was not the first social scientist to make this observation; however, his study was the first to be based on extensive historical and comparative data. After reviewing changes in family structure in Europe and North America during the preceding seventy-five years, Goode concluded that the smaller family unit composed of a married couple and their children (i.e., the conjugal family) was increasingly dominant in industrial societies. For Goode, the change from the larger extended family to the smaller and more geographically mobile nuclear family was part of an even larger worldwide revolution in which people are demanding greater control over the conditions that shape their lives.

From the standpoint of the family, this "revolution" translates into demands for freedom to select one's mate, to decide where to live after marriage, to decide whether to have children and how many to have, and even to terminate the marital relationship. Such choices were often impossible in earlier family systems, in which marriages were arranged, the married couple was expected to live within a larger extended family, and couples were expected to have numerous children.

According to Goode, the driving forces behind the large-scale changes in family structure in this century were economic and technological. The more families had to adapt to an economy in which income was earned outside the family, the more the family had to be mobile and flexible. Families must be willing to move from one place to another in search of employment. Geographic mobility, in turn, meant that children would not be able to maintain households in which their parents could live, that is, extended families consisting of "three generations under one roof." And because children no longer worked in the home or on the farm, they became less important in economic terms than they had been in earlier epochs; families therefore had fewer children.

In the three decades since Goode's study appeared, there has been a wealth of new research that has further developed the idea of a transition from extended to nuclear family systems as a result of industrialization. More recent studies often focus on issues related to defining the family, studying family history, and distinguishing between ideal and actual family patterns.

PROBLEMS OF DEFINITION   If one studies who lives in households (i.e., who lives together and eats together more or less regularly), the traditional or "Dick and Jane" family (Mom, Dad, Dick, Jane, and their dog, Spot) appears to be the most prevalent family form. However, if one also considers patterns of interaction with others, the family unit might include, say, a grandmother living in a nearby apartment with an unmarried aunt, as well as a divorced uncle in a nearby community. This approach is illustrated in a volume titled *Beyond the Nuclear Family Model* (Lenero-Otero, 1977), which compares patterns of family structure and interaction in several industrialized societies and finds a wide range of possible patterns. For example, although families may not live with "three generations under one roof," they may live in nuclear family units in close proximity to one another, a pattern that continues to sustain large extended families. Technologies like the telephone and jet travel allow family members to see one another fairly frequently when they are separated by geographic distance. And when divorce breaks apart a nuclear family and the parents remarry, the reconstituted family may be embedded in a larger set of extended-family relations that may occupy even more of the members' time. None of these patterns was predicted in the theories of Goode and others who studied the revolution in family structure.

STUDIES OF FAMILY HISTORY   Studies of family form and patterns of family interaction over time have found a good deal of evidence that challenges the conclusions of Goode's research. For example, demographer Peter Laslett found that in some parts of England the emergence of the nuclear family seems to have preceded industrialization by many decades. When people migrated to new agricultural regions, they often left behind extended kin groups and became more dependent on the smaller nuclear-family group. Laslett and other researchers have found that modern technologies like the telephone or the automobile enable members of smaller family units, who formerly might have lost touch with their extended families, to maintain their kinship ties.

Similarly, in her research on industrialization in the mill towns of Massachusetts, Tamara Hareven found evidence that extended families often sent family members whom the land could not support, especially young women, to the towns. There they might marry and form urban families, but often they returned home and married into farm families. In most cases the urban workers managed to maintain close ties with their rural kin, especially through letters and visits to friends.

In the case of the black family, research by social historian Herbert Gutman on the effects of slavery and industrialization has shown that slaves often formed extended families that included strong nuclear units. During the Reconstruction period after the Civil War, many families that had been torn apart by slavery were reunited. Toward the end of the nineteenth century, however, migration caused by the industrialization of agriculture in the South and the demand for unskilled labor in large northern cities created instability in many black families, a pattern that would become prevalent in later decades of the twentieth century. In sum, therefore, the theory that industrialization creates a single dominant family form and predictable patterns of family interaction is no longer widely accepted in the social sciences.

IDEAL VERSUS ACTUAL FAMILY PATTERNS   When politicians and government officials talk about "preserving family values," they often have in mind the traditional two-parent nuclear family. To many people this remains the ideal family form. In reality, however, as Table 1 shows, such families are less prevalent today than they were in earlier decades. Increasing numbers of families are headed by a single parent, usually the mother but sometimes the father. Moreover, two-parent families may actually be reconstituted, that is, created by remarriage after divorce or the death of a spouse. Thus what appears to be a conventional nuclear family is really a far more complicated family form with extended ties among parents and siblings in different nuclear families.

Among lower-income people these patterns are especially prevalent—so much so that some researchers have concluded that families without fathers are a direct consequence of poverty. Although they tend to share the same norms of family life as other members of society, poor people bear added burdens that make it difficult, if not impossible, for them to actually meet those norms. In particular, men in such families may not be able to provide their expected share of family income and hence may become demoralized and unable to maintain family relationships. This is especially true when teenagers father children before they are adequately prepared to take economic responsibility for them. Thus, in poor families the father often is not a central figure, and female-headed families are the dominant family form.

Contemporary social–scientific research on family structure and interaction increasingly focuses on issues like those just described. At the same time, there

TABLE 1   FAMILY COMPOSITION IN THE UNITED STATES, 1970–2000

Type of Family	1970	1990	1995	2000
All families (in millions)	51.2	64.5	68.0	71.7
Total	100.0%	100.0%	100.0%	100.0%
Married couple with children	49.6	36.9	36.2	34.5
Married couple without children	37.1	41.7	41.8	42.8
Female head with children	5.7	10.2	10.0	9.7
Male head with children	0.7	1.8	2.2	2.7
Other families	6.9	9.4	9.8	10.3

Source: Ahlburg and DeVita, 1992.

is growing recognition that the actual form the family takes may vary greatly at different stages of the life course. For example, as the proportion of elderly people in the population increases, more families must decide whether to care for an aging parent at home. Let us therefore take a closer look at how families change throughout the "family life cycle."

THE FAMILY LIFE CYCLE

Sociologist Paul Glick, an innovator in the field of family demography and ecology, first developed the concept of the *family life cycle,* the idea that families pass through a sequence of five stages:

- Family formation: first marriage
- Start of childbearing: birth of first child
- End of childbearing: birth of last child
- "Empty nest": marriage of last child
- "Family dissolution": death of one spouse

These are "typical" stages in the life cycle of conventional families. Although there are other stages that could be identified within each of these—such as retirement (the years between the time of retirement and the death of one spouse) or the "baby stage" (during which the couple is rearing preschool-age children)—the ones that Glick listed are most useful for comparative purposes.

As the "typical" family structure becomes ever more difficult to identify owing to changes in family norms, the stages of family development also vary. In fact, the stages of the family life cycle have become increasingly useful as indicators of change rather than as stages that all or most families can be expected to experience. The Census Bureau estimates, for example, that there are at least three million heterosexual couples in the United States who are cohabiting. This number represents a sixfold increase since 1970, when an estimated 500,000 cohabiting couples were counted. (Note also that the census figures include only heterosexual couples and therefore vastly underestimate the total number of cohabiting couples.) Although the majority of cohabiting couples will eventually marry, many others will break up or continue to live together without marrying. Fifty-five percent of white women and 42 percent of black women in their first cohabiting union will marry their male partner.

When sociologists look at the median age at which people experience the various stages of the family life cycle, significant trends emerge. Consider age at first marriage. In 1890 the median age of Americans at first marriage was 26.1 years for men and 22 years for women; by 1965 it had reached the historic low of 22.8 and 20.6. Then it began rising again slowly, until by 1986 it was 25.5 for men and 23.3 for women, approaching the pattern of a century ago (see Table 2). Age at first marriage tends to be somewhat higher for males than for females and is associated with educational attainment; more highly educated people are more likely to delay marriage. There is also a tendency for members of minority

FAMILY

TABLE 2   ESTIMATED MEDIAN AGE AT FIRST MARRIAGE: UNITED STATES, 1890–1985

| | Median age at first marriage | |
Year	Men	Women
1890	26.1	22.0
1900	25.9	21.9
1910	25.1	21.6
1920	24.6	21.2
1930	24.3	21.3
1940	24.3	21.5
1950	22.8	20.3
1960	22.8	20.3
1970	23.6	21.8
1980	24.7	22.0
1990	26.3	24.1

Source: Census Bureau, 1992.

groups to marry later, owing to the proportionately lower income levels of these populations. People with lower incomes tend to delay marriage or not to marry because they lack the material means to sustain a marital relationship.

As it passes through the family life cycle, every family experiences changes in its system of role relations. In analyzing these changes, social scientists often modify Glick's stages so as to focus more sharply on interactions within the family. An example is the set of "developmental" stages shown in Table 3. There are major emotional challenges at each of these stages. For example, families with adolescent children must adapt to the children's growing independence. This may involve going through a stage of negotiation over such issues as money, cars, and dating. But researchers who study family life note that parents are often confused about how to interact with their adolescent children. They may assume that it is normal for adolescents to leave the family circle and to become enmeshed in their own peer groups, which often get into trouble. However, as Carol Gilligan has pointed out, adolescents also want the continuing guidance and involvement of adults.

Earlier research by Erikson and Bettelheim also found that too much emphasis on adolescence as a time of separation from the family can be a form of social cop-out in which adults fail to provide meaningful goals and activities for adolescents. Many social scientists feel that adolescence is a time for building interdependence as well as independence. By this they mean that adolescents need to become involved in prosocial interactions such as assistance in caring for elderly or younger family members, or involvement in community agencies or social movements.

TABLE 3 Stages of the Family Life Cycle

Stage	Emotional process	Required changes in family status
1. Between families: The unattached young adult	Accepting parent–offspring separation	a. Differentiation of self in relation to family of origin b. Development of intimate peer relationships c. Establishment of self in work
2. The joining of families through marriage: The newly married couple	Commitment to new system	a. Formation of marital system b. Realignment of relationships with extended families and friends to include spouse
3. The family with young children	Accepting new generation of members into the system	a. Adjusting marital system to make space for child(ren) b. Taking on parenting roles c. Realignment of relationships with extended family to include parenting and grandparenting roles
4. The family with adolescents	Increasing flexibility of family boundaries to include children's independence	a. Shifting of parent–child relationships to permit adolescents to move in and out of system b. Refocus on midlife marital and career issues c. Beginning shift toward concerns for older generation
5. Launching children and moving on	Accepting a multitude of exits from and entries into the family system	a. Renegotiation of marital system as a dyad b. Development of adult-to-adult relationships between grown children and their parents c. Realignment of relationships to include in-laws and grandchildren d. Dealing with disabilities and death of parents (grandparents)
6. The family in later life	Accepting the shifting of generational roles	a. Maintaining own and/or couple functioning and interests in face of physiological decline; exploration of new familial and social role options b. Support for a more central role for middle generation c. Making room in the system for the wisdom and experience of the elderly; supporting the older generation without overfunctioning for them d. Dealing with loss of spouse, siblings, and other peers, and preparation for own death. Life review and integration

Source: McGoldrick and Carter, 1982.

The severe economic recession of the early 1990s had a major impact on the transition from dependence to independence for many young American adults. The Population Reference Bureau reports that "compared with the 1970s, more young adults (ages eighteen to twenty-four) are living at home with their parents. . . . Over half (54 percent) of all eighteen–twenty-four year olds lived with their parents in 1991." This trend will change as the economy improves, but many young adults will continue to live with their family of orientation and be frustrated in their desire to become independent and form their own families.

In later stages of family life the parents must be willing to watch their grown children take on the challenges of family formation while they themselves worry about maintaining their marital roles or caring for their own parents. The latter issue is taking on increasing importance in aging societies like the United States. And since women are still expected to be more nurturing and emotionally caring than men, it often falls to women to worry about the question of "where can Mom live?" According to Elaine Brody, a leading researcher on this issue, "It's going to be primarily women for a long time. Women can go to work as much as they want, but they still see nurturing as their job." Moreover, "with many more very old people, and fewer children per family, almost every woman is going to have to take care of an aging parent or parent-in-law."

As if these stages were not stressful enough, consider the complications resulting from divorce, remarriage, and the combining of children of different marriages in a new family. It is increasingly common, for example, for teenagers and young adults to have parents who are dating and marrying, and for children to have four parental figures in their lives instead of two. These more complex family systems also pass through the stages of the family life cycle. On television, a wholesome family like the "Brady Bunch" accomplishes this with modest resources and lots of love. In reality, however, such families may experience severe stress. Children in such families often learn to maintain a cheerful demeanor so that adults will not worry about them, but inside they generally experience far more emotional turmoil than children who have not been through the experience of family breakup. The difficulties such children experience—for example, in trying to feel at home in more than one place and having to carry their belongings back and forth—are only now beginning to be understood.

The difficulties faced by children in "intact" as well as troubled families raise the age-old questions of how people decide whom to marry and what makes marriages last. Couples normally do not think they will split up when they marry, nor can they understand the emotional and social consequences of divorce before they have children, but the more people understand some of the reasons for selecting particular individuals as mates and the reasons that some relationships are more lasting than others, the more insight they gain into their own relationships. In the next section, therefore, we examine the sociology of mate selection and marriage.

In the animal kingdom, mating involves only the two partners. For man-kind, it is the joining of two enormously complex systems. We may think of mate selection and marriage as matters that affect only the partners themselves, but in reality the concerns of parents and other family members are never very far from either person's consciousness. And, as we will see shortly, the values of each partner's extended family often have a significant impact on the mate-selection process.

MARRIAGE AS EXCHANGE People in Western cultures like to think that interpersonal attraction and love are the primary factors in explaining why a couple forms a "serious" relationship and eventually marries. But while attraction and love are clearly important factors in many marriages, social scientists point out that in all cultures the process of mate selection is carried out according to basic rules of bargaining and exchange. Sociologists and economists who study mate selection and marriage from this exchange perspective ask who controls the marriage contract, what values each family is attempting to maximize in the contract, and how the exchange process is shaped by the society's stratification system.

Among the upper classes of China and Japan before the twentieth century, marriage transactions were controlled by the male elders of the community—with the older women often making the real decisions behind the scenes. In many societies in the Middle East, Asia, and preindustrial Europe, the man's family negotiated a "bride price" with the woman's family. This price usually consisted of valuable goods like jewelry and clothes, but in some cultures it took the form of land and cattle. Throughout much of Hindu India, in contrast, an upper-class bride's family paid a "groom price" to the man's family. Although such norms appear to be weakening throughout the world, "arranged marriages" remain the customary pattern of mate selection in many societies. The following account describes factors that are often considered in arranging a marriage in modern India:

> Every Sunday one can peruse the wedding ads in the classifieds. Many people still arrange an alliance in the traditional manner—through family and friend connections. Caste is becoming less important a factor in the selection of a spouse. Replacing caste are income and type of job. The educational level of the bride-to-be is also a consideration, an asset always worth mentioning in the ad. A faculty member at a college for girls has estimated that 80 to 90 percent of the students there will enter an arranged marriage upon receiving the B.A. Perhaps 10 percent will continue their studies. In this way, educating a daughter is parental investment toward securing an attractive, prosperous groom.

In all of these transactions the families base their bargaining on considerations of family prestige within the community, the wealth of the two families and their ability to afford or command a given price, the beauty of the bride and the attractiveness of the groom, and so on. Different cultures may evaluate these qualities differently, but in each case the parties involved think of the coming marriage as an exchange between the two families. But do not get the idea that only selfish motives are involved in such marriages. Both families are also committing themselves to a long-standing relationship because they are exchanging their most precious products, their beloved young people. Naturally, they want the best for their children (as this is defined in their culture), and they also want a climate of mutual respect and cooperation in their future interfamily relationships.

NORMS OF MATE SELECTION

ENDOGAMY/EXOGAMY   All cultures have norms that specify whether a person brought up in that culture may marry within or outside the cultural group. Marriage within the group is termed **endogamy;** marriage outside the group is termed **exogamy.** In the United States, ethnic and religious groups normally put pressure on their members to remain endogamous—that is, to choose mates from their own group. These rules tend to be especially strong for women. Among Orthodox Jews, for example, an infant is considered to have been born into the religion only if the mother is Jewish. Children of mixed marriages in which the mother is not Jewish are not considered Jewish by birth. The conflict between Orthodox and Reformed Jews over the status of children born to non-Jewish mothers who have converted to Judaism is an example of conflict over endogamy/exogamy norms. Many African tribes have developed norms of exogamy that encourage young men to find brides in specific villages outside the village of their birth. Such marriage systems tend to promote strong bonds of kinship among villages and serve to strengthen the social cohesion of the tribe while breaking down the animosity that sometimes arises between villages within a tribe.

HOMOGAMY   Another norm of mate selection is **homogamy,** or the tendency to marry a person from a similar social background. The parents of a young woman from a wealthy family, for example, attempt to increase the chances that she will associate with young men of the same or higher social-class standing. She is encouraged to date boys from "good" families. After graduating from high school she will be sent to an elite college or university, where the pool of eligible men is likely to include many who share her social-class background. She may surprise her parents, however, and fall in love with someone whose social-class, religious, or ethnic background is considerably different from hers. But when this happens she will invariably have based her choice on other values that are considered important in the dating and marriage market, values like outstanding talent, good looks, popularity, or sense of humor. She will argue that these values outweigh social class, especially if it seems apparent that the young man will gain upward mobility through his career. Often the couple will marry and not worry about his lower social-class background. On the other hand, the untalented, homely, poor man may aspire to a bride with highly desirable qualities, but he cannot offer enough to induce either her or her family to choose him, for they can find a groom with more highly valued qualities.

Numerous sociologists have studied the phenomenon of homogamy. In a post-World War II study entitled *Elmtown's Youth,* for example, August

Hollingshead found that 61 percent of the adolescents in a small midwestern city dated within their social class and 35 percent dated members of adjacent classes. In two out of three cases in which a boy crossed class lines, he dated a girl from a lower social-class background. And in two out of three cases in which a girl crossed class lines, she went out with a boy from a higher social class. Those who dated members of a higher class were found to have special qualities in terms of looks, popularity, leadership skills, or athletic ability. Many other studies of dating and mate selection have demonstrated the same patterns of social-class homogamy and the same kinds of departures from that norm. It is reasonable to conclude, therefore, that cultural norms that stress homogamy in dating and marriage also tend to reproduce the society's system of social-class stratification in the next generation.

Homogamy in mate selection generally serves to maintain the separateness of religious groups. Because the Census Bureau does not collect systematic data on religious preferences, it is extremely difficult to obtain accurate data on religious intermarriage. Yet sociologists and religious leaders agree that, although parents continue to encourage their children to marry within their religion, there is a trend away from religious homogamy, particularly for Protestants and Catholics.

The norm of homogamy also applies to interracial marriage. Before 1967, when the United States Supreme Court struck them down as unconstitutional, many states had laws prohibiting such marriages. After that decision, marriages between blacks and whites increased by about 26 percent, from about 51,000 in 1960 to about 65,000 in 1970, and their number continues to increase. Yet as a proportion of all marriages, black–white marriages remain only 4 percent of the total and are less common than other types of interracial marriages. Thus the norm of racial homogamy remains relatively strong in the United States.

ROMANTIC LOVE

Although exchange criteria and homogamy continue to play a significant role in mate selection, for the past century romantic attraction and love have been growing in importance in North American and other Western cultures. Indeed, the conflict between romantic love and the parental requirement of homogamy is one of the great themes of Western civilization. "Let me not to the marriage of true minds / Admit impediments," wrote Shakespeare in a famous sonnet. The "star-crossed lovers" from feuding families in *Romeo and Juliet,* and the lovers who have forsaken family fortunes to be together in innumerable stories and plays written since Shakespeare's time, attest to the strong value we place on romantic love as an aspect of intimate relationships between men and women.

In his review of worldwide marriage and family patterns, William J. Goode found that compared with the mate-selection systems of other cultures, that of the United States "has given love greater prominence. Here, as in all Western societies to some lesser degree, the child is socialized to fall in love." Yet although it may be taken for granted that people will form couples on the basis of romantic attachment, important changes in the structure of Western societies had to occur before love as we know it could become such an important value in our lives. In particular, changes in economic institutions as a result of industrialization required workers with more education and greater maturity. These changes, in turn, lengthened the period of socialization, especially in educational institutions. This made it possible for single men and women to remain unattached long enough to gain the emotional maturity they needed if they were to experience love and make more independent decisions in selecting their mates.

However familiar it may seem to us, love remains a mysterious aspect of human relationships. We do not know very much—from a verifiable, scientific standpoint—about this complex emotional state. We do not know fully what it means to "fall in love" or what couples can do to make their love last. But two promising avenues of research on this subject can be found in Winch's theory of complementarity and Blau's theory of emotional reciprocity.

COMPLEMENTARY NEEDS AND MUTUAL ATTRACTION Robert F. Winch's theory of complementary needs, based on work by the psychologist Henry A. Murray, holds that people who fall in love tend to be alike in social characteristics such as family prestige, education, and income but different in their psychological needs. Thus, according to Winch, an outgoing person often falls in love with a quiet, shy person. The one gains an appreciative audience, the other an entertaining spokesperson. A person who needs direction is attracted to one who needs to exercise authority; one who is nurturant is attracted to one who needs nurturance; and so on.

Winch and others have found evidence to support this theory, but there are some problems with this research. It is difficult to measure personal needs and the extent to which they are satisfied. Moreover, people also show a variety of patterns in their choices of mates. Some people, in fact, seem to be attracted to each other because of their similarities in looks and behavior rather than because of their differences.

ATTRACTION AND EMOTIONAL RECIPROCITY Blau's theory of emotional reciprocity as a source of love is based on his general theory that relationships usually flourish when people feel satisfied with the exchanges between them. When people feel that they are loved, they are more likely to give love in return. When they feel that they love too much or are not loved enough, they will eventually come to feel exploited or trapped and will seek to end the relationship. In research on 231 dating couples, Zick Rubin found that among those who felt this equality of love, 77 percent were still together two years later, but only 45 percent of the unequally involved couples were still seeing each other. As Blau explained it, "Only when two lovers' affection for and commitment to one another expand at roughly the same pace do they mutually tend to reinforce their love."

Blau's exchange approach confirms some popular notions about love—particularly the ideas that we can love someone who loves us and that inequalities in love can lead to separation. And yet we still know little about the complexities of this emotion and how it translates into the formation of the most basic of all social groups, the married couple. This is ironic, because books, movies, and popular songs probably pay more attention to love than to just about any other subject.

Francesca M. Cancian, a leading researcher on love in a changing society, notes that a price of the high value men and women place on individuality is "a weakening of close relationships." As people spend time enhancing their own lives they may become more self-centered and feel less responsible for providing love and nurturance. Cancian's research on loving relations among couples of all kinds has convinced her that people are increasingly seeking a form of love that "combines enduring love with self-development." She regards this kind of relationship as based on "interdependencies" in which each member of the couple attempts to assist the other in realizing his or her potential and at the same time seeks to strengthen the bond between them. But she finds that, in order to foster a loving interdependent relationship, couples often need to sacrifice a certain amount of independence and career advancement—not a simple matter in a culture that places a high value on individual achievement.

The nature of loving relationships is likely to be a subject of highly creative sociological research in coming years. Since capacity to love and be loved depends on individual characteristics as well as on social conditions, much of the research in this area will be done by social psychologists (see Box 1 on page 366).

MARRIAGE AND DIVORCE   More than any other ritual signifying a major change in status, a wedding is a joyous occasion. Two people are legally and symbolically joined before their kin and friends. It is expected that their honeymoon will be pleasant and that they will live happily ever after. But 20 percent of first marriages end in annulment or divorce within the first three years. Of course, divorce can occur at any time in the family life cycle, but the early years of family formation are the most difficult for the couple because each partner experiences new stresses that arise from the need to adjust to a complex set of new relationships. As Monica McGoldrick and Elizabeth A. Carter point out, "Marriage requires that a couple renegotiate a myriad of personal issues that they have previously defined for themselves or that were defined by their parents, from when to sleep, have sex, or fight, to how to celebrate holidays, and where and how to live, work, and spend vacations." For people who were married before, these negotiations can involve former spouses and shared children, resulting in added stress for the new couple.

In the United States and other Western societies, the rate of divorce rose sharply after World War II, accelerated even more dramatically during the 1960s and 1970s, and has decreased only slightly since then (see Table 4). These statistics often lead sociologists to proclaim that there is an "epidemic of divorce" in the United States. But demographer Donald Bogue has concluded that "the divorce epidemic is not being created by today's younger generation. It has been created by today's population aged thirty or more, who married in the 1960s and before." This generation was noted for its search for self-realization, often at the expense of intimate family relationships. It is not yet clear whether subsequent generations, who appear to be somewhat more pragmatic, will continue this trend. If they do, we can expect high divorce rates to continue.

BOX I   LOVE OF A LIFETIME?

USING THE SOCIOLOGICAL IMAGINATION

It takes a lot of imagination to sustain love. Insight into both oneself and one's mate is vital, but so is a sociological imagination. It is not hard to know how social conditions affect a person's feelings in the long and short term, but it is surprising how few people develop the capacity to see the world the way those close to them see it. When caught up in the early passion of love this may not be a problem. But as the relationship de-velops they need as much imagination and understand-ing as possible. An awareness of the various dimensions of intimate love may help.

COMMITMENT

Level

Time

Social psychologists who study love in married and unmarried couples are finding new evidence that con-firms what many people have long known intuitively: It is in fact quite difficult for couples to maintain the level of passion they experienced in the early stages of their marriage. "People don't know what they are in for when they fall in love," asserts Yale's Robert Sternberg. "The divorce rate is so high, not because people make foolish choices, but because they are drawn together for reasons that matter less as time goes on."

Sternberg believes that love has three components: intimacy, passion, and commitment. The first is a shared sense that the couple can reveal their innermost feelings to each other even as those feelings change. Passion is largely a matter of physical attraction and sexuality. Commitment is a shared sense that each member of the couple is permanently devoted to the other. Research shows that the fullest love demands all three of these qualities, but that over a long relationship passion is the first to fade; intimacy develops slowly and steadily as a result of shared experiences and values; and com-mitment develops more gradually still (see graphs).

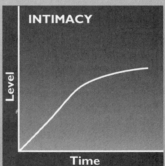

INTIMACY

Level

Time

In the early stages of a love relationship, the couple may become so caught up in their passion that they do not help each other develop as autonomous individuals. This can produce serious problems in later stages of the relationship. At the same time, commitment alone can-not substitute for the other two qualities of love. "You have to work constantly at rejuvenating a relationship," Sternberg explains, "You can't just count on its being

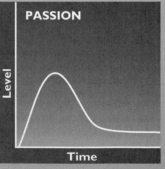

PASSION

Level

Time

OK, or it will tend toward a hollow commitment, devoid of passion and intimacy. People need to put the kind of energy into it that they put into their children or ca-reer." Studies by Sternberg and many others find that children who have been deprived of parental love, especially by the parent of the opposite sex, often have trouble devel-oping commitment and sharing intimacy. Often they avoid feeling vulnerable and de-pendent on another person by avoiding strong emotional ties altogether.

TABLE 4 DIVORCE RATES FOR SELECTED COUNTRIES, 1960–1988				
	Divorces per 1,000 married women			
Country	1960	1970	1980	1988
United States	9.2	14.9	22.6	20.7
Canada	1.8	6.3	10.8	12.6
France	2.9	3.3	6.3	8.4
Germany (western)	3.6	5.1	6.1	8.8
Japan	3.6	3.9	4.8	4.9
Sweden	5.0	6.8	11.4	11.4
United Kingdom	2.0	4.7	12.0	12.3

Source: *Statistical Abstract,* 1991.

Most states in the United States now have some form of no-fault divorce that reduces the stigma of divorce by making moral issues like infidelity less relevant than issues of child custody and division of property. While the growing acceptance of divorce helps account for why divorce rates are so much higher in the United States than in other nations with highly educated populations, Americans today also place a higher value on successful marriage than their parents may have. This means that they often divorce in the expectation of forming another, more satisfying and mutually sustaining relationship.

TRIAL MARRIAGE   In the 1980s it was widely believed that the practice of "trial marriage," or cohabitation before marriage, would result in greater marital stability: Couples who lived together before marriage would gain greater mutual understanding and a realistic view of marital commitment, and this would result in a lower divorce rate among such couples after they actually married. However, as the 1990s approached, it became evident that these expectations were unfounded; in fact, the divorce rate among couples who had lived together before marriage was actually higher than the rate for couples who had not done so. Within ten years of the wedding, 38 percent of those who had lived together before marriage had divorced, compared to 27 percent of those who had married without cohabiting beforehand.

On the basis of an analysis of data from a federal government survey of over 13,000 individuals, Larry Bumpass and James Sweet concluded that couples who cohabit before marriage are generally more willing to accept divorce as a solution to marital problems. They also found that such couples are less likely to be subject to family pressure to continue a marriage that is unhappy or unsatisfactory. In addition, cohabitation has become a predictable part of the family life cycle, not only before marriage but in the interval between divorce and remarriage. Among individuals who remarried between 1980 and 1987, 60 percent lived with a person of the opposite sex beforehand.

FAMILY

Summary

THINK ABOUT IT CRITICALLY

During the 1992 presidential election campaign family policies and "family values" were used as "wedge issues" to create divisions in the electorate. These issues were raised by some candidates to suggest that people in single-parent or gay families are deviant or otherwise threatening to the nation's values. From what you have learned in this chapter, why did the appeal to "family values" seem to fail so badly?

A *family* is a group of people related by blood, marriage, or adoption, and the role relations among family members are known as *kinship* relations. The smallest unit of family structure is the *nuclear family,* consisting of two or more people, related by consanguineous ties or by adoption, who share a household. The nuclear family in which one is born and socialized is one's *family of orientation,* and the nuclear family one forms through marriage or cohabitation is one's *family of procreation.* An *extended family* includes an individual's nuclear family plus all the nuclear families of his or her blood relatives.

The traditional household consisting of two parents and their children is no longer the typical American family. Since the 1940s there has been a dramatic increase in female-headed single-parent families and in nonfamily households, as well as in the numbers of women and men living alone and in the numbers of unmarried same-sex couples.

Studies of changes in family structure have shown that family units become simpler as societies undergo industrialization. Economic and technological changes require the family to adapt to an economy in which income is earned outside the family; this means that families must become smaller, more mobile, and more flexible. More recent research has found that nuclear families have not entirely replaced extended families, although extended families do not always live under one roof. Modern technologies like the telephone and the automobile enable members of smaller family units to maintain kinship ties with their extended families.

The typical stages of the family life cycle are family formation, start of childbearing, end of childbearing, "empty nest," and family dissolution (i.e., the death of one spouse). As it passes through this cycle, every family experiences changes in its system of role relations. These changes present major emotional challenges, which are often complicated by divorce, remarriage, and the combining of children of different marriages in a single family.

In all cultures the process of mate selection is carried out according to basic rules of bargaining and exchange. In many societies the customary pattern of mate selection is the "arranged" marriage, in which the families of the bride and groom negotiate the marriage contract. All cultures also have norms that specify whether a person brought up in that culture may marry within or outside the cultural group. Marriage within the group is termed *endogamy;* marriage outside the group is termed *exogamy.* In societies in which marriages are based on attraction and love, individuals tend to marry people similar to themselves in social background, a tendency that is referred to as *homogamy.* Homogamy generally serves to reproduce the society's system of social-class stratification in the next generation and to maintain the separateness of religious and racial groups.

Compared with the mate selection systems of other cultures, that of the United States gives love greater prominence. Yet, from a scientific standpoint, little is known about this complex emotional state. It appears that people who fall in love tend to be alike in social characteristics but different in their psychological needs; however, this is not always the case. There is also considerable evidence that love relationships are more lasting when the partners' affection for each other is roughly equal.

In the United States and other Western societies, the rate of divorce has risen sharply since World War II. In the 1980s it was widely believed that the practice of cohabitation before marriage would result in greater marital stability, but in fact the divorce rate among couples who had lived together before marriage was actually higher than the rate for couples who had not done so.

Glossary

ENDOGAMY   a norm specifying that a person brought up in a particular culture may marry within the cultural group

EXOGAMY   a norm specifying that a person brought up in a particular culture may marry outside the cultural group

EXTENDED FAMILY   an individual's nuclear family plus the nuclear families of his or her blood relatives

FAMILY   a group of people related by blood, marriage, or adoption

FAMILY OF ORIENTATION   the nuclear family in which a person is born and raised

FAMILY OF PROCREATION   the nuclear family a person forms through marriage or cohabitation

HOMOGAMY   the tendency to marry a person who is similar to oneself in social background

KINSHIP   the role relations among people who consider themselves to be related by blood, marriage, or adoption

NUCLEAR FAMILY   two or more people related by blood, marriage, or adoption who share a household

FAMILY

WHAT DID I LEARN FROM PREVIEWING?

Now reflect for a moment on what you learned by previewing this chapter. For example, the title, "The Family," certainly brought to your mind many associations. All of the examples of family types, structures, and cycles are quite familiar to us. Our task, then, is to learn and apply the technical terms of sociology to the real-life situations we already know. Only by doing this can we make and understand statements and predictions about the family in general. Subtitles such as "Defining the Family," and "The Family Life Cycle" gave you a good idea as to the content of the chapter. The key terms the author thinks you should know are written in bold-face type. Many of the key terms are elaborated in tables. A summary paraphrases the highlights of the chapter. The key terms are repeated for you in a glossary at the end of the chapter.

Now that you have previewed the text, return to the chapter and give it your first reading.

UNDERLINING AND ANNOTATING

Previewing and reading the chapter through one time have prepared you to really study the important ideas it contains. The best way to master the information in a textbook is to underline and annotate the chapters. To review these skills, turn to Appendix B. Then underline and annotate this chapter, "The Family." Be sure to discuss and compare your annotated chapter with those of your classmates. Discuss any differences you may have. If you were to take a real exam on this material, you could study simply by reviewing what you marked in the text.

VOCABULARY

In this textbook, the author indicates the key terms—important words he thinks you should know and remember—both by using bold-face type in the text itself and in a glossary at the end of the chapter. Be sure to find and mark each term in the text. Remember to mark any term you don't understand so you'll remember to ask a classmate or the instructor for an explanation. It is also a good idea to keep a special section of your notebook where you write the terms and their meanings.

EXAM QUESTIONS

Test your understanding of the many ideas in this chapter by answering the questions that follow. This chapter, "The Family," was taken from a textbook that is used in introduction to sociology courses. These exam questions are the actual ones given by instructors who teach the course.

SHORT ESSAY QUESTIONS

1. Distinguish between the family of orientation and the family of procreation.
2. List the stages of the family life cycle as developed by Glick.

3. Explain the exchange factor in mate selection.
4. Explain the relationship between endogamy and homogamy.

Multiple Choice Questions

Directions: Choose the letter of the best answer for each question.

_____ 1. The network of role relations among people who consider themselves to be related by blood, marriage, or adoption is referred to as

   a. consanguinity.
   b. family.
   c. kinship.
   d. siblings.

_____ 2. Fictive kin are

   a. blood relatives within the nuclear family.
   b. people who are considered to be kin despite the lack of blood ties.
   c. people who become relatives as a result of adoption.
   d. relatives that one acquires through marriage.

_____ 3. Two or more people related by blood, marriage, or adoption who share a household are

   a. a conjoint family.
   b. a conjugal family.
   c. an extended family.
   d. a nuclear family.

_____ 4. The nuclear family in which one is born and socialized is one's family of

   a. indoctrination.
   b. initiation.
   c. orientation.
   d. procreation.

_____ 5. The nuclear family that one forms through marriage or cohabitation is one's family of

   a. indoctrination.
   b. initiation.
   c. orientation.
   d. procreation.

_____ 6. The practice of marrying someone from one's own cultural group is termed

   a. endogamy.
   b. exogamy.
   c. monogamy.
   d. polygamy.

FAMILY

_____ 7. Mark and Katherine are very much in love and plan to marry. He is the son of devout Presbyterians; Katherine is the daughter of practicing Catholics. In sociological terms, their marriage would be

    a. ambiguous.
    b. endogamous.
    c. exogamous.
    d. homogamous.

_____ 8. In recent years the median age of Americans at first marriage has

    a. decreased.
    b. fallen dramatically.
    c. remained the same.
    d. risen slowly.

_____ 9. Which of the following statements about marriage is _always_ true?

    a. Interpersonal attraction and love are the primary factors in explaining why people marry.
    b. Marriage affects only the partners themselves.
    c. Marriage is primarily an economic relationship.
    d. Mate selection is carried out according to basic rules of bargaining and exchange.

_____ 10. The tendency to marry a person similar to oneself is termed

    a. heterogamy.
    b. hexogamy.
    c. homogamy.
    d. hyperogamy.

_____ 11. Which of the following theories argues that people who fall in love tend to be alike in social characteristics, like family prestige, education, and income but different in their psychological needs?

    a. complementary needs
    b. emotional reciprocity
    c. mutual attraction
    d. social determinism

_____ 12. What proportion of all first marriages end in annulment or divorce within the first three years?

    a. 20 percent
    b. 40 percent
    c. 50 percent
    d. 75 percent

THE HUMAN RESOURCE

A Chapter from the Textbook *Business*

Louis E. Boone and David L. Kurtz

Remember, your first step in studying a textbook chapter should always be to preview. Be sure to review Appendix A, "Previewing," if you need to. The questions and suggestions below will enhance what you learn from the usual previewing steps.

1. Note the many helpful features in this chapter, beginning with a short case study highlighting a human resource problem and its solution. Case studies like this stimulate our interest and show us real-life applications of the concepts discussed in the chapter.
2. To continue previewing, list the subheadings of the chapter.
3. a. In addition to the real-life story that begins the chapter, the authors include many other interesting and helpful features. List a few of them.
   b. Does the chapter include any tables, charts, or graphs? What do they contain?
4. How do the authors indicate the words or terms they feel are important?

THE HUMAN RESOURCE

LEARNING GOALS

1. Explain the importance of human resource management and the responsibilities of a human resource department.

2. List the different needs in Maslow's hierarchy.

3. Distinguish among Theory X, Theory Y, and Theory Z managers.

4. Explain how recruitment, selection, orientation, training, and evaluation contribute to placing the right person in a job.

5. Explain the concept of job enrichment and how it can be used to motivate employees.

6. Outline the different forms of compensation.

INTRODUCTION

EMPLOYEE LAYOFFS can be devastating to employee morale, but management may face a "cut costs or else" ultimatum if the survival of the firm is at stake. Cost-cutting efforts have cost hundreds of thousands of jobs this decade in large corporations and small businesses alike. A few firms, however, have found a way for their workers—who might otherwise have been laid off—to continue drawing a paycheck.

Take the case of Rhino Foods, a $5 million specialty-dessert maker based in Burlington, Vermont. When President Ted Castle faced the unpleasant prospect of a temporary layoff recently, he asked his fifty-five employees to think of solutions to the staffing overcapacity. A series of brainstorming sessions produced an idea that might save twenty-six workers from unemployment: an employee-exchange program with other distributors and producers in the region.

Rhino's human resource director, Marlene Dailey, was given the task of identifying possible clients and determining their needs. Ben & Jerry's Ice Cream, Rhino's biggest customer, was one of the first to take on workers—and that's how bakers became order-takers in Ben & Jerry's food-production division.

Since the hiring companies were also Rhino customers, management made it clear to the twenty-six employees who volunteered to enter the exchange program that they had to perform their new assignments with the same commitment to excellence they had displayed at Rhino. Although Rhino would be consulted in any disciplinary decisions, the contracting firms had authority over these employees. As one worker in the program explained, "If we get fired there, we get fired here."

At the beginning, contract lengths were kept short. For example, assignments at Gardener's Supply were limited to three weeks. However, the arrangement worked so well that Gardener's Supply management asked that the contract be extended. Rhino workers earned the same wage as other employees doing the same job. If the contract wage rate was lower than the worker's previous pay, Rhino made up the difference.

Contract workers continued to receive health and dental insurance coverage from Rhino in addition to benefits required by law, such as worker's compensation. A key factor in the program's success was keeping communications open between Rhino and its contract employees. Often these workers later rejoined Rhino with quality-improvement ideas. On completing a job at Ben & Jerry's, one worker suggested rotating breaks on the production line.

Rhino's employee exchange program is a win–win situation for the community, the employer, and workers alike. The company was able to reduce its work force temporarily and also avoid losing its well-trained employees. For their part, contract workers frequently learn new skills and remain loyal to the company since they still are employed. President Castle also was able to demonstrate his firm's principles in a tangible way: "The company's relationship with its employees is founded upon mutual trust and respect within an environment for listening and personal attention." This innovative program earned Rhino the 1994 Blue Chip Enterprise Award from the U.S. Chamber of Commerce.

CHAPTER OVERVIEW

The importance of people to the success of any organization is stressed in the very definition of *management:* the use of people and other resources in accomplishing organizational objectives. This chapter addresses the critical issue of human resource management. We will examine the way an organization recruits, trains, and motivates people. We also will discuss employee training, development, and counseling, and will consider issues in labor–management relations. Finally, we will take a look at human resource concerns of the next century, including the opportunities and challenges in managing older workers, two-career couples, part-time employees, and an increasingly diverse work force.

HUMAN RESOURCE MANAGEMENT: A VITAL MANAGERIAL FUNCTION

In this chapter we emphasize people—the human element—and their importance in accomplishing an organization's goals. Most organizations devote considerable attention to **human resource management,** which can be defined as (1) *the process of acquiring, training, developing, motivating, and appraising a sufficient quantity of qualified employees to perform the activities necessary to accomplish organizational objectives;* and (2) *developing specific activities and an overall organizational climate to generate maximum worker satisfaction and employee efficiency.*

While the owner–manager of a small organization is likely to assume complete responsibility for human resource management, larger organizations use company specialists called *human resource managers* to perform these activities in a systematic manner. The position is becoming increasingly important because of increased competition, growth in the use of outsourcing and part-time workers, a new emphasis on cost control, complex wage and benefit programs, and a changing work force. These human resource managers assume primary responsibility for forecasting personnel needs, recruiting, and aiding in selecting new employees. They also assist in training and evaluation, and administer compensation, employee benefits, and safety programs.

We can view human resource management in two ways. In a narrow sense, it refers to the functions and operations of a single department in a firm: the human resource, or personnel, department. Most firms with two hundred or more employees establish such a department. In a broader sense, though,

---

THEY SAID IT
"Daughters of lions are lions, too." —*Swahili proverb*

A hundred years ago, companies hired workers by posting a notice outside the gate, stating that a certain number of workers would be hired the following day. The notice might list skills, such as welding or carpentry, or it might simply list the number of workers needed. The next morning, people would appear at the front gate—a small number in prosperous times, large crowds in periods of high unemployment—and the workers would be selected. The choices were often arbitrary; the company might hire the first four in line or the four people who looked the strongest or healthiest. Workers operated under a precise set of strict rules. This is one turn-of-the-century example of such a list.

RULES FOR CLERKS, 1900

1. This store must be opened at sunrise. No mistake. Open at 6:00 A.M. summer and winter. Close about 8:30 or 9 P.M. the year round.
2. Store must be swept and dusted; doors and windows opened; lamps filled and trimmed; chimneys cleaned; counters, base shelves, and showcases dusted; pens made; a pail of water and the coal must be brought in before breakfast; if there is time to do it and attend to all the customers who call.
3. The store is not to be opened on the Sabbath day unless absolutely necessary and then only for a few minutes.
4. Should the store be opened on Sunday the clerks must go in alone and get tobacco for customers in need.
5. Clerks who are in the habit of smoking Spanish cigars, being shaved at the barber's, going to dancing parties and other places of amusement, and being out late at night will assuredly give the employer reason to be overly suspicious of employee integrity and honesty.
6. Clerks are allowed to smoke in the store provided they do not wait on women while smoking a "stogie."
7. Each store clerk must pay not less than $5.00 per year to the church and must attend Sunday school regularly.
8. Men clerks are given one evening a week off for courting and two if they go to prayer meeting.
9. After the fourteen hours in the store, leisure hours should be spent mostly in reading.

human resource management involves the entire organization, even when a special staff department exists. After all, general management also is involved in training and developing workers, evaluating their performance, and motivating them to perform as efficiently as possible.

The core responsibilities of human resource management include human resource planning, recruitment and selection, training/management development, performance appraisal, and compensation and employee benefits. Trained specialists from the human resource department typically are involved in carrying out each of these responsibilities. However, such responsibilities usually are shared with line managers, ranging from the company president (who is involved in overall planning) to first-line supervisors (who may be involved in preliminary interviews with applicants and in employee training), and—in companies practicing worker empowerment—even operative employees on the shop floor. By accomplishing these critical tasks, the human resource department achieves its overall objectives of (1) providing qualified, well-trained employees; (2) maximizing employee effectiveness in the organization; and (3) satisfying individual employee needs through monetary compensation, employee benefits, advancement opportunities, and job satisfaction.

HOW NEEDS MOTIVATE PEOPLE

From his examination of twenty top American firms, Robert Leering, author of *A Great Place to Work*, concludes that any manager can turn a bad work place into a good one through what he calls "the three Rs." The first of these is granting workers more and more *responsibility* for their jobs. The second R involves sharing the *rewards* of the enterprise as equitably as possible. The third R is ensuring that employees have *rights.* These include establishing some kind of grievance procedure, allowing access to corporate records, and giving employees the right to confront those in authority without fearing reprisals.

The presence of the three Rs in an organization should contribute to employee morale. **Morale,** *the mental attitude of employees toward their employer and job,* involves a sense of common purpose with respect to other members of the work group and to the organization as a whole. High morale is a sign of a well-managed organization, because workers' attitudes toward their jobs affect the quality of the work done. One of the most obvious signs of poor manager–worker relations is poor morale. It lurks behind absenteeism, employee turnover, slowdowns, and wildcat strikes. It shows up in lower productivity, employee grievances, and transfers.

Burnout, a byword in business today, is evidenced by low morale and fatigue. The most likely burnout candidates are those who care most about their jobs and the company. They experience burnout when they feel a sense of futility and a lack of accomplishment. Kenneth Pelletier, a stress-management consultant and psychiatrist, believes a manager can inspire workers and prevent burnout by showing appreciation for effort. Appreciation is, according to Pelletier, "the most underestimated benefit."

What factors lead to high employee morale? Interestingly, managers and employees give different answers. In one classic study (see Table 1), managers thought that the most important factors involved satisfying employees' basic needs for money and job security. Employees, however, want to be appreciated, to be treated sympathetically, and to feel like part of a team.

Other studies agree with these results. An Opinion Research Center survey found that many Americans would rather work for a small company than a large corporation. Says one researcher, "This desire is interesting, when you consider that benefits and pay are generally better in big corporations, and most people know that."

THE HUMAN RESOURCE

TABLE 1   What Contributes to High Morale?

	Most important	Less important	Least important
Manager opinions	Good wages Job security Promotion and growth with company	Good working conditions Interesting work Management loyalty to workers	Tactful disciplining Full appreciation for work done Sympathetic understanding of personal problems Feeling "in" on things
Employee opinions	Full appreciation for work done Feeling "in" on things Sympathetic understanding of personal problems	Job security Good wages Interesting work	Promotion and growth with company Management loyalty to workers Good working conditions Tactful disciplining

Managers and employees have quite different opinions regarding what factors contribute to high morale.

Maintaining high employee morale also means more than just keeping employees happy. A two-day workweek, longer vacations, or numerous work breaks easily could produce happy employees. But truly high morale results from an understanding of human needs and the ability of the organization to make satisfying individual needs consistent with organizational goals.

Each of us is motivated to take actions designed to satisfy needs. A **need** is simply *the lack of something useful.* It reflects a gap between an individual's actual state and his or her desired state. A **motive** is *the inner state that directs us toward the goal of satisfying a felt need.* Once the need—the gap between where a person is now and where he or she wants to be—becomes important enough, it produces tension and the individual is *moved* (the root word for *motive*) to reduce this tension and return to a condition of equilibrium.

Let's look at an example. If you have been in class or worked at your job until 1 P.M., your immediate need may be for food. Your

lack of lunch is reflected in the motive of hunger. So you move—literally—to address your need by walking to a nearby restaurant where you buy the $2.69 special (hamburger, fries, and soft drink). By 1:20 you have satisfied your need for lunch. Now you are

THE MOTIVATION PROCESS

Need → **produces**

Motivation → **which leads to**

Goal-directed behavior → **resulting in**

Need satisfaction

ready to satisfy your next need: getting to your 2:00 class on time! The principle behind this process is that a need produces a motivation, which leads to goal-directed behavior, resulting in need satisfaction.

Maslow's Needs Hierarchy

Psychologist Abraham H. Maslow developed a widely accepted list of human needs based on the important assumptions listed on the next page.

MASLOW'S HIERARCHY OF HUMAN NEEDS

Self-Actualization Needs
Accomplishment, opportunities for advancement, growth, and creativity

As a young man, Sid Craig wrote his goals on his bathroom mirror every morning (a frequent entry: "Become the owner of the company"). After a career that included teaching ballroom dancing and owning five Arthur Murray franchises, Craig and his wife, Jenny, built the enormously successful chain of Jenny Craig diet clinics in the United States and Australia. Craig not only realized his dream of building and running a successful business, but he and his wife's ownership shares are now worth almost $500 million.

Esteem Needs
Recognition, approval of others, status, increased responsibilities

When Union Carbide's CEO asked for volunteers to develop new business ideas, 10 percent of the two thousand-member specialty chemicals staff signed up. Some sixty-six new-venture ideas dreamed up by these volunteers are being studied by Union Carbide.

Social (Belongingness) Needs
Acceptance, affection, affiliation with work groups, family, friends, co-workers, and supervisors

Autoworkers at the Fremont, California, assembly plant operated as a joint venture between GM and Toyota are referred to as *team members*. Team members rotate jobs and work together in an atmosphere of "mutual trust." They produce almost defect-free cars.

Safety Needs
Protection from harm, employee benefits, job security

IBM, AT&T, Xerox, and Johnson & Johnson created stress-management programs for employees that include everything from exercise and meditation to counseling and referrals.

Physiological Needs
Food, water, and shelter

In the early 1900s, Henry Ford aided his employees in satisfying physiological needs by paying them $5 a day—twice the going wage.

Maslow's hierarchy of needs illustrates the order in which needs are satisfied.

- People are wanting animals whose needs depend on what they already possess.

- A satisfied need is not a motivator; only those needs that have not been satisfied can influence behavior.

- People's needs are arranged in a hierarchy of importance; once one need has been at least partially satisfied, another emerges and demands satisfaction.

Everyone has needs that must be satisfied before higher-order needs can be considered. On the bottom level of Maslow's hierarchy of needs are *physiological needs*—the most basic needs, such as the desire for food, shelter, and clothing. Since most people in industrialized nations today can afford to satisfy their basic needs, however, higher-order needs are likely to play a greater role in worker motivation. These include *safety needs* (job security, protection from physical harm, and avoidance of the unexpected); *social needs* (the desire to be accepted by members of the family and other individuals and groups); and *esteem needs* (the needs to feel a sense of accomplishment, achievement, and respect from others). The competitive urge to excel—to better the performance of others—is an esteem need and an almost universal human trait.

At the top of the hierarchy are *self-actualization needs*—the needs for fulfillment, for realizing one's own potential, for using one's talents and capabilities totally. Different people may have different self-actualization needs. One person may feel fulfilled by writing a poem, another by running a marathon, and someone else may not attain self-actualization until listed in the *Guinness Book of World Records*. For Steve O'Donnell, a writer with the David Letterman TV show, self-actualization means "a pat on the back, making Dave happy, the thrill of hearing the audience laugh—that's what matters most." Organizations seek to satisfy employees' self-

actualization needs, whatever they may be, by offering challenging and creative work assignments and opportunities for advancement based on individual merit.

A major contribution of the needs-hierarchy concept is that, for most people, a satisfied need is no longer a motivator. Once physiological needs are satisfied, the individual becomes concerned with higher-order needs. There obviously will be periods when an individual is motivated by the need to relieve thirst or hunger, but interest most often is directed toward the satisfaction of safety, belongingness, and the other needs on the ladder.

Theories X, Y, and Z

Maslow's theory became popular with managers because it is relatively simple and seems to fit the facts. (After all, few of us are interested in self-actualization when we're starving.) Business organizations have been extremely successful in satisfying the lower-order physiological and safety needs. The traditional view of workers as ingredients in the production process—as machines, like lathes, drill presses, and other equipment—led management to motivate them with money. Today's managers have been forced to reconsider their assumptions about employees and how best to motivate them.

Psychologist Douglas McGregor, a student of Maslow, proposed the concepts of Theory X and Theory Y as labels for the assumptions that different managers make about worker behavior and how these assumptions affect their management style. **Theory X** *assumes that employees dislike work and must be coerced, controlled, or threatened to motivate them to work.* Managers who accept this view feel that the average human being prefers to be directed, wishes to avoid responsibility, has relatively little ambition, and wants security above all. Such managers are likely to direct their subordinates through close and constant observation, continually holding over them the threat of disciplinary action, and demanding that they closely follow company policies and procedures.

If people behave in the manner described by Theory X, this may be because the organization satisfies only their lower-order needs. If, instead, the organization enables them to satisfy their social, esteem, and self-actualization needs, too, employees may start to behave differently. McGregor labeled this thinking **Theory Y,** *an assumption that workers like work and, under proper conditions, accept and seek out responsibilities to fulfill their social, esteem, and self-actualization needs.* The Theory Y manager considers the expenditure of physical and mental effort in work as natural as play or rest. Unlike the traditional management philosophy that relies on external control and constant supervision, Theory Y emphasizes self-control and direction. Its implementation requires a different managerial strategy that includes worker participation in major and minor decisions previously reserved for management.

The trend toward downsizing, empowering, and increased employee participation in decision making has led to a third management style, labeled **Theory Z.**

This approach *views involved workers as the key to increased productivity for the company and an improved quality of work life for the employee.* Theory Z organizations blend Theory Y assumptions with Japanese management practices. Long-term employment for employees and shared responsibility for making and implementing decisions are characteristics of such organizations. Evaluations and promotions are relatively slow, and promotions are tied to individual progress rather than to the calendar. Employees receive varied and nonspecialized experience to broaden their career paths.

The move toward the participative management style that characterizes the Theory Z approach is dramatically reshaping U.S. corporations. Many companies are adopting the matrix form of organization to reap the benefits of the team approach to solving problems. Increasingly, managers are asking workers how to improve their jobs—and then giving them the authority to do it.

William Malec, chief financial officer of the Tennessee Valley Authority, goes to unusual lengths to learn how TVA workers feel about their jobs. He spends one day every month actually doing the job of one of his two thousand

DID YOU KNOW?

Conducting personal interviews in Belgium or Switzerland requires you to be able to speak four different languages.

Many American recruiters consider a willingness to "look you in the eye" an important personality trait for job applicants. In Japan, though, children are taught never to look directly at a person with superior status. Japanese workers frequently lower their eyes when speaking with superiors as a sign of respect.

At Nissan USA there are no privileged parking spaces and no private dining rooms. The president's desk is in the same room with a hundred other white-collar workers.

Many Spanish offices, shops, and restaurants close for *siesta* between 1:30 and 4:00 P.M. And visitors to Madrid should prepare for late dinners. Restaurants there don't open until at least 9:00 P.M., and *Madrileños* often sit down to a full-course dinner at midnight.

The cost of living for an international manager is highest in Tehran, Tokyo, and Abidjan; the lowest-cost cities are Warsaw, Harare, Zimbabwe, New Delhi, and Mexico City.

THE HUMAN RESOURCE

employees. This practice helps him see the company from an employee's point of view and identify areas for improvement. A stint as a clerical worker taught him that employees had to fill out too many forms to rent a company car; he changed the rules so that they only had to show their company badge and Social Security number. While cleaning offices one night, he learned that janitors wasted a great deal of time plugging and unplugging their vacuum cleaners. He bought them battery-powered sweepers. Explains Malec, "When you get down into their jobs they will tell you things you don't normally hear."

BUILDING THE TEAM

Given the importance of a well trained, high-quality employee team in achieving organizational success, it is not surprising that human resource management is such an important function. The entertainment industry visionary Walt Disney expressed it this way: "You can dream, create, design, and build the most wonderful place in the world, but it requires people to make the dream a reality."

Not just people, but well-trained, well-motivated people are required. The recruitment and selection process plays a major role in convincing such people to become a part of the organization. Writer Leo Rosten made this observation, "First-rate people hire first-rate people. Second-rate people hire third-rate people."

Recruitment is expensive; it can include interviews, tests, medical examinations, and training. The human resource manager must ensure that potential employees have the necessary qualifications for the job, since an employee who leaves the firm after a few months can cost a company up to $75,000 in lost productivity, training costs, and em-

ployee morale. A poor employee who stays with the company can cost even more.

To ensure that potential employees have the necessary qualifications for the job and that they either possess needed skills or are capable of learning them, most firms use a six-step approach to recruitment and selection. Rejection of an applicant may occur at any of these steps.

Businesses use both internal and external sources to find candidates for specific jobs. Most firms have a policy of *hiring from within*—that is, considering their own employees first for job openings. If qualified internal candidates are not available, management must look for people outside the organization. Outside sources for potential job applicants include colleges, advertisements in

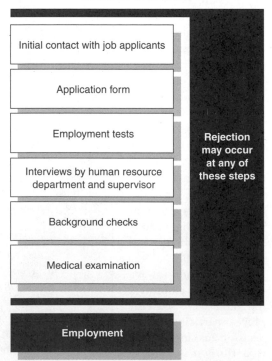

STEPS IN THE RECRUITMENT AND
SELECTION PROCESS

| Initial contact with job applicants |
| Application form |
| Employment tests |
| Interviews by human resource department and supervisor |
| Background checks |
| Medical examination |

Rejection may occur at any of these steps

Employment

newspapers and professional journals, public employment agencies (such as state employment services), unsolicited applications, and recommendations by current employees.

Management of Sbarro, a seven hundred-store international chain of cafeteria-style Italian restaurants, can attest to the importance of hiring—and promoting—from within whenever possible. When the Commack, New York, supplier of lasagna, pizza, cheesecake, and the like, went outside the company for management talent, morale sagged, sales per store declined, and profits fell below expectations. As Mario Sbarro admits, "Many of our own people had the qualifications to do the job. It was a case of 'the grass always looks greener.'" Today, Sbarro promotes almost exclusively from within and seeks new employees based on recommendations of its work force.

A number of federal and state laws aimed at prohibiting discrimination in hiring practices have been enacted over the last three decades. Failure to follow these requirements may prevent the firm from profiting from the strengths of its own diverse work force; it also can result in stiff penalties and bad publicity. In addition to these laws, employers must be aware of various other legal restrictions governing hiring practices. For instance, some firms try to screen out high-risk employees by requiring drug testing for job applicants, particularly in industries where employees are responsible for public safety, such as airlines and public transportation companies. Drug testing is controversial, however, due to concerns about privacy. Furthermore, positive test results may be inaccurate; traces of legal drugs, such as prescribed medications, may chemically resemble traces of illegal substances. Several states have passed laws restricting drug tests.

The use of polygraph (lie detector) tests is prohibited in almost all pre-hiring deci-

sions, as well as in random testing of current employees. The only organizations that are exempt from this law are federal, state, and county governments; firms doing sensitive work under contract to the Defense Department, FBI, or CIA; pharmaceutical companies handling controlled substances; and security-guard services.

Employees, for their part, must be aware of legal restrictions governing their own behavior. For instance, a growing number of communities ban smoking in work places and public areas. Many employers have policies against hiring smokers; some penalize current employees who smoke by charging higher premiums for health insurance and other benefits.

Orientation, Training, and Evaluation
Newly hired employees usually complete an orientation program, which is the joint responsibility of the human resource department and the department in which the person will work. Another major function of the human resource department is developing and maintaining a well-trained, productive labor force. Employee training should be viewed as an ongoing process throughout an employee's tenure with the company.

On-the-job training, in which *employees are trained for job tasks by allowing them to perform them under the guidance of an experienced employee,* is a frequently used method. A variation of this approach is *apprenticeship training,* a program wherein an employee learns a job by serving as an assistant to a trained worker for a relatively long time period. Formal training programs—and particularly apprenticeship programs—are much more common in Europe than in the United States. While U.S. apprenticeship programs currently involve only 200,000 people out of a total work force of almost 120 million, almost 70 percent of Germans enter the work

...rce through apprenticeships. Other differences exist between U.S. and European training approaches. European apprentices start younger (between ages sixteen and nineteen, compared with age twenty-seven in America) and involve many white-collar professions (in contrast to U.S. programs that usually focus on blue-collar trades.)

Off-the-job training involves some form of *classroom training,* in which classroom techniques—lectures, conferences, audiovisual aids, programmed instruction, or special machines—are used to teach employees difficult, high-skill jobs. A **management-development program** is *training designed to improve the skills and broaden the knowledge of current and potential managers.* Such programs often are conducted off the company premises. General Motors, Holiday Inn, McDonald's, and Xerox are among the dozens of giant companies that have established college-like institutes that offer specific programs for current potential managers.

Another important human resource management activity, **performance appraisal,** is *the evaluation of an individual's job performance by comparing actual performance with desired performance.* This information is used to make objective decisions about compensation, promotion, additional training needs, transfers, or terminations. Such appraisals are not confined to business. Professors appraise student performance through assignments and examinations, while students appraise instructors by completing written evaluations.

Effective training programs often include both training and performance appraisal. Consider the Hewlett-Packard Interactive Network, which combines a classroom training format with interactive video. H-P instructors present the telecourses in special studios; the information is beamed to Hewlett-Packard offices and factories around the world. Students provide feedback to instructors by speaking into microphones at their desks, or by typing responses into networked computers. Instructors, who have electronic seating charts for each on-line site, provide immediate performance appraisals by polling students; test results can be displayed instantly on computer-generated charts. Since the company began using the interactive network, the cost of the new-product seminars has fallen by more than 98 percent. The network is so cost effective that Hewlett-Packard has turned it into a profit-maker by selling the service to other companies.

Employee Compensation

One of the most difficult functions of human resource management is to develop an equitable compensation and benefits system. Because labor costs represent a sizable percentage of total product costs, wages that are too high may result in products that are too expensive to compete effectively in the marketplace. But inadequate wages lead to high employee turnover, poor morale, and inefficient production.

The terms *wages* and *salary* often are used interchangeably, but they do have slightly different meanings. *Wages* represent compensation based on the number of hours worked or the amount of output produced. Wages generally are paid to production employees, retail salespeople, and maintenance workers. *Salary* is employee compensation calculated on a weekly, monthly, or annual basis. White-collar workers, such as office personnel, executives, and professional employees, usually receive salaries.

A satisfactory compensation program should attract well-qualified workers, keep them satisfied in their jobs, and inspire them to produce. The compensation policy of most companies is based on five factors: (1) salaries and wages paid by other companies in the area that compete for the same personnel, (2) government legislation, (3) the cost of living, (4) the ability of the company to pay, and (5) the workers' productivity.

Many employers seek to reward superior performance and motivate employees to excel by offering some type of *incentive compensation,* an addition to a salary or wage given for exceptional performance (see figure below). Effective incentive compensation plans reward employees for goals related to quality as well as productivity; ineffective plans can backfire. Robert Rodin, CEO of Marshall Industries, a California-based electronics distributor, admits that his company's old compensation program was counterproductive; he used to reward top performers with cars or trips. Recalls Rodin, "We used to have people shipping ahead of schedule just to make a number or win a prize. In this day of quality, you can imagine our customers were not too happy about getting product early." Today, in addition to their salaries, every Marshall employee earns the same percentage bonus—up to 20 percent of annual salary—based on the firm's profits. While the new compensation plan costs the company 15 percent more than the old one, sales are up $250 million.

Employee Benefits

The typical organization furnishes many benefits to employees and their families besides wages and salaries. **Employee benefits** are *rewards such as pension plans, insurance, sick leave, child care, and tuition reimbursement given at all or part of the expense of the company.* Some benefits are required by law; most employers must contribute to each employee's federal Social Security account. In addition, they make payments to state employment insurance programs that assist laid-off workers and to worker's compensation programs that

provide compensation to persons suffering from job-related injuries or illnesses.

One desirable employee benefit is job protection for workers who need emergency time off to care for dependents or for themselves if they are too ill to perform their work. The *Family and Medical Leave Act of 1993* requires covered employers to give up to twelve weeks of unpaid, job-protected leave to eligible employees. The law applies to all public agencies, including state, local, and federal employers and schools.

Other benefits may be provided voluntarily. Examples include health insurance, pensions and retirement programs, paid vacations and leave time, and employee services, such as tuition-reimbursement programs. In 1995, two Marriott hotels in Atlanta joined forces with a local Omni hotel to help solve the 300 percent annual turnover

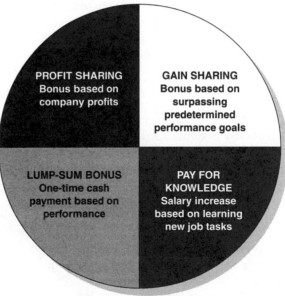

FOUR FORMS OF INCENTIVE COMPENSATION

PROFIT SHARING Bonus based on company profits

GAIN SHARING Bonus based on surpassing predetermined performance goals

LUMP-SUM BONUS One-time cash payment based on performance

PAY FOR KNOWLEDGE Salary increase based on learning new job tasks

These four types of incentive compensation are designed to reward exceptional performance by the individual work team.

THE HUMAN RESOURCE

rate among low-income, entry-level employees. They subsidized construction of a round-the-clock child-care and family services center and reserved 80 percent of the slots for low-income employees and their families.

Employee benefits are a large and rapidly growing component of human resource costs. Wages account for only 61 percent of the typical employee's earnings; the other 39 percent takes the form of employee benefits. A major reason why benefit costs have been rising faster than wages and salaries during the past ten years is the soaring cost of medical benefits. Even though employees' vacations and leaves of absence take the biggest chunk of a company's benefits budget, medical costs are increasing much more rapidly.

An increasingly common method of controlling benefits costs is to offer *flexible benefit plans*. This so-called "cafeteria plan" is a system of flexible benefits in which employees are provided with specific dollar amounts of benefits and are allowed to select areas of coverage. They are well-suited for two-income households wanting to avoid duplicate coverage and for single people who do not need a more expensive family insurance plan. Also, their flexible nature permits employees to adjust their benefits packages through various stages of their lives.

A vital employee benefit for all workers is safe working conditions. All employees deserve a safe work

> ### THEY SAID IT
>
> "If you hit a pony over the nose at the outset of your acquaintance, he may not love you, but he will take a deep interest in your movements ever afterwards."
>
> —*Rudyard Kipling (1863–1936), English novelist*

place, but every year an estimated ten thousand workers die from on-the-job injuries—about thirty per day. Another seventy thousand are disabled permanently from job-related injuries or illnesses. Some of the most dangerous industries are steel, shipbuilding, logging, construction, and food processing.

Recognition of the importance of a safe work environment led to the creation of the *Occupational Safety and Health Administration (OSHA)*, a federal agency whose purpose is to assure safe and healthful working conditions for the U.S. labor force. Employers are responsible for knowing and complying with all OSHA standards that apply to their work place. Employees must be informed of their rights and responsibilities under the law.

Job Enrichment

In their search for ways to improve employee productivity and morale, a growing number

WHERE THE EMPLOYEE BENEFIT DOLLAR GOES

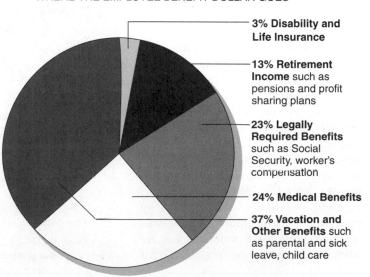

3% Disability and Life Insurance

13% Retirement Income such as pensions and profit sharing plans

23% Legally Required Benefits such as Social Security, worker's compensation

24% Medical Benefits

37% Vacation and Other Benefits such as parental and sick leave, child care

TECHNOLOGY

VIRTUAL PERSONNEL

For centuries people have had to adapt to technological changes, from the invention of the wheel to the discovery of electricity and the combustion engine to the proliferation of today's world of computers. In the short run, workers often are left unemployed as machines perform many of the functions previously done by humans. In the long run, the labor force adapts to technological changes and, as new applications are found, new jobs are created.

While most small businesses today still have a person to answer the phone, most medium- and large-sized organizations have changed to computerized telephone systems. More recently, computer technology has moved up the managerial ladder to replace white-collar workers. This new computerized work force is referred to as *virtual personnel*.

U.S. drug giant Merck & Co. began a transition to virtual personnel in its human resource management division back in 1990. At an initial cost of $3 million, Merck converted its universal employee health insurance plan to a flexible package of benefits managed by a new computerized system. Kiosks, resembling automated teller machines with computer screens, were installed, enabling 15,500 headquarter employees to enroll themselves in the plan. Without this system, Merck would have had to double its human resource staff to forty people.

The project was such a success that Merck invested another $1 million to install twenty-four more kiosks at each of the firm's fifteen U.S. locations. Companywide enrollment took just five weeks and no additional clerical workers were needed.

Employees choose the benefits they want simply by entering their Social Security number and Merck ID number. Since employees can take care of personnel matters themselves, Merck has been able to reassign employees and redesign tasks. Although computers can't counsel employees, they are excellent for routine, programmed clerical tasks.

Plans for new applications are already on the table. The next goal is to merge three systems—payroll, benefits, and personnel records—into one integrated system. This system is expected to save Merck a cool $1.7 million a year.

Virtual personnel will handle many more tasks in the near future. Specialized software soon will allow Merck employees to take care of retirement planning, and the company is considering posting job openings on the system as well.

SOURCE: Carolyn T. Geer, "For a New Job, Press #1," *Forbes,* August 15, 1994, 118–19.

of firms are focusing on the motivational aspects of the job itself. Rather than simplifying the tasks involved in a job, they seek to enrich the job by making it more satisfying and meaningful. **Job enrichment** involves *redesigning work to give employees more authority in planning their tasks, deciding how the work is to be done, and allowing them to learn related skills or trade jobs with others.*

A recent survey of seventy-seven major companies found that job enrichment plays a crucial role in determining which new products succeed and which did not. Successful product-development teams that succeed

THE HUMAN RESOURCE

enjoy full support from top management and are given the authority to manage the project themselves. An example is the team that developed Thermos's popular Thermal Electric Grill that uses a new, clean-burning technology to give food a barbecued taste. According to team member Frederick Mather, "Our reward is that the team owns the project from beginning to end, and that gives us a sense of pride. The real reward is a new product that gets up and flies."

Job enlargement sometimes is used interchangeably with job enrichment, but it differs in that it is merely an expansion of a worker's assignments to include additional, but smaller, tasks. Rather than performing two tasks, a worker might be given four similar tasks. Enlarging a job might lead to job enrichment, but not necessarily. Job enrichment occurs only when the new tasks give an employee greater authority and responsibility for the end result. Enrichment means that employees have more opportunity to be creative and to set their own pace within the limits of the overall schedule.

Flexible Work Schedules

According to a recent study of 7,437 employees, ranging from clerks to managers, the number one stress factor for U.S. workers is time pressure. This helps explain why flexible work schedules are a good way for companies to attract and motivate talented employees and enrich their jobs. Flexible schedules include flextime, compressed workweeks, job sharing, and home-based work.

A work-scheduling system that allows employees to set work hours within constraints specified by the firm is called **flextime.** Most employers offering flextime designate certain "core hours" when employees are required to be on the job,

such as between 9 A.M. and 3 P.M. Meetings typically are scheduled during these core hours. In general, flextime is more common in insurance, finance, retailing, and government positions than in manufacturing jobs. Its use is more widespread in Europe than it is in the United States; an estimated 40 percent of the work force in Switzerland and 25 percent in Germany have flexible schedules, compared to roughly 12 percent in the United States. Other alternative work-scheduling practices include a *compressed workweek*— where employees work the same number of hours in fewer than the typical five days— and *job sharing,* the division of one job assignment between two or more employees.

More and more companies offer employees a fourth option of **home-based work**— *working the same jobs, but doing the work at home instead of in the office.* Home-based workers sometimes are called telecommuters because they may "commute" to work electronically by being hooked up via home computer to the company's computer system. Technologies, such as personal computers, electronic mail, and facsimile machines, make working at home easier than ever before.

The number of company employees who work at home rose 15 percent last year to reach 7.6 million. While most home-based workers like the arrangement, some people adapt better than others. At US West Inc., for example, employees who want to become telecommuters must go through a rigorous screening process to make sure they—and their supervisors—will be able to make the arrangement work. Successful telecommuters need to be self-disciplined, reliable, computer literate, and able to do without much supervision; they also need bosses who are comfortable with setting goals and managing from afar.

WHAT DID I LEARN FROM PREVIEWING?

Reflect for a moment on what you learned by previewing. First, consider the title. Perhaps you did not know the exact meaning of the term *human resource.* Whenever you encounter a word in a title that you do not know, it is essential that you find its meaning before you proceed. In this case, your first step would have been to check the glossary at the end of the textbook. There you would have found this definition: *human resources*—"All the people employed in producing a good or service." If the book did not contain a glossary, you would have gone immediately to the dictionary. In the *Merriam Webster Collegiate Dictionary,* you will find *human resources* defined as "personnel."

Your listing of the subheadings gave you a clear idea of the content and organization of the chapter. The key terms are written in bold-face type. Much of the information in the text is summarized for you in tables and charts. Spending a few minutes previewing this chapter saved you a great deal of time in the long run. Reading the actual text is now so much easier because you know what to expect and you are ready to comprehend and remember.

Return to the chapter now and read it through quickly.

UNDERLINING AND ANNOTATING

Now that you've previewed the chapter and read it through, you are ready to underline and annotate. These are intensive study activities and are the best way to master the ideas in your textbooks. To review these skills, turn to Appendix B. Then underline and annotate "The Human Resource." Discuss your annotation with your classmates. Your discussion of the text is true active studying—the mose productive way to study in college.

VOCABULARY

In this textbook, the authors give you a list of the *Key Terms* and a quiz to help you master them immediately. But don't forget to find and mark each term in the text yourself. Put a question mark or some other special symbol next to any term you don't understand. Then you will be sure to remember to ask a classmate or the instructor for an explanation. If you are keeping a special section of your notebook for important terms and their meanings, write them there also.

Key Terms Quiz

Directions: Match each of the terms below to its definition on the following page.

employee benefits	morale	management-development program
on-the-job training	motive	
need	human resource management	Theory Y
job enrichment		Theory Z
Theory X	performance appraisal	

_____   1. Process of acquiring, training, developing, motivating, and appraising a sufficient quantity of qualified employees to perform necessary activities; and developing activities in an organizational climate conducive to maximum efficiency and worker satisfaction.

_____   2. The mental attitude of employees toward their employer and job.

_____   3. Lack of something useful; discrepancy between a desired state and the actual state.

_____   4. Inner state that directs individuals toward the goal of satisfying a felt need.

_____   5. Managerial assumption that workers dislike work and must be coerced, controlled, or threatened to motivate them to work.

_____   6. Managerial assumption that workers like work and, under proper conditions, accept and seek out responsibilities to fulfill their social, esteem, and self-actualization needs.

_____   7. Management approach emphasizing employee participation as the key to increased productivity and improved quality of work life.

_____   8. Training employees for job tasks by allowing them to perform them under the guidance of an experienced employee.

_____   9. Training designed to improve the skills and broaden the knowledge of managers and potential managers.

_____   10. Defining acceptable employee performance levels, evaluating them, and then comparing actual and desired performance to aid in determining training, compensation, promotion, transfers, or terminations.

_____   11. Employee rewards, such as pension plans, insurance, sick-leave pay, and tuition reimbursement, given at all or part of the expense of the company.

_____   12. Redesigning work to give employees more authority in planning their tasks, deciding how they are to be done, and allowing them to learn related skills or to trade jobs.

EXAM QUESTIONS

In this textbook, used in introduction to business courses, there are many types of questions included to help you master the material. At the end of each chapter are *Review Questions* and *Discussion Questions* in addition to the *Key Terms Quiz* above. Review questions are meant to help you examine and reinforce the ideas presented in the text. Discussion questions generally require that you take information you learned from the text and apply it to other areas. Such questions often ask you to give a personal reaction or an opinion based on information in the text. Following are examples of all the types of exam questions you are likely to encounter.

Review Questions

1. Explain the primary functions of a human resource department. Which of these responsibilities are most likely to be shared with line departments?
2. Based on Maslow's hierarchy of human needs, which needs are being referred to in the following statements?

   a. "The new General Motors labor agreement will guarantee the jobs of at least 80 percent of all GM workers through 2008."
   b. "This is an entry-level job here at Marx Clothiers, and we pay minimum wage for the first six months."
   c. "We have just organized a company basketball team. Why don't you try out Thursday afternoon after work?"
   d. "Judy won our Employee of the Month award this month due to her exceptional performance."
   e. "We pay a 20 percent bonus for employees who work the midnight shift."

3. List several methods of work structuring that should result in job enrichment. Can you think of situations where job-enrichment programs would not be effective? List them and explain your reasoning.

Discussion Question

1. A survey of 2,010 workers performing 23 different jobs conducted by the Institute of Social Research of the University of Michigan gave the following "Most Boring" awards: assembly-line workers, forklift-truck driver, machine tender, and monitor of continuous-flow production. By contrast, these jobs were ranked at the "Least Boring" end of the scale: physician, professor, air traffic controller, and police officer. Identify some common characteristics of each group of jobs that appear to explain their rankings.

True/False Questions

_____ 1. The management style labeled Theory X views involved workers as the key to increased productivity for the company and an improved quality of life for the employee.

_____ 2. The majority of firms use the polygraph test for all prehiring decisions as well as in random testing of current employees.

_____ 3. Incentive compensation is an addition to a salary or wage given for exceptional performance.

_____ 4. According to a recent study of employees, the number one stress factor for United States workers is job security.

Multiple Choice Questions

_____ 1. The human resource manager's position is becoming increasingly important for the following reasons, *except for*

    a. increased competition
    b. growth in the use of outsourcing and part-time workers
    c. new emphasis on cost control
    d. complex wage and benefit programs
    e. marketing research

_____ 2. Human-resource managers assume primary responsibility for the following, *except for*

    a. forecasting personnel needs
    b. hiring decisions
    c. recruiting
    d. aid in selecting new employees
    e. training and evaluation

_____ 3. The human resource department achieves one of its overall objectives—satisfying individual employee needs—through all of the following, *except*

    a. monetary compensation
    b. disciplinary procedure
    c. employee benefits
    d. advancement opportunities
    e. job satisfaction

_____ 4. Evidenced by low morale and fatigue, a byword in business today is

    a. burnout.
    b. apathy.
    c. distrust.
    d. distress.
    e. turnover.

_____ 5. At the pinnacle of Maslow's hierarchy of needs are

    a. psychological needs.
    b. physiological needs.
    c. self-actualization needs.
    d. hygiene factors.
    e. maintenance factors.

_____ 6. Business organizations have been extremely successful in satisfying the lower-order or physiological and _____ needs.

    a. psychological
    b. safety
    c. social
    d. affiliation
    e. achievement

_____ 7. What theory assumes that employees dislike work and must be coerced, controlled, or threatened to motivate them to work?

    a. Theory X
    b. Theory Y
    c. Theory Z
    d. Expectancy Theory
    e. Equity Theory

_____ 8. Unlike the traditional management philosophy that relies on external control and constant supervision, _____ emphasizes self-control and direction.

    a. Theory Y
    b. Theory X
    c. Reinforcement Theory
    d. Systems Theory
    e. Contingency Theory

_____ 9. When employees are trained for job tasks by performing under the guidance of an experienced/senior employee, this is

    a. job instruction training.
    b. vestibule school.
    c. case method training.
    d. computer instruction training.
    e. on-the-job training.

_____ 10. A program where an employee learns a job by serving as an assistant to a trained worker for a relatively long time period is

    a. sensitivity training.
    b. vestibule school.
    c. job instruction training.
    d. apprenticeship training.
    e. T-group training.

_____ 11. Compensation based on the number of hours worked or the amount of output produced is

    a. salary.
    b. perks.
    c. incentives.
    d. wages.
    e. E.S.O.P.

_____ 12. The Family and Medical Leave Act of 1993 requires covered employers to give up to twelve weeks of unpaid, job-protected leave to eligible employees and applies to the following public agencies, *except for*

    a. state agencies
    b. local agencies
    c. federal agencies
    d. schools
    e. religious institutions

_____ 13. A major reason benefits costs have been rising faster than wages and salaries during the past ten years is the soaring cost of

    a. pension benefits.
    b. paid holidays.
    c. tuition reimbursement.
    d. medical benefits.
    e. child-care benefits.

_____ 14. The Occupational Safety and Health Administration's purpose is to assure workers

    a. a fair minimum wage.
    b. equal pay for equal work.
    c. non-discrimination of employees.
    d. aged employee protection.
    e. safe and healthful working conditions.

_____ 15. _____ means employees have more opportunity to be creative and to set their own pace within the limits of the overall schedule.

    a. Job enlargement
    b. Job evaluation
    c. Job enrichment
    d. Performance appraisal
    e. On-the-job training

THINKING AND LANGUAGE

A Chapter from the Textbook *Psychology in the New Millennium*, 6th ed.

Spencer A. Rathus

PREVIEWING

Begin your study of the chapter by previewing. Review previewing in Appendix A if you need to. For this chapter, read, don't skim, the short introduction, "What Is Thinking?" on page 396. It will introduce you to the author's writing style and thus make reading the rest of the chapter easier. You will usually find that you can read a textbook with greater and greater ease as you progress through the chapters. Partly, this is due to your increasing familiarity with the author's way of thinking and writing. In the case of this particular textbook, the author has a warm and personal style; he injects some subtle humor into his text. His style is pleasant to read, but this is unusual for a college text! After you read the introduction, follow the usual previewing steps.

Before you begin, write your own definition of the word *thinking*. In addition to your usual previewing questions, consider the following:

1. Note that the key terms are written in bold-face type. But the author has highlighted the key terms in another way, too. What is it?

2. As you read along you'll be tempted by some of the author's stories and puzzles to stop previewing and start to read carefully. Don't worry—it can't hurt. But don't let it tempt you to omit the next important step in studying the chapter—the careful *second* reading of the chapter.

3. You will encounter many new words and phrases in the chapter. Terms like *heuristics, algorithm,* and *means-end analysis* may give you a fright upon first reading. But they are all clearly defined and used in examples in the text and should give you no problem after a bit of study.

THINKING AND LANGUAGE

WHAT IS THINKING?

At the age of nine, my daughter, Jordan, hit me with a problem about a bus driver that she had heard in school. Since I firmly believe in exposing students to the kinds of torture I have undergone, see what you can do with her problem:

> *You're driving a bus that's leaving from Pennsylvania. To start off with, there were 32 people on the bus. At the next bus stop, 11 people got off and 9 people got on. At the next bus stop, 2 people got off and 2 people got on. At the next bus stop, 12 people got on and 16 people got off. At the next bus stop, 5 people got on and 3 people got off. What color are the bus driver's eyes?*

Now, I was not about to be fooled when I was listening to this problem. Although it seemed clear that I should be keeping track of how many people are on the bus, I had an inkling that a trick was involved. Therefore, I first instructed myself to remember that the bus was leaving from Pennsylvania. Being clever, I also kept track of the number of stops rather than the number of people getting on and off the bus. When I was finally hit with the question about the bus driver's eyes, I was at a loss. I protested that Jordan had said nothing about the bus driver's eyes, but she insisted that she had given me enough information to answer the question.

One of the requirements of problem solving is paying attention to relevant information. To do that, you need some familiarity with the type of problem it is. I immediately classified the bus-driver problem as a trick question and paid attention to apparently superfluous information. But I wasn't good enough.

The vast human ability to solve problems has allowed people to build skyscrapers, create computers, and scan the interior of the body without surgery. Some people even manage to keep track of their children and balance their checkbooks. Problem solving is one aspect of thinking. **Thinking** is mental activity that is involved in understanding, processing, and communicating information. Thinking entails attending to information, mentally representing it, reasoning about it, and making judgments and decisions about it. The term *thinking* generally refers to conscious, planned attempts to make sense of things. Cognitive psychologists usually do not characterize the less deliberate cognitive activities of daydreaming or the more automatic usages of language as thinking. Yet language is entwined with much of human thought. The uniquely human capacities to conceptualize mathematical theorems and philosophical treatises rely on language. Moreover, language allows us to communicate our thoughts and record them for posterity.

In this chapter we explore the broad topics of thinking and language. We begin with concepts, which provide building blocks of thought. We wend our way toward language, which lends human thought a unique richness and beauty.

Before we proceed, I have one question for you: What color were the bus driver's eyes?

CONCEPTS AND PROTOTYPES: BUILDING BLOCKS OF THOUGHT

I began the chapter with a problem posed by my daughter, Jordan. Let me proceed with a riddle from my own childhood: "What's black and white and read all over?" Since this riddle was spoken, not written, and since it involved the colors black and white, you would probably assume that "read" was spelled "red." Thus, in seeking an answer, you might scan your memory for an object that was red although it also somehow managed to be black and white. The answer to the riddle, "newspaper," usually met with a good groan.

The word *newspaper* is a **concept.** *Red, black,* and *white* are also concepts— color concepts. Concepts are mental categories used to class together objects, relations, events, abstractions, or qualities that have common properties. Concepts are crucial to cognition. They represent aspects of the environment and of ourselves. In the cases of imagination and creativity, concepts can represent objects, events, activities, and ideas that never were. Much of thinking has to do with categorizing new objects and events and with manipulating the relationships among concepts.

We tend to organize concepts in hierarchies. The newspaper category includes objects such as your school paper and the *Los Angeles Times.* Newspapers, college textbooks, novels, and merchandise catalogs can be combined into higher-order categories such as *printed matter* or *printed devices that store information.* If you add CD-ROMs and floppy disks, you can create a still higher category, *objects that store information.* Now consider a question that requires categorical thinking: How are a newspaper and CD-ROM alike? Answers to such questions entail supplying the category that includes both objects. In this case, we can say that they both store information. That is, their functions are similar, even if their technology is very different. Here is another question: How are the brain and a CD-ROM alike? Yes, again, both can be said to store information. How are the brain and a CD-ROM different? To answer this question, we find a category in which only one of them belongs. For example, only the brain is a living thing. Functionally, moreover, the brain does much more than store information. The CD-ROM is an electronic device. People are not electronic devices. Could we, however, make the case that electricity is involved in human thinking?

Prototypes are examples that best match the essential features of categories. In less technical terms, prototypes are good examples. When new stimuli closely match people's prototypes of concepts, they are readily recognized as examples. Which animal seems more birdlike to you? A sparrow or an ostrich? Why?

Thinking Mental activity that is involved in understanding, manipulating, and communicating about information. Thinking entails paying attention to information, mentally representing it, reasoning about it, and making decisions about it.

Concept A mental category that is used to class together objects, relations, events, abstractions, or qualities that have common properties.

Prototype A concept of a category of objects or events that serves as a good example of the category.

Exemplar A specific example.

Positive instance An example of a concept.

Negative instance An idea, event, or object that is *not* an example of a concept. Concept formation is aided by presentation of positive and negative instances.

Which of the following better fits the prototype of a fish? A sea horse or a shark? Both self-love and maternal love may be forms of love, but more people readily agree that maternal love is a kind of love. Maternal love apparently better fits their prototype of love.

Many lower animals can be said to possess instinctive or inborn prototypes of various concepts. Male robins attack round reddish objects that are similar in appearance to the breasts of other male robins—even when they have been reared in isolation and have thus never seen another male robin. People, however, generally acquire prototypes on the basis of experience. Many simple prototypes such as *dog* and *red* are taught by **exemplars.** We point to a dog and say "dog" or "This is a dog" to a child. Dogs are considered to be **positive instances** of the dog concept. **Negative instances**—that is, things that are not dogs—are then shown to the child while one says, "This is *not* a dog." Negative instances of one concept may be positive instances of another. So, in teaching a child, one may be more likely to say "This is not a dog—it's a cat" than simply, "This is not a dog."

Children may at first include horses and other four-legged animals within the dog schema or concept until the differences between dogs and horses are pointed out. (To them, the initial category could be more appropriately labeled "fuzzy-wuzzies.") In language development, the overinclusion of instances in a category (reference to horses as dogs) is labeled *overextension.* Children's prototypes become refined as the result of being shown positive and negative instances and being given verbal explanations.

Abstract concepts such as *bachelor* or *square root* are typically formed through verbal explanations that involve more basic concepts. If one points repeatedly to *bachelors* (positive instances) and *not bachelors* (negative instances), a child may eventually learn that bachelors are males or adult males. However, it is doubtful that this show-and-tell method would ever teach them that bachelors are adult human males who are unmarried. The concept *bachelor* is best taught by explanation after the child understands the concepts of maleness and marriage.

Still more abstract concepts such as *justice, goodness, beauty,* and *love* may require complex explanations and many positive and negative instances as examples. These concepts are so abstract and instances so varied that no two people may agree on their definition. Or, if their definitions coincide, they may argue over positive versus negative instances (things that are beautiful and things that are ugly). What seems to be a beautiful work of art to me may impress you as meaningless jumbles of color. Thus the phrase, "Beauty is in the eye of the beholder."

REFLECTIONS

Now that you have read the opening sections of the chapter, reflect on the following questions:

- What strategy were you using to try to solve the bus driver problem? Were you misled or not? Why?

- When you were a child, some people were probably introduced to you as Aunt Bea or Uncle Harry. Do you remember when you first understood the concept of *aunt* or *uncle*? Can you think of ways of teaching these concepts to small children without using verbal explanation?
- Which concepts in this textbook have you found the most simple or most difficult to understand? Why?

PROBLEM SOLVING

Now I have the pleasure of sharing something personal with you. One of the pleasures I derived from my own introductory psychology course lay in showing friends the textbook and getting them involved in the problems in the section on problem solving. First, of course, I struggled with the problems myself. Now it's your turn. Get some scrap paper, take a breath, and have a go at the following problems. The answers will be discussed in the following pages, but don't peek. *Try* the problems first.

1. Provide the next two letters in the series for each of the following:

    a. ABABABAB??
    b. ABDEBCEF??
    c. OTTFFSSE??

2. Draw straight lines through all the points in part A of Figure 1, using only *four* lines. Do not lift your pencil from the paper or retrace your steps. (The answer is given in Figure 4.)

3. Move three matches in part B of Figure 1 to make four squares of the same size. You must use *all* the matches. (The answer is shown in Figure 4.)

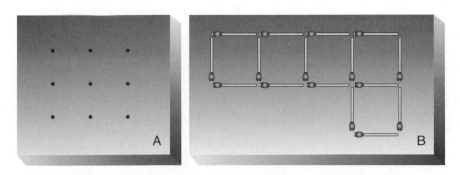

FIGURE I • Spotlight on Two Challenges to Problem-Solving Abilities Draw straight lines through all the points in Part A, using only four lines. Do not lift your pencil or retrace your steps. Move three matches in Part B to make four squares equal in size. Use all the matches.

THINKING

TABLE 1   WATER-JAR PROBLEMS

| | Three Jars Are Present with the Listed Capacity (in Ounces) | | | |
Problem	Jar A	Jar B	Jar C	Goal
1	21	127	3	100
2	14	163	25	99
3	18	43	10	5
4	9	42	6	21
5	20	59	4	31
6	23	49	3	20
7	10	36	7	3

For each problem, how can you use some combination of the three jars given, and a tap, to obtain precisely the amount of water shown?

Source: Adapted from *Rigidity of Behavior,* by Abraham S. Luchins and Edith H. Luchins, 1959, Eugene: University of Oregon Press, p. 109.

4. You have three jars—A, B, and C—which hold the amounts of water, in ounces, shown in Table 1. For each of the seven problems in Table 1, use the jars in any way you wish to arrive at the indicated amount of water. Fill or empty any jar as often as you wish. How do you obtain the desired amount of water in each problem? (The solutions are discussed on pages 404, 406, and 409.)

Approaches to Problem Solving: Getting from Here to There

What steps did you use to try to solve parts a and b of problem 1? Did you first make sure you understood the problem by rereading the instructions? Or did you dive right in as soon as you saw them on the page? Perhaps 1a and 1b came easily, but I'm sure that you studied 1c very carefully.

After you believed you understood what was required in each problem, you probably sought to discover the structure of the cycles in each series. Series 1a has repeated cycles of two letters: *AB, AB,* and so on. Series 1b may be seen as having four cycles of two consecutive letters: *AB, DE, BC,* and so on.

Again, did you solve 1a and 1b in a flash of insight, or did you try to find rules that govern the advance of each series? In series 1a, the rule is simply to repeat the cycle. Series 1b is more complicated, and different sets of rules can be used to describe it. One correct set of rules is that odd-numbered cycles (*1 and 3,* or *AB* and *BC*) simply repeat the last letter of the previous cycle (in this case *B*) and advance by one letter in the alphabet. The same rule applies to even-numbered cycles (*2 and 4,* or *DE* and *EF*).

If you found rules for problems 1a and 1b, you used them to produce the next letters in the series: *AB* in series 1a, and *CD* in series 1b. Perhaps you then evaluated the effectiveness of your rules by checking your answers against the solutions in the preceding paragraphs.

Question: What alternate sets of rules could you have found to describe these two series? Would you have generated the same answers from these rules?

In this section, we explore approaches to problem solving. We begin where you may have begun with the letters series: understanding the problem. Then we discuss various strategies for attacking the problem, including the use of algorithms, heuristic devices, or analogies.

Understanding the Problem.   Let us begin our discussion of understanding problems by considering a bus driver problem that is very similar to the one my daughter, Jordan, gave me. This one is "official," however, That is, it appeared in the psychological literature:

> *Suppose you are a bus driver. On the first stop, you pick up 6 men and 2 women. At the second stop, 2 men leave and 1 woman boards the bus. At the third stop, 1 man leaves and 2 women enter the bus. At the fourth stop, 3 men get on and 3 women get off. At the fifth stop, 2 men get off, 3 men get on, 1 woman gets off, and 2 women get on. What is the bus driver's name?*

Both versions of the bus driver problem demonstrate that a crucial factor in understanding a problem is focusing on the key information. If we assume that it is crucial to keep track of the numbers of people getting on and off the bus, we are focusing on information that turns out to be unessential. In fact, it distracts us from focusing on the crucial information.

When we are faced with a novel problem, how can we know which information is relevant and which is irrelevant? Background knowledge in the problem area helps. If you are given a chemistry problem, it helps if you have taken some courses in chemistry. If my daughter, Jordan, gives you a problem, it is helpful to expect the unexpected, or to head for the hills. (In case you still haven't noticed, by the way, the critical information you need to solve both bus driver problems is indicated in the first sentence.)

Understanding a problem means constructing a coherent mental representation of the problem. I'll beat a horse to death by reminding you that psychologists cannot directly measure a person's mental representation of a problem or of anything else. However, psychologists make inferences about people's mental images from what people say and what they do—in this case, how they describe a problem and how they go about solving it.

The mental representation of the problem can include symbols or concepts, such as algebraic symbols or words. It can include lists, graphs, and visual images. Successful understanding of a problem generally requires three features:

1. *The parts or elements of our mental representation of the problem relate to one another in a meaningful way.* If we are trying to solve a problem in geometry, our mental triangles should have angles that total 180 degrees and not 360 degrees.

2. *The elements of our mental representation of the problem correspond to the elements of the problem in the outer world.* If we are neutralizing an acid to wind up with a salt and water, our mental representation of water should be H_2O and not OH. The elements of our mental representations must include the key elements for solving the problem, such as the information in the first sentence of the bus driver problem. We prepare ourselves to solve a problem by familiarizing ourselves with its elements and defining our goals as clearly as possible. Part of understanding algebra and geometry problems is outlining all of the givens.

3. *We have a storehouse of background knowledge that we can apply to the problem.* We have taken the necessary coursework to solve problems in algebra and chemistry. The architect has a broad understanding of building materials and styles to apply to the problem of designing a particular structure for a particular site. A broad knowledge base may allow us to classify the problem or find analogies. When given a geometry problem involving a triangle, one may think, "Does this problem seem to be similar to problems I've solved by using the quadratic equation?"

Algorithms.   An **algorithm** is a specific procedure for solving a type of problem. An algorithm will invariably lead to the solution—if it is used properly, that is. Mathematical formulas—such as the Pythagorean Theorem—are examples of algorithms. They will yield correct answers to problems *as long as the right formula is used.* Finding the right formula to solve a problem may require scanning one's memory for all formulas that contain variables that represent one or more of the elements in the problem. The Pythagorean Theorem, for example, concerns triangles with right angles. Therefore, it is appropriate to consider using this formula for problems concerning right angles but not for others.

Consider anagram problems, in which we try to reorganize groups of letters into words. Some anagram problems require us to use every letter from the pool of letters; others allow us to use only some of the letters. How many words can you make from the pool of letters *DWARG?* If you were to use the algorithm termed the **systematic random search,** you would list every possible letter combination, using from one to all five letters. You could use a dictionary or a spell-checking computer software program to see whether each result is, in fact, a word. Such a method might be plodding, but it would work.

Systematic random searches are made practical in many cases by using a computer. If you were to use a computer to solve the DWARG anagram problem, you might instruct it to engage in a systematic random search as follows: First, instruct it to list every possible letter combination, using from one to five letters. Second, instruct it to run a spell-checking program on the potential solutions. Third, instruct it to print out only the combinations that are identified as words by the spell-checking program.

Did you develop an algorithm for solving the bus driver problem? Did it involve rereading the problem slowly, checking every word to determine whether it held a clue to the solution? Have you developed an algorithm for doing well in this course? Does it involve smiling at your professor now and then and keeping your fingers crossed, or something a bit more . . . substantive?

Heuristics.   **Heuristics** are rules of thumb that help us simplify and solve problems. Heuristics, in contrast to algorithms, do not guarantee a correct solution to a problem. They are shortcuts. When they work, they allow for more rapid solutions. A heuristic device for solving the anagram problem would be to look for familiar letter combinations that are found in words and then to check the remaining letters for words that include these combinations. In *DWARG,* for example, we can find the familiar combinations *dr* and *gr.* We may then quickly find *draw, drag,* and *grad.* The drawback to this method, however, is that we might miss some words.

It is not true that using the "tried and true" formula is the most efficient way to solve a problem.

Using a tried and true formula—that is, an algorithm—may be less efficient than using a heuristic device.

One type of heuristic device is the **means-end analysis.** In using this heuristic device, we assess the difference between our current situation and our goals and then do what we can to reduce this discrepancy. Let's say that you are out in your car and lost. You know that your goal is west of your current location and on the other side of the railroad tracks. A heuristic device would be to drive toward the setting sun (west) and, at the same time, to remain alert for railroad tracks. If the road comes to an end and you must turn left or right, you can scan the distance in either direction for tracks. If you don't see any, turn right or left, but then, at the next major intersection, turn toward the setting sun again. Eventually you may get there. If not, you could use that most boring of algorithms: Ask people for directions until you find someone who knows the route.

When an inexperienced chess player is stuck for a move, she or he could engage in a systematic random search. That is, she could examine each piece remaining on the board and visualize every move the rules will allow each piece to make. Lengthy. She could make the process even lengthier by imagining every possible countermove to each move, several moves hence. If there are many pieces on the board, it is not difficult to imagine the combinations quickly running into the billions. Chess players—even inexperienced chess players—tend to use heuristic devices or rules of thumb, however. The ultimate goal is to win the game. Chess players focus on subgoals, for example, such as trying to capture the center of the board, protecting the king, or trying out a Sicilian defense. They also use means-end analysis. They consider their subgoals and imagine ways of reducing the discrepancies between their current positions and their subgoals (for example, trying to castle to protect the king). Experienced players also search their memories for games that entailed similar or identical positions.

As we see in playing chess, one strategy of achieving a sizable goal is to break it up into more manageable subgoals. The goal of writing a term paper on psychological ways of managing stress can be broken down into subgoals such as

Understanding Constructing a coherent mental representation of a problem.

Algorithm A systematic procedure for solving a problem that works invariably when it is correctly applied.

Systematic random search An algorithm for solving problems in which each possible solution is tested according to a particular set of rules.

Heuristics Rules of thumb that help us simplify and solve problems.

Means-end analysis A heuristic device in which we try to solve a problem by evaluating the difference between the current situation and the goal.

THINKING

making a list of the subtopics to be included (relaxation, exercise, and so forth), taking notes on recent research on each topic, creating a first draft in each area, and so on. This approach does not mean there is less work to do. However, it provides direction and helps outline a number of more readily attainable goals. It is thus easier to get going.

A few expert chess players are capable of reflecting on similar positions in classic games in historic chess matches. As we see in the following section, experts search for analogies that will help them achieve their goals.

Analogies.   An *analogy* is a partial similarity among things that are different in other ways. During the Cold War, some people in the United States believed in the so-called domino theory. Seeing nations as analogous to dominoes, they argued that if one nation were allowed to fall to communism, its neighbor would be likely to follow. In the late 1980s, a sort of reverse domino effect actually occurred as communism collapsed in Eastern Europe. When communism collapsed in one nation, it became likely to collapse in neighboring nations as well.

The analogy heuristic applies the solution of an earlier problem to the solution of a new one. We use the analogy heuristic frequently, whenever we try to solve a new problem by referring to a previous problem. Consider the water-jar problems in Table 1. Problem 2 is analogous to problem 1. Therefore, the approach to solving problem 1 works with problem 2. (Later we consider what happens when the analogy heuristic fails.)

Lawyers look for analogies (called *precedents*) when they prepare cases for argument. Precedents inform them as to what types of arguments have and have not worked in the past. Psychologists and physicians consider analogies (usually in the form of case studies) when they are attempting to understand a new case and create a treatment plan. Knowing what does *not* work can be as important as knowing what works.

The chess player might think, "Karpov was in a similar [analogous] position in 1977 and was checkmated in four moves when he moved his king." (Yes, she truly might summon up such a game.) People who are good at solving math problems tend to categorize the problem properly. That is, they recognize what *type* of problem it is—and thus summon up the right formulas. Solving a problem by analogy requires locating or retrieving relevant prior problems and adapting the solution of earlier problems to the current problem.

Let us see whether you can use the analogy heuristic to your advantage in the following number series problem: To solve problems 1a, 1b, and 1c on page 399 you had to figure out the rules that guide the order of the letters. Survey this series of numbers and find the rule that guides their order:

$$8, 5, 4, 9, 1, 7, 6, 3, 2, 0$$

Hint: The problem is somewhat analogous to problem 1c.[*]

[*] The analogous element is that there is a correspondence between these numbers and the first letter in the English word that spells them out. What would you do to the words to arrive at this order?

Factors That Affect Problem Solving

The way in which you approach a problem is central to how effective you are at solving it. Other factors also affect your effectiveness at problem solving. Three of them—your level of expertise, whether you fall prey to a mental set, and whether you develop insight into the problem—can be conceptualized as residing in you. A couple of problem characteristics also affect their solution: the extent to which the elements of the problem are fixed in function, and the way in which the problem is defined.

Expertise.   To appreciate the role of expertise in problem solving, unscramble the following anagrams taken from Novick and Coté. In each case, use all of the letters to form an actual English word:

> *DNSUO*
> *RCWDO*
> *IASYD*

How long did it take you to unscramble each anagram? Would a person whose native language is English solve each problem (unscramble each anagram) more efficiently than a bilingual person who spoke another language in the home? Why or why not?

Experts solve problems more efficiently, more rapidly than novices do. (That is why they are called *experts*.) Although it may be considered "smart" to be able to solve a particular kind of problem, experts do not necessarily exceed novices in general intelligence. Their areas of expertise may be quite limited. For example, the knowledge and skills required to determine whether a Northern Renaissance painting is a forgery are quite different from those that are used to find words that rhyme with elephant or to determine the area of a parallelogram. Generally speaking, experts at solving a certain kind of problem have a more extensive knowledge base in the area, have better memories for the elements in the problems, form mental images or representations that facilitate problem solving, relate the problem to other problems that are similar in structure, and have more efficient methods for problem solving. These factors are interrelated. An art historian, for example, acquires a data base that permits her or him to understand the intricacies of paintings. As a result, her or his memory for paintings—and who painted them—expands vastly. People whose native language is English are likely to have a more extensive data base of English words, which should make them more efficient at unscrambling anagrams of English words. Their extensive English data base should also facilitate their learning and memory of new English words.

Novick and Coté found that the solutions to the three anagram problems seemed to "pop out" in under two seconds among "experts." The experts apparently had more efficient methods than the novices. Experts seemed to use parallel processing. That is, they dealt simultaneously with two or more elements of the problems—in this case, the anagrams. In the case of DNSUO, for example, they may have played with the order of the vowels (*UO* or *OU*) at the same time they tested which consonant (*d, N,* or *S*) was likely to precede them, arriving quickly at *sou* and *sound.* Novices were more likely to engage in serial processing—to handle one element of the problem at a time.

Mental Sets.   Jordan hit me with another question: "A farmer had 17 sheep. All but 9 died. How many sheep did he have left?" Being a victim of a mental set, I assumed that this was a subtraction problem and gave the answer 8. She gleefully informed me that she hadn't said "9 died." She had said *"all but* 9 died." Therefore, the correct answer was 9. (Get it?) Put it another way: I had not *understood* the problem. My mental representation of the problem did not correspond to the actual elements of the problem. I resolved to actually pay attention when Jordan riddled me in the future.

Return to problem 1, part c, on page 399. To try to solve this problem, did you seek a pattern of letters that involved cycles and the alphabet? If so, it may be because parts a and b were solved by this approach.

The tendency to respond to a new problem with the same approach that helped solve earlier, similar-looking problems is termed a **mental set.** Mental sets usually make our work easier, but they can mislead us when the similarity between problems is illusory, as in part c of problem 1. Here is a clue: Part c is not an alphabet series. Each of the letters in the series *stands* for something. If you can discover what they stand for (that is, discover the rule), you will be able to generate the ninth and tenth letters. (The answer is in Figure 4 on p. 410.)

Have another look at water-jar problem 6. The formula $B - A - 2C$ will solve this problem. Is that how you solved it? Note also that the problem could have been solved more efficiently by using the formula $A - C$. If the second formula did not occur to you, it may be because of the mental set you acquired from solving the first five problems.

Insight: Aha!   To gain insight into the role of insight in problem solving, consider the following problem, which was posed by Janet Metcalfe:

> *A stranger approached a museum curator and offered him an ancient bronze coin. The coin had an authentic appearance and was marked with the date 544 B.C. The curator had happily made acquisitions from suspicious sources before, but this time he promptly called the police and had the stranger arrested. Why?*

I'm not going to give you the answer to this problem (drat?). Instead, I'll give you a guarantee. When you arrive at the solution, it will hit you all at once. You'll think "Aha!" or "Of course!" or something a bit less polite. It will seem as though there is a sudden reorganization of the pieces of information in the problem so that the solution leaps out at you—in a flash.

Problem solving by means of insight is very important in the history of psychology. Consider a classic piece of research by a German psychologist who was stranded with some laboratory subjects on a Canary Island during World War I. Gestalt psychologist Wolfgang Köhler became convinced of the reality of insight when one of his chimpanzees, Sultan, "went bananas." Sultan had learned to use a stick to rake in bananas placed outside his cage. But now Herr Köhler (pronounced *hair curler*) gave Sultan a new problem. He placed the banana beyond the reach of the stick. However, he gave Sultan two bamboo poles that could be fitted together to make a single pole long enough to retrieve the delectable reward.

As if to make this historic occasion more dramatic, Sultan at first tried to reach the banana with one pole. When he could not do so, he returned to fiddling with the sticks. Köhler left the laboratory after an, hour or so of frustration (his own as well as Sultan's). An assistant was assigned the thankless task of observing Sultan. But soon afterward, Sultan happened to align the two sticks as he fiddled. Then, in what seemed to be a flash of inspiration, Sultan fitted them together and pulled in the elusive banana. Köhler was summoned to the laboratory. When he arrived the sticks fell apart, as if on cue. But Sultan regathered them, fit them firmly together, and actually tested the strength of the fit before retrieving another banana.

Köhler was impressed by Sultan's rapid "perception of relationships" and used the term **insight** to describe it. He noted that such insights are not acquired gradually. Rather, they seem to occur "in a flash" when the elements of a problem have been arranged appropriately. Sultan also proved himself to be immediately capable of stringing several sticks together to retrieve various objects, not just bananas. It appeared that Sultan understood the principle of the relationship between joining sticks and reaching distant objects.

Soon after Köhler's findings were reported, psychologists in the United States demonstrated that even rats are capable of rudimentary forms of problem solving by insight. E. C. Tolman, a University of California psychologist, showed that rats behaved as if they had acquired **cognitive maps** of mazes. Although they would learn many paths to a food goal, they would typically choose the shortest. If the shortest path was blocked, they would quickly switch to another.

Bismarck, one of University of Michigan psychologist N. R. F. Maier's laboratory rats, provided further evidence of insight in laboratory rats. Bismarck had been trained to climb a ladder to a tabletop where food was placed. On one occasion, Maier used a mesh barrier to prevent Bismarck from reaching his goal. But, as shown in Figure 2, a second ladder to the table was provided. The second ladder was in clear view of the animal. At first, Bismarck sniffed and scratched and made every effort to find a path through the mesh barrier. Then Bismarck spent some time washing his face, an activity that apparently signals frustration in rats. Suddenly, Bismarck jumped into the air, turned, ran down the familiar ladder around to the new ladder, ran up the new ladder, and then claimed his just desserts. It seems that Bismarck suddenly perceived the relationships between the elements of his problem so that the solution occurred by insight. He seems to have had what Gestalt psychologists have termed an "Aha! experience."

It is not true that only people are capable of solving problems by means of insight.

Classic research evidence shows that lower animals, including apes and rats, are also capable of insight (a sudden reorganization of the perceptual field).

Insight   In Gestalt psychology, a sudden perception of relationships among elements of the "perceptual field," permitting the solution of a problem.

Cognitive map   A mental representation or picture of the elements in a learning situation, such as a maze.

THINKING

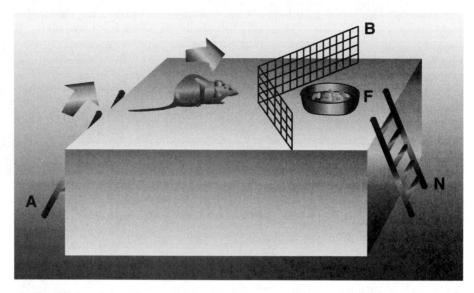

FIGURE 2 • Bismarck Uses a Cognitive Map to Claim His Just Desserts Bismarck has learned to reach dinner by climbing ladder *A*. But now the food goal (*F*) is blocked by a wire mesh barrier (*B*). Bismarck washes his face for a while, but then, in an apparent flash of insight, runs back down ladder *A* and up new ladder *N* to reach the goal.

Let us return to the problems at the beginning of the section. How did you do with problem 1, part c, and problems 2 and 3? Students tend to fiddle around with them for a while, as Sultan fiddled with his sticks. The solutions, when they come, appear to arrive in a flash. Students set the stage for the flash of insight by studying the elements in the problems carefully, repeating the rules to themselves, and trying to imagine what a solution might look like. If you produced and then tried out solutions that did not meet the goals, you may have become frustrated and thought, "The heck with it! I'll come back to it later." Standing back from the problem may allow the **incubation** of insight. An incubator warms chicken eggs for a while so that they will hatch. Incubation in problem solving refers to standing back from the problem for a while as some mysterious process in us seems to continue to work on it. Later, the answer may occur to us in a flash of insight. When standing back from the problem is helpful, it may be because it provides us with some distance from unprofitable but persistent mental sets.

It is not true that the best way to solve a frustrating problem is to keep plugging away at it.

It may be better to distance oneself from the problem for a while and allow it to "incubate." Eventually you may solve the problem in what seems to be a flash of insight.

Have another look at the possible role of incubation in helping us overcome mental sets. Consider the seventh water-jar problem. What if we had tried all sorts of solutions involving the three water jars, and none had worked? What if we were then to stand back from this water-jar problem for a day or two? Is it not possible that, with a little distance, we might suddenly recall a 10, a 7, and a 3—three elements of the problem—and realize that we can arrive at the correct answer by using only two water jars? Our solution might seem too easy, and we might check Table 1 cautiously to make certain that the numbers are there as remembered. Perhaps our incubation period would have done nothing more than unbind us from the mental set that problem 7 *ought* to be solved by the formula $B - A - 2C$.

Functional Fixedness.   **Functional fixedness** may also impair your problem-solving efforts. For example, first ask yourself what a pair of pliers is. Is it a tool for grasping, a paperweight, or a weapon? A pair of pliers could function as any of these, but your tendency to think of it as a grasping tool is fostered by your experience with it. You have probably only used a pair of pliers for grasping things. Functional fixedness is the tendency to think of an object in terms of its name or its familiar usage. Functional fixedness can be similar to a mental set in that it can make it difficult for you to use familiar objects to solve problems in novel ways.

Now that you know what functional fixedness is, let's see if you can overcome it by solving the Duncker candle problem. You enter a room that has the following objects on a table: a candle, a box of matches, and some thumbtacks (see Figure 3). Your task is to use the objects on the table to attach the candle to the wall of the room so that it will burn properly. (The answer is shown in Figure 4.)

You may know that soldiers in survival training in the desert are taught to view insects and snakes as sources of food rather than as pests or threats. But it would be understandable if you chose to show civilian functional fixedness for as long as possible if you were stuck in the desert.

Incubation In problem solving, a hypothetical process that sometimes occurs when we stand back from a frustrating problem for a while and the solution "suddenly" appears.

Functional fixedness The tendency to view an object in terms of its name or familiar usage.

FIGURE 3 • The Duncker Candle Problem Can you use the objects shown on the table to attach the candle to the wall of the room so that it will burn properly?

THINKING

The Definition of the Problem.   Problems can be well-defined or ill-defined. In a **well-defined problem,** the original state, the goal, and the rules for reaching the goal are all clearly spelled out. The water-jar problems are well-defined in that we know the size of each jar (the original state), each goal state (exactly how much water is to be obtained), and the rules (how we may use the water jars to reach the goal). Well-defined problems also have specific ways in which we can determine whether we have reached a solution. For example, we know that we have solved the anagram problem, RCWDO, when we arrive at a correctly spelled English word—*crowd.*

> **Well-defined problem**
>
> A problem in which the original state, the goal, and the rules for reaching the goal are clearly spelled out.
>
> **Ill-defined problem**
>
> A problem in which the original state, the goal, or the rules are less than clear.

In an **ill-defined problem,** the original state, the goal state, or the rules are less than clear. Consider the (unlikely) possibility that an architect is simply asked to design a house. You might think that an architect would savor such an ill-defined problem because of the freedom it grants. Yet, it is difficult for the architect to know when she or he has been successful. Of course, given the inadequate definition of the problem, the architect could always claim that, under the circumstances, any design is a success. In the real world, an architect would likely be given a site for a house, a budget, a requested number of bedrooms, and information about the housing styles (for example, Georgian colonial or contemporary) that a client prefers.

There are various strategies for approaching ill-defined problems. One involves dividing the problem into subproblems. The architect might begin by thinking, "Let me begin by designing an ideal master bedroom." Or one could implant structure on the problem where none existed. The architect might think,

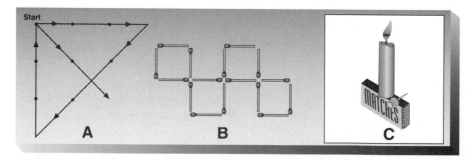

FIGURE 4 • Answers to Problems For problem 1C, note that each of the letters is the first letter of the numbers one through eight. Therefore, the two missing letters are *NT,* for *n*ine and *t*en. The solutions to problems 2 and 3 are shown in this illustration. Solving the Duncker candle problem requires using a thumbtack to pin the matchbox to the wall, then setting the candle on top of the box. Functional fixedness prevents many would-be problem-solvers from conceptualizing the matchbox as anything more than a device to hold the matches. Wrong answers include trying to affix the bottom of the candle to the wall with melted wax and trying to tack the candle to the wall.

"Let me assume that I must design a contemporary house for a bluff that sits high above a bay." Or one could just get started and stop when she or he has arrived at a solution. The architect could simply start sketching and see what happens.

REFLECTION QUESTIONS

1. How did you go about solving the problems presented at the beginning of the section on problem solving (p. 399)? Which did you get right? Which did you get wrong? Why?
2. Did you develop an algorithm for solving the bus driver problem? What was it? Did you attempt to use heuristic devices? What were they?
3. How can you use subgoals to develop a strategy for doing well in this course? For doing well in an athletic event?
4. Are you an expert at solving math problems? Social problems? Automobile problems? Musical problems? How did you get to be an expert?
5. Can you think of an example in which a mental set or functional fixedness interfered with your ability to solve a problem?
6. Can you think of an example in which you were struggling and then suddenly developed insight into a problem or an academic subject?

SUMMARY

1. **What is thinking?** Thinking is cognitive activity that is involved in understanding, processing, and communicating information. Thinking refers to conscious, planned attempts to make sense of the world.
2. **What are concepts?** Concepts are mental categories that group objects, events, or ideas with common properties. We tend to organize concepts in hierarchies.
3. **What are prototypes?** Prototypes are good examples of categories. When new instances closely match people's prototypes of concepts, they are readily recognized as examples.
4. **How do people approach problem solving?** People approach problem solving by first attempting to understand the problem. Then they use various strategies for attacking the problem, including algorithms, heuristic devices, and analogies.
5. **What are algorithms and heuristic devices?** Algorithms are specific procedures for solving problems (such as formulas) that will work invariably as long as they are applied correctly. Heuristics are rules of thumb that help us simplify and solve problems. Heuristics are less reliable than algorithms, but when they are effective, they allow us to solve problems more rapidly.
6. **What are some factors that affect problem solving?** Five key factors are one's level of expertise, whether one falls prey to a mental set, whether one develops insight into a problem, functional fixedness, and the definition of the problem.

THINKING

WHAT DID I LEARN FROM PREVIEWING?

Think about what you learned from previewing this chapter. You should have paid special attention to the word *thinking*. Have you ever considered the meaning of the word *think* before? Common words like *read* and *think* and *language* and *concept* are basic and yet the most difficult to define. How did the author's definition of *thinking* compare to yours?

From your previewing you learned that one of the major goals of the chapter is to discuss problem solving. Many small problems are presented for your consideration. Most students are eager to return to the chapter so they can wrestle with the many interesting questions the author poses. Finally, you noted that many of the key points are summarized for you at the end. In addition to the underlining and annotating you will do, this summary will be among your most valuable study aids when it comes time to take an exam or to write a paper.

Return to the chapter now and read it carefully.

UNDERLINING AND ANNOTATING

Now that you have previewed and read the chapter once, you are ready to underline and annotate. Underlining and annotating your textbooks are your most powerful study activities. To review these skills, turn to Appendix B. Then underline and annotate this chapter, "Thinking and Language." Don't forget to discuss your annotation with your classmates. This discussion of the text, of what is most important and what is less important, is true active studying—the most valuable kind of studying you can do.

VOCABULARY

As noted, the key terms are listed in bold-face type and are also highlighted in boxes in the margins. Don't forget to find and mark each term in the text yourself. Put a question mark or some other special symbol next to any term you don't understand. This will remind you to ask a classmate or the instructor for an explanation. If you are keeping a special section of your notebook for important terms and their meanings, write them there also.

EXAM QUESTIONS

In this textbook, used in introduction to psychology courses, the author asks many questions along the way to stimulate your thinking about what you've learned. Another feature of the book is *Reflection Questions,* questions that take the concepts in the text and ask you to apply them to yourself. Also, instructors who actually teach the course develop exam questions for their students. Following are examples of multiple choice exam questions you are likely to encounter when you take an actual introduction to psychology course that uses this text.

Multiple Choice Questions

_____ 1. Even Rathus, the text author, was tricked by the problem of determining the color of the bus driver's eyes because the simple solution was hidden

    a. in complicated wording.
    b. through the order of presentation of clues.
    c. by extra, unneeded information.
    d. in a complex code.

_____ 2. The bus driver problem indicates the importance of

    a. rote repetition of mental representation of the elements of a problem.
    b. prototypes.
    c. the availability heuristic.
    d. paying attention to relevant information.

_____ 3. The term _thinking_ generally refers to

    a. a conscious, planned attempt to make sense of things.
    b. formal problem solving.
    c. any mental activity.
    d. spontaneous use of one's native language, either silently or aloud.

_____ 4. _____ may be considered the building blocks of thought.

    a. Words and phrases
    b. Problems and answers
    c. Unconscious and conscious ideas
    d. Concepts and prototypes

_____ 5. Prototypes are defined as _____ that best match the essential features of categories.

    a. positive instances
    b. negative instances
    c. examples
    d. concepts

_____ 6. If Angela remembers what the word _amphibian_ means by picturing a creature that exemplifies an amphibian's essential features, she is using a(n)

    a. pragmatic.
    b. extender.
    c. premonition.
    d. prototype.

THINKING

_____ 7. In the context of language development, _____ refers to the tendency to include wrong instances in a category.

    a. overcategorization
    b. prototypezation
    c. overextension
    d. re-reflection

_____ 8. The water-jar problems in the chapter indicate the role of _____ in problem solving.

    a. heuristic devices
    b. functional fixedness
    c. incubation
    d. mental sets

_____ 9. According to the text, _____ a problem is defined as constructing a coherent mental representation of the problem.

    a. understanding
    b. incubating
    c. solving
    d. defining

_____ 10. A mathematical formula for solving a problem is an example of a(n)

    a. mental set.
    b. analogy.
    c. algorithm.
    d. heuristic device.

_____ 11. Seventeen of the forty students in a teacher's class earned an "A" on the last test. To calculate what percent this represents, she divides seventeen by forty, using a(n)

    a. approximation.
    b. analogy.
    c. heuristic device.
    d. algorithm.

_____ 12. The main advantage of using a heuristic device in problem solving is that it will

    a. guarantee reaching a solution.
    b. be quick, easy, and possibly effective.
    c. apply to a wide variety of different problems.
    d. demand little thought.

_____ 13. When her car would not start, Joan began to solve her problem by turning on the headlight to see if the battery was dead. Her approach is an example of a(n)

   a. first guess.
   b. algorithm.
   c. heuristic.
   d. analogous application.

_____ 14. An advantage of breaking a sizeable goal into subgoals is that this will

   a. show a person which part of the goal is most important.
   b. usually make each subgoal easier to reach than the previous one.
   c. provide direction and make it easier to get going.
   d. show you how to put the subgoals together again.

_____ 15. If Ralph tells you, "I had pretty much the same problem with the college records office last year and had to see the registrar to straighten it out. You ought to talk with her," he is proposing that you use a(n)

   a. subgoal analysis.
   b. algorithm.
   c. biorhythm.
   d. analogy heuristic.

_____ 16. If Lisa tells you, "If you have a problem with the college records office, the only way to straighten it out is to go to your academic advisor, then to the dean, and then to the registrar," she is proposing that you use a(n)

   a. subgoal analysis.
   b. algorithm.
   c. biorhythm.
   d. analogy heuristic.

_____ 17. Consider this problem: "A farmer had 17 sheep. All but 9 died. How many sheep did he have left?" If a person who is good at math arrives at the wrong answer, it is probably because of

   a. creativity.
   b. a mental set.
   c. functional fixedness.
   d. overconfidence.

_____ 18. If you are confused by a multiple-choice test question because you notice that several choices are correct, but fail to notice that the

THINKING

question asks "Which answer is *not* correct?" you have experienced the effect of

a. overanticipation.
b. a mental set.
c. cereal processing.
d. insight.

_____ 19. U.S. psychologists Tolman and Maier independently demonstrated that _____ are capable of solving problems through insight.

a. soldiers
b. rats
c. toddlers
d. chimpanzees

_____ 20. Which of the following is *not* true about insight?

a. It comes gradually as one reviews possible problem solutions.
b. It may result in a person's overcoming an ineffective mental set.
c. Some label it an "Aha! experience."
d. It often comes after an incubation period.

_____ 21. You cannot get in the front door of your house because the front door key will not turn in the lock. Which of the following choices would be the best example of using insight to solve your problem?

a. systematically trying every other key you have in the lock
b. spraying some lubricant into the key hole
c. kicking at the door to try to break the lock
d. going in the back door

_____ 22. All of the following help individuals solve problems, *except*

a. insight
b. incubation
c. heuristic devices
d. functional fixedness

_____ 23. Which of the following is *not* spelled out in a well-defined problem?

a. a final solution
b. the original circumstances
c. rules for reaching a solution
d. what would represent a solution

Essay Question

Return to the Reflection questions on pages 398 and 399. Choose one of the questions and answer it completely in one or two well-organized paragraphs.

APPENDIX A

PREVIEWING

A Strategy for Reading and Understanding Textbooks

Does this sound familiar? It's your first week of a new semester. You've just spent a wheelbarrow-full of money on your new books. You are full of enthusiasm and have promised yourself you are really going to study hard this term. You open a book to do your first reading assignment and begin to study and what happens? Your mind begins to wander. You come to the end of a page, and even though you know your eyes have passed over every single word on the page, you have no idea what you've read.

Of course, this has happened to everyone: don't panic! There are ways to help yourself, but be prepared: reading for school is different from reading for pleasure. It requires more effort, more concentration—and a plan.

One reason we sometimes find it hard to absorb what we read is that we are reading materials totally new to us. This is especially true in college introductory courses where we are beginning a subject we may never have studied before. Have you noticed that it's easier to read a difficult, perhaps very technical, article about a subject you know well (say baseball, or computers, or fashion), than it is to read a very simple article on an unfamiliar topic (like ecology, perhaps, or astronomy)? The reason is simple: the more you know about a topic, the easier it is to read about that topic. In other words, the more background information you possess, the easier it is to read.

How is this going to help you when you're confronted with a college textbook on a subject you're not familiar with? Previewing the material before reading it is a first step toward acquiring background knowledge. Previewing will introduce you to the goals of the book, its structure, and helpful tools for learning that are contained in the book. Previewing will also "turn on the engine" of your brain, get you thinking, help you remember anything you *do* know about the topic, and, in general, get you ready to study.

PREVIEWING THE TEXTBOOK

These are the steps to follow to get ready to read your textbook:

First, read and think about the book's title. Are there any words in it you don't know? Look them up. Try to remember what you already know about the subject.

Second, quickly skim the preface or introduction. The author may give some helpful information about the goals and structure of the book.

Third, skim through the table of contents. This will show you the organization of the book and the topics that will be covered.

Fourth, check the table of contents for a glossary. It can appear either at the end of the book or after each chapter. A glossary can be very helpful; it contains definitions of important words used in the book. Using the glossary saves you the time of looking up words in the dictionary and the confusion that often results when a dictionary lists more than one definition; the glossary will list only one—the one used in the textbook.

Fifth, check the table of contents for an index. An index lists all the topics mentioned in the book in alphabetical order, plus their page numbers. Using an index can save lots of time when you are looking for information on one specific subject.

Sixth, check to see if there is an appendix. What does it contain? Sometimes the information in an appendix can be very helpful. For example, a history text's appendix may contain maps to help orient you; an accounting text's appendix may include sample financial statements.

Finally, look quickly through the book. Check to see if there are helpful features, such as summaries at the ends of chapters, or headings and subheadings.

Now spend a moment thinking about what you've just done. Are any of the topics in the title or table of contents familiar to you? Try to remember anything you can about them. Ask yourself what you expect to learn from this book.

You've probably spent four or five minutes previewing the textbook—a small investment of time that will speed up your studying in the long run.

PREVIEWING EACH CHAPTER

When you are ready to study a chapter in a textbook, you'll find previewing a very helpful strategy to "turn on" your brain, help you remember what you already know about the subject, and get ready to absorb new information. These are the steps to follow to prepare yourself to read a chapter:

First, read the title. Think about what it means. If you know anything about the subject, spend a moment to recapture from your memory as much information as you can. If there are any words you don't understand, look them up in the glossary or dictionary.

Second, read the headings and subheadings. This will show you the organization of the chapter and introduce you to the topics to be covered.

Third, see if there is a summary. If there is, read it carefully. It should provide you with a good overview of the chapter and will probably be the most useful part of the chapter later, when it comes time to review.

Fourth, check any questions or exercises before or after the chapter. These questions generally are meant to highlight the most important ideas in the chapter, so it is helpful to keep them in mind as you read.

Previewing the chapter will probably take you three or four minutes. Sometimes, students are impatient and say they'd rather spend these few minutes "really reading" rather than previewing. Studies have shown, however, that students who preview first will read faster, with better comprehension, and remember more. Not a bad return on a few minutes' investment!

GUIDE QUESTIONS

Directions: Write answers to the questions in your notebook or on a separate sheet of paper if your instructor wishes to collect them.

1. a. Describe the problem many students have when they study a textbook.
   b. Do you ever have this problem?
2. a. Which topic would you find it easier to read about: television or U.S. geography? Why?
   b. Which topic would be easier to read about, baseball or the Bible? Why?
3. Explain why previewing can help you read better.
4. List the steps in previewing a textbook.
5. List the steps in previewing a chapter.

APPLICATION

Directions: Now that you have read and understood the ideas in "Previewing," it's important to use them at once. The following exercises, "Previewing a Textbook" and "Previewing a Chapter," will help you apply the methods you have just read about.

Previewing a Textbook

Directions: Choose one of the textbooks you will be using this term and answer the following questions about it.

1. State the title of the textbook.
2. Name the author or authors.
3. Name the course in which you will use this book.
4. Who is the instructor of the course?
5. Identify the publisher of the book.
6. Cite the publication date.
7. Quickly skim the Preface (which may also be called Introduction, Foreword, or To the Student). What does the author say is his or her goal in writing the book?
8. Turn to the table of contents. Into how many parts is the book divided?
9. List three of the topics in the table of contents.
10. Does the book have a glossary?
11. Does the book have an index?
12. Does the book have an appendix? What does it contain?
13. Flip through the book. Do the chapters have any helpful features, such as bold-face type, headings, summaries, questions, or illustrations? State which features the book has.

14. How much of the book are you expected to read this term? All of it? (Ask your instructor if you don't know.)

Previewing a Chapter

Directions: Preview a chapter of this book or a chapter from one of the other textbooks you are using this semester by answering the following questions. Your instructor will tell you which chapter to preview.

1. Read the title and subheadings (if any).

   Are there any words you don't know?

   What are they?

   Look them up and write their meanings.

   What topic will be discussed?

   What do you already know about the topic?

2. Does the chapter contain a summary?
3. Does the chapter include comprehension questions or other exercises? What are they?
4. List helpful features that the chapter contains, such as bold-face type, illustrations, a glossary, margin notes, and so on.

APPENDIX B

Underlining, Annotating, and Summarizing

WHAT IS UNDERLINING?
Underlining is marking or highlighting the parts of a text that you feel are of major importance and wish to remember. Many students use a pen to do their underlining; others use a felt-tip pen to highlight material. Probably the best thing to use is a pencil, for obvious reasons: if you make a mistake, it is easy to erase and correct.

Why Underline? Underlining your reading assignments in school will help you in several ways. First, underlining as you read forces you to be actively involved in your reading. It is easy to fool ourselves into thinking we are studying when all we are really doing is passing our eyes over the printed page, especially if the material is difficult or not very interesting to us at the time. This helps explain why, sometimes, we can read a whole chapter of a book and realize at the end that we can't remember a single thing we've read! If we are physically involved—by underlining—we are forced to be involved with, and learn from, the text.

A second benefit of underlining is that it helps you determine what is important to learn and remember, and what is not. Third, an underlined textbook is an asset when it comes time to study for an exam. The major ideas are already noted for you to review. And, certainly, reviewing your underlining is more efficient than rereading every word of the text.

How to Underline Follow these steps to underline effectively:

1. Read the material very quickly first without underlining anything. If the text is long, divide it up into sections, and attack one section at a time. *Never* underline while reading something the first time! You will certainly make mistakes. It is impossible to know what is important (and thus what should be underlined) if you don't first have a good feel for the author's point.
2. Underline the information you want to learn and remember. Don't underline things simply because they are interesting. Here are some tips for choosing important ideas to underline:
   a. Use the headings and subheadings. Usually they will give you the topics to be discussed in the text. Look for information that explains the information in the headings and subheadings.

b. Pay special attention to the first sentences of paragraphs. Sometimes the author's major point is found in the first sentence of a paragraph.

c. Note words printed in bold-face or italic type. The author has used special type for these terms because he or she wants to call attention to them.

d Pay close attention to lists. They usually include information that you must know.

e. Look for words that signal major ideas. The following words and others like them usually indicate important points: *first, second, third,* and so on; *next, furthermore; another; finally; in addition; therefore; to summarize.*

Warning Be careful not to underline too much! We have all seen books that look like yellow daisies because almost every line has been highlighted. It may be colorful, but it is useless as a study aid. The student might just as well have underlined nothing.

Practice Underlining Read the following selection and, following the steps above, underline the major points.

JOB STRESS: WOMEN COPE BETTER

Women are by no means the weaker sex when it comes to handling on-the-job stress. Research done by psychiatrists reveals that while working women are subject to more on-the-job pressure than men, they are able to cope with it better.

Studies show that women are not as likely to suffer stress-related illnesses as men in similar jobs because females find it easier to vent their anger and verbalize their frustration at work. Researchers conclude that women are more open about their feelings. They are less ashamed to display emotion and more willing to discuss their problems with peers and bosses.

Men, on the other hand, are afraid to express their feelings about work. Because of cultural conditioning, men feel it is a sign of weakness to admit dissatisfaction and disappointment. Even if they feel unsure of themselves, even if they hate their jobs, they believe they must keep their feelings to themselves to maintain their "macho" image. Consequently, they bottle up their emotions. Rather than directing them at their peers and bosses, men direct their frustrations at their heart, arteries, and stomach.

The working woman versus wife-and-mother conflict is a major cause of stress. In our society, work has always been more important than home for men. It is acceptable for a man to spend most of his time working, or to be away from his family for days traveling on business, but not for a woman. Men can pick and choose which family responsibilities they care to take on. Women don't have such selectivity. They have the responsibility for the entire family—taking care of children, maintaining the house, shopping, cooking, and so on. These time-consuming chores must be fit into a working woman's schedule, adding to her stress.

A business dinner with a client is a neutral situation for men but is a sexually charged one for working women, turning what is an accepted part of the job for men into another stress factor for career women. The situation is even more complicated when business travel is considered. The world of hotels, restaurants, and relative freedom is accepted for men but is still filled with taboos for the business woman.

A final stress point is an economic one. The male role has traditionally been that of the economic provider for the family, while the woman's role was as the caretaker of home and children. What happens when the wife makes a larger salary than her husband? Even a single woman making lots of money may find many men unwilling to choose her, even for a date.

Model Underlining This is an example of how you might underline the selection.

JOB STRESS: WOMEN COPE BETTER

Women are by no means the weaker sex when it comes to handling on-the-job stress. Research done by psychiatrists reveals that <u>while working women are subject to more on-the-job pressure than men, they are able to cope with it better</u>.

Studies show that women are not as likely to suffer stress-related illnesses as men in similar jobs <u>because females find it easier to vent their anger and verbalize their frustration at work. Researchers conclude that women are more open about their feelings</u>. They are less ashamed to display emotion and more willing to discuss their problems with peers and bosses.

Men, on the other hand, are afraid to express their feelings about work. <u>Because of cultural conditioning, men feel it is a sign of weakness to admit dissatisfaction and disappointment</u>. Even if they feel unsure of themselves, even if they hate their jobs, they believe they must keep their feelings to themselves to maintain their "macho" image. Consequently, they bottle up their emotions. Rather than directing them at their peers and bosses, men direct their frustrations at their heart, arteries, and stomach.

<u>The working woman versus wife-and-mother conflict is a major cause of stress</u>. In our society, work has always been more important than home for men. It is acceptable for a man to spend most of his time working, or to be away from his family for days traveling on business, but not for a woman. <u>Men can pick and choose which family responsibilities they care to take on. Women don't have such selectivity. They have the responsibility for the entire family</u>—taking care of children, maintaining the house, shopping, cooking, and so on. <u>These time-consuming chores must be fit into a working woman's schedule, adding to her stress</u>.

<u>A business dinner with a client is</u> a neutral situation for men but is a sexually charged one for working women, turning what is an accepted part of the job for men into <u>another stress factor for career women</u>. The situation is even more complicated when <u>business travel</u> is considered. The world of hotels, restaurants, and relative freedom is accepted for men but <u>is still filled with taboos for the business woman</u>.

<u>A final stress point is an economic one</u>. The male role has traditionally been that of the economic provider for the family, while the woman's role was as the caretaker of home and children. <u>What happens when the wife makes a larger salary than her husband?</u> Even a single woman making lots of money may find many men unwilling to choose her, even for a date.

WHAT IS ANNOTATING?

As you underline the important ideas in your books, you should also annotate the text. Annotating simply means such things as:

1. making notes in the margin of the page;
2. circling unfamiliar words or ideas;
3. double underlining or putting a mark next to important ideas;
4. placing a question mark next to statements or concepts that you don't understand or would like to discuss in class.

You can also use annotation to remind yourself to look up words or ideas or to ask your instructor about things you found confusing, debatable, or especially important.

Why Annotate? Annotating, like underlining, is a way of interacting with the text. It helps you to be an active reader because you will not simply be passing your eyes over the words on the page. You must be actively involved in order to mark your text meaningfully. Annotating is a way of talking back to the author: asking questions, arguing a point, commenting on what you are reading.

An Example of Annotated Text Following is the essay you just underlined, as you might annotate it. Remember, as in underlining, be careful not to mark too much. A page covered with marks, with every other line underlined or circled, is distracting and will be difficult to read when you return to review the material.

Model Annotating This is an example of how you might annotate the selection.

JOB STRESS: WOMEN COPE BETTER

Women are by no means the weaker sex when it comes to handling on-the-job stress. Research done by psychiatrists reveals that <u>while working women are subject to more on-the-job pressure than men, they are able to cope with it better.</u>

} *Main idea*

Is this true?

Studies show that women are not as likely to suffer stress-related illnesses as men in similar jobs <u>because females find it easier to vent their anger and verbalize their frustration at work. Researchers conclude that women are more open about their feelings</u>. They are less ashamed to display emotion and more willing to discuss their problems with peers and bosses.

Why women cope better

Ask teacher about this

Men, on the other hand, are afraid to express their feelings about work. <u>Because of (cultural conditioning) men feel it is a sign of weakness to admit dissatisfaction and disappointment</u>. Even if they feel unsure of themselves, even if they hate their jobs, they believe they must keep their feelings to themselves to maintain their "macho" image. Consequently, they bottle up their emotions. Rather than directing them at their peers and bosses, men direct their frustrations at their heart, arteries, and stomach.

Why men don't cope as well

<u>The working woman versus wife-and-mother conflict is a major cause of stress</u>. In our society, work has always been more important than home for men. It is acceptable for a man to spend most of his time working, or to be away from his family for days traveling on business, but not for a woman. <u>Men can pick and choose which family responsibilities they care to take on. Women don't have such selectivity. They have the responsibility for the entire family</u>—taking care of children, maintaining the house, shopping, cooking, and so on. <u>These time-consuming chores must be fit into a working woman's schedule, adding to her stress.</u>

Major source of "extra" stress for women

Examples of extra stress women have

<u>A business dinner with a client is</u> a neutral situation for men but is a sexually charged one for working women, turning what is an accepted part of the job for men into <u>another stress factor for career women</u>. The situation is even more complicated when <u>business travel</u> is considered. The world of hotels, restaurants, and relative freedom is accepted for men but <u>is still filled with taboos for the business woman.</u>

<u>A final stress point is an economic one</u>. The male role has traditionally been that of the economic provider for the family, while the woman's role was as the caretaker of home and children. <u>What happens when the wife makes a larger salary than her husband?</u> Even a single woman making lots of money may find many men unwilling to choose her, even for a date.

I disagree

WHAT IS A SUMMARY?

A summary is a brief, concise statement, in your own words, of the most important points of a passage (a chapter, an article, an essay, a paragraph, etc.). We summarize in our day-to-day life all the time. For example, if a friend asks you to tell about the two-hour movie you saw last night, you don't spend two hours telling her—you summarize. If you write a letter to a relative telling him what you did last week, you obviously summarize the information: you are brief, concise, and include only the high points. Other examples of summaries are when you write down a telephone message or make a list of the things you must accomplish today. So, most of us are already experienced summarizers. Now you must learn to apply the skill you already have to your college reading.

Why Summarize? Summary writing provides many advantages for the college student. The first is that it forces you to truly understand what you have read. If you do not understand, you will not be able to put the text into your own words. Second, writing a summary will help you to remember what you have read. Third, the summaries you write of your textbook chapters or articles are excellent tools for studying when exam time comes along. Wouldn't it be easier to reread your own summaries than to plow through the entire text again? Finally, writing summaries will help you to improve your writing skills, because a good summary must be clear and coherent, just as we would like all our writing to be.

Steps in Writing a Summary

1. *Read* the material one time quickly. This will give you a good overall feel for the information in the text.
2. *Reread* the material slowly and carefully, this time noting the thesis (main idea) and the important supporting points. Underline or take notes on the main points.
3. *Write* on a separate piece of paper the author's main idea. Sometimes the main idea is clearly stated, but if it is not, you must create a main idea statement.
4. *Write* the important supporting ideas that you have underlined or noted under the main idea.
5. *Rewrite* the main idea and supporting ideas in your own words.
6. *Check* your summary against the text to make sure it is accurate and complete.
7. *Eliminate* unnecessary details, such as explanations, examples, statistics, and repetition. Make sure you have no unnecessary words. Remember: a summary is *not* a composition. Many of the features of compositions are not appropriate in a summary—for example, transitional phrases, introductory phrases, conclusions that repeat the thesis, and so on.
8. *Proofread* your summary and *write* the final draft.

Practice Practice the steps for writing a summary by applying them to the article that follows.

Step 1—Read the Article:

HUMAN RELATIONS IN BUSINESS

Lorence Long
LaGuardia Community College

Think of the human relations challenges in business! Here are just a few:

Telling the boss she is wrong, without getting her angry;

Encouraging a subordinate to tell you what you need to know to solve a problem that involves your own behavior;

Helping a customer to make a purchase, without overdoing it;

Expressing your criticism of a peer who is not carrying his share of the work, without turning the rest of the office against you (or him);

Handling your supervisor's overtures, which the supervisor says will improve your position in the office, but which might cost you some self-respect.

Some students (and some instructors) may focus so intently on the skill and knowledge of preparing for the business world that they neglect the human relations dimensions of the work situation.

Recent research indicates that human relations are very important in business. Last October, *The Wall Street Journal* asked 782 company chief executives to identify the most important personal traits linked to success. The executives specified "integrity" and "ability to get along with others" as by far the most important success-related characteristics.

Further, when these same people were asked to identify the failings of weak managers in their firms, they cited "inability to understand others" and "inability to work with others" as two of three most common failings. (The most common fault was described as "limited point of view.")

Many people think that they are constitutionally unable to learn how to relate to people more effectively. "I'm just a numbers person," they say in explaining their uncomfortable dealings with others. But human relations skills are like any others: they can be learned, and practice helps to improve performance.

One skill that is helpful in working with people is being able to observe accurately. Most of the time, we see events around us from a very personal viewpoint. Our observations are usually laced with assumptions and inferences that distort our ability to see what is happening. Practice in accurate observation helps us to respond more appropriately to the people around us.

A second skill is that of listening. A major corporation—Sperry—has been spreading across the advertising pages its conviction that listening to each other is the most important skill we can learn. We can learn to hear what the other person is saying without defensiveness or judgmental attitudes. We can learn ways to respond, so that the other person knows that we have heard what he or she was trying to say.

A third area for learning in human relations is that of assertiveness: expressing our needs, feelings, and ideas clearly, but without stifling others or putting them down. Many interpersonal problems arise from our inability to say what is on our minds in a way that other people—bosses, subordinates, peers—can accept.

A fourth area is related to our ability to recognize the culturally conditioned values of people we work with, and to be able to take them into account. Especially when these values clash with our own, we need to be sensitive to the implications of this conflict for our work.

Human relations skills are as important as any other to business success and are worthy of serious study.

Step 2—Reread the Article, Noting the Main Points In this example, we will underline the ideas we think are important.

HUMAN RELATIONS IN BUSINESS

Think of the human relations challenges in business! Here are just a few:

Telling the boss she is wrong, without getting her angry;

Encouraging a subordinate to tell you what you need to know to solve a problem that involves your own behavior;

Helping a customer to make a purchase, without overdoing it;

Expressing your criticism of a peer who is not carrying his share of the work, without turning the rest of the office against you (or him);

Handling your supervisor's overtures, which the supervisor says will improve your position in the office, but which might cost you some self-respect.

Some students (and some instructors) may focus so intently on the skill and knowledge of preparing for the business world that they neglect the human relations dimensions of the work situation.

Recent research indicates that human relations are very important in business. Last October, *The Wall Street Journal* asked 782 company chief executives to identify the most important personal traits linked to success. The executives specified "integrity" and "ability to get along with others" as by far the most important success-related characteristics.

Further, when these same people were asked to identify the failings of weak managers in their firms, they cited "inability to understand others" and "inability to work with others" as two of three most common failings. (The most common fault was described as "limited point of view.")

Many people think that they are constitutionally unable to learn how to relate to people more effectively. "I'm just a numbers person," they say in explaining their uncomfortable dealings with others. But human relations skills are like any others: they can be learned, and practice helps to improve performance.

One skill that is helpful in working with people is being able to observe accurately. Most of the time, we see events around us from a very personal viewpoint. Our observations are usually laced with assumptions and inferences that distort our ability to see what is happening. Practice in accurate observation helps us to respond more appropriately to the people around us.

A second skill is that of listening. A major corporation—Sperry—has been spreading across the advertising pages its conviction that listening to each other is the most important skill we can learn. We can learn to hear what the other person is saying without defensiveness or judgmental attitudes. We can learn ways to respond, so that the other person knows that we have heard what he or she was trying to say.

A third area for learning in human relations is that of assertiveness: expressing our needs, feelings, and ideas clearly, but without stifling others or putting them down. Many interpersonal problems arise from our inability to say what is on our minds in a way that other people—bosses, subordinates, peers—can accept.

A fourth area is related to our ability to recognize the culturally conditioned values of people we work with, and to be able to take them into account. Especially when these values clash with our own, we need to be sensitive to the implications of this conflict for our work.

Human relations skills are as important as any other to business success and are worthy of serious study.

Step 3—Write a Main Idea (Thesis) Statement In this case the author has written a main idea statement for us. The kernel of the first sentence of the third paragraph is an "umbrella" sentence that "covers" all the information in the article:

. . . human relations are very important in business.

Step 4—Write the Important Points That Support the Thesis or Main Idea In this case you need only copy the sentences you have already underlined in the article.

. . . human relations skills are like any other: they can be learned, and practice helps to improve performance.

One skill that is helpful in working with people is being able to observe accurately.

A second skill is that of listening.

A third area for learning in human relations is that of assertiveness: expressing our needs, feelings, and ideas clearly, but without stifling others or putting them down.

A fourth area is related to our ability to recognize the culturally conditioned values of people we work with, and to be able to take them into account.

Step 5—Rewrite the Main Idea and Important Supporting Ideas in Your Own Words This simply means to paraphrase the information you've just copied:

Human relations skills are important to success in the business world. These skills can be learned and improved with practice. The first important human relations skill is the ability to observe accurately. The second important skill is listening well. A third skill is assertiveness—expressing ourselves without hurting or offending others. A fourth skill is the ability to recognize and appreciate the values of other people, especially if they differ from our own.

Step 6—Check Your Summary against the Original to Make Sure It Is Accurate and Complete Compare the paragraph in step 5 with the article again just to be sure you haven't left anything out or misstated any ideas.

Step 7—Eliminate Unnecessary Material from Your Summary Note, for example, that we did not include any of the quotes at the beginning of the article. These serve as introduction and as examples to catch the reader's interest; they are not necessary in a summary. We also left out the statistics from *The Wall Street Journal* survey of chief executives. Details such as this normally are not appropriate in a summary. Finally, we did not include the last sentence, "Human relations skills are as important as any others to business success, and are worthy of serious study," because this simply repeats the information in the main idea. Remember, a summary is different from an essay.

Step 8—Proofread, Then Write the Final Draft

APPENDIX C

DIRECTION WORDS

Direction words are words used frequently in college. You will see them on exams and homework assignments and hear them in lectures. It is important to know how to respond properly to these words. The following is a list of the most common direction words and their meanings.

analyze To break down into parts in order to better understand the whole. Example: *Analyze* the job requirements of an assistant-manager position at Macy's.

cite To **list**, to **name**, to **state** something. Example: *Cite* three causes of the Civil War.

compare To state the similarities between two things. Example: *Compare* reading for pleasure with reading for study purposes.

contrast To state the differences between two things. Example: *Contrast* high school and college.

define To give the meaning of a word, as in the dictionary. Example: *Define* the word *synonym.*

describe To paint a picture using words. Example: *Describe* the sunset on a warm summer night at the beach.

evaluate To examine something and then judge its worth or value. Example: *Evaluate* the budget proposed by the president in his speech.

explain To make something understandable, to give reasons for something. Example: *Explain* how previewing a textbook chapter can help you understand it more easily.

identify To name or state something. Example: *Identify* the course requirements for a Computer Science major.

illustrate To give examples that will help explain something. Example: *Illustrate* the use of mathematics in the work of a baker.

paraphrase To put something into your own words. Example: *Paraphrase* the old saying "Never judge a person until you have walked a mile in his shoes."

react   To state your view of an issue and the reasons you feel the way you do. Example: *React* to the news that taxes will be raised in the coming year.

summarize   To give a condensed version of a longer text; to give only the main points or highlights. Example: *Summarize* the speech given by the president last night.

PRACTICE USING DIRECTION WORDS

Directions: Read and study each direction word and its definition and example. When you are convinced that you know what each word requires, do the following exercise.

1. *Identify* three authors of reading selections on the topic of *culture* in this textbook.
2. *Illustrate* what is meant by the statement "Life is 10 percent what happens to you and 90 percent how you react to it."
3. *Describe* one of the other students in this class.
4. *Define* education.
5. *Paraphrase* the old saying "Genius is 90 percent perspiration and 10 percent inspiration."
6. *Explain* the value of good communication skills.
7. *Name* the instructors of the courses you are taking now.
8. *Compare and contrast* your experiences in high school and in college.
9. *Summarize* the requirements for your major as they are stated in the school catalog.
10. *List* three courses outside your major that you would like to take.
11. *React* to the statement "Every student in the United States should study a foreign language."
12. *Cite* three reasons that some college students drop out of school.

APPENDIX D

FIGURATIVE LANGUAGE

Figurative language is used so much in English that it is hard to imagine a conversation in which at least one example does not appear. "The line at the bursar's office was a zoo!" "The air conditioning broke down and the office was an oven." "My little brother is a pain in the neck!" Stevie Wonder sang, "You are the sunshine of my life . . ." "Excuse me, I have a frog in my throat." "The bottom line is you can't pass this course if you don't pass the final exam."

One type of figurative language, the simile, is extremely common. Similes generally use the words *like* or *as*. Similes usually involve a simple comparison: "Whew! I worked like a dog last night!" "She eats like a horse, but stays as thin as a rail." "The news of the air crash spread like wildfire." "Searching for my dropped contact lens at the beach was like looking for a needle in a haystack." Forrest Gump observed that "Life is like a box of chocolates; you never know what you're going to get."

Another type of figurative language, the metaphor, is a bit more complex. Like the simile, it involves a comparison of one thing to another, but in a pure metaphor, the comparison is more complicated, more layered. Think about Shakespeare's *Romeo and Juliet.* As Romeo sees Juliet come onto her balcony at dawn, he says, "What light through yonder window breaks? It is the east and Juliet is the sun!" Romeo is comparing Juliet to the sun, but it is not a simple comparison. If Romeo compares his beloved to the sun, it is not the same as simply saying she is bright or warm. What does his metaphor make us think, make us feel? The sun is so many things: it gives light; it is bright; it gives warmth; it is beautiful; it is dependable. The sun is the giver of life! So, when Romeo says these scant four words, "Juliet is the sun," we learn a wealth of things about his feelings for her. Metaphor allows us to say a lot in few words; it makes our speech and writing so much more interesting.

Figurative Language in Poetry Below are examples of figurative language written by famous poets. Explain what you think each poem means.

> *Hope is the thing with feathers*
> *That perches on the soul,*
> *And sings the tune without the words,*
> *And never stops at all.*
>
> —Emily Dickinson

> *A wicked whisper came and made my heart as dry as dust.*
>
> —Samuel Taylor Coleridge

> *Last summer you left*
> *my life quivering*
> *like a battlefield.*
> *I wore headaches like garments.*
>
> —Colleen McElroy

> *An aged man is but a paltry thing,*
> *a tattered coat upon a stick, . . .*
>
> —William Butler Yeats

Metaphor in Prose Here are some famous examples of metaphor by prose writers. Explain what each one means.

> *Hope is a good breakfast, but it is a bad supper.*
>
> —Francis Bacon

> *Speak softly and carry a big stick.*
>
> —President Theodore Roosevelt

> *A house divided against itself cannot stand.*
>
> —President Abraham Lincoln

What comparison is each of these writers making? What effect does the comparison have on the reader?

AN EXERCISE IN RECOGNIZING FIGURATIVE LANGUAGE

Now keep in mind what you've learned as you read the newspaper, listen to TV and radio, and talk with friends over the next few days. You should encounter many examples of metaphor (including similes). Write them in the chart below (you should have at least six).

Write the example and its source. The first one is done for you as a model.

Metaphor	Source
1. "Microsoft's rivals want a bigger piece of the pie"	An article in *The New York Times* Business Section, Oct. 14.
2.	
3.	
4.	
5.	
6.	

AN EXERCISE IN UNDERSTANDING FIGURATIVE LANGUAGE IN POETRY

Below are two famous poems written by the great American writer Langston Hughes. Discuss each of the poems in view of what you have learned about figurative language.

ISLAND

Wave of Sorrow,
Do not drown me now:
I see the island
Still ahead somehow
I see the island
And its sands are fair:
Wave of Sorrow,
Take me there.

HARLEM

What happens to a dream deferred?
Does it dry up like a raisin in the sun?
Or fester like a sore—and then run?
Does it stink like rotten meat?
Or crust and sugar over like a syrupy sweet?
Maybe it just sags like a heavy load.
Or does it explode?

What comparisons does the writer make? What do you think his poem means? Why do you think he used the comparisons he did?

GLOSSARY

abstract   An abstract word refers to a quality, condition, or idea that cannot be perceived by the senses. Abstract is the opposite of concrete. Examples of abstract words: love, happiness, thinking, justice, truth, fear. See *concrete*.

allusion   An allusion is a reference to another idea, something the writer assumes the reader is familiar with.

analogy   An analogy is a comparison of one thing to another thing. Analogies are generally used to explain the nature of something unfamiliar to us by comparing it to something we already know. For example, in the novel *Being There*, author Jerzy Kosinski describes the economy by using the analogy of a garden; just as there are cycles (or seasons) in a garden, there are cycles (times of growth and times of stagnation) in the economy. Note that, while analogies can be helpful in understanding a difficult concept, they are not always *true*. (The economy and the garden are quite different things.) Other examples of analogies: comparing the human mind to a computer, the heart to a pump, life to a journey.

antonym   An antonym is a word that is opposite in meaning from another word. Examples of pairs of antonyms: hot/cold; high/low; sharp/dull.

argument   In discussions, an argument is a reason given to support a position or opinion.

concrete   Something concrete is something you can see, touch, hear, smell, or taste. Concrete is the opposite of abstract. Examples of concrete words: chair, wine, elephant. See *abstract*.

connotation   Connotation refers to the emotional effect a particular word or phrase has on a person. Two words can have the same denotation, but different connotations. For example, *thin* and *skinny* have basically the same denotation, but different connotations. Likewise, *fat, chubby, heavy-set,* and *full-figured* all have the same basic meaning, but arouse different feelings or attitudes in the mind of the listener or reader. See *denotation*.

denotation   The denotation of a word is its literal, dictionary meaning.

jargon   Jargon is the specialized language of a specific group or profession. The fields of law, medicine, and computers are well-known for their jargon. The jargon of a group is usually unfamiliar to people outside the group.

metaphor   A metaphor is a figure of speech that compares one thing to another by saying that thing *is* the other. Shakespeare is the source of many of our most familiar metaphors: "All the world's a stage"; "What's in a name? . . . a rose by any other name would smell as sweet." Calderón de la Barca said "Life is a dream." Other familiar metaphors: "Life is just a bowl of cherries"; "Time is money."

oxymoron   An oxymoron is a word or phrase that combines two opposites in meaning. Examples: "James Bond was a well-known secret agent"; "The menu offered fresh-frozen jumbo shrimp" (two oxymorons in one phrase). A famous oxymoron is the Greek word *sophomore,* which is a combination of two words: *wise* and *fool.*

paradox   A paradox is a statement that seems to contradict itself, but is nevertheless true. One of the most famous paradoxes in literature is the opening of *A Tale of Two Cities,* by Charles Dickens: "It was the best of times, it was the worst of times, it was the age of wisdom, it was the age of foolishness, it was the epoch of belief, it was the epoch of incredulity, it was the season of Light, it was the season of Darkness, it was the spring of hope, it was the winter of despair, we had everything before us, we had nothing before us, we were all going direct to Heaven, we were all going direct the other way . . ."

simile   A simile is a figure of speech in which a comparison is made using the words *like* or *as.* Examples: "I was as hungry as a bear"; "Her tears flowed like wine."

synonym   A synonym is a word that means the same as another word. Examples of synonym pairs: old/elderly, doctor/physician, teacher/instructor, student/pupil.

AUTHOR/TITLE INDEX

ACKNOWLEDGMENTS OF PERMISSION

Mortimer Adler. "How to Mark a Book," by Mortimer Adler, *Saturday Review,* July 6, 1940. Reprinted by permission of the author.

American Anthropological Association. Excerpt from "Body Rituals among the Nacirema," by Horace Miner. Reproduced by permission of the American Anthropological Association from *American Anthropologist* 58:3, June 1956. Not for further reproduction.

Barbara Brandt. "Less Is More: A Call for Shorter Work Hours," by Barbara Brandt. Originally published for the Shorter Work-Time Group, © 1991. Reprinted by permission.

The Chicago Tribune. "A New Genetic Test Can Foretell Agonizing Death: Would You Take It?" by Peter Gorner, *The Chicago Tribune,* August 4, 1988. Copyrighted, Chicago Tribune Company. All rights reserved. Used with permission.

Rose Del Castillo Guilbault. "Hispanic USA: The Conveyor-Belt Ladies," by Rose Del Castillo Guilbault, *San Francisco Chronicle,* April 5, 1990. Reprinted by permission of the author.

Nicholas Gage. "The Teacher Who Changed My Life," by Nicholas Gage, originally appeared in *Parade Magazine,* December 17, 1989. Copyright © 1989 by Nicholas Gage. Reprinted by permission of Parade Magazine and the author.

Dow Jones. "Culture Shock Affects Steelworker Who Switched to White-Collar Job," by Carol Hymowitz, *The Wall Street Journal,* June 1983. Reprinted by permission of The Wall Street Journal, © 1983 Dow Jones & Company, Inc. All rights reserved worldwide.

Harcourt Brace & Company. Excerpt from *Looking Out/Looking In: Interpersonal Communication,* Eighth Edition, by Ronald B. Adler and Neil Towne, copyright © 1996 by Holt, Rinehart, and Winston, Inc., reprinted by permission of the publisher.

Harcourt Brace & Company. Excerpt from *Looking Out/Looking In,* Eighth Edition Activities Manual and Study Guide, by Mary O. Wiemann, copyright © 1996 by Harcourt Brace & Company, reprinted by permission of the publisher.

Harcourt Brace & Company. Excerpt from *Business* by Louis E. Boone and David L. Kurtz, copyright © 1995 by Harcourt Brace & Company, reprinted by permission of the publisher.

Harcourt Brace & Company. Excerpt from *Business,* Fourth Edition, by Louis E. Boone, David L. Kurtz, and Thomas Lloyd, copyright © 1995 by Harcourt Brace & Company, reprinted by permission of the publisher.

Harcourt Brace & Company. Excerpt from *Sociology in a Changing World,* Third Edition, by William Kornblum, copyright © 1994 by Holt, Rinehart, & Winston, Inc., reprinted by permission of the publisher.

Harcourt Brace & Company. Excerpt from *Sociology in a Changing World,* Third Edition Test Bank by Carol Boggs, copyright © 1994 by Harcourt Brace & Company, reprinted by permission of the publisher.

Harcourt Brace & Company. Excerpts from *Psychology in the New Millennium,* Sixth Edition, by Spencer A. Rathus, copyright © 1996 Holt, Rinehart, and Winston, reprinted by permission of the publisher.

Harcourt Brace & Company. Excerpts from *Psychology in the New Millennium,* Sixth Edition Test Bank by Harry Tiemman and Mara Merlino, copyright © 1996 Harcourt Brace & Company, reprinted by permission of the publisher.

ICM. Excerpt from "Crack and the Box," by Pete Hamill, *Esquire,* 1990 and "Death of a Salaryman," by Pete Hamill, *Esquire,* 1994. Reprinted by permission of International Creative Management, Inc. Copyright by Pete Hamill.

Lippincott-Raven. "Nursing Practices—England and America," by Mary Madden, *American Journal of Nursing,* April 1968. Used with permission of Lippincott-Raven Publishers, Philadelphia, PA.

Christopher Lovrien/Janelle Anderson. "The Economics of Immigration," by Christopher Lovrien and Janelle Anderson, originally published in *The Informed Argument,* fourth edition, by Robert Miller. Reprinted by permission of the authors.

MacDonald Communications. "Cultural Diversity in Today's Corporation." First appeared in *Working Woman* in January 1991. Written by Audrey Edwards. Reprinted with the permission of Working Woman Magazine. Copyright © 1991 by Working Woman Magazine.

The New York Times. "School vs. Education," by Russell Baker, September 9, 1975; "On Language: A Taste for Scrambled English," by Bill Bryson; "Darkness at Noon," by Harold Krents; "Who Needs Love! Many Couples in Japan Don't," by Nicholas D. Kristof, February 11, 1996; "African Woman in France Battling Polygamy," by Marlise Simons, January 26, 1996; "About Men/One Man's Kids," by Daniel Meier, November 1, 1987; "Hers Column/Women in Science," by K. C. Cole, December 3, 1981; "Op-Ed/Why Spanish Translations?" by Mauricio Molina, March 12, 1980; and "As a Pampered Generation Grows Up, Chinese Worry," by Patrick E. Tyler, June 25, 1996. Copyright © *The New York Times* 1975, 1976, 1980, 1981, 1984, 1987, 1990, 1996 by The New York Times Company. Reprinted by permission.

Newsweek. "Knowing Isn't Everything," by Sally Spaulding, April 3, 1995; "The Last Days of Eden," by Spencer Reiss, December 3, 1990; and "Sexism in the Schoolhouse," by Barbara Kantrowitz, February 24, 1992, from *Newsweek,* © 1990, 1992, 1993, 1995, Newsweek, Inc. All rights reserved. Reprinted by permission.

North America Syndicate. "What True Education Should Do," by Sydney J. Harris. Reprinted with special permission of North America Syndicate.

Psychology Today. "Overcoming an Invisible Handicap," by Thomas Cottle, *Psychology Today,* 1980. Reprinted with permission from Psychology Today Magazine, copyright © 1980 Sussex Publishers, Inc.

Putnam. Excerpt reprinted by permission of The Putnam Publishing Group from *A Not Entirely Benign Procedure,* by Perri Klass. Copyright © 1987 by Perri Klass.

Science News. "A Case of Dwarfism," "A Case of Paternity," "A Question of Privacy," and "A Case of Who Decides," from *Science News,* June 8, 1991. Reprinted with permission of Science News, the weekly newsmagazine of science. Copyright © 1991 by Science Service.

Gary Turbak. "Let's Make English Official," by Gary Turbak, originally published in *VFW,* April 1996. Copyright © 1996 by Gary Turbak. Reprinted by permission.

U.S. News & World Report. "One Nation, One Language," by Susan Headden, *U.S. News & World Report,* September 25, 1995. Copyright U.S. News & World Report.

Wadsworth. Excerpt from *Sociology: A Global Perspective,* Second Edition, by Joan Ferrante. Reprinted by permission of Wadsworth Publishing Company.

William Morrow. "On Friendship," from *A Way of Seeing* by Margaret Mead and Rhoda Metraux. Copyright © 1961, 1962, 1963, 1964, 1965, 1966, 1967, 1968, 1969, 1970 by Margaret Mead and Rhoda Metraux. Reprinted by permission of William Morrow & Company, Inc.

William Morrow. "The Future of English," from *The Mother Tongue* by Bill Bryson. Copyright © 1980 by Bill Bryson. Reprinted by permission of William Morrow & Company, Inc.

William Morrow. Excerpt from *You Just Don't Understand,* by Deborah Tannen. Copyright © 1990 by Deborah Tannen. Reprinted by permission of William Morrow & Company, Inc.